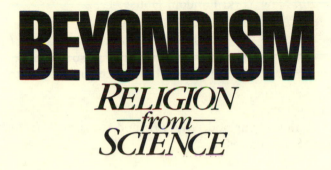

BEYONDISM
RELIGION
—from—
SCIENCE

Chapter 5:
Omar Khayyam. "The Rubaiyat, XLVI." From *The Rubaiyat of Omar Khayyam*. New York: Random House, 1952.

Chapter 7:
Sir Henry Newbolt. "The Volunteer." From *The Sailing of the Long Ships*. Great Britain: John Murray, 1902. Also in *Selected Poems*. London: Hodder & Stoughton, 1981. Reprinted by permission of Peter Newbolt.

Chapter 10:
William Henley. "England, My England." From *Selected Poems*. London: Scribner, 1900.

Chapter 11:
John Dryden. "Absalom and Achitophel." From *Best of Dryden* (L. Bredvold, Ed.). London: Nelson, 1933.

Chapter 11:
Dean Inge. From *Assessments and Anticipation*. London: Cassell, Ltd., 1929. Reprinted by permission of Macmillan, New York.

Chapter 12:
Sir Henry Newbolt. "Clifton Chapel." From *The Island Race*. Great Britain: Elkin Mathews, 1898. Also in *Selected Poems*. London: Hodder & Stoughton, 1981. Reprinted by permission of Peter Newbolt.

Chapter 15:
Table 15.1. "Marriage Choice and Racioethnic Origin." From N. E. Morton, C. S. Chung, and M. P. Mi. *Genetics of Interracial Crosses in Hawaii*. Basel, Switzerland: Karger, 1967. Reprinted by permission of N. E. Morton.

Chapter 17:
Omar Khayyam. "The Rubaiyat, LXXI." From *The Rubaiyat of Omar Khayyam*. New York: Random House, 1952.

Notes:
A. E. Housman. "The Welsh Marches." From *The Collected Poems of A. E. Housman*. New York: Holt, Rinehart and Winston, 1965.

G. K. Chesterton. From *Wine, Water & Song*. London: Methuen, 1915.

Rudyard Kipling. "The Gods of the Copy-book Headings." From *Inclusive Verses, 1885-1932*. New York: Sundial, 1940.

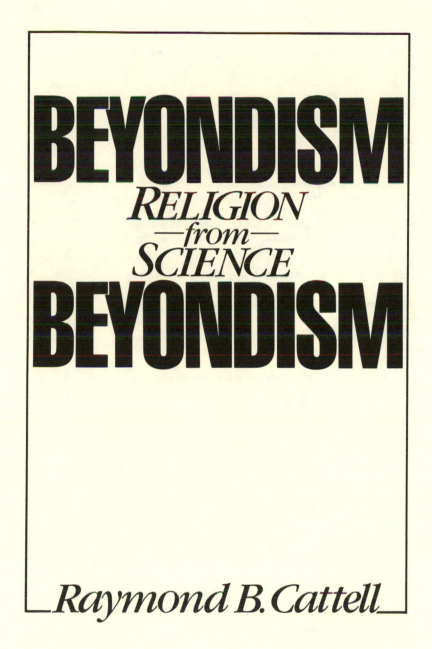

BEYONDISM

RELIGION —from— SCIENCE

BEYONDISM

Raymond B. Cattell

PRAEGER

New York
Westport, Connecticut
London

Library of Congress Cataloging-in-Publication Data

Cattell, Raymond B. (Raymond Bernard), 1905-
    Beyondism : religion from science.

    Bibliography: p.
    Includes indexes.
    1. Science and ethics.   2. Religion and science—
1946-   I. Title.
BJ57.C36   1987   171'.7   87-17885
ISBN 0-275-92431-9 (alk paper)

Library of Congress Catalog Card Number: 87-17885
ISBN 0-275-92431-9 (alk. paper)

First published in 1987

Praeger Publishers, One Madison Avenue, New York, NY 10010
A division of Greenwood Press, Inc.

Printed in the United States of America

∞™

The paper used in this book complies with the
Permanent Paper Standard issued by the National
Information Standards Organization (Z39.48-1984).

10 9 8 7 6 5 4 3 2

CONTENTS

Concluded on next page

Contents *(Concluded)*

Tables

Figures

This book is a sequel to *A New Morality From Science: Beyondism*, in which I outlined the historical roots of the Beyondist movement, and explicated its differences from revealed religions, national religions such as Shinto, the Asian religions, and the relatively modern philosophical creations of Utilitarianism, Spencerian Darwinism, and Marxism. Its intellectual ancestry begins with rationalism, but it does not cease with the rational but unempirical line of such as Diderot, Rousseau, Locke, Hegel, Russell, Veblen, Marx, Sartre, or Spengler. Rather it takes its momentum from Bacon, Bentham, Darwin, Mill, Comte, Haeckel, Spencer, and those who have seen with increasing clarity the integration of ethics possible through science.

With my 1972 book thus available for those who seek scholarly roots and references, I am freed here to reconnoiter further ahead and to state the principles with less documentary encumbrance and with more help from recent science. The new steps here arise partly from new analytical thought and partly from new data. I now also have the company of some intellectual comrades who, with unusual cool courage, have also prepared themselves to derive ethics and spiritual values from science.

As Weyl (1972) points out, the line of Spencer, Tennyson, and others in seeking some reconciliation of evolution and religion had evaded or ignored what became the main development in my book (and in earlier articles)—the laws of *natural selection of groups* of men *as* groups. A substantial scientific background of observations for such a theme was provided in timely fashion by Wilson's *Sociobiology*, appearing only three years (1975) after my own, from which I have drawn excellent aid from natural history to proceed in the present sequel.

Meanwhile, this galaxy of able pioneer writers, to which I referred as recently appearing, boldly broke loose from traditional viewpoints (often tied to academic sociology). They created independent but generally fragmentary contributions that proved happily integrable into the Beyondist viewpoint. I think particularly (including somewhat earlier writers) of Ardrey, Baker, deBenoist, Darlington, Eysenck, Eisenstadt, Gedda, Graham, Hardin, Huntington, Jencks, Jensen, Keith, Lenski, Lindzey, Loehlin, Lorenz, Lynn, Monod, Muller, Norling, Oliver, Osborne, Pearson, Pendell, Putnam, Roberts, Rummel, Salk, Spuhler, Toffler, Waddington, Weyl, and Williams (See References). Through these progressive writers, the general public has begun to open its eyes to realities in education, genetics, physiology, ethnology, social structure, and lessons of history to which it has long been blinded by religious and political prejudice, by scientific ignorance, and particularly by the stereotyped irrelevances of political "right" and "left."

Some pure background research scientists (whose detached but indispensable contribution in this field are of the highest quality and significance) have tended to chide me on adopting the designation, *Beyondism*. It suggests, they say, a belief in an afterlife! It was Pareto, in his "residues," who noticed the social psychological fact that a pattern of emotional satisfactions built up around one cognitive system may serve well to sustain a superseding set of cognitive perceptions. As the reader will see, I think *the emotional restraints and expectations which Christianity, in particular, has built up, can be sustained, in part, on a quite different basis of logical derivation.* The *future life* understood by Beyondism is a widely *different* cognitive concept from that of revealed religion, but much of the emotional meaning for the individual is the same. The aptness of Beyondism comes also from a quite different and purely technical basis. "Progressivism" would never do, because the essence of evolution is that we do not know what progress is until it has been brought about, weighed, and accepted or rejected. The basic condition of progress is that people should realize that stagnation is obsolescence, and that the categorical imperative commands a readiness to go *beyond* the present.

An alternative criticism I have met is that "If this construct is something that is reached simply by following the paths of objectivity, data gathering, and reasoning, surely it needs no label, being a part of science itself?" I reply that acceptance of present scientific knowledge could lead to quite a variety of ethical systems. I sense differences, at least in ethical emphasis, in, for example, the explorers Darlington, Keith, Hardin, and Salk. There is no evidence yet that all social and biological scientists are ready to find their way to this same Beyondist position. Intellectually it has the status of a theory that will have its supporters and its critics. Actually the label is of little importance. But the time has surely come when those rationalists, thinking liberals, sociobiologists, and scientifically progressive, educated persons of all origins, begin to gather the strength for social and spiritual leadership that comes of being united. (Independent thinkers are frequently so temperamentally independent that they get nowhere when opposed to the solid, self-effacing members of the phalanxes of traditionalists.)

We must keep open the possibility that the model of science, as it has been known until now, will not always entirely apply. Some physicists (such as Planck and Heisenberg) have been forced to conclude that precise causality does not exist for particulars, and that the laws of science are probabilistic. Compared to those of physics, the sociobiological laws are so approximate that it will take some time to become aware of such fine deviations, if they exist. I have addressed these questions in *Personality and Learning Theory,* Volume II (1980, p. 572), where I also point out that the social sciences (and any evolutionary phenomena) are embedded in an ongoing process, beginning before we started observations. The process thus denies us complete, necessary knowledge of all antecedents and therefore the capacity to predict all consequences. Consequently, at present—and for some time indefinitely into the future—the derivation of an ethical system from science must have the property of an approximation.

However, the admission of this approximateness, as well as of the necessity of great advances in the sociobiological sciences before we can patently direct socio-ethical affairs with their aid, does not forbid us to follow this path. As discussed more fully in Chapter 16, we have to operate like another science that comes to man's aid—medicine—in part as an art, recognizing that decisions of razor-edge precision and complete dependability are not possible, that most actions for greater benefit have minor undesirable side effects, and that, nevertheless, on the whole we are far better off with it than without it.

It is thus not claimed that Beyondism yet has scientific certainty in its ethical values, but only that it points to ways of becoming more objective and exact, and offers, to a world staggering through loss of its underpinnings in the revealed, dogmatic religions, a "fair trust" basis for its ethical and social decisions. It is at present a primitive compass—a mere lodestone—but better for navigation in the social and ethical fogs of emotion than no compass at all.

In the 1972 exposition of Beyondism, an academic statement of position and a scholarly review of intellectual roots was all that was tried. The present book enters, further, upon the planning of an initial social organization of Beyondism as a movement. Such an organization is needed on the one hand to direct, strategically, the imaginative and sophisticated research needed to reach firmer ethical values, and, on the other, to bring influence to bear on social and political decisions presently made by traditional institutions. For some time to come, Beyondism may have to operate by giving aid to existing progressive groups, and, meanwhile, to work toward a centralized international research center by undertaking social science research by aid from existing trusts.

Finally, a word regarding the structure of the book may be helpful to the reader. It is an old but sound maxim in teaching that for ease of assimilation one should proceed from the concrete to the abstract. Here, as in a Euclidean presentation, I have had to challenge the reader's fortitude by proceeding in logical rather than psychological order, beginning necessarily with the principles and abstract concepts on which the arguments for particular social conclusions drawn later depend. The arrangement is unusual also in that it proceeds in the spirit of a catechism, centering each chapter on a major question—an "issue"—raised at its opening.

For improvements and clarifications over the first volume of Beyondism, I am grateful first to certain eminent psychologists—often companions in technical research—notably, Professors John Horn, John Nesselrode, Richard Lynn, Richard Gorsuch, John Loehlin, Alan Welford, James Schuerger, Charles Cloninger, Garrett Hardin, as well as to Richard Herrnstein, John McArdle, Gregory Boyle, Arthur Jensen, Ronald Johnson, Joseph Royce, E. O. Wilson, Robert Woliver, C. D. Darlington, W. B. Shockley, Revilo Oliver, Geoffrey Ashton, and Rudolph Rummel, as well as Drs. Robert Graham, Nathaniel Weyl, Herbert Eber, Ivan Scheier, Wilmot Robertson, Roger Pearson, and John Gillis. Needless to say, they are not responsible for the final positions in this book, though I am indebted to them for improvements. Finally, the perspectives on popular reactions to ideas, illuminated by my wife, Dr. Heather Cattell, from the standpoint of a practicing psychologist, have been indispensable.

Chapter 1

New Direction or Ancient Drift
in the Ethical Guidance of Morality?

This book seeks an answer to the question of how to find the highest ethical values and to convert them into morality. A tentative answer has been put forward 50 years ago (Cattell, 1938), and expanded a decade ago (Cattell, 1972), in the basic principles of *Beyondism*.

What, briefly, is Beyondism? It is a system for discovering and clarifying ethical goals from a basis of scientific knowledge and investigation, by the objective research procedures of scientific method. This does not deny it emotional richness, but in fact calls for the deepest, most genuine emotional satisfaction and loyalty, unaided and unbetrayed by myths and illusions. It believes that the difficult and honest thinking that has given us power, light, warmth, speed of travel, and world-wide instant communication by the physical sciences, and health and longevity by the medical sciences, is capable of giving us definiteness of values, true social progress, and peace of mind, in our individual, national, and international behavior.

Since most thoughtful people even today draw their moral values ultimately from religious systems, it calls, in a troubled age, for re-examination of those systems. Among the more independently thinking citizens, there has already been a quiet withdrawal from what are properly designated the "revealed" and ethically dogmatic religions into some kind of existentialism, or a benign and humanity-proud humanism, or a variety of hashes cooked from arbitrarily chosen fragments of Christianity, Islam, Buddhism, Shintoism, etc. These hashes can all be called "morally relativistic" in that their followers claim that all values are "relative," lack any objective basis, and can be modified to suit the individual. The choice appears to be between suppressing independent reasoning and curiosity and accepting the absolutes of traditional religions, on the one hand, or, on the other, of cutting oneself adrift on a pilotless stream of "modern thought" in which close examination reveals presently, at best, a basis in only a vague, liberal humanitarianism.

We witness that many of the mounting ills of our time are due to the increasing secession from firm revealed religions into relativisms, and the associated plain disillusionment and confusion, generally begetting a boundless, self-serving permissiveness. Social research has failed to find the increase in alcoholism, drug addiction, and crime, and the decrease in motivation and achievement in work (as shown by inflation) and school (as shown by thorough objective test examinations), to be explicable by economic and other causes commonly first considered. The answer is almost certainly that these evils are associated with a more general decay in morale and ethical certainty. This process began for educated people with the "debunking" of religion by science in the mid-nineteenth century, and has now filtered down from the educated (who retained socialized attitudes without the aid of hell fire) through the general population and down to the less intelligent and the uncontrolled.

To claim to have reasoned to one's own ethical values is generally praiseworthy, especially if one is wary of narcissism and rationalization. But even brilliant philosophers like Bertrand Russell failed to avoid the latter. The path of rugged facts that we have to follow is one for scientists, not verbally intoxicated philosophers. The average citizen, unless it involved his special, endorsed qualification, would not presume to repair a self-focussing camera or a computer, or to diagnose and prescribe for a particular form of cystinuria or cancer. Yet the complexities of social science, as in, for example, syntality calculations in social psychology, that he needs to understand in order to infer the ultimate consequences of a given form of social action, are at least as complex as those in the physical organism.

In setting out here to develop an ethical system based on the consequences of individual and mass actions of various kinds, we cannot hope at once to reach the firm conclusions that proper attention to science in this domain can hope eventually to reach. It is our aim only to reach clear general principles, with a sufficiency of illustrations, handled at a presently less exacting level, to clarify arguments in a new territory.

Chapter 2

Where Do We Go for the Source of Moral Values?

The basic questions a thinking person asks as he considers the human lot are: "What am I?" and "Where am I?" and "What should I do?" I have reviewed elsewhere (1972) the psychology of religions in their struggle toward answers to these questions. A thousand years ago religion offered (apart from some insight from the likes of Aristotle and Eratosthenes) the most systematic available answers to these profound questions. Today there is little doubt that science answers them more reliably and completely, and with less emotional distortion present in religion from an agglomeration of myths and rituals.

Among professional scientists, research has until recently confined itself to Questions (1) and (2). Actually, despite the doubts of many scholarly philosophers, and the professional anathemas of priests, it has full rights to proceed logically to the third. As to the first, we see, in approximate terms, that our status may be "a little lower than the angels," but it is certainly a little higher than the primates, despite our sharing with them a prehensile forelimb and the emotions expressing comparable instincts. Just as the first question brings us to biological evolution, so the second brings us to the cosmic evolution of the universe. So it is not surprising that Beyondism draws its meaning, and the basis of its ethics from the wonder and glory that the broadest view of science offers: that of an evolutionary process.

Sometimes it is said that the difference between science and religion is that the latter demands acts of faith, whereas the former, as Bacon (1893) advocated, begins with doubts. "If a man begins in certainties he shall end in doubts; but if he will be content to begin with doubts, he shall end in certainties." This wise comment we shall meet again in this book. But, meanwhile, as far as religious certainties especially are concerned, we shall begin with doubts, starting with a clean sheet even though our quest aims ultimately at comparative certainty. The

3

dogmas of the "universalistic religions" are as beset with acts of faith as a frequent earthquake area with geological faults. However, to be epistemologically realistic, we must admit that science also has its acts of faith, though they are very few and surely less obviously questionable.

In all areas science has its explicit *assumptions, models,* and axioms. But these are tentative explanations, always subject to checking by empirical fact. It *does* have one or two broader assumptions that must long remain items of faith. Notably, science has to deny Berkeley's option of considering the external world a dream, and accept Descartes' argument for its being a reality. In addition, our senses are not equipped to tell us all that is going on. We cannot, for example, receive radio waves. But, there seems no limit to our ability, by sufficient ingenuity, to convert the rest into our sensory ranges. However, it is in the realm of interpretation that Beyondism demands an act of faith by which it may seem to stand or fall. The Berkeley-Descartes issue we are content to answer with "The universe exists." What Beyondism requires in addition is the interpretation that "Evolution exists as a paramount fact within this universe." Thus, if we wish to be as tightly logical as a Euclidean proposition—which we need if we claim our position to be logically sound—we have to recognize these two assumptions or presuppositions.

Of the second assumption—the existence of evolution—it can be said that it has a fail-safe status. This is because there are scientific problems in the universe that cannot be solved just by accumulation of data and the strict application of scientific method, but demand also an evolution of the human species in intelligence. Thus, to see if evolution is what we think it is, we have ourselves to evolve. Furthermore, even if a man is not prepared to give full acceptance to the primacy of evolution as we now understand it, he is compelled to accept it as a contingent basis for finding out whether it is the genuine goal of action and ethics.

Of course, since man has free will, and the maladjusted often have an excess of egotistical contrasuggestibility or contentiousness, it is possible for puny man to say, "I do not accept that I am a part of evolution, or agree to cooperate with it." He is in effect saying, "Stop the world! I want to get off," and he can do this, by suicide or by a sybaritic life deliberately leaving no children.

There is thus admittedly an act of faith or a broad assumption in accepting evolution and committing oneself to it as the paramount principle. Once this is done, however, an astonishing richness of conclusions follows, for social and ethical action, each with the firmness of a scientific finding. These we shall explore in the rest of the book.

4

Chapter 3

Must Natural Selection Have Its Ultimate Action Among Groups, Not Individuals?

Beginning fundamentally with "What am I?" "Where am I?" and "What ought I to do?" we have reached the conclusion that the sustaining of human evolution is necessarily the central purpose of mankind. As Haeckel observed at the opening of Darwin's impact (1890), "Evolution is the key word that will either answer all the riddles which surround us, or put us on the way to their solution."

The two forms of evolution—biological and cultural—are in complex interaction—an interaction that we must ultimately seek to understand as far as is possible today. However, since we have to begin somewhere, and since they have great similarity in essential form, let us grasp first the bases of biological evolution. For these bases have been far more scientifically studied and developed. We need to take a look also at a sense in which the Lamarckian view that striving creates progress is true. The giraffe's striving to reach its head higher into the trees does nothing to its germ plasm. But if a spontaneous mutation to a longer neck occurs, it will be given more advantage *in the striving atmosphere.* Mutations may die unrecognized where there is no environmental pressure in the direction that they favor. In this sense, the Lamarckian view that stiving and adventure produce mutations is true: they at least give scope for mutations to show their advantageousness.

There has been great progress in genetics recently, but fundamentals remain as Darwin, Huxley, Spencer, and others described them a century or more ago. The basic requirements of biological evolution are two: (1) the occurence of new variations (mutations and recombinations) in the biological make-up, as determined by gene changes, and (2) exposure to natural selection, under which some forms survive

5

better than others, through better adaptations to the given environment.

The selection has finally to operate, literally, on *individuals*, but often the results are well summarized and understood by considering the effect on groups—either as (1) a species, interbreeding and having common characteristics, or (2) an organized group, with roles, rules, and social structure—say a nation. A species, though it is not just "a classification in the mind of man," is only an interacting group to a limited degree (except in certain social insects—and even there different nests may separate as organized groups and indulge in conflict).

In a species to a limited extent and in an organized group to a large extent, the survival of the group depends on *capacities for interaction* that are not relevant, or necessary, simply for the survival of the individual *as such*. For example, in all species, capacities to court and mate and, in many, ability to look after the young, are necessary to survival of the species. Indeed, the development of a genetic mutation that increased the strength and capacity of the individual to survive would disappear if it interfered with the necessary modes of interacting with others in the species.

In organized groups, as, for example, in primate and human societies, the possible relations and results are somewhat more complex. Thus, although all survival ultimately takes place as survival of *individuals*, it is overconcrete and unsubtle thinking to overlook that it is nevertheless the ultimate interactive properties of the species or group *as such* that greatly determine evolution. The concrete view would say that the death of an individual, for example, is nothing more than the death of a lot of cells, yet obviously something more important than the cell dies. The individual cell, it is true, contains the plan of the whole body, but when the body dies all cells must die. In the analogue of the whole social body this is only approximately true, but close enough for us to find a considerable reduction in the population type when a culture dies.

Natural selection is going on *simultaneously* between groups and among individuals within groups. As we shall see, within-group selection has to conform to the demands of between-group selection. This was not understood when Darwin and Wallace first put forward the theory of evolution by natural selection, for people thought it rested principally on conflict among individuals. On the other hand, the kind-hearted Tennyson (1908) refused to believe that "nature red in tooth and claw" could be the rule of human interaction, while the convention-wrecking Nietzsche (1930) thought this meant the superman, lording it over his fellows as an individual, "beyond good and evil." It surely needs no extended illustration to accept the basic premise of Beyondism that evolution must produce superior individuals who are *fitted to work in organized groups*. Hobbes's oft-quoted statement in his *Leviathan* (1958) that the life of an isolated man, a savage, is likely to be "nasty, brutish, and short" is relevant here. By all means, let us select for greater individual mental capacity, in intragroup selection, but let us remember that the greatest scientific genius could accomplish very little without the small army of technical aids, and the industrial world still further beyond them, that make a scientific laboratory possible. The transmission of the education that has given powers to his mind, his defense against disorder and violence, and all else, comes from the action of survival on a survival-worthy *group*.

Our basic position that natural selection does and should act on groups to produce the human beings and the cultural developments, for a higher life, is often attacked at a superficial level by three objections: (1) that everyone belongs to several groups—national religious, racial, economic— not one; (2) that we *know* what group progress and reform are, without the need for any verdict from natural selection; and (3) that natural selection applied to groups means competition and eventually war.

The first—the problem of overlapping groups[1]—is complex, but for the present we shall say, approximately, that the survival of the individual and his particular cultural attitudes is a function of the relative survival of the several groups to which he belongs. The parallel to this in everyday life is the insurance company which calculates an individual's risk in terms of group categories, of known characteristics, to which he belongs.

With the second objection—that we know what progress is and can accordingly abolish group natural selection—Beyondism is in fundamental disagreement. We can peer ahead a little way, with the help of historical perspective and reasoning—and even penetrate the fog a little farther when a truly potent social science is built up—but the wisest never could, and probably never will, be able to foresee the ultimate effect of inventions and social legislations. Evolution is no more a straight line than the course of a ship sounding its way through uncharted channels. History books could be, and have been, filled with the untoward and ludicrous results of labors of well-intentioned but unimaginative social reformers, who "know what's best."

The basic position of Beyondism is simply that we have to *go beyond what is*, and that the two basic requirements of evolution apply (1) to groups as to individuals and (2) to cultural as to biological evolution.

That is to say, (1) *There must be natural variation*, in which groups agree to take diversified paths, racially and culturally. As the geneticist Dobzhansky (1962) reminded us, "We cannot evade indefinitely the problem of where we're evolving, and where we want to evolve." Each group must "put its money down." (2) *There must be natural selection among groups*, in which some survive and some do not, though this difference of survival may be in relative rather than absolute terms.

Ensuing inferences from this basic stance are distasteful to many arrested at humanistic, relativistic-ethical positions, but largely because of incorrect inferences. All one can answer is that if anyone knows another way to human advance he should declare it to science. (The proviso always exists in the above description of evolution that the successful adaptation is only to a *given* or conceivable environment: a proviso we shall return to in due course.)

The third antipathy to the basic position is mentioned above—the fear that competition implies war, a particularly distressing notion at the present level of war's destructiveness. Our answer to this is that when Beyondism is universally adopted the whole process of variation and selection among groups will be embraced as a single cooperative undertaking in what we shall call "cooperative competition." Agreed competition for the best results is familiar to us already in sports (as perhaps an artificial example) and in manufacturing competition to give the best quality at lowest cost to the customer (here this aim is complicated by secondary principles). War is not a part of the best competition, but a breakdown therein, like the petulant, immature chess player who upsets the board. But wasteful and horrible as war is, and to be avoided at almost all costs, to reject competition because it has some risk of war[2] is to throw away the baby with the bath water. It would be a supreme blasphemy of denying life because life has possibilities of pain.

However, as Solzhenitsyn, an expatriate from Russia, has sized up Western culture (commencement address at Harvard), "To defend oneself one must be ready to die. There is little such readiness in a society raised in the cult of material well-being. Western thinking has become conservative: 'the world situation should stay as it is at any cost.' This debilitating dream of a status quo is the symptom of a society which has come to the end of its development." This "status quo" philosophy is completely out of touch with Beyondism.

What we have to make clear here is the relation of natural selection among individuals to that among groups. The contribution between group and individual is a two-way affair. In an obvious sense, a group cannot exist without individuals, and it has been argued that an individual who is to come to fullest use in progress cannot exist without a group. It is thus true that we have a causal chain in what systems theorists call a "feedback" action, in which individuals help shape the group, and the group helps shape the individual. (One says "helps" because both individual and group get part of the shaping from the physical environment.) This statement of course applies to both cultural and genetic shaping, recognizing that different genetic predispositions will respond differently to schooling. It follows from the above that we do not have a complete symmetry where natural selection comes in. If the genetic and cultural shaping of individuals *must* yield a viable group, *then that shaping has to be something that fits the survival of the group in its interactions with other groups and the environment.* The conditions of survival of the group must determine the conditions for survival of the individual—not vice versa. That is the discovery of the present chapter, and should be called the second principle of Beyondism—the first being the acceptance of evoluation as the ultimate goal.

A sociobiologist will see some additional minor principles calling for further thought. Some must be left to later chapters, but the issue just mentioned—that fitness is always definable only in relation to an environment—needs considering directly with the main mechanisms—variation (of groups), and natural selection (of groups), by differential survival.

The *environment* of any group, such as a nation or a business corporation or a religious sect, is partly (a) the collection of other groups and (b) the physical universe. Putting aside variance due to size, natural resources, etc., we shall accept here and elsewhere, from the evidence of correlations in modern nations and of history, that nations, tribes, and other groups *tend* to rank in the same order in (1) competing with other groups and (2) in their mastery of their environment. This is not merely because mastery of the environment gives better economic and military weapons, but because the general intelligence that begets one *tends* to beget the other. The argument is parallel to that in the psychology of individuals, that Spearman's (1937) general intelligence factor simultaneously raises learning level in both verbal and numerical skills.

There exist also discrepancies, and, as we must study later, nations advanced in, say, physical science are not at just the same level in success in war. Similarly, success in war is not fully correlated with cultural level in the special sense (arts, music, literature and other subjective satisfactions). These war and competence relationships have been calculated and used in the concept of group syntality dimensions (Cattell, 1949, 1950, 1960, 1980. See Chapters 6 and 10 here).

What we are seeing further in human historical terms here is a broader principle running through all biological observations, and relevant to the outcome of all the mechanisms of variation and natural selection. It has to do with the remarkable fact that some species do not evolve at all for millions of years. A frequently quoted instance is the common horseshoe crab which has apparently remained unchanged in form and behavior on the seashores of the world for 50 million years. There are many other members of this conservative club, adapted to special unchanging niches in various corners of the earth.

On the other hand, the record of the rocks shows that far more species have passed away than presently exist. The firmest criterion of evolutionary success is that a species has survived. However, as we have seen, this can be called success only relative to an environment. Change in the form of the species to meet a changing environment is often, as by some standard of potency of equipment, actually a regression, as in creatures who adapt to the "niche" of dark caves and lose their eyes. Simple survival is a first condition of success in the biological world, but we shall later (Chapter 5) attempt to add a second score, for more *positive* achievement. Spencer (1897) and others who have carefully studied the tree of evolution, attempt to define "advance" (over and above survival per se) as an increasing complexity of organization, as an organism. This is consistent, up to a point, with the definition of advance we develop later (Chapter 7) as successful *adaptation to a broader span of environment, rather than a narrower niche.*

The upset of a long-lasting equilibrium comes from (a) genetic mutations in the species which change to fit the environment, (b) physical changes in the environment (the ice ages would be prominent in the modification of man), and (c) changes in the pattern of symbiotic or parasitic relation with a variety of other species (often affecting the food chain). The production of a *better* or more extended fit by mutations (a) is very slow because more than nine-tenths of mutations are blindly unfitting. Within (b) we must also include initiative in the species in moving itself into new environments. That from (c) is perhaps the most active, because the balance among several species in the same environment necessarily magnifies, from its several species sources, the effects due to (a) and (b) directly on one species.

The above perspective over the biological field is necessary at this point, but the essential theme of this chapter is that organized human groups are subject to the same selection as individuals—history being a tale of the birth and fall of such groups, instanced in tribes, nations, religions, and empires. And although we later consider some differences between the genetic and cultural elements operating in evolution, the basic laws of variation, natural selection, and evolutionary shift, studied most closely in the genetic model, apply to both, in their interactive products. Consequently, we see human progress as having to depend on natural selection among organized groups.

Those organized groups tend to be nations. As Sir Arthur Keith (1914) summarizes, "Most of my colleagues regard a nation as a political unit, with which anthropologists have no concern, whereas I regard a nation as an 'evolutionary unit' with which anthropologists ought to be greatly concerned. The only live races in Europe today are its nations." The great size of the nation, relative to the small familial tribes among which the evolution of group qualities formerly took place, slows up the natural selective process, but that is necessary to produce the "large group" characters we now need.

It is true, however, that, as recognized above, individuals experience, *within* the group, also an interindividual natural selection operating on laws of its own, and that individuals shape groups and groups shape individuals. But the natural selection of individuals has to fit the natural selection among groups, else the group disappears. Darwin, in his letters, pointed out that a tribe "superior in patriotism, fidelity, sympathy . . . and readiness to sacrifice" will be selected for survival, other traits being equal, relative to a tribe low in those qualities. Groups survive to the extent (among other things) that their members practice an ethic of mutual love among citizens and self-sacrifice for the group. Hence the familiar form of the development of ethics derives from intergroup natural selection. This is the essential perception on which we base the need for *continuing selection by groups*, in the interest of advancing ethics.

Chapter 4

What Has Group Competition To Do With Ethics, Morality, and Progress?

If a number of human groups are in competition in much the same environment, it is easy to see that several different factors will determine their relative survival: size, natural resources, level of scientific technological development, effectiveness of social structure and organization, level of education, proportion of genetically highly gifted citizens, diplomatic skill in alliances, and level of morale. For the present we shall focus on the last, setting aside the others and, indeed, for analysis, assume they are much the same in the countries compared. The question of their importance *relative* to morale in begetting success we must also set aside, noting though the comment of Napoleon and other military leaders who have assessed the situation—that in war, at least, morale is more important than anything else.

Morale and morality are, of course, distinguishable concepts, but social psychological research, alike in small (Cattell & Stice, 1960) and in larger national groups (Cattell & Gorsuch, 1965), shows that the morale of a group, as shown in its cohesion in face of attempts to dissolve and destroy the group, is appreciably correlated with the level of interindividual morality. One must distinguish also—though again often correlated—the level of the ethical rules themselves as adopted by a group, and the level of the population's conformity to those rules, which may be called its morality. The work of Gorsuch and many others reveals, clearly, substantial differences in existing nations in their population morality levels, as measured by such mutually correlated social indices as rates of homicides per 100,000, low venereal disease rates, low alcoholism, fewer illegitimate births, lower death rates from tuberculosis and typhoid fever (more attention to community care), and absence of licensing of prostitution.

13

It surely needs no array of illustrations to show that from football teams to nations the soundness of the ethical system and the mutual concern and respect of individuals regarding ethical requirements are very significant determinants of group success—against other groups, or against nature, as in the crew of a storm-tossed ship. The biologist, incidently, points to the rise of the same problem of balance when single cells ceased to live on their own and became parts of a colony and eventually of a structured body. Cells had to learn a new mode of existence, giving up freedoms and acquiring new modes of group belonging —such as they lose, for example, in cancer. The life of the body depends on each cell's capacity to cooperate. Similarly, deep in the instinctive inheritances of man we find a strong tendency to xenophobia—the dislike of the unlike—society—and a natural tendency to recognize and defend the territory of the tribe (shown also by Carpenter (1934) in his studies of rhesus monkeys) against strangers. These are the basic, instinctive "amity" and "enmity" moral imperatives of Herbert Spencer.

It is not unreasonable to assert, from the drawings of the cave man and the anthropologists' modern studies of preliterate tribes, that the virtues enshrined by the great religions—by Christ, St. Paul, Mohammed, Buddha, and Tao—were recognized, codified, and taught as local developments long before the universalist religions arose. The latter only gave to them an aura of divine origin, a dramatic artistic elaboration around the life of an individual, and a cult to keep the ethical development alive. There had to be emotional, not to say superstitious, overtones, and Moses had to bring the tablets down from the magic mountain, though the commandments would have been just as valuable in themselves if he had carved them in the shed.

A religion which fostered love and self-sacrifice and general humaneness (and did not degenerate into sacrificial orgies such as finished the Carthaginians and the Incas) was a most potent force for relative survival in the groups that possessed it. Ethical and religious values consequently grew into human society through the natural selection by which evolution eternally operates. In recognizing that the morality of a people and the rectitude of its governing class is a powerful factor in survival, we are not overlooking, incidentally, that other factors, such as the natural resources and the intelligence which uses natural resources, are also important in success, but selection operates on all.

Considering this fact, that selection by groups rather than individuals has begotten concern for ethical values (usually tied in historical development to a religion) two questions arise(Eibel-Eibesfeldt, I., 1979):

(1) Is it not necessary to retain competitive individual selection also *within* the group, to assist forward movement, and, if so, are there (a) some optimum levels for such and (b) special rules necessary to that end?

(2) By the ethic of evolution, should competition between groups proceed with no overflow into it of the mutual love ordained among individuals? Should it perhaps set up entirely different moral rules, yet rules derived consistent from the same basic evolutionary premise?

These questions require answers by deeper penetration into the findings of psychology and socio-biology, in subsequent essays in this book. What has to be said categorically in this chapter is that the bio-ethics of Beyondism does not lead to "nature red in tooth and claw" as the rule of life for men and women interacting within their community. It leads to all the commandments of love and forebearance which mosts religions have taken over. And, whatever subtle points remain to consider in the laws of interaction of nations, it definitely condemns the aims of a Hitler, a Napoleon, a Ghengis Khan, or a Stalin. For these men sought a world dictatorship, destroying natural biocultural experiments. This is the deadliest of dangers to evolution, yet let us not be so naive as to see no possibility of danger to creative variation also in other imperialisms, notably of religions, or the purely economic goals of multinational corporations.

The problem throughout history has been to attach sufficient emotional appeal to the group ethics to enable ethical appeals to overcome the obstinate selfishness and impulsiveness of the individual. The alternatives for control are fear produced by force—the king's law and the police—or fear and other emotional appeals established in taboos, superstitions, and religions. Our argument here is that the Ten Commandments, or the taboo on incest, and the like, have grown up in the first place by trial and error, in a learning process of group failure and success, survival and nonsurvival. The slowness of ethical growth is evident to anyone who attempts to read history. A U.S. Presidential candidate, Barry Goldwater, confesses (in *With No Apologies*, 1979), "when we scrape away the varnish of wealth, education, class, ethnic origin, parochial loyalties we discover that however much we've changed the shape of man's physical environment, man himself is still sinful, vain, greedy, ambitious, lustful, self-centered, unrepentant, and requiring of restraint."

The improvement of morality through group natural selection is bound to be very slow, because of the multitude of other factors that determine group survival, and because of the large size of modern national groups. Later we shall (see Chapter 16) discuss ways of making it more efficient. In any case, we must recognize that in the past, ethical standards have been incorporated in, and sustained by, religion, through the insights and the inventions of religious leaders. The process of blind discovery (natural variation) along with conscious ratification is one of small step-like alternations and iterations, not a simple first and second stage as initially described. In that iterative process, the ethical innovations have probably almost as frequently come from "revealed" religion, with ideas confirmed as a good "theory," by experience, as initially stumbled upon pragmatically by group experience. Any kind of group learning mechanisms are of so much lower an efficiency level than *individual* means-end-learning (instrumental conditioning) that the process of discovering the most efficient ethical laws has been, and is, likely to be extremely slow. For the same reason, many taboos and rituals justifiably annoying to rationalists have remained embedded in otherwise functionally effective ethics. (For example, the "deceased wife's sisters bill" was supported by the church until, only fairly recently, legislation removed the ban on such a marriage). Hardin's (1982) *Grounded Reason versus Received Formulas* studies this further.

Probably the great religions—such as Zoroastrianism, Taoism, Buddhism, Christianity, Islam (and such hybrids as the doctrines of Asoka, of Shintoism, of Confucius, of Marx, and some of the French Encyclopedists' rituals of Reason)—advanced ethics more rapidly than would have occurred through the painful process of sheer blind group trial and error alone. Against the gain from this indispensable help to ethics from religion and reason, one must debit:

(1) The obstinate intellectual maintenance of various myths that have stood in the way of a true answer to two of our three primary questions: "What am I?" and "Where am I?" as instanced in Galileo being threatened with the rack.

(2) The introduction of reward and punishment systems, e.g., Paradise and hellfire, to maintain morality. With the sudden puncturing of these fantasy myths, a severe readjustment problem to ethical control is forced traumatically upon us.

(3) Each religion succumbed to an imperialist ambition to be called a "universal" religion. Universal is here to be considered in contrast to a nationalistic loyalty (as in Shintoism, Hebrewism, and simple

patriotism). In the first place, the claim to being a religion and an ethical system that is universally correct is shown to be questionable by the fact of seven or eight different systems competing for the claim. Secondly, we would argue that the mode of origin of these ethical systems—actually by discovery of the values that aid the survival of a group in competition—does not fit them to reach the correctly separated-out *universal* values. (See Figure 8-1). That the "universal" religious ethics are a blind continuation of values found desirable *within* a group is shown in a practical way by:

(a) the countries which adopted them becoming more formidable as nations than those which did not (the Christian countries of Europe and the U.S. commanded the world in the nineteenth century),

(b) the great difficulty they experienced in entering a country like Japan, with a strictly patriotic religion, too similar in values to call for replacement, and

(c) the ethical obscurity in which they leave the conscientious objector to war, for example, in his values of loyalty to his own culture. What one should not "render unto Caesar" is unclear because the system is *derived* from within group ethics.

If we believe, from Beyondism's scientific approach to ethics, that natural selection among groups is the real basis of development of interindividual ethical rules within groups, then the ethical rules governing group interacting with group, and of in-group member with out-group individual, remain to be studied on their own, by evolutionary requirements, and could conceivably be appreciably different from those now supposed. In fact, our conclusion when we pursue this further in Chapter 8 is that the requirements *are* different. The concepts of a universal religion, as they have grown up historically in its existing forms, are therefore definitely mistaken, from a Beyondist point of view, in ways that will be further clarified as we proceed.

Setting aside at this stage of investigation just what the relations of human beings need to be in broadest roles, we conclude in this section that *within-group ethics, governing the behavior in interactions of group members, are to be derived from research on what behavior contributes to the survival of the group.* This may appear—and is meant to be—an uncompromising position and one completely different from that of any form of "revealed" religion (with or without claim to universality). That is to say, it is proposed that the basis of ethics in the intuitions of revealed religions, and issuing in dogmas claimed to be beyond questioning by reason, should be replaced by *research results from the social sciences tracing what group consequences follow from varieties of individual behavior.* Incidentally, it is common sense to make that social substitution of Beyondist for revealed religious values a gradual one, with the slow progress of a difficult science. One is altering a house in which he goes on living. It may well be that it will take social psychology, sociobiology, sociology, behavioral genetics, economics, cultural anthropology, and other branches of social science longer to reach the necessary methodological sophistication than one likes to think. But the principle is clear that ethics can and should become a branch of evolutionary science.

If one had space to give some close reasoning here on social science data and technical calculations of probability, one could almost certainly show that the major injunctions for ethical behavior from the revealed religions are supported by social science. Intuition has often been useful in science itself when confirmed by later calculation. But in dealing with the ever-present rejection of morals by recalcitrant and egotistical human nature, using comfortable and ingenious relativistic rationalizations, it is one thing to attempt to lay down values on the basis of some apostolic authority, and quite another to lead to them by an explicit chain of scientific evidence.

At this point, one can see that Beyondism is in the position of a religion, but, unlike certain species that perplex biological systematists, it defies generic classification because it is also a science. The question of whether it can offer the same emotional stability and satisfaction as religions have done must be examined in Chapters 13, 14, and 15. What distinguishes it from historical religions at this point, besides its scientific basis, is that it is a religion of progress, directed to the human adventure of progress, not a religion of conservatism, negation, and resignation. It asserts that what is good and bad must be evaluated by its contribution to human progress, genetic and cultural. As pointed out in the Preface, a reader might then ask why it is not called, say, Progressivism, rather than Beyondism? This would satisfy the idealistic reformer, the liberal, perhaps the Marxist, and all who are immediately concerned with abolishing the presumed evils of the world. The reason is very clear: that the reformer only *thinks* he knows that what he is bringing about is really progress. The doctrinaire writers behind the French revolution inadvertently brought about some dreadful things in the pursuit of "progress." Furthermore, the notion that progress is "more of the same" has repeatedly, indeed commonly, been a wrong assumption. The answer to public transport in 1800 would have seemed bigger and better stagecoaches. The answer to biological evolution of primates might have seemed to a gorilla to be toward a bigger and better gorilla—not a stunted, hairless little protohuman. Many an avant guarde reformer has turned sick on seeing 50 years later the actual product of the reform for which he fought so hard.

Progress ultimately emerges from changes in many directions, many of which were never thought of as progress. It occurs basically by cultural experiment and variation, followed by natural selection for successful survivals analogously to biological selection in Darwinian terms. Of course, one can be guided by superior insights, from the sociobiological sciences, in judging when reform will advance, i.e., some insights are likely to give a survival rate that will be better than chance. But still, *all moves toward progress are, in the last resort, blind. Thus, the basic principle emerges that the believer in progress, who is a believer in evolution, must begin with the premise only that we have to go beyond what we are.*

Along with that must go concern for the development of research that will evaluate survival levels attained. We shall see that, if this is taken as the basic creed, there will follow interesting developments. This has implications for changes of values in several social, religious, and political fields differing from those now prevalent. Even in the anti-eugenic attitude of Russia, we see the dawning of doubt and a recognition that genetic competition may become real. We note Toffler's (*Future Shock*, 1970) notice of Dr. Nefshk, of the Soviet Academy of Science, saying that "the world will soon witness a genetic equivalent of this arms race," implying that the Soviet should be doing something about it. With the present USSR "party-line" denial of individual genetic differences, that development is more likely to come in Britain and the U.S.A. than in Russia.

Anyone familiar with the current movements in thought will recognize that some are quite out of keeping with Beyondism as thus defined and that others, like "right-" and "left-" wing politics, being merely historical and arbitrary conglomerates of values, have no relevance. There is, however, a family, generic resemblance of Beyondism to such current movements as Social Darwinism and sociobiology, that needs to be examined. On scrutiny, one realizes that there is no identity but only resemblance appearing in some overlap of constituent concepts, not in the way they are put together. To avoid misunderstandings and caricatures, it is necessary, because of some confused current writings, forthwith to distinguish them.

"Social Darwinism" is a curious label in that it has received clear definition only by its critics, who define it as competition between man and man for survival, pursued, if one is consistent, *a lóutrance.* This is a gross parody of the subtle and more extended and complex group doctrine that is Beyondism. Beyondism touches Social Darwinism only in accepting evolution, but derives from that acceptance an altogether different and more refined view of what the implications are for human ethics.

Sociobiology differs in another way. It is solely a new science, combining the social and biological sciences. It is not a system of organized social and ethical values, as Beyondism becomes. Its great service to the science of man, as contributed, for example, by the writing of E. O. Wilson (1975), Ardrey (1961), Herrnstein (1971), Barash (1982), Hardin (1977), Lenski (1981), and others, has been to compel sociologists, many of whom have been notorious for deliberately and tendentiously ignoring genetics, to recognize the role of the human biological make-up in shaping societies. Beyondism recognizes that both cultural history *and* the innate tendencies and needs of the species, shape society.

As we come in Chapter 6 to study the interaction of the biological and the cultural, we get perspective from the fact that in different species they take different proportions, but though man is extreme in the proportions of behavior influenced by culture, it is a colossal mistake to ignore the genetic forces in his culture. And as Havelock Ellis long ago reminded us, "there is nothing so fragile as civilization, and no high civilization has long withstood the manifold risks it is exposed to" (1910). The genetic survives.

Evolution, then, combines *cultural* and *biological* evolution. As stated, one notes that in different species their proportionate roles are different. In insects, like the ant and the bee, the "culture" and the form of society itself is entirely genetically determined. We see in some birds, however, that the accidents of environment bend to new forms the genetic patterns, while in man the historical traditions and school learning may seem superficially to command the whole culture. But one sees also that they affect biological evolution.

Beyondism thus aims at finding the laws for evolution, cultural and genetic. It demands greater research endowment than the social (in contrast to the physical) sciences presently receive, first, to cover cultural and biological evolution and, secondly, to educate mankind to the goal of evolutionary advance. This latter education requires a re-evaluation of what many admired leaders (Aristophenes, King David, Christ, Schiller, Russell, and Einstein) have told us—explicitly that "we are all God's children," and presumably should therefore not enter into competition. Group competition, is, however, from the standpoint of Beyondism, the central requirement of ethical life.

Chapter 5

Can We Quantify "Relative Survival" and Employ the Evidence in Evaluating and Evolving Higher Morality?

The successful survival of a group requires, among other things, that individual morality reach an adequate level based on an ethic that requires people to sacrifice the crude satisfaction of impulse, to curb self-indulgence, and, in the last resort, to give their lives for the sake of the group to which they belong.

In the animal and vegetable kingdoms, generally, difference in species in probability of survival, often foreshadowed in an increase or diminution of population or area of established living (territory), can be recognized by a skilled biologist. In the end, a perceived decline may eventually result in a total extinction that is absolute, and one can then say that this, this, and this species or genus, e.g., the pterodactyls, disappeared after such and such a specific geological epoch. On the other hand, some species through gene mutations and trial and error in somewhat different environments had a form of continuity as a completely new, segregated species.

The narcissism of man, retreating into fantasy and other defense mechanisms from that faint new growth which psychologists call reality thinking, strongly prefers to believe that his race and culture cannot become extinct. Indeed, he is inclined to consider that genocide—even the necessary and fair-minded genocide by nature, not the amateur and illegitimate genocide by man—is intrinsically evil!

One wonders whether, in the name of humanitarianism, and the avoidance of unnecessary stress and waste, the process of natural selection could be kept effective between groups without individual groups actually having to go to the ultimate discard. (*Individual groups* certainly do not need to suffer if eugenics is practiced.) But in terms of cultures, could advanced social science research, by what might be

21

called the practice of political medicine, detect societies that are ill or moribund, and (a) save them from extinction, as well as (b) obtain evidence of sources of illness that would be of benefit to societies in general?

In standing for competition, one must parenthetically also note the danger that intensive competition, as among people in a race, tends to narrow the meaning of excellence. There is an old saying that "Competition, like alcohol, begins by stimulating but ends by bringing all to the same dull and brutish level." Evolution demands a different race, in which those who diverge from the track may win. That is to say, originality may lead to survival; and diversity is to be encouraged. But one constant goal of a good society is to maintain the tension of a moral purpose.

From a broad perspective, the chances of indefinite survival of the same group are not good. The relationship of human beings to a group is analogous to that of cells to a body. Without any actual disease, each person as a group of cells seems inevitably to age and die. What happens to individuals seems to happen, historically, to species, races, and cultures. It is estimated that 95% of the distinct biological life forms that ever existed are now extinct. Whole races of men have disappeared, and history is full of the demise of cultures (Eisenstadt, 1967). E. O. Wilson (1975) estimates that in nature some 10,000 species a year die out, finally. It is an unmistakable law of evolution, alike on the individual and on the group level, that progress occurs through the scrapping of individual organisms. But let us not begrudge, and call cruel, a process which in racial evolution has ensured that we are not the low-browed Neanderthal savage of 50,000 years ago or the hominids of three million years back. And, in cultural evolution, that we do not have to live, say, in Charlemagne's empire around 800 A.D., where the average life expectancy was about 35 years.

The importance of knowing what constitutes this syndrome of decay and death in a racio-cultural experiment arises from the fact that critics of Beyondism harp upon the difficulty or impossibility of *objectively* rating cultures for success. It is difficult, admittedly, but one way of calculating success is to recognize that it is the opposite direction on the scale from moribundness and death. Success, with groups as with individuals, may go in different directions, and the diseases that carry them in the opposite directions may be different; but death means in all cases loss of breathing and the stoppage of the heart. There are numerous excellent analyses by historians, from Gibbon's *Decline and Fall* (1910) to Eisenstadt's *Decline of Empires* (1967), of what causes and constitutes group decline,[3] but we still lack the quantitative laws and insights into dynamics with which some brilliant social psychologist may yet provide us. In Chapter 19 here, we urge that Beyondists work for a truly adequate international research center that may discover what happens in the aging of societies and their forms of disease, but for the present we shall simply argue on principle that diagnoses are intrinsically *possible*.

A researcher skilled in multivariate techniques will not make the mistake of supposing that the vitality of resistance to decay of a society is dependent only on its choice of interindividual ethical rules and the level of morality in aspiring to them. But despite economic and other conditions, it will *in part* do so, and it is with that part that we are concerned. Actually, history shows that a society *can* die from poor morale *alone*, as presumably in Sodom and Gomorrah, and, indeed, in Carthage and in the Roman Empire. Our concern is to reach a diagnostic skill that will recognize decay and point to the ethical aberrations that are contributing to it. But, if the Beyondist should fail to get public attention, and the necessary research, focused on this development of refined diagnosis, he can still rest satisfied that the necessary evolutionary principles will continue to operate effectively, though more harshly, in terms of the final *total collapse* and removal of societies with really low ethical standards. Indeed, though scientific debate may paralyze decision and early action in some borderline cases, the ultimate verdict of maladaption is always objectively given, beyond cavil, by nonsurvival of the society.

As indicated, social scientists are as yet in a state of comparative ignorance about the fine signs that indicate a declining and moribund society, and even about the natural history of *total* collapse we are not fully clear. When a human being dies, there is the death of a body and of a mind, but, in the analogue of the dying society, is there nonsurvival *both* of a race and a culture? What happens is obviously more complex in that *all* the racial, genetic substrate does not disappear, and elements of the culture, though not the unique total pattern, do *not* vanish. In short, natural selection of societies is not quite so simple in action as natural selection of individuals.

History apparently records that, when a particular culture in a particular group develops some faulty morality or nonadaptive habit which causes it to fail to survive, parts of its value system may still go on. As Gibbon (1910) describes the decline of the Roman Empire, partly through the indigestibility of a mixture of Roman and Christian virtues, there was a decay not only of administration and defense, but also of many values and customs now superseded and replaced by others in Western Culture. However, on the contrary, Roman law was embodied in several new cultural groups, such as when it was polished up by the Code of Napoleon to fit liberty, equality, and fraternity. Countless examples could be given of a positive "cannibalization" of decaying cultures that is a part of culture-borrowing generally, though in such a situation of decadence the borrower should beware. In short, on the cultural side, the collapse of a society does not bring the simple, generally total genetic and cultural extinction that occurs to a completely failing biological species. Nevertheless, apparently more of its customs die with it than survive, and although cultural evolution by trial and error and natural selection is thus a more confused and inefficient operation than the biological one, one can conclude that *on the whole* it leads to the better survival of cultures and of *cultural elements* that are better adapted to maintaining the economic, military, and biological life of the borrowing groups and other groups in the same situation.

As we turn to the genetic basis of the group, we see likewise that the direct extinction of the *species*, such as occurs in natural selection at the biological level in nature, also is modified. Indeed, it seems theoretically *possible* for a culture to expire culturally without any reduction in the gene pool that supported it. However, whenever counts of population have been possible, there seems to be an almost general rule that the decease of a culture pattern is accompanied by a reduction in the population that supported it. It is true that the dramatic reductions in native populations where their own culture was replaced, as took place in the Hawaiians and the Red Indians, can be partly attributed to such specifics as measles and alcoholism, but, as Margaret Mead (1955) convincingly argues, there is a malaise that occurs "when the cup of the culture is broken." The decay of the Roman Empire was accompanied by population reduction and, in a more conscious and intelligent action, the population of Japan ceased to grow as rapidly as before (30% reduction since World War II) when it lost in World War II.

In the era of classical Greek and the Old Testament histories, destruction of a national tribal culture almost always meant extinction (by massacre) or enslavement and reduced reproduction of the associated peoples. We see this in Carthage, the empire of Genghis Khan, the Indian tribes of North America, the Incas, the ancient Egyptians, and countless other examples. But the genetic displacement from the cultural victory is only partial and, except in more race conscious cultures, is further reduced by interbreeding of the defeated with the victors. Thus, to this day we are probably carrying genes from Neanderthal as well as Cro-Magnon races, though as a whole we are moved to being a new breed.

What has most frequently happened historically to genetic, racial components when a national culture is broken, is a genetic shrinkage, especially at the level of the aristocracy or governing classes, more so than at the level of the common people. As many observers have noted, it has been the rule rather than the exception—at least till the last few centuries—for the aristocracy to be racially differentiated from the common subjects. Thus, the Chinese were for a long time the subjects of the Huns; the Hyksos tribes ruled Egypt; and the Romans ruled over racially different populations. In the considerably changing relative success of Visigoth, Frankish, Ostrogoth, Avar, Vandal, and Lombard kingdoms through the Middle Ages, it was, for example, the Ostrogoth military caste, and not the Slavic race they controlled, that was mostly wiped out in their collapse. And if some superior Continental power had defeated England in, say, 1100 A.D., it would have been the Normans not the Saxon peasants who would have lost the substrate of their existence as a genetic pool. One must not exaggerate this difference; but it is worth noticing as a secondary systemic modifier of the tendency to reduction of a race with the downfall of its political group and its culture.

From the standpoint of keeping biological perspective, we must note that this incompleteness of co-selection of a genetic type and a behavioral life style is almost peculiar to breeds and *races* that lie within the same internally mating species. It *scarcely* exists in selection between truly different *species*, within a genus. This is largely because there is no cross fertility between species. As among breeds of man the genetic selection process might be called inefficient, or, at least, interrupted, hesitant, and confounded by cultural circumstances. By contrast, when a species becomes extinct, all its peculiar genes die with it. They are not usually carried on massively in other species, and the genes of any that do continue in other species can be only those way back in the common genus. Vavilov's principle of homologous development from internal genetic restraints is important here.

These technical asides on the blurring of the completeness of both genetic and cultural natural selection, and of their coordination, among human societies, introduce us to various further minor complexities that the general reader will not need to pursue in detail in following the main argument. Nevertheless, if the mechanisms of evolution are complex and yet central to our understanding of ethics, they must eventually be inspected and researched, for our main thesis in this chapter is that group natural selection is the crucible in which ethical advance is created. Spengler, in *The Decline of the West* (1928), lists 27 other civilizations preceding ours in decline. We must needs, therefore, take a "philosophical" attitude to the extinction of an ethnic (genetico-cultural) group. We should preserve what is preservable from the standpoint of filling out scientific knowledge; but there is no point in everywhere setting up little dams to stop the river of evolution. The due perspective is well caught, as regards individuals, in Omar Khayyam's

> And fear not lest Existence closing your
> Account, should lose or know the type no more.
> The Eternal Saki from the Bowl has pour'd
> Millions of Bubbles like us, and will pour....

The process of moral advance has two aspects. One must distinguish between (1) consciously discovering what ethical values are important for survival, and (2) the effective historical production of social values by natural selection, with or without our insight, for either will produce evolutionary advance. It is basically sufficient for both forms of the process that certain groups fail to survive. But in the more insightful learning we can recognize two sources of progress or change:

(1) Post mortems that historians and other thoughtful leaders make on the failing societies. Therefrom mankind can find out what is good only by discovering and excluding what is bad. Such lessons can come only after the event and with no benefit to the particular society that has taken the primrose path.

(2) Correlational statistical studies relating measures over time of the vitality vs. moribundness of the society to the extent of practice of and existence of various laws of morality. The correlations can properly be undertaken over a large sample of nations.

Although historians and political scientists have plenty of ideas about what indices they would use to assess vitality vs. moribundness, the deeper probings of social psychologists to analyze out and establish the *totality of dimensions* on which a nation's profile can be understood in developmental terms has only just begun, with the researches of Adelson (1950), Cattell and Brennan (1952), Cattell, Breul and Hartman (1952), Cattell and Gorsuch (1965), Graham (1970), Jonassen (1961), Lynn (1977), Rummel (1972), Russett (1968), Sawyer and Levine (1966), Cattell and Woliver (1980), and others. Graham tells us of evolution, "If we fix on scientific achievement (as a dimension of change) we discover a world transformed for human use and happiness; but if we think of political history we peer into mires of passion, hate and murder." And, checking with this discrepancy, we get estimates that the human population has stood at a total around a million through millions of years, whereas now we add a million to the world population in less than one week! Many dimensions of change may occur to one, but the check of factor analysis shows there is sufficient consistency (Cattell & Woliver, 1980) on the nature of the important broad dimensions to show that these methods are on the right track. A concrete illustration of profiles so derived is given by Figure 5-1, though comprehensive account of the nature of the various dimensions must be seen elsewhere (Chapter 12).

Figure 5-1

PROFILES OF CULTURAL TYPES
Contrast of Central Tendencies in Three Major Culture Patterns

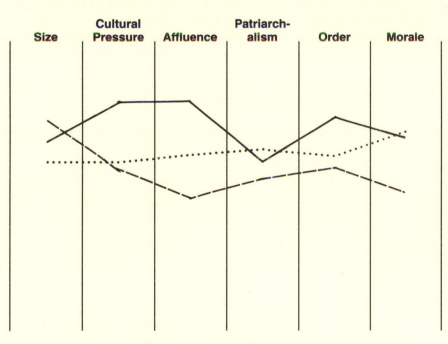

_____ The American-British-Australian Pattern
- - - - - - - The China-India-Liberia Pattern
· · · · · · · · · · The Russia-Argentina-Arabia Pattern

The vertical scale is in standard score units for each factor, but is not set out numerically.

Technically, we are in a region demanding what is called "partial correlation" and recognition of pattern effects, if we are to tease out the various historical causal actions. For, presumably, all dimensions of a nation contribute to the decision on its survival, whereas in the present chapter we are, for the time being, concerned only with the weights to be given to the population *morale* dimension, i.e., the aptness of the particular ethical rules, and the extent to which, in morality, they are practiced. And, as a last caveat, one must recognize that we are speaking of the internal conditions affecting success and survival in *all* societies, not those concerned with advancing the unique direction of development aimed at by each society, for which ethical values will also be specific. In the analogue presented by an individual, the corresponding distinction would be between his soundness in health and as a good citizen, on the one hand, and his fitness in his special profession, on the other. It would suffice to take us a long way if we achieve evaluation of the former, the group's basic survival fitness and the ethical rules that ensure it. And, as to the total evolutionary aim, we may temporarily lean on Erick Kohler's summary (*The True, the Good, the Beautiful*, 1980) "We have ... a perfectly reliable criterion of evolution ... and that is extension of score, extension of range of living."

That extension, like most "pulled out of a hat" by historians, may be too vague and nonoperational for measurement. But, in Figure 5-1 of this chapter, we see in the operationally discovered dozen or more dimensions of nations a real basis for estimating, in a profile, the factors in survival.

Nevertheless, we are far from being able to anticipate the future, and all the research institutes discussed in Chapter 18 may only advance us a little. In 1933 the U.S. President set up a group of distinguished experts to anticipate the innovations of the next quarter century. They overlooked the massive movements due to electronics, antibiotics, and space flight, among others. We cannot all think with the imagination of an H.G. Wells—a proven prophet. However, we are developing measurement and P-technique methods likely to give us "relative survival" estimates that exceed present ignorance.

In later discussion we reject dictatorial "global government" in favor of national, compartmentalized experiments, from the creations and the creative errors in which all humanity can learn. But true experiment requires quantitative measures of culturo-genetic success—and that is what we have been asking about in this chapter.

Chapter **6**

What Are the Properties of Biological and Cultural Evolution, and How Do They Interact?

It has been recognized earlier that the characteristics of biological and cultural evolution through group natural selection are less efficient or, at least, less free of temporary "error" than corresponding processes with individuals. The failure of a racio-cultural group does not fully eliminate, but only reduces, the population proportion of that genetic pool in the world gene total, and though its less fortunate elements of cultural custom and practice may be looked at askance by intelligent surviving cultures, they are likely to linger here and there, embedded in other cultures for a comparatively long time.

Purely biological selection, both of individuals within a group and among groups themselves, is scientifically, comparatively well understood through the rapid advance of genetics and behavior genetics over the last hundred years. By contrast, the field of cultural evolution has been trampled by the feet of so many diverse methodologists—cultural anthropologists, historians, sociologists, political scientists, and journalists—that a succinct statement of findings and principles reached today is unlikely to satisfy all.

There was first the battle between *diffusionists*, on the one hand, arguing that the observed common cultural elements across groups arose by "copying" in some form, and on the other, the *independent origin* investigators who believe that the wheel, the bow and the arrow, the smelting of bronze, totem worship, priesthood, and kingship were repeatedly reinvented in response to the same problems and through the nature of man's mind and his environment. Scientific evidence gradually came to put more weight on the diffusionist position. It is at least clear that inventiveness is more rare than we had supposed. (Not so, perhaps, today, when invention is a self-conscious professional activity—but still there are blind spots, e.g., in ethics where the idea of inventive progress has not cognitively been entertained.) True, the Mediterranean and the Chinese civilizations independently invented the domestication of the horse, the military sword and shield, and the smelting of metals. But invention of paper, the "agriculture" of silk, and a crude form of printing appeared first in China. I am inclined to argue with Coon (1962) that the diffusionist position has been overstated, though before, say, 5000 B.C., man was extraordinarily slow to invent and more subject to the chance migratory diffusion processes.

The next battle of emphasis was between what is sometimes called the *materialist* school and what might be called the *leader* or "heroic" school, in regard to the origin of social mutations. The former argues in the manner of Hegel and Marx, that massive economic influences, e.g., from a change in mode of production, population pressures, disease epidemics, climatic changes, and organizational influences, act with a deterministic inevitability, and that the role of individual ideas is small in relation to these. For example, the Black Death in Europe certainly helped bring the feudal system to an end, and the increase of trade and life in cities (initially walled and defensive) helped the rise of social power in a middle class. By contrast, the leader school (as in Carlyle's heroes, and the great man school of history) ascribes major changes to the leadership of outstanding individuals and their ideas.[4] On this a quantitative solution seems impossible, and the only error a social evolutionist can make is to deny granting substantial influences to both.

If we are to reach some understanding of the integration of biological and cultural evolution—the mixture which *finally* determines events—we must first give more attention to the natural history of cultural change, because, as just stated, we can take the main biological laws of change as comparatively settled. Diffusion first needs our attention, for in spite of poor communication, geographical barriers, and the slowness of migrations, it worked rather well in prehistoric times (see Pearson, *Anthropology*, 1974).

Cultural elements can move around by voluntary imitation by the adopting culture or by the coercions of war, migration, and missionary propaganda. Most "developing" countries in our own time have believed they see advantages in Western Culture and have willingly imitated. After a slight contretemps requiring the interference of Admiral Perry, Japan in the mid-19th century also imitated willingly. In the Russia of Peter the Great, only a few Russians joined him with any enthusiasm in deliberate culture borrowing from the West, and the rest resisted, in vain. In the countries conquered by Rome, the new culture patterns of Roman law, etc., were imposed, as were those of Britain on India. Striking examples of coercion were Charlemagne's bringing Christianity with mass executions, to the Saxons, Napoleon's imposition of his legal code on Europe, and the allies' imposing democracy in World War II on Germany and Japan.

There are doubtless interesting differences in the stability and the manner of absorption of new culture patterns according to whether these patterns were reached via admiration and willing borrowing or were imposed by economic, missionary, and military pressures; and whether the culture patterns were adopted without any racial substitutions and admixtures or with racial migration and supplanting. Such differences should be researched, but, meanwhile, other more basic questions need to be addressed. Among these more basic aspects let us note that the diffusion itself is one thing, mainly based on economics or fallible human appreciations, while the evolutionary check that decides whether the borrowing shall lead to more permanent prevalence is quite another. For in willing borrowing there can be foolish borrowing, as King James rightly said of Raleigh bringing the tobacco-smoking Caribs to Europe. Nevertheless, as in interindividual admiration, there is some probability of the more adjustive and prospering customs being among those consciously imitated. In the above instance we took from the new world also the potato, Indian corn, and cotton. One must say "some," because there are conspicuous examples (besides smoking!) of the superficial passion we call "fashionableness" leading to diffusions that are, in the end, inimical to survival, and so, when all accounts are in, become discarded. Did the Holy Roman Empire do better to copy the authoritarianism of Rome than the democracy of Greece from those two available classical ruins?

Cultural evolution by borrowing is a chancy affair to the extent that it depends on human judgment faced with altogether too complex a choice. Its only guaranteed probablity of advance is that the borrowing is more frequently from live than dead cultures, and that there is more chance for cultural habits that caused collapse to be carried into oblivion.

A second complication in cultural evolution is that, in the frequently occurring borrowing of *single* elements, the borrowed element may prove indigestible, functionally inconsistent, and disruptive of the existing pattern in the borrower. This seems to have happened a lot with importing of superior technology without social or religious values that have been the generator for, and therefore probably in some dynamic sense consistent with, the imitated technology. A recent instance is Iran's taking in American technical skills but finding the rest of the pattern quite unacceptable. In that case, and some others, the borrowing process is stopped, but one suspects that there is at least an inherent tendency, in general, for the adoption of one element to lead in step-like fashion to the adoption of the *whole* internally dynamically consistent new pattern.

Besides changes of culture by materialistic, natural pressures and by voluntary and involuntary borrowing, we must recognize the third major contribution to cultural evolution—that from invention by individuals. This was slow and infrequent in early times—Zoser's engineers' invention of the pyramid and Akhenaten's introduction of monotheism seem the only major developments in 2,000 years (say 2650 B.C. to 650 B.C.) of Egyptian culture, a culture sufficiently isolated to demonstrate what comes from invention alone. Yet, for reasons needing investigation, the last thousand years, at least in Western culture, has seen invention by individuals, or small groups of individuals, as seemingly the main source of cultural change.

We are speaking here of invention defined on a broad front—mechanical, biological, political, and artistic—especially since the Renaissance. The important social psychological principle here is that frequently the "side effects" have been quite different from and greater than the intended use of the original invention. Becquerel's discovery of radioactivity, important enough in physics, actually led to its largest effects socially, for example, in medicine and warfare. Luther's 95 theses, intrinsically theological, altered the political shape of Europe and its colonies. Nickolaus Otto's construction of the internal combustion engine in his garden shed, changed the form of cities (and perhaps the art of lovemaking!).

To the surviving materialists and diffusionists of the last generation, we may seem to be regressing to the old simple-minded view of progress as a series of new ideas, but that is not what we are saying, and, moreover, we are talking of mankind since, say, 100 A.D., not of the millenia that went before, when, as Bury (1920) points out, the idea of deliberate progress scarcely existed in the common man, and in most others. But as of now, and conceived here with major side effects, we give it an altogether larger role in cultural evolution than did, say, Marx, Hegel, and Keith.

Moreover, it is this inventive action in cultural evolution that brings the latter more closely to the corresponding biological model. The change produced by invention by the inspired individual is initially instant and specific, but it can still be advantageous or disadvantageous for survival, the decision remaining to be made, as in other modes of cultural change, by group natural selection. One would probably have to concede that unlike genetic mutations, *most* of these cultural mutations are as beneficial as they were intended to be. But it is conceivable that such inventions as Dr. Guillotine's machine for rapid decapitation, the adjusted income tax, Hitler's introduction of mass genocide in war, "pot" smoking, papal infallibility, and the custom of accepting monopolies in labor and management groups, will prove to be inventions inimical to evolution.

Recognition of the major importance of conscious inventions (and their unforeseen side effects) mainly resulting from highly original and independent individuals, necessarily points to a different balance in what would otherwise be the desired conclusion on the relative importance of individuality and group conformity, as studied in Chapter 10 below.

Incidentally, because we give this growing importance to deliberate intellectual and conscious creation, let no one assume that our concept of culture is that it is a world of conscious ideas only. Each and every culture pattern contains vast amounts of unconscious "wisdom," i.e., trusted and tried emotional adaptiveness, not verbalized, and scarcely capable of defense by reason. (Hence the limitations of Rationalism, little understood by the 18th-century rationalists.)

With this admittedly too-condensed overview of the sources of alteration in culture per se, let us turn to the intriguing scientific issue of the mode of interaction of genetic and cultural processes in weaving the warp and the weft of the many-patterned carpet of history. As to the role of the former, many academic sociologists and cultural anthropologists—but few historians or practical politicians in close contact with actual events—have written and theorized as if race played no part whatever in the adjustment, or effective contribution to progress, by various human groups. It was, for various emotional reasons, fashionable around the middle of this century to discount group genetic differences entirely. To make clear that we need not get involved in these racist prejudices one way or the other, we shall use the term *racial composite* for any given *gene pool*, since a "pure race" national gene pool is virtually unknown. The presently physically recognized central tendencies in the classical race types developed largely by geographical isolations since the later ice ages (Coon, 1962; Hooton, 1946; Baker, 1974). They may have little importance for the new world developments in cultures. But it is also possible that cultures will develop new races.[5] Certainly we must agree with the naturalist, Baker (*Race,* 1974) that "It is scarcely possible to believe that two ethnic taxa, differing in many genes affecting various parts of the body, could be identically similar in all those genes that affect the development and function of the nervous system."

The necessary research to tell us what the true position is regarding the interaction of race and culture would need to begin with an appraisal of their relative magnitudes, and continue into more specific effects. In simplest form, such an enquiry would begin with an analysis of variance as sketched in Figure 6-1(a). The horizontal rows would be a representative sample of races differing on some characteristics such as stature, resistance to malaria, performance in tests of spatial ability, and so on. The vertical rows would represent, correspondingly, a spread over some cultural characteristics such as typical number of years of education, degree of freedom of divorce, amount of animal diet, and so on.

Figure 6-1

RACE AND CULTURE AS CONTRIBUTIONS TO GROUP PERFORMANCE

(a) Procedure for Analysis of Variance of Group Performance Due Respectively to Genetic Variance and Cultural Variance

		Races			
		1	2	3	4
Cultures	1	5 7 6 10	3 3 5 6	4 8 10 16	2 3 5 6
	2	3 6 6 9	2 3 6 6	5 10 10 12	7 4 5 5
	3	7 8 10 12	4 5 7 9	6 9 12 18	3 3 6 8

(b) The Distribution of a Sample Where There Is Interaction Such That Race and Culture Are Correlated

		Races							
		1		2		3		4	
Cultures	1	2 4	2 5	2 4	3 6	1 5	2 5	3 5	4 5
	2	2 6	3 7	3 5	3 9	3 6	4 6	3 6	5 7
	3	4 7	4 9	4 8	5 8	4 5	4 6	7 8	7 9

Four countries for illustration have their scores placed in each cell.

If 48 cultures were collected to fill in the cells (squares) in Figure 6-1, we would have the ideal material for answering the question "What is the relative contribution of this genetic, racial trait and that cultural trait to this group's particular performance?" ("the dependent variable"). But if the argument below is true that a cultural element may be accepted by one race more readily than by another, we shall have instead the distribution shown in Figure 6-1(b) when we correctly sample the population by (a). This "scattergram" shows here that there is a positive correlation of the two sources, e.g., increase of height of head might be correlated with more musical emphasis in the culture. In that case, the splitting of the two contributions becomes a little more complex. Incidentally, it is the existence of such correlations that popularized the term "ethnic group," because that term recognized that a racially distinct group is, in fact, generally culturally distinct too, so that they have to be taken together, in practice though not in scientific analysis.

It follows that an important question regarding human evolution concerns whether such a tie-up of a genetic pool with a cultural pattern is an historical accident of migrations, wars, etc., or derives from an inherent basis in that some cultures can be more suitable, and more easily acquired, by some races than others. The taboo on good analytical studies of race, brought on by Hitler's travesties, around 1940, and continuing in the conventional mind to perhaps 1970, has been broken by the fine scientific studies of Baker, Coon, Hooton, Jensen, Lynn, and other bold thinkers and experimenters; but our understanding still remains, unfortunately, backward and befogged because of that period of blackout.

The psychology of individual differences leaves absolutely no doubt (despite Watson's (1914) nonsensical conclusions in reflexology) that individuals with different genetic make-up have differing difficulties in acquiring learned cultural performances. The tone-deaf individual cannot become a good violin player. The person with poor spatial ability (which many studies—see Vandenberg [1965]—have shown is substantially inherited) will reach poorer achievement in mechanical engineering. A person with a manic-depressive diathesis will vary unstably in his daily outlook and attitudes. And a low-I.Q. high school student tends to be averse to more analytical subjects.

It is also possible that in two groups, one all of, say, I.Q. 80 and the other of I.Q. 120, an *emergent*, interactional effect arises that makes group performance difference greater than what one would expect from the central level of the constituent individuals. And if there is a normal distribution in such groups, instead of all standing at the group average, the differences in the sheer number of very high and of very low I.Q.s will be much greater between these groups than a small difference of average would lead a nonstatistician to expect (See Figure 6-2).

Research on cultural associations between the racial character (gene pool) of groups and the cultures they successfully adopt is rare and recent, but by no means absent.[6] Cattell and Brennan (1983) have shown relations of culture-fair intelligence levels of populations to national cultural productivity as also has Lynn (1971) for regional sections of a country—Great Britain. But the relations of the broader traits that historians and cultural anthropologists talk about rest more on psychologists' hunches than on empirical researches. Thus, McDougall (1921) made a first rough analysis claiming to show that the outline of the Nordid race distribution in Europe determines pretty well the boundaries of the Protestant form of Christianity. In France, he showed also that other indicators, such as alcoholism, introversion, suicide, and scientific rather than artistic interests, are related across the nation to racial distributions. Kretschmer (1931) pointed to areas running across countries that seem to tie musical productivity, and especially interest in opera, to amount of Alpinid race settlement. Tastes in pictorial art are more ephemeral, yet both Eysenck and the present writer have noted preference for bright, clear colors among extroverts and more sombre, subtle painting among introverts.

None of these psychologists denies the role of history, propinquity, and economic causes in producing overlaying effects that blur the rela-

Figure 6-2

DISTRIBUTION OF INTELLIGENCE

**Large Differences in Frequency of Really High and Low IQs
with Small Difference of Group Means**

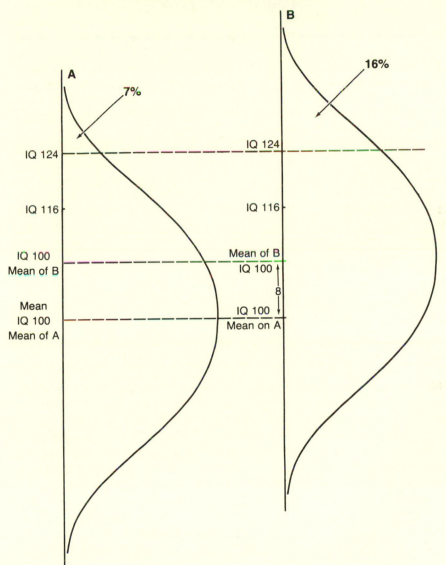

An increase of 8 points of IQ in the mean of the group A results in IQs in B above 124
as increasing from 7% to 16%. The ratio of increase in B of IQs above 130 is still greater.

tions with race. This realistic scientific evaluation is, however, very different from that of a species of environmentalists which glibly denies any attention to possible racial contribution.[7] A study is long overdue on the hypothesis that a cultural feature perhaps most closely tied to race is the form of religion most readily culturally adopted. Besides McDougall's study, above, one notes, for example, that despite great Christian missionary efforts in Africa, Africans seem to identify more readily with Islam. And despite Buddha starting his work in India, Buddhism today distributes itself much more according to the boundaries of the Mongoloid race. Buddhism has briefly been described as a religion that combines comfort with resignation, reminding one of the recent experiments with Caucasian and Mongolian year-old infants (Freedman, 1971) in which the former show more dynamic behavior and less tolerance of interference. We may note also the description by Sheldon (W. Sheldon, an authority on temperament, says in *The Varieties of Temperament* (1947), "In Buddhism we usually find relaxation, love of sleep and ease, tolerant complacency, pleasure in digestion, deliberate ceremoniousness, and orientation toward kin—in short, viscerotonia—deified."

In essence, what we are saying here is no different from William James's (1963) persuasive argument that the philosophical systems of philosophers are most determined by their temperaments. It is also very reasonable to expect that a choice among religions, in a group exposed to diverse missionary pressures, will be substantially decided by the temperament of the people. As an anthropologist of great experience, Sir Arthur Keith, in *A New Theory of Human Evolution* (1949), says, "Tradition is important but I cannot conceive a people nursing and handing down a tradition that is not compatible to their inborn mental qualities." In a more restricted, but more closely historically documented area—that of occupations, guilds, ruling classes, and so on—Darlington (1969), with pedigrees, makes a case for some tie-ups of cultural specialization with genetic pools, including, for example, leaders in the industrial revolution. Perhaps even the circles of diplomats and the types active in politics collect groups not only by the obvious social connections, but by genetic talents in families. The Churchills in England and the Kennedys in America offer instances for study. When Harold Macmillan became British Prime Minister, Gunther (1927, p. 459) notes that he "found he was related (by marriage and family) to no fewer than sixteen members of the House of Commons and had blood ties with seven of the nineteen members of the cabinet." Since nepotism is, substantially, strictly prevented from raising its ugly head in British appointments, this must be, at least in part, a tending of suitable genetic gifts to accumulate in a particular area of cultural activity. Such examples may not be of mass importance, and, like the Roman Emperors and the European aristocracies, may well represent more family influence than genetic aptness for the occupations; but they at least illustrate on a small scale a shaping of gene pools by cultural standards and expectations when acting over many generations. For although these emperors and aristocracies may have been inadequate to their tasks, studies of them as individuals (Woods, H., *Mental & Moral Heredity in Royalty*, 1906) show them to be well above the average capacity in the population.

The most basic principle in the interaction of genetic and cultural influences is that it is a two-way affair. A long-continued cultural demand, with fall-out of those who do not meet it, can mold genetic levels, and the genetic level of a people can affect the final form of its cultural adoption. The former is evident when a culture selects, by migrations and differential birth rates (if eugenic), the types best suited to it. The latter includes the influence of new genetic mutations, and the racial changes through what geneticists call "genetic drift," and immigrations. A sufficient genetic change can obviously upset the cultural-genetic equilibrium and modify the culture afresh. But, in general, the culture decides the direction in which natural selection will most vigorously take place, genetically.

The action of the former—culture molding race—one would expect to find well documented, but the above examples are presently all one can glean. But its occurrence in humans is clearly indicated by its powerful role in horticulture and husbandry, where, in a space of a century or two, the Guernsey Herd Society creates and fixes the quite special properties of Guernsey cows, or a Peking palace breeds the canine curiosity we call a Pekinese dog. There is thus little doubt that if within-group natural selection prevailed in the direction of better fitting the people to the culture genetically (before educational influences take on) the largely geographically generated races as we now know them could, in perhaps as few as 20 generations, give way to *new* races differing in more important ways.

This has scarcely begun to happen. The Jews, and the English in their colonizations, have in the main kept a race-conscious ideal, but otherwise it is difficult to point to examples where, over some hundreds of years, a traditional commitment to segregation, without any assertion of superiority, has operated sufficiently to produce a type. A minimum general requirement for this perception is that for *between-*

group survival the natural selection *within* a group must be adjusted to that goal. This understanding seems to have been as remote from the grasp of politicians and the mediocre man in the street as, say, the medical understanding in 1900 that the common precursor of rheumatic fever was streptococcal sore throat. Even when perceived, as men like Darwin and Spencer perceived it, the conscience of the public and the politicians in regard to the next generation has been insufficient to produce action. This is seen, for example, in the fact that the larger families are being produced by the sub-average in intelligence. This fact has been established by psychologists for 50 years, without any sign of adequate discussion of socio-political counter measures.

Up to the present, perhaps the main effect of within-group selection in relation to between-group survival has been a slight lowering of I.Q. (only since differential death rates were eliminated) and the spread of a more domesticated and dependent form of the human animal. Perhaps in the period of prehistory clever archeologists will substantiate instances of culture, e.g., hunting or agricultural, molding the genetic pool by within-tribe natural selection. Yet the practical likelihood clearly exists, of self-molding, and, we would argue that the reformed cultural groups of the future will, in fact, mold the genetic pool of each group in a way analogous to that in which the external environment and climate have already produced the races we know today.

The interactions of genetic and cultural evolution we have to consider are two-way, but in general they act by gentle restraint and modification rather than by some absolute prohibition by one of a development in the other. (The latter might have arisen if we tried to teach Neanderthal man the culture of advanced physics or if the members of the Mensa society had to try to adapt themselves to the harsh physical life of a tribe of Australian aborigines.) A useful analogy, and perhaps even a workable theoretical model, for understanding mutual adjustment of race and culture is to consider the former as the hardware and the latter as the software (programs) in terms of computer technology. On applying a complex and exacting culture to a race to whom it is not particularly suitable in virtue of their average mental capacity, we may expect the memory storage to be inadequate to the program, and certain subroutines to be missing, so that only a fragmentary imitation of the original program is possible. The changes in Christian theology and ritual—including those in hagiology—which some Catholic missionaries have had to accept in preliterate peoples may be of this type.

Culture borrowing may thus be subject to the same limitations and distortions as in shifting a program from one machine to another, or in translating from a more developed language to a cruder one. The fact that psychologists have pointed to no *absolute* prohibition in teaching a borrowed culture to a racially different group thus does not mean that important partial deformations do not take place. They have simply not been quantitatively investigated. However, in the miniature society of school classes, it is demonstrated by what happens if even the most devoted teacher tries to teach, say, advanced algebra to, say, a 6th-grade class composed of children of I.Q. 70 to 75.

The existence of cultural effect on gene pools means that we may ultimately have to recognize the genetic effect of *individuals* of considerable cultural impact. The character and ability of St. Paul, Peter the Great, and Faraday so powerfully modified the environment of their societies as probably to produce genetic selection in the direction of their own personalities. And, in the same direction, the culture brought to Russia in the Mongol invasions probably resulted in such suicide of the freedom-demanding Nordid types as to lead to a disproportionate genetic representation of Mongoloid Stalin types in the eventual genetic pool.

In seeking further general principles about the interaction of the processes of biological and cultural evolution, we must keep in focus the basic proposition that *both* processes have two steps of (1) variation (mutations) followed by (2) natural selection. (The "insights" toward improved culture which constantly occur and which seem to deny that all is trial and error, are, after all, only human insights, as blind in the longer perspective and the last resort as the effect of cosmic rays upon chromosomal mutations.) There is a further culture parallel to genetics in that the genetic variation in a group may come about by hybridization, paralleling cultural variations that occur by borrowing of cultural elements between groups, producing a mixed culture and new derivatives from the mixture. The chief difference is that the biological process is slower and more lasting. One might be tempted to say it is more irreversible,[8] but it may be that cultural change is, also, *strictly*, irreversible. (The "restoration" of Charles II did not reinstate the kingship conditions of Charles I.) And so "the moving finger writes, and having writ moves on."

The basic difference is that although a culture pattern exists (except as a concept) only in the behavior of a *substrate of people, it does not depend solely for its survival on the survival of a particular genetic group.* Inasmuch as it can be diffused and borrowed readily (if sufficiently desired), it has a free-floating existence in itself and a separate subjection to selection. It is a soul needing a body, but able to settle in virtually any, except for the slight genetic interaction above. Should it fail to command a substrate, it lives on only in the anemic understanding of its full-blooded nature that is abstracted in the print of history books. But the cultural natural selection may essentially be understood to operate on ideas.

The true *survival value* of a culture cannot, however, be calculated (as from Figure 6-1) as a complete abstraction from its biological substrates, because of the interaction phenomena just discussed. Because of the resistance of some sociologists and cultural anthropologists to this concept, one must take an extreme example and ask if the early human *homo erectus* (or the almost prehuman *Pithecanthropus*), with perhaps half the brain capacity of the more educable humans today, could have adopted and maintained a culture of librarians, computers, complex taxation laws, and nuclear power? Even in the last couple of centuries we have seen cultural diffusion occurring in a definitely racially determined fashion. Let us first recognize that it is reasonable to assume that a group with a well-developed pre-existing *complex* culture will offer more resistance to intrusion of a new culture than will one whose culture is so crude as to be almost a vacuum. Then let us note that some races with closer historical and geographical connections to Europe than Japan ever had are today much behind Japan in fulfilling their intention to develop essentially European cultural complexities in technology and social organization. What data exists on relatively culture fair intelligence tests suggests that in this case the mean and distribution of intelligence in the biological bases of the population here compared is the deciding factor (Jensen, 1973; Lynn, et al., 1987).

So far as the genetic contribution to racio-cultural survival is concerned, an index based on the average and standard deviation of I.Q. in each nation's racial composite calls for correlational research on the relation of mean intelligence to the cultural mean. Low but significant correlations have been found (Cattell & Brennan, 1981). But one would not expect the statistically significant correlation between intelligence and culture to be large, because of interaction effects, and because the qualities of the purely cultural contribution to performance linked with the genetic contribution would vary substantially. The outcome in terms of survival for a particular cultural mutation is as beset by chance influences as a blown seed falling on good or poor earth. In the cultural innovation and propagation of monotheism by the two Egyptian geniuses Akhenaten and Moses, was the latter lucky in trying it on an idolatrous Hebrew people?

Any analysis and calculated estimate of the survival values of racial gene pools and cultural patterns will be highly complicated by reason of the above-mentioned interaction effects which occur first within the two parts themselves: (1) the hybrid interaction in the gene pool and (2) the hybrid adaptations when diverse cultural elements are brought together. These effects exist before the new combination of genetic and cultural patterns themselves is brought about. There are going to be nice problems concerning mathematical models for those who tackle this field.

Meanwhile, one has to recognize what can only be called inherent inefficiences in the group natural selection process as it occurs in the natural, hitherto unmonitored, historical process. For the increase or decrease by natural selection to be maximally responsive to the soundness of either a genetic pool or a cultural style, it would be desirable that no "unlucky" tie-up of, say, a good culture with a poor race should occur. One sees that a racial degenerative failure (such as the presumed breeding out of the capable managerial class in later Rome) may collapse the associated culture, and, conversely, that a poor cultural choice may bring the end of a promising race. As the balanced design of analyses of variance in Figure 6-1 shows, a human experimenter with some control over his experiment could avoid odd results and get an efficient process going. There are at the moment some 150 self-governed countries in the world, a number large enough to reduce chance "unlucky" survival judgments. Apart from what nature decides, human scientists could on this number obtain some reliability of estimate of what various culture types and gene pools are doing.

Some further questions arise concerning the inefficiences and tragedies of the unmonitored historical process and their possible rectification—or, at least, understanding. First, let us recognize that any effective use of the above design in assessing the contributions of the two contributors to survival supposes that we do not have to wait for nonsurvival but can develop an index of vitality—vs.—moribundness that is a reasonably valid dependent variable. Social science still has to confirm this.

Secondly, there is a serious, systematic, evolutionary problem in the proper feedback of benefits to a more inventive and enlightened group from its life style. In the rapid communication and imitation that is increasingly possible, originality and inventiveness as such—which are extremely valuable to mankind—count for little, since an obviously successful device is immediately copied by less creative races, and by cultures of a style inherently inimical to originality. In terms of the successful survival of a better culture little objection can be raised, because the borrowing *is* the survival of that element—though even then in perhaps dangerously poor company, as when a backward country acquires nuclear arms. The inefficiency of reinforcement lies in the genetic part, in that little reward goes to the biological quality behind inventiveness and creativity. The fate of nations in this respect is not so different from the true and tragic story of many inventive individuals, less shrewd than Edison and Marconi, who die in the attic, while financiers with cunning promotional knowledge (the kind that Edison, Ford, Wells, and many true creative people have hated) scoop the profits.

For most of the now closing century the percent of the national income contributed to *basic* scientific and medical research by such countries as Germany, Denmark, Sweden, and Switzerland has been ahead of virtually all other countries. These expenders of public subscription on scientific knowledge for its own sake are now more closely followed by England, France, the U.S., and, in the last generation, Russia and Japan. Their findings benefit the health, standard of living, and defense capacity of very different countries, racially and culturally, whose cultural values cause them to put more into, say, luxury, outworn religions, or expensive recreations than into scientific institutions and the cultivation of dedication to truth. The vitally important condition of cultural evolution—just as in individual learning—is that *rewards should be fed back specifically* to the behavior that actually begets such rewards.

The response of the knee-jerk "feeling liberal" to this situation is that science is international, and the idealistic scientist is happy to think that he is helping all mankind. Basic research is supported by either charity or by the taxpayer, and it is little comfort, surely even to the scientist-idealist to know that his willing supporters may be blown up by his own invention, pirated by a very different culture that gives no regard or support to "science for its own sake." The situation repeats itself on a smaller scale among business corporations whose leaders support more basic research, while those which are interested only in profits and use spies are parasitic upon the former. Incidently, the public demand for cheap nonprescriptive drugs has contributed to drying up the sources of purely exploratory research, and is another instance of the lack of realization that the goose that lays the golden eggs in pure research tends to go unreinforced and unfed.

Since secrecy is quite impracticable and defeating in basic research, a social device that could convince us that the rewarding action of natural selection need not be lost in this field is eagerly sought but not easy to find. As far as one can presently see, the only advantage that can come to the more creative life style and genetic endowment is the advantage of an *earlier* start,[9] which, however, in the typically long evolutionary perspectives is too brief for leverage. What happens is shown in the English establishment of constitutional limits to monarchy in the Magna Carta, the European invention in the 15th century of the ocean-going vessel, the Middle Ages invention of the stirrup, the horse collar, and the moldboard plow, the German creation of the jet airplane, and, say, the English invention of the steam engine. The last one gave England a head start in the industrial revolution, and the possession of trained occupational groups associated with their research has given nations a year or two advantage in war. In each case, these inventions did happen to give increased survival value for some time, until effectively imitated. This happened in the case of social inventions by reduction of costly internal friction, and in physical inventions by access to earth's resources, and by capacity to support a larger population at a comparatively good standard of living.

However, many examples of a much more trivial or completely absent gain, relative to other groups, from the precious quality of creativity could be cited. The early white settlers in the U.S. drove the Indians westward sustained from hunger by the great Indian "invention" of maize. On the other hand, the Shang dynasty in China, 1000 B.C., had planned cities, writing paper, silk, horses, metal swords, kings, and priests, yet these were not imitated in Europe for most of a thousand years. As world communication of all kinds speeds up and imitation is more immediate, the advantages of first invention become slight. In war there have been instances of the originator being penalized by his own invention, e.g., the German invention of antimalarial atabrine was used to strengthen the power of troops fighting against Germany in tropical Africa. Patents and copyrights, when internationally observed, preserve some natural selection for creativity. But mainly it is only in the military field that the deliberate preservation of secrecy succeeds in giving some advantage to the more creative.

A third interference with the effective action of evolution at the group level arises again from the onset of rapid communication and trade. It concerns the spread of "sameness"—the danger of a total run-down into entropy in the domain of evolution. Unless, or until, nations have expressively developed their particular, firm, racio-cultural ideas, there is a risk that the current fashionable magpie adoption of alien culture patterns, as well as freedoms of invasion by immigration, will reduce the basic diversity that natural selection needs, in many groups, for its operation. Obviously, if all countries were reduced to the same—incidentally monotonous—style of culture, no scientific basis would remain to enable the relative effectiveness of designs to be evaluated. This biological form of the law of entropy in thermodynamics as far as I know has not yet been investigated in terms of the dependence of evolution on the range of deviation among breeds, cultures, and species. As far as ethics is concerned, theoretically one could have sameness in genetic and most cultural traits, including also the form of the ethical system, i.e., in morality. This situation might appeal to some as an ideal concentration on raising morality; but human progress is much more than increasing moral adherence to a particular, transient, arrested ethical system. Just as the useful economic capital of a society is not increased by everyone borrowing indiscriminately from everyone else, so an overactive and indiscriminate culture borrowing destroys the motive power of the evolutionary mechanism.

In conclusion to this section, we must recognize the limits of the present research. It is evident that classical biological evolution, on the one hand, and free-floating cultural-element evolution, on the other, operate by partly different models and that they interact in ways science has not yet investigated. Unfortunately, the students in sociology and anthropology who might now be coming to effective research therein have been exposed to the loud and self-righteous assertion that the genetic pool—race—can have no effect on culture patterns. But we see here, in fact, a two-way action in which genetic patterns affect the acceptance of culture patterns, and culture patterns help to mold genetic pools. One consequence is that although separate survivals—of genetic features and culture pattern elements—predominate, the prevalent degree of interaction means that an unadapted culture may reduce the survival level of a potentially well-adapted race, and a declining racial pool may contribute to the failure of a good culture. Nevertheless, although manipulative experiments on the requisite scale cannot be set up, the multivariate experimenter has statistical means whereby he can assess what effects arise separately from genetic and cultural sources.

Chapter 7

How Are Interindividual Ethics and Selection To Be Adapted to Intergroup Selection for Survival?

Beyondism has uncovered the principle—in studying the six issues to this point—that since the ethics and morality of members are one component in group survival, these qualities are enhanced by the continuance of intergroup natural selection. However, lest one lose a sense of proportion, it is necessary to point out that a second principle also enters— namely, that selection among individuals, sometimes modifying the interindividual behavior, is also necessary for long-term group survival genetically. Ethics and eugenics may, indeed, have come into conflict. The altruism and self-sacrifice which strengthen the group immediately, may weaken it in the long run, if they aid the survival of the weak at the expense of the strong.

In considering this subtle interplay of two principles, we must also keep in mind a second duality—that of *universal group survival characters* (UGSC) and *specific group survival characters* (SGSC). The first cover the development of characters which aid the survival of *any* group—such as group cohesiveness. The second is necessitated by the position Beyondism has taken that each group should go out on its own adventure, in the necessary diversification of groups for natural selection to act upon. There will thus be *some* ethical laws within each group devoted explicitly to the survival of its particular life style, and not required in other groups. For example, regard for education in mathematics may be ethical in a U.S. or U.S.S.R. group, but irrelevant in a primitive Papuan society.

As to the mode of origin of different SGSC value systems, history is full of examples of the special leadership of subgroups and individuals. However, we might pause to note an almost chance effect that occurs at the genetic level in what has become recognized as "genetic drift." A first glimpse of this came to science in the biological field, through the sharp eye of Darwin. When he visited the Galapagos Islands he noted that the South American parent stock had, in several instances, developed into a new species (sometimes only a new breed), distinctive for each island. He was surprised to find that in these islands, being highly similar, "neither the nature of the soil, nor height of the land, nor the climate..." (1917) could account for these differences as being *adaptive.* Each type was, if we like thus to speak of it, as the result of the "life force" seemingly varying for "variation's sake." A geneticist today would speak of chance mutations, and the "genetic drift" that then occurs in small colonies. Such is essentially the nature of what we here call "a specific group adventure," except that we here speak of both spontaneous genetic specificity and genetic specificity caused by cultural specificity, in combination, determining a group's unique path. Much minor variation has been "nonadaptive."

Let us consider the first, more difficult question—that of the clash of ethical and eugenic principles—first. The rise of ethical rules for group survival takes place partly unconsciously, e.g., in the rules against incest, and partly with community religious co-action, e.g., in rules against theft and murder. The prohibitions against theft, incest, adultery beyond the recognized monogamous or polygamous marriage, and murder, are virtually common to the "Ten Commandments" and taboos of practically all known cultures. Had we the space, we should at this point demonstrate by example that these UGSC (Universal) characters arise almost everywhere and by experience of the group weakness and confusion that arise on their absence. However, the reader must be referred to original sources in anthropological works like the Bible, Frazer, Darlington, Eisenstadt, Gibbon, Huntington, Keith, Norling, and Oliver. The reader will note, as we have said, that some injunctions can be perceived clearly to have social survival value, whereas others are obscure and have been tentatively adopted and re-adopted over thousands of years of experience. For example, though promiscuity and homosexuality were automatically condemned by Victorians, anyone who tries to do so today, in public and on a rational basis, will almost certainly fail to convince his opponent. The verdict on these and other questions can be reached only by research on the survival potential of countries with and without these prohibitions. And the causal chains from individual behavior to group health effects[10] will involve complex networks of quantitative argument.

The SGSC (special group) values rest on the same research methods, but here we shall expect that interindividual behavior rules will be contributory only to a specific group goal and situation. The island situation of Britain required praise of sailors and begot those who could colonize at the end of a "far flung battle line." Whereas Germany, surrounded at every frontier by a possible enemy, begot military and authoritarian values.

The UGSC values in nations are obviously those of sacrifice, loyalty, patriotism, and so on, while in religious groups they are reverence, obedience, and charity. But one has only to think of the ideal citizen type in, say, Britain, France, Italy, Russia, and Japan, or of Protestantism and Catholicism, to see that specific values are cherished in inter-individual behavior that are quite diverse and shaped to the survival of a particular group.

In both UGSC and SGSC values, we are presently at a point of individualistic thinking where something more than custom or religious intuition is required to clarify the necessity of ethical ideals, and, in particular, to give strength to morality. For doubt as to which is the correct target makes good marksmanship rather superfluous.

Because *any* ethical system harasses the id, it will tend to be criticized, and it is not surprising that from the Neolithic and Bronze Ages on, and through the various family systems, a constant preoccupation of society has been simply to get morality—the obeying of the *given* ethics—established. It is not our task to enter on the vast problem of how best to educate the superego,[11] but our concern to establish rational bases for ethical laws is the first part of the problem.

When ethical laws are examined more closely, one finds that they can be considered as a hierarchy of object loyalties. These are set out for clarity in Table 7-1 below. For the follower of the revealed religions, God stands at the head of the hierarchy and under that comes concerns and loyalties to his fellow citizens, and, after that, to mankind in general. This hierarchical form has caused both philosophical confusion and conflict in practical life for the average man. As examples of the former we can take philosophies from Plato's to Nietzsche's *Beyond Good and Evil*, which have played with the idea that the differences are best understood as different rules for *different groups within society*. History certainly produces instances of different ethical rules for knightly aristocracies, guild craftsmen, villains, and the like, and slaves. To illustrate from a multitude of instances, one may choose the Samurai, versus other Japanese, or the Visigothic aristocracy versus the native Roman population. Euric, becoming "emperor," commanded, in the last instance, that a single system apply to both, instancing that the whole movement of universal religions such as Christianity has always been toward that goal.

Table 7-1

CONNOTATIONS OF THE FACTOR OF MORALE AND MORALITY AS A DIMENSION OF NATIONAL CULTURES

Variable
(High standard of inter-individual morality)
Low frequency of syphilis
Low frequency of homicides
Low death rate from alcoholism
Low death rate from typhoid fever
More eminent men eminent outside the field of politics
Small proportion of births illegitimate
Better education and civil rights for women
Fewer families per single house
No licensing of prostitution
Fewer deaths from tuberculosis
No absolute restriction on divorce
Low divorce rate
Low gross birth rate
Low gross death rate

Variables are here arranged in declining order of loading, averaged over two or more researches. Thus the first listed variables are more closely connected with the action or genesis of morale than the last.

What we are arguing for is a universality of a complex object system, basing the differences among the objects essentially on a transcendental *contract* difference. In any case, "laws equal for all persons" must recognize that people stand in different roles. The high court judge who sentences a murderer to execution is not himself a murderer. However, the main value differences we have to deal with are not due to role differences, but to differences in the value system of particular independent groups. Here we have to take note of the mechanisms of reward and punishment that are used to implement the positive and negative (restrictive) values of a country. A current myth of the feeling liberal is that punishment does not affect antisocial behavior. The reader should get this denial of punishment into true perspective by reading Skinner's *Beyond Freedom and Dignity* (1971) on the social application of learning laws. Socially instituted punishment has three main functions: (1) to change the habits of the criminal; (2) to act as a deterrent to those on the border of succumbing to temptation ("Pour encourager les autres" as the French say); and (3) to satisfy what some would represent as "the revenge and vindictiveness of the outraged society." The last has sometimes been condemned, but in the dynamics of maintaining difficult inhibitions, the superego of society also needs its rewards if it is to be maintained. It may bring a glow of virtue to the feeling liberal to argue that if the effective treatment of one convicted of "robbery with violence" happens to be pleasant, society should forego its revenge. As a psychologist, I see the present knowledge of means of reform to be so lacking in substance that almost anything can be argued for. With the dismal practical failure of reformed reform therapy, we cannot deny the importance to society of its expressed indignation.

One thing is clear: that any method likely to produce personality change in a criminal is, like "brain washing," likely to require intrusion on the individual's "right to privacy" and perhaps even of dignity. Our democratic indignation when a communist country treats political dissidents at a mental hospital for psychiatric brainwashing should be tempered by the reminder that we essentially brainwash our dissident children who cause trouble in schools. The same is part of normal education in monolithic Communist and Catholic schools. In the U.S. the individual has at least the choice of being a conforming Democrat or a conforming Republican!

Let us consider next the conflict of ethical and eugenic rules. It is an immediate ethical advantage if each member is prepared to lay down his life for others. This occurs, for example, in the soldiers storming a breach. But if the more ethical individual is more frequently eliminated, and conscience and altruism have a moderate genetic element, then the society over generations will come to lack morale. It is evident that the *ethical* laws must include a sophisticated regard for *eugenic* laws. Society is out to survive, but over generations as well as immediately. The mechanisms to help this result we discuss in Chapters 16 and 17. Meanwhile it is evident that the ethics of society require within-group success and within-group survival to be tied to the possession of *above-average* qualities. In essence, but not in every detail, this requires the recognition of society as a *meritocracy.* This means free social mobility and free competition that differentially reward degrees of talent, hard work, and honesty.

It is an unrealistic speculation that all people, out of sheer idealistic ethics, will do their best, without reward, in whatever their abilities bring them to do. The clerk working mechanically all day, and the garbage collector, need an immediate extra reward to keep them busily at their jobs. What is needed is a growth in society of greater respect for lowly jobs. At present, respect for an occupation, and the mean I.Q. of those who practice it, are highly correlated. We have a problem here that can only be solved by a meritocracy respecting effort and good will as much as intelligence—while still recognizing individual differences in capability (Young, 1958; Herrnstein, 1971).

Meritocracy, as the last part of the word tells us, implies *government* by the more intelligent, as the result of a fair and efficient promotion scheme. Better methods of selecting politicians than those we now practice have been suggested (Shaw, 1944), but they imply arresting a power game in full play and substituting a more just psychological selection. The problem is as old and intractable as when Plato suggested the selection of his guardians of society, by their explicit lack of interest in power per se. There is more to it than the obvious introduction of psychological selection methods. We must study history and the statistical comparison of countries with different systems. Then there is the question, not only of the effects of different ethical systems, but also of the degree to which they are followed—the origins of morale and morality.

In view of our recognition from the beginning that survival is multiply determined, e.g., by natural resources, population size, etc., and not by morality level alone, it is somewhat unexpected to find that the actual verdict of research (see Cattell & Gorsuch, 1965) is the existence of a fairly definite dimension of morale in the existing nations of the world, which correlates with social indices as shown in Table 7-1.

It is noteworthy that it includes several variables having to do with general social responsibility, besides freedom from murders, prostitution, alcoholism, etc. A similar "goodness of living" factor was found by Thorndike in comparing 300 American cities, and we have ventured to add to Table 7-1 from this and other sources other variables that theoretically we would expect to find there.

If the breakdowns of societies from crime, parasitism, and lack of morale are as frequent as history suggests, it is at first a little surprising that the genetic and personally acquired behaviors which lead to breakdown have not been more rapidly eliminated. The ruins and desolate spaces encountered over the earth where once were flowering cultures —from the Pyramids to the Roman provinces of North Africa, to Angkor Vat, and Teotihuacan—tell us as much as the bones of extinct species. And where history reaches back, as to Sodom and Gomorrah and the days of Nero, the correspondence of collapse with decay of morale is evident. Other causes of decay, such as a failing economy, excessive wars, population resources of "management capacity" growing by low birthrates "thin on top," environmental assaults as with malaria, plague, and drought, are not forgotten, but it is hard to find instances of total decay in a society of high morale.

The influences of decay in the large and complex national group have, for our easier study, a more easily demonstrable analogue in the business corporation, which may go bankrupt from various combinations of defects, e.g., poor technical practice, high wage demands from unions, managerial inefficiency, embezzlement by a director, etc. However, certainly in nations, the further evils are clearly more generally consequences of the morale decay itself. This apparently lay at the root, in the final collapse of the Roman empire, of such individual events as the aqueducts falling into disrepair, the unwillingness to face military service, filling the army with offspring of slaves, malarial mosquitoes causing abandoned farms, taxation becoming ruinous to support priesthoods and bureaucracies which no one felt it was his personal task to protest against and control, and, in the case of Rome, women from able patrician families declining to inconvenience themselves with childbirth.

Probably four *major* influences have in general contributed to declines of morale: (1) A rise in distraction luxuries, through slave labor, or, in modern times, scientific production of machines and goods. (2) The advent of "pluralistic ethics," i.e., few values in common over different ethnic groups in the same national culture. (3) The attrition of the reality principle by the pleasure principle, through intellectual rationalization steadily gnawing at "the outworn, puritanic traditions of right and wrong." This last is essentially what we have called "moral relativism" and arises in the permissive, relaxed phase of a civilization, which Toynbee (1947) recognized as alternating with tighter demands in what the Chinese call the succession of Yin and Yang. (4) The inherent negative eugenic individual survival value of moral conduct.

Social psychology is beginning to have some insightful and dependable things to say on each of these. The first—the submerging of essentials in a sea of trifles—needs little comment. Probably the recently documented decline in school achievement on "basics" in a growing curriculum of fads is a representative case. As to the second, we have recognized on the one hand that there are *legitimately* "local" ethical varieties that derive from the same basic principle worked out in different situations. But, especially in the case of unabsorbed diverse ethnic groups, or too bigotted religious subcults, the probability seems to be that the morale of the organic total group suffers from Pluralism. The correlations show this fragmentation of culture to be (partially) greater simply in larger nations, like the U.S.A., India, and Russia. Later (Chapter 18) we shall discuss possible advantages in ethnic pluralism in other respects, notably contribution to genetic hybridization "experiments" and the possibilities of comparative cultural experiments available within the group. But general historical observation suggests serious disservice of pluralism to morale and morality. The first World War began over the attempt of the Austrian Empire to contain too many diverse cultures in its basket; India has suffered in its reforms through 500 language groups, and in religions it saved itself only by the great loss of life in separating Pakistan from India proper. The U.S.A. currently for religious reasons finds social agreement on such things as planned abortion difficult to reach, while on an ethnic basis millions of its immigrant citizens are demanding that school instruction be given in their particular languages, at government expense! And it is not unusual for a psychologist dealing with individual delinquents to find that an adolescent who has been exposed to a kaleidoscope of many subgroup values will conclude that there is no basis to any of them. This, in addition to Tarde's "anomie" of big city life, is probably the main cause of "alienation." Alienation, as a feeling of loneliness and not belonging, is distressing to the individual and a prime cause of low morale and disregard for identification with the values of the culture.

Although religious freedom is an essential for cultural integrity, the fact seems to be that the country is fortunate which does not have to put up with religions too diverse in values. Some of the strongest leadership has been given by countries where patriotism is bound by a single religion, as in the theocracies of Israel and the New England colony, while Spain, Japan, and Britain have come near thereto. In this respect, Beyondism is in a unique position in that, insofar as its social values and imperatives derive from science, it offers a possibility of resolution between clashing systems that are based on revelation and dogmatic assertion of subjective values. It has to admit, instead, only the "approximations" that reside in the growing edge of science.

The third source of attrition in morale is inherent in the assaults which the psychoanalytic id will continually make on the hard realism of the ego and the resolute demands of the superego. Among the defenses by which the ego comes to terms with the gnawing demands of the id is rationalization, and no section of society is more cunning at impressive rationalizations than the intellectuals of the "phantasy" p-cultures—literature, art, and the theater. Such high intellectual gifts as, say, Bertrand Russell had, did not prevent him, and many like him, suggesting behavior in national life, love, and education that stood, for ethical support, on no realistic psychological evidence. The "defection of the intellectuals" is a well-known accompaniment of revolution (detested by the same "intellectuals" when the comfort upset in revolution actually occurs!). What is less obvious and more in need of social psychological study is the slow undermining of values over decades and centuries which the rationalizing "intellectual" brings about. As when the ocean attacks the shore, the undesirable reef and the desirable harbor wall disappear together. In making a study of humor in *Punch* over a hundred years, I could not help being impressed by the role of the intellectuals' humor in the erosion process.

The fourth and last influence at work in the running down of a culture is what we may call the *altruism drain*. By the very nature of conscientiousness and altruism, the individual high in these qualities sacrifices himself to the group more than do other individuals. He and his kind therefore tend to diminish, both as to numbers possessing certain educational standards of altruistic social concern, and genetically as ingredients in the gene pool. As regards the latter, biologists have studied closely what happens on a number of species, especially insects, where some members, e.g., the workers in the beehive, naturallly do not reproduce. Their "biological evaluation" is, in that case, made through the selection evaluation of their close relatives. Biologists have pointed out that in mammals, for example, altruistic sacrifice of individual life, e.g., of a vixen for her cubs, remains effective for continuing the hereditary altruistic trait provided the heredity of the saver and the saved are close enough. Sir Arthur Keith's contribution to understanding how altruistic traits advance in human society was in pointing out that over perhaps 500,000 years of intertribal (and even interfamily) competition, the benefit of self-sacrificing reverted pretty quickly to evolutionary gain in the relative success of any group, among such numerous *small* groups, i.e., with close genetic affinity of members.

With the huge modern nations, this mechanism, however, becomes inefficient almost to futility, as Keith (1968) points out, and this may be why moral decline, after some centuries, is almost the rule of large societies. It therefore behooves such a group deliberately to institute forms of within-group selection that favor the altruistic in spite of the natural tendency of the altruistic to be replaced by the egoistic and the parasitic. The anguished cry of the biblical prophet that "the wicked flourish" is a true perception. Yet with a large group, just as with a small one, if it is permitted for the ethical sanctions that favor the survival of individuals to be contrary to those necessary for the survival of the group, these collision courses of evolution will meet ultimately head-on, and the verdict will be given by collapse of the group.

The battle between the forces of idealism and law within the group, on the one hand, and those of ruthless selfishness and uncontrol on the other, of course, shifts in favor of one or the other continuously. But there is reason to believe that there are insidious processes which in most cases cause the latter to triumph—or at least gradually gain ground—in many historical eras. This produces, as it were, regularly a senile society, in which the impulses of idealism are dead. If this continues, a point is reached at which the group literally dies—like a human cell invaded by a virus and turned to manufacturing a foreign substance instead of its own nourishment. Or, if the group does not actually fall to pieces, it undergoes such a loss of survival potential relative to other groups that it suffers, internationally, economic and political setbacks harmful to its members, or is thrust into unfavorable positions relative to other nations through defeat in war.

The tragedy of this is that the few good citizens perish with the many who have thrown aside moral values. But the redeeming feature of this process is that it puts an inescapable end to the degenerative process, whenever it occurs. It is the one hope we have that no matter how long the era in which vice triumphs over civic virtue it will eventually meet a sudden end. Both the genetic carriers of the antisocial trends and the defective social customs themselves, will be wiped out—so long as intergroup competition efficiently prevails.

In considering the readiness of the individual to reach moral standards, and the selection among individuals which is part of the necessary interindividual, within-group ethical system, we shall stand by the position adopted throughout this book, and recognize that the individual pursuing antisocial, unconscientious behavior does so partly by genetic defects and partly by unfortunate values and habits that he has acquired. Students are taught by many sociologists that criminal behavior can have no genetic contribution, because crimes are all so different in different cultures. Yet they are obviously given a single name—crimes—because they do have much in common, with poor self-control and selfishness especially defining them.

If anyone has difficulty in envisaging the genetic component in crime, let him reflect that spelling ability, dealing with a performance highly specific to a culture, is, as Thurstone (1977) showed, substantially inherited. A disability here can show as poor spelling in a diversity of culturally taught languages. The twin studies of Lange, Lykken, Rosanoff, Stumpfl, and Franz, as well as other than twin methods of evaluating heredity (See Cattell, 1982), *strongly suggest* that individuals may inherit a "mental defect" or "lack" in whatever it takes to be conscientious and concerned about duties and the personalities and needs of other people. Further psychological research points more specifically to the roots of the deficiency in a collection of multiple personality factor deviations, notably $C-$, $G-$, $M+$, $O-$, and Q_2+, while true psychopaths are also high on E. In rough popular terms this means a type marked by emotional instability and subjectivity of demands, with poor superego development and high assertion. Note we are not arguing for a *predominance* of genetics in antisocial behavior, but only for a partial role greater than the zero role which some sociologists have absurdly maintained. For although C and Q_2 have substantial heredity, E, G, and O are more environmentally determined.[12]

One might easily get from the above an implication that man is genetically unadapted to an altruistic, society-centered life. Montaigne (1958) stresses the contrast of the demands of a rational society with "this infinite number of passions to which we are incessantly a prey." As the psychologist sees it, however, man, along with the primates, has, in general, excellent natural equipment for altruistic and social behavior. He has a natural ergic impulse ("instinct") toward tender, parental, protective behavior and toward sympathetic gregariousness ("herd instinct"). The problem lies in intelligent handling of these instincts in a complex society, because pity and good fellowship are just as likely to be mishandled in their social effects as any other emotional resources. However, in later study (Chapter 12) we recognize that there can additionally be a "genetic lag," notably in that the overall strength of the primate sex and pugnacity ergs, in particular, can be in excess of civilized needs. The adjustment of morals to ethics thus calls also for some genetic breeding.

As far as a positive response to this situation is concerned, the Beyondist within-group ethic calls for devices, considered in more detail in Chapters 16 and 18, whereby both the genetic and educational parts of the ethical counter influence can be strengthened. These measures are considered in the hope of demonstrating that *the decline of nations is not an inherent necessity.* Selection within the group to meet between-group competition, of course, involves production of a whole pattern of traits and people, but part thereof is a raising of this and a lowering of that level on a particular population variable, e.g., an increase of intelligence, and a reduction of psychotic instabilities under stress. Education can operate on both levels and patterns, e.g., it can raise literacy and produce, say, a pattern of more scientists than lawyers, or vice versa. Eugenics can mainly only raise levels in the raw material that education and culture will shape to required patterns. But in the example of inheritance of personality factors above, it is clear that desirable direction can be worked out at the genetic level (Chapter 16).

Without these counter measures, we argue, any large and highly organized group tends to enter on a downward course after a time, in both socially desirable inheritable qualities, and, in a cultural sense, in favoring the survival of selfish acquired attitudes, habits directed to purely personal gain, neglect of charitable social services, and spreading the scoffing humor of social cynicism. The issue of national decline involving other population qualities than moral ones, notably intelligence, is discussed elsewhere, though in studying decline, as such, they must be focussed together.

If we are to argue that some of the decline in morale is due to a slow, long-term dysgenic trend in the basis of *positive moral attitudes*, we must explain why the replacement rate among the more conscientious becomes subnormal. One can very likely show that this is the case in regard to those who give greatest community service in peace and those who more readily defend their group in war.

There are historians who suggest that one cause of national decline is war, and that, after excessively severe wars, nations regularly decline. The reader will think of many examples. The decline in cultural, economic, and political strength could be due to economic and other causes, but the majority of writers on this topic ascribe it to loss of the more enterprising, the physically and mentally fit, and the dedicated, among a whole generation. As Barrie lamented in a famous speech, "The spring of the year is buried in the fields of Flanders."

In any case, war offers a more easily studied, probably more simple, instance of the negative selection that goes on more obscurely in the processes of cultural stress at a more steady peaceful level. The late Chancellor of Stanford University, David Jordan, noted that before conscription there were quite disproportionately high volunteering and casualty rates in university students compared to other classes, and Toynbee (1947) bemoans the same heavy losses of young men in his contemporaries at Oxford and Cambridge. Even under conscription it is still the physically and mentally fit who are chosen. However, in spite of the almost uniform conclusion of writers that war is dysgenic, my own examination of data, e.g., the relative casualty rates of officers and men, leaves me, if I am to be a cautious social scientist, still not

58

clearly convinced of this. It is possible that we are too affected by the pathos of it, as expressed in such poets as Wilfred Owen and Rupert Brooke, and in the lines of Newbolt (*The Volunteer*):

> "*He leapt to arms unbidden,*
> *Unneeded, over-bold;*
> *His face by earth is hidden,*
> *His heart in earth is cold.*

But, if the majority is right, then the sinking of great nations into second rate status, after an undue number of wars—even when all were successful wars—could be explained by the loss of the more intelligent, healthy, and, especially, enterprising and idealistic. Let it be repeated here, however, that this refers to culturally acquired as much as genetic qualities. Psychologists have demonstrated that basic values are values passed on more by the family than school or church. Those buried in the fields of war may not only be relatively childless, but, if fathers, have been absent from the setting of intimate values for their children. Conceivably, over several generations, wars can gradually deprive nations of cultural vigor and ultimate survival capacity. (It is sardonic comfort that if there are nuclear wars in the future they will reduce the fit no more than the unfit.)

Peace, in an advancing culture, however, has its other socio-genetic costs, possibly no less deplorable than those of war. If earnings determine the size of family that can be supported and educated, i.e., if we consider countries where welfare and socialistic aids apply only to a quite small incompetent minority, then we still find various more altruistic callings that will under-reproduce. The priest, the worker who gives money and time to community activities, the researcher, the artist or musician, and probably the school teacher and the nurse, as well as many others more obscure, are underpaid relative to the businessman, his associated workers, and all who can appeal directly to the consumer. The film star, the prize fighter, the seller of liquor, the pornographic specialist, and all who are simply prepared to take all that can be acquired by selling to an ignorant, ill-educated, self-indulgent market place, will, by contrast, prosper. This is no criticism of the open market, with its *general* functionality, but only a note on its abuses, and an observation that altruism, especially outside beaten paths, results, in any form of society, in taxing the life energies of the altruist—even when it does not crucify him. Incidentally, this is the element of truth in the Christian and Buddhist worship of poverty: that it permits men to do what is necessary for society regardless of whether it is paid. But a Beyondist society can surely intelligently anticipate valuable activities that need to be supported, without the mistake of perpetuating poverty as such.

This problem brings us into glancing contact with the issue of the "consumer economy" we shall analyze more comprehensively later (Chapter 18). Politically, Beyondism cuts across and transcends the game of right and left wing. Socialism and communism have two main planks: interference with market-earning levels differentiating the more and the less needed workers, in favor of the latter; and controlling directions of production by a government elite rather than by consumer demand. Beyondism agrees with the second but not the first. *Most* governments, despite a slogan of "consumerism," agree with the second to the extent of heavily taxing liquor and tobacco, and by subsidizing a level of child education that few consumers would be willing to pay for, if left to their own consumer choices.

If we ask whether societies are at present aiming at such within-group ethical values and selections as are necessary for the survival of the group, the answer is that the advanced countries are doing so reasonably well in terms of what is needed culturally and educationally, but poorly in terms of what is needed through ethics applied to genetics. That is why in this chapter much more detailed argument and illustration has been given to the latter—not as an expression of its greater relative importance, but through the need to rescue it from total neglect.

On yet another flank we have to consider the impediments to clean *intergroup* natural selection presented by international business/corporations and international finance in the International Monetary Fund. The former mix and confuse survival potentials of different nations; the latter is a banking organization to supply loans to various countries arrested in some proposed progress, by lack of funds. In both cases it is argued that without aid "world recovery" would be slowed down. But what is meant by "world recovery" other than "more trade"? Heightening of world activity in trade is an objective very different from the effective pursuit of natural selection, and may operate *against* natural selection in certain instances.

What emerges is that within-group ethics require, but in a different proportion, the combination of interindividual cooperation and competition that we study more closely in the next chapter as *cooperative competition among groups*, and *eugenic laws*. That is to say, the cooperation among individuals to produce group survival involves the style of ethics which religions have long approached, with an added selection on the cultural level by the requirements of meritocracy and on the genetic level to defeat the wastage that seems endemic in large societies.

/ / **/ / / ■ ■ ■ ■ ■ ■ ■ ■ ■ ■ ■ ■ ■ ■ ■ ■ ■**

Chapter 8

The Six Targets of Ethical Responsibility: What lies beyond within groups and world values?

The survival of groups as such is decided by their behavior to one another and to their environments. The latter is not an ethical matter except insofar as it affects other groups, e.g., through pollution, extravagant use of resources, etc. What we have specifically to ask about here, therefore, is the ethics of behavior among groups, as organized groups with governments. This is the next logical step following the derivation of ethics *among* members of a group, studied as a first principle in Chapter 4.

It is a common assumption, mainly from the influence of would-be universalistic religions, that the same ethical rules apply to intergroup as to interindividual behavior. We shall argue that this is erroneous, not only because groups do not have the same kinds of behaviors to control as individuals do (for example, they cannot commit adultery!), but because evolution applies to them in a different manner. (The former—the dissimilarity of behavior—is actually only incidental, since the same principles could cover the two different domains of derivatives.)

The criterion of ethical *interindividual* behavior is that it shall be consistent with the survival of the group, and for that purpose a high degree of cooperation, mutual help, and self-sacrifice is normally indicated. It is not required that the consequences of behavior shall always be favorable to the individual; indeed, he may be required to give his own life in ethical service.

In the group, on the other hand, if its ethical *internal* laws and standards are to be maximally improved, *it is important that all consequences of its behavior—its institutions and morality—should feed back to it directly in terms of survival or nonsurvival.* This self-sufficiency would be an absolute requirement, demanding no cooperation among groups akin to that required among individuals, if there were no analogue to a society of individuals in the form of an association of groups. That groups will develop their own peculiar moralities is obvious. Nietzsche (*Joyful Wisdom*, 1960) reminds us, "As the conditions for the maintenance of our community have been very different from those of another community, there have been very different moralities." Until the rise, first of the League of Nations, and then of UNO, there was no worldwide society of nations having "rights." However, whether such an organization existed or not, the general principle has always existed that the competition among groups could be fatal without some regard for all groups. This we now consciously recognize, in concluding that competition has to operate with some restrictions, over and above the above *primary* principle that a group should be independent enough of others to stand or fall, unaided, in natural selection by its own internal health as a group of interacting people.

Whatever "feeling liberals"[13] may wish to believe about idealistic action among nations, in the spirit of self-styled "universalistic" religious values, not a glimmer of such charity, or even mercy, in intergroup action has existed through known history—at least until a fitful spark appeared in rational governments during the last century. Any historian, any diplomat, can cite countless instances of the rule of sheer force—and of some instances of apparent charity which, on realistic examination, prove to be roundabout but unquestionable examples of self-interest. So long as no world society of nations existed in fact, and more importantly, no risk arose in international competition of destruction of the human species, this all-out, unhampered competition for survival was, indeed, a Beyondist first principle. It was the most efficient basis for improving group structure, technical advance, interindividual ethics, and individual within-group altruism in the human species.

If we accept—as our arguments will suggest—the need for an "Earth Society" of originally independent nations, to avoid total destruction and to support a common research institute to evaluate the level of survival potential of all countries (as a guide to their internal ethical effectiveness), then a more definite, sound form for international ethics, than this first free competition, can be scientifically reached.

What we then have in the world is a society of two tiers:
(1) Single organized societies within which must prevail what we may call Ethical System 1 among the members. (Revealed religious ethics and social legislation now in being begin to converge on this concept.)

(2) A worldwide society among organized societies, having what we shall define as Ethical System 2 in this chapter.

It then becomes evident from this similarity of form that although interindividual and intergroup ethics must differ substantially, they will do so *in degree, not in kind*. In *System 1*—among individuals—the demand for cooperation and mutual self-sacrifice within the group puts limits to, and requires special devices for accommodating the action of natural selection. In *System 2*—between group ethics—the need for selection of individuals and ethical and cultural customs in such a way as to *favor the group producing and cherishing advanced human types*, is by contrast, paramount. For the necessary machinery here remains such that the group shall receive the feedback of its own qualities.

At the outset it is necessary to reaffirm here that intergroup ethics is not concerned *only* with intergroup behavior. One must not fall into the familiar error of thinking that intergroup competition is solely or even mainly expressed as a direct struggle *among* groups. Intergroup maneuvering plays its part; but groups are being judged by something less humanly fallible than their peers, namely, by the natural environment itself. Just how much the survival of groups as groups, under the process of natural selection, is determined respectively by political, economic, and military success in interaction, and how much by mastery over nature we do not yet know. It is a similar problem to finding how much relative success among farmers is due to their technical skill in farming and how much to shrewdness in marketing procedures. So long as nations remain at different levels in their scientific advance and their technological control of the natural environment, natural selection will act desirably upon the genetic qualities responsible for this and will also spread the more successful cultural elements. But as technology and successful forms of social organization, e.g., nuclear energy and the provision of schools, become more evenly diffused by imitation (as is presently happening), the basis of selection is likely to shift more to differences of (a) skill in direct competition with other groups rather than with nature, and (b) planning genetic differences. The present writer has frankly adopted the blind value prejudice that it would be better if conquest of nature rather than diplomatic and military action increasingly became the decider in group competition, but let us attempt to evaluate realistically how likely that is to happen.

With this in mind we must examine the ethical conditions desirable in intergroup natural selection. At first glance it might seem that maximum efficiency of intergroup natural selection should continue what in fact has prevailed up to this century—a completely ruthless power struggle. Incidentally, it testifies to present confusion about the basic difference of between-person and between-state ethics, that many citizens, e.g., conscientious objectors to defense by war, are unable to grasp the real change of values when they step outside the protective shell of their own cultural group into the realities of intergroup power struggles. And, even in this century of the League of Nations and the UNO, we must not be so naive as to interpret every "helping hand," e.g., by foreign aid, as charity rather than a push of pawns in the power struggle. Indeed, anyone who doubts the new level of ruthlessness in intergroup relations might reflect that just in the last decade, and among countries of advanced civilization, there have been planned assassinations of leaders and agents in competing countries, and, indeed, also the execution of millions of innocents, as in Stalin's and Hitler's treatment of political opposition and subject populations.

In agreeing with the "feeling liberal," that this *is* the present reality to be dealt with, we do not argue that it *should* be. Its very persistent existence, however, points to the possibility that even *ideally* the evolutionarily required ethical code between groups should be systematically different from that among individuals. Indeed, as introduced above, we accept as basic that a process of differential survival among groups must be maintained to ensure (a) the evolution of the best possible style of interindividual altruistic ethics among group members, (b) the elimination of genetic and cultural experiments that have taken a fruitless direction, and (c) the shaping of whatever system of interindividual selection, genetic and in viewpoints, that goes on *within* groups, will fit the survival of the group.

Little has been introduced here yet to deny that the processes involved *should*, for greatest efficiency, be carried on within an ethic of completely ruthless competition, with no limits to the forms of competition and no succorance of cultures that prove misguided. Closer attention to total consequences, however, while not denying this as the primary law, indicates the need for secondary, qualifying, superimposed laws. We have pointed out that the aim of culture-genetic *diversification* and group *natural selection* is the greatest need for the evolutionary advance of the human species. However, it is obvious that, for such experiment to proceed, its total elements—the human species and the planetary society itself—must survive! Not only does this call for such conditions of intergroup competition as would eliminate the possibility of destrucion of *all* groups, but also, in face of severe natural catastrophes, e.g., a sudden ice age, a large meteoric collision, that all must combine in mutual support.

Logically, a second catastrophe that could put an end to evolutionary action is the disappearance of all groups but one, terminating variation and natural selection. This could occur by catastrophe or by world conquest or by universal merging. The last I have discussed more fully elsewhere (1972) under the concept of the Hedonic Pact.

Most people today are inclined to what appears to be a mid course between two possible political extremes—acceptance on the one hand of completely sovereign nations, isolationist, totalitarian, and governed in their relations only by the realities of power, and on the other hand, a one-world political organization. In its extreme form the latter would often be accompanied by complete genetic and cultural uniformity among groups and cessation of competition. What could emerge in practice from a Beyondist ethic might look like a mere middle course between these extremes, but is in fact something more complex. Certainly it is very different from the disastrous solution by "racial and cultural slumping," which is all that some self-styled progressive social movements presently envisage.

To show more clearly what a Beyondist ethic requires in the interaction of within-group and between-group ethics, we need some digression into the scientific study of the natural history of group interactions operating in natural selection among groups. To begin with, we need to look at the ecological principles that naturalists study in the food chains, the effects of limits of natural resources, and the symbioses and the parasitisms that are powerful determiners of ultimate survival in the animal and plant world.

Nations plan their survival by industrial advance, by military alliances, by trade (paradoxically often with "cold war" opponents), by education and health measures, by struggle for possession of vital natural resources, and so on. Since, for evolutionary ends, it is the *quality* rather than the *size* of the experimental group that *should* be the basis of natural selection, we have here an additional argument against war, in which size counts. But, meanwhile, a shrewd "ecological" tendency, for smaller to attach to larger groups, functions in the interests of the security of quality, e.g., presently, Israel's attachment to the U.S.A. (This comment on size does not mean (a) the cultural capacity to organize in larger units, as the states of the U.S. did, is not itself an achievement, and (b) that a successful culture will tend better to support, at an acceptable standard, a larger population.) However, such intergroup alliance tends to bring about some cultural alignment of the more dependent with the more independent group, offering a specific influence in that natural selection of cultural elements by imitative spread that we have already discussed.

A major problem in deciding what values and practices need to be encouraged or discouraged in an intergroup ethic is tied up with a distinction between symbiosis and parasitism. Naturalists, e.g., Thomas (1979), have made much recently of the network of mutual services between living things as if all of it were benign symbiosis (a sort of Sunday School lesson to humanity) rather than parasitism. When the alligator opens his mouth wide for birds to pick his teeth, the advantage is mutual and we have symbiosis. When the malaria protozoa makes a home in the blood of man, or man keeps cows or shoots home-raised pheasants for food, we have what is, broadly, parasitism. Either symbiotic deals or parasitisms, but particularly the latter, create a problem in assessing the survival value of one party in distinction from the other, and in deciding what forced interactions are ethical and which are not. Among nations there are and have been a great variety of interactions that are questionably ethical from the standpoint of maximal possible evolutionary advance. (Was Britain in the 19th century symbiotic with or parasitic upon India? Probably *both* countries benefited.)

It is not within the scope of this book to cover in scientific terms the varieties of interaction of groups and environments—for which new substantial research and a large volume would be necessary. Our purpose is, instead, to consider principles in (a) the ethical laws needed for fulfilling the evolutionary purpose, and (b) the possibility of evaluation of the rise and fall of groups, before actual collapse might occur. Since the first requires longer discussion, let us make a first foray into the second, leaving the first to be encountered in more detail later on.

The basic principle in evolution must first be kept in mind that *fitness is relative to an environment* and the environment includes most other living organisms. Any estimate of the fitness of one culture-genetic experimental group is therefore tied up with, and *in part* a function of, its interaction with other associated groups. This adds a complexity to the calculation of "worthiness," but one that future social evolutionists will doubtless reduce to clear principles. The important point is that, if time curves can be plotted on *potential for survival*, as contrasted with decadence and collapse, laws are likely to appear that the Beyondist International Research Center described in Chapters 16 through 20 can use in diagnosis. Thereby, nations or other institutional groups can advance without the competition with environment and other groups having to await the incontestable proof from complete dissolution of the ailing culture.

Nevertheless, let us restate that neither the introduction of such "humane" diagnostic accessories, nor the condition that competition must always stop short of any risk of destruction of the total world community of groups, denies that intergroup natural selection can act efficiently in only one condition. It is that the intergroup ethic *permits each group fully to receive the consequences of its own acts*, without other groups either specially aiding it or taking advantage of its vulnerability when it is in trouble. Whatever the initial human sentimental impulses may be on this matter, e.g., in providing aid in famines, the reality is that it is impossible, from the needs of evolution, to see justification *for any other basic and primary intergroup ethic.* Of course, as we have admitted, there will be secondary, subprinciples which, on closer inspection, derive from the first. For example, an advanced, more successful group may by apparent charities induce a failing group to imitate its values, e.g., a fascist state to turn to democracy. And since, as we have seen, cultural evolution leans appreciably on lucky imitation, such "charity" is a contribution to evolution. "Charitable cultural lending" is in fact, when well based on prior proof of effectiveness of an element, a direct form of cultural evolutionary advance—though with the danger of producing excessive homogeneity. In short, we have to recognize that the whole network of trading, military alliances, and cultural migration which occurs among nations makes the definition and the operation of intergroup natural selection more complex, without, however, destroying its main effects and values.

Let us return to finish discussion of the first of the two issues above and ask whether there are desirable human laws regarding group competition that would be compatible with, and increase the efficiency of, the weighing of groups by their internal structure and morale, through *intergroup* competition. The primary aims of such regulations in international law would be (a) to avoid whatever might destroy the world society and end the human race, and (b) to outlaw such forms of competition as are "unfair" in the sense of making natural selection less effective. The first is obvious; the second could have several forms. For example, it would seem we should outlaw the sudden turning of a heavily armed large country upon an unsuspecting smaller neighbor, if *long-term* fitness is the real criterion and if an infant culture of great future promise could be wiped out by such action. Or, again, a country with poor values and poor control of population size, of contagious diseases, and so on, might feel free to ship its surplus, less-successful population to a country struggling for higher standards (as indeed the hideously wrong inscription on the idol in New York Harbor invites!).

There thus seems little doubt that the community of nations must impose certain intergroup laws on its members as a single group does on its citizens. However, there are important differences. First, different nations, in the interest of basic evolution, should be under no restriction of the goal of being as diverse as possible. Their racio-cultural adventures as such should be restrained as little as possible. There should be as high a degree of independence and freedom from conformity as is compatible with noninterference with others.

As to the danger of total disappearance of the human race, or total cessation of its evolution, there are three sources: (1) a totally destructive war; (2) a vast natural catastrophe—perhaps a comet of lethal gas, in which groups fail to come to one another's assistance; and (3) what I have called elsewhere (1972) "the Hedonic Pact." This last is an agreement to abolish all competition among groups, in order that they may enjoy greatest hedonistic life styles. This would stop natural selection and leave humanity at an arrested level at which it would be unable to meet the more monstrous challenges of environment that may come, as well as it could have done had it progressed.

One must pause to ask how serious this risk of the obliteration of mankind by its own actions is. For decisions on the desirable extent of international control depend thereon. Against falling into the pitfall of the Hedonic Pact, no existing ethical system gives greater insurance than Beyondism itself, and we shall assume the risk is not great. Against an almost overwhelming natural catastrophe, we can only work for the most efficient evolution of man's mental capacity whereby he can defeat that threat.

If mankind should be destroyed by any one of these three, what are the hopes for the evolution of intelligence elsewhere? Cosmologists, taking heart from the enormous probability of earth-like planets elsewhere, are prepared almost to swear (as Sagan and Schlowskii [1966], for example, tell us) that intelligent life is developing elsewhere. I have asked (1972) why, if so, we have received no messages, and I have suggested certain explanations, such as an inherent failure of societies, due to an inevitable Hedonic Pact, to pass beyond a certain technical stage, that might account for this.

Someone could argue that if there are, for certain, other intelligent worlds successfully developing, we can, as devoted participators in the whole evolutionary process, afford on earth to take a more daring, faster, riskier, course than if the future of mind rested entirely on ourselves. That is to say, under risks (1) and (3) above we could on the one hand enter a more intensive intergroup competition despite its risks of bringing about destructive war, and we could allow adventurous diversity to be tamed more by central world authority, despite risks of essentially an Hedonic Pact.

With the question of the existence of other locations of life and mind answerable only at a probability level, mankind, like a wise investor, will divide its capital into a conservative and a suppositions fraction. The conservative plan is to assume that we *may* be the only promising source of developing intelligence, and that variety of directions must be maintained among *us*. But even if this argument for avoiding racio-cultural fusion and mediocrity were not sustained by stellar evidence, we should still, as one source of mind among many, find it desirable, as a condition of evolutionary advance *here*, to maintain experimental diversity.

Those who believe universal brotherly love will be provided by a "one-world" philosophy, however established, should reflect that an end possesses the quality of the means. The movements toward effectively establishing one political world have rested on the insane ambitions of a Ghenghis Khan, a Napoleon, or an Alexander, ruthlessly seeking sheer power. What the Beyondist concept requires, instead, is a *federation* of independent, distinctive states, jealous of the significance of their individuality.

At a popular level, the retreat into the fold of "one world" is largely motivated by fear of war. All agree that war is wasteful, brutal, and hideously cruel, yet if we stop healthy competition because it has a danger of degenerating into war, we are "throwing out the baby with the bath water." Even when considering this ghastly breakdown, let us keep perspective. Decidedly more people are killed in equally ghastly automobile accidents than war, yet no one parades in favor of unconditionally giving up automobiles. The number of humans who die painful natural deaths in bed likewise far exceeds deaths in war; but no one suggests that the risk of such deaths requires that we should not beget any more people. We must almost certainly proceed contingently with the assumption that losses in war are dysgenic, from abrasion of the more enterprising in the emotional make-up of a people. But we shall proceed under the assumption that with a real international police force at work war is no argument whatever against the basic necessity of an intergroup competitive agreement.

Even apart from war, however, there are arguments for regulation of international competition in ways conducive to "law and order." But does not *any* restriction on mode of competition lessen the breadth of racio-cultural selective advance? Let us suppose that in some way, before the appearance of color vision in certain animals, it had been decreed that in hunting, mating, and other aspects of survival, glasses must be worn that filter out colors. Almost certainly color vision would not have become a newly selected capacity. Or culturally, if an international agreement forbad rockets in warfare, how retarded the development of astronautics would be! Artificiality was not unknown in classical and primitive times where, in the interests of saving life, sometimes the verdict was left to a tournament between two champions. Even when warfare is permitted, the decision actually, in the modern complex world, rests more broadly on diplomatic, economic, genetic, and cultural influences that are hard in any case to restrict and control. As the endless debates on national expenditure on armaments versus an expanding "welfare state" expenditure remind us, a war is won or lost by values and actions outside the battlefields.

The role of war in natural selection among nations is, in any case, changing. Even as late as Greek and Roman times, it often led to extermination of a population—genocide—or a wholesale enslavement of noncombatants that greatly reduced their continuation as a racial gene-pool. In taking over land area, it resulted in expansion of the more successful gene-pool and culture. These consequences have practically disappeared, except through economic means; but the imposition of cultural elements continues, as in the recent establishment of democracy in Germany, Italy, and Japan.

Winning world opinion, by whatever psychological, rhetorical tricks are necessary, is an increasingly powerful factor in the relative survival of cultures. Psychological warfare is nevertheless old, and, of course, the same techniques have long played a part in business advertising, with a slight change in goal, and, indeed, in courtship and all human attempts to win in competitive situations. It is a feature which tinges intergroup competition with a dishonesty not present in the second realm of survival—the control of nature. Admittedly, one succeeds better managing a crowd, as in managing an engineering feat, if one has more intelligence and understanding of the thing itself, but a side effect in the first is that the psychological warfare specialist becomes dishonest to the people concerned. The remedies, of course, are an education in perceiving the rhetoric, the false appeals to emotion and the slanted use of words, together with better school education in science and statistics. Unfortunately, in psychological warfare, the *average* intelligence of a democracy is exposed to propaganda, whereas in a dictatorship the opposed view is stopped at the level of the scoffing dictator and never reaches the public. It is a "one-sided free trade!" An interesting study of World War I concerned "The trail of deceit" (Tuttle, 1951), showing how an atrocity myth started to whip up war feeling, ran on for many years, poisoning all kinds of attitudes, with results ultimately as costly to the creators as to the maligned.

The question of how much and what kind of intergroup competition one should ideally design, i.e., in Beyondist ethics, and attempt to control is a vast issue, which we have illustrated above in regard to physical warfare and to psychological warfare. Our conclusion is that the less regulation the better, beyond an initial forceful regulation of threat based on size. Yet, if common force fails against a very advanced and powerful group, then we must recognize that just as *successful* treason against a king or government ceases to be treason, so a reality of power, military or psychological, will transcend the existing rules. Nevertheless, the ideal final intergroup structure must be federation, not an hegemony.

In demonstrating that even the evolutionarily desirable rules of ethics among groups, i.e., between governments, are in part definitely different from those among within-group individuals, we have perhaps seemed to spend undue time on particulars where the general principle is all one needs for the overview of essentials. But many a reader, encountering, say, the issue of war, will have felt the need for expanded reaction.

What we have to complete in this chapter, however, is a step from the recognition of the *two* levels of ethical inference—individual and group—to what is the truly comprehensive analysis of ethical systems and obligations. It is obvious that, if one starts with any monistic general principle, it will lead to different subsystems in different situations. If a central electric power system is compelled to economize on output, it may do so in, say, an area of factories by cutting out certain hours of supply, and in the region of domestic houses by reducing the voltage to dim lights, and so on. The specific injunction will arise from the situation.

There are six distinct *entities* among which ethical rule systems can logically appear:

1. A citizen in a society
2. A government of a group
3. A world government
4. The goal of evolution
5. A citizen of the world, i.e., outside the given society, member of another.

6. The set of individuals committed to a Beyondist Ethic.

Parenthetically, there are, of course, an almost infinite number of subsets corresponding to the roles of individuals as parents, children, policemen, and so on, defining what is ethical behavior in each; but here we are operating at the level of the most generalized, main relations.[14]

To handle this ethics issue comprehensively and exhaustively, we begin by recognizing that among six entities there will be 15 diadic relations, as shown in Figure 8-1. Additionally, there are four "internal relations," of members of one entity class to other members of the same class, i.e., when the entity is not single and unique as is the world government and the principle of evolution in the universe.

Since all but the last entity involve people, the obligations are two way, except in the last, where arrows could consequently be drawn only one way instead of two.

The ethical systems of the main revealed religions—Christianity, Buddhism, Islam, and so on—have stressed their universality of values, urging "Love for all men under the sun" and that all are "God's children," i.e., they claim to be System III, obligations among all humans, in Figure 8-1. Yet the ethical subsets defined above are nevertheless recognized by these religions (with confusion) in some historical situations. For example, System IV, which defines special relations among believers, was well recognized by both sides in the crusades. System I and System II are recognized in Christ's "Render unto Caesar...." System II is in the forefront of the present-day attempt to achieve agreement on some ethical rules among nations, in the United Nations organization. The Jesuits and equivalent theological experts in other religions have drawn some realistic fine distinctions, and every church member gets some instruction on why it is right to kill in defense of his country (System II, "My country right or wrong," as an American patriot said), though murder is wrong (System I). The modern "feeling liberal" and "feeling conservative"—as we designate those who feel, according to conformity, rather than think independently—have actually regressed from these insights, and it is an uncommon sociologist who insists as does Nathaniel Weyl (1973) that "What is moral conduct toward one man or group may be immoral when applied to a different individual or group." Regarding the duty to values of a particular group, we need the perspective of Nietzsche that "a people perishes when it confuses its duty with duty in general" (*The Antichrist*, 1930) and of Walter Otto "The most significant event in the life of a people...is the emergence of a mode of thought that is peculiar to it. ... by which it

Figure 8.1

ETHICAL RULE SUBSYSTEMS DEVELOPING
FROM A BEYONDIST PRINCIPLE

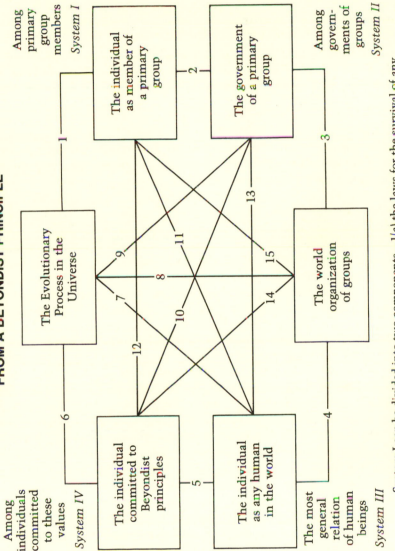

System I can be divided into two components—1(a) the laws for the survival of any group and 1(b) the laws appropriate to the behavior of individuals in the particular adventure for survival of the given group.

is henceforth distinguishable in the world's history" (*The Homeric Gods*).

It is not our aim to expand adequately here on the Ethical Rule Subsystems in Figure 8-1, which some Beyondist could well do in a whole book. We aim only to point to the multi-principle, and to suggest that some terms and labels be used for each—such as we have begun. These labels would greatly clarify discussion of what the true values are in various settings. If the average religious man complains of the seeming complexity, we can only say that we are discussing ethics as a natural science.

Each of these subsystems brings about—or should—a system of attitudes, duties and values built into the individual's emotional life, on which his ethical decisions can be made without confusion.

If we consider the educated use of the term "God" to apply to a basic purpose and direction in the universe, which we put at the head of Figure 8-1 as "the evolutionary purpose," then we can approach the vexed question of whether the love of man and the love of God (System I and No 1) are the same. The question has haunted various very practical political debates, sometimes with a Christian assertion that love of God is *entirely* love of fellow man, and sometimes, as in the view of an intellectual Catholic, G.K. Chesterton, that they are very distinct.[15] The Beyondist position, as in Figure 8-1, is that they are distinct. The tendency of totalitarian, secular societies, like Communism or Fascism, is to put total emphasis on service to fellow man, as he is. The drawback is that this gives priority to living man as he is. It is a system that makes martyrs of dissidents, who believe that man and society have a goal *beyond* the present group.

One would deduce from Figure 8-1 that as far as an individual's attitude and obligations to another human being are concerned there are three subsystems: (1) System I, to other citizens in his society; (2) to other members of the group devoted to Beyondist principles, System IV; and (3) to any human in the world, System III. There is a widespread secular humanistic belief, evident in much modern writing, that the more basic morality is in the third. But what do members of this group have in common but a basic physiology (largely shared with the primates and other mammals)? This is not to be belittled, as an emotional understanding shared with all mankind and higher animals, but it is, from a Beyondist standpoint, the merest beginning of the richer obligations and shared values in the other two systems (I and IV).

The analyses above may seem to some readers an abstract and even merely academic exercise.[16] Nevertheless, it is the basis of solution for many moral dilemmas that wrench the emotions of the individual and cloud public policy. However, in claiming to be a science, the system implies that empirical research is necessary to complete it. What, indeed, are the practices that in each subsystem contribute to its goal as here indicated? An attempt has been made, looking at social psychology and history, to differentiate and crystallize some of these rules as they concern within-group (System I) and between-group (System II) behavior; but the rest remains for the social sciences to work upon.

/ / / ▪ ▪ ▪ ▪ ▪ ▪ ▪ ▪ ▪ ▪ ▪ ▪ ▪ ▪ ▬ ▬ ▬ ▬ ▬

Chapter 9

How Benign Is Nature, and How Does This Affect the Emotional Roots of Beyondist Ethics?

Through the eight chapters to this point we have pursued a definition of Beyondist Ethics based rigorously on a scientific appraisal of what is essential to human evolution. Since most readers will have social beliefs and religious feelings from long-established sources, there will undoubtedly have been clashes between those and some of the abruptly new concepts— from an argument necessarily followed with Euclidean logic and economy.

From this point, through the next 10 chapters, it is proposed, however, thoroughly to explore and analyze what the personal emotional adjustments and the social attitudes of individuals and policies of groups need to be in response to the logical framework of Beyondism. First, let us recognize that this procedure of sequence of argument from scientific, cosmic views to inner emotional life is the complete reverse of what has happened with the great revealed religions. Despite their new names appearing in the last two thousand years or so, they are actually parts of a step-like growth of beliefs, myths, rituals, and ethical laws going back to primitive ages (as shown for example in Frazer's classical *Golden Bough* (1890). The result is that the habits have been tooled and fitted to the needs of human nature, to practical guidance in standard affairs of life, and to the ineffable yearnings that arise from sublimations of all the frustrated forces of the unconscious. They reason from within outward: we from the outer universe to inner beliefs.

The cognitive constructs that go with "revealed" religions, corresponding to the cognitive framework that goes with Beyondism, have not been reached by scientific observation, as in the above chapters, but by a continuous, rather blind social trial and error, aided by the insights of inspired leaders, and, in Christianity, by theological conventions set up to define true belief and heresies. (And like the American Constitution, the Bible still has its Supreme Court of academic theological analysts, like Tillich, Curran, and others.)

A more extended treatment than these brief chapters would enquire into what these religions have done in fashioning their mythology and beliefs to human emotional cravings, e.g., to retaining a child's dependence on a father figure into the turmoil of adult life, and also into the dynamics they have created to sustain inherently unpalatable ethical controls.

Almost all such religions contain a benign ruler of the universe. The major hurdle that will make the path of popular acceptance of Beyondist concepts a difficult one is that it is unquestionably a more austere belief system than the rooted religions, demanding a higher level of emotional maturity because of the abandonment of numerous such comforting myths. It is a trusim to say that we always pay painfully in the end for the falsity of our comforting illusions; but it is also a psychological truism that humans prefer the nearer satisfactions of a myth to the remoter goals of truth. Religions that imposed themselves before it was possible to give a logical, factual, scientifically informed account of why the given ethical restraints and sacrifices were needed, had to make strong emotional appeals if their ethical restraints were to work at all. Paradise, hell, a loving father in the sky who answered personal prayers, and expected worship, and many rituals that an enlightened, educated person today would call superstitions, were essential devices in the emotional appeal. Indeed, it is the increasingly widespread recognition of the superstitions in religion—without the needed simultaneous current perception of the new avenues available in Beyondism—that has put us today in mortal peril of that weakening of morality, with degeneration into "moral relativism," which is today of such concern to intelligent people. Indeed, the loss of morale now proceeding gives an especial urgency to the building of such a firmly scientifically based ethic as Beyondism.

It is not proposed here to examine the lesser myths and rituals, and what might replace those existing, but to begin by examining the basic mythical conception of a benign universe ruled by a God responding to the appeals of his favorite children—the human race. Since the concept of deity is more closely scrutinized and analyzed in Chapters 13 and 14, let us examine here a roughly defined power of that kind, in the wider context of a benign universe.

Psychologically it is surely to be expected when a person devoted to goodness is overwhelmed by evidence of human falsity and self-seeking and the inevitable suffering that ensues, that he or she should turn to belief in an understanding God. The martyrs for spiritual values have been so sustained down the ages. Yet if a scientist—say an astronomer or a biologist—looks at the universe, though he admittedly sees on the one hand an awe-inspiring power, and a superhuman complexity, he must truthfully say that he sees no particular evidence of a *merciful* God, or of response to human prayers, or of mankind being "the apple of God's eye." As Darwin wrote to Asa Gray, on the subject of a "benign universe," "I own that I cannot see as plainly as others do, and as I would wish to do, evidence of ... beneficence on all sides of us." Appalling cruelty or, more objectivly described, endless suffering, prevails throughout the animal world, and it is quite clear that man is exempted only to the extent that he intelligently avoids it by his own efforts. What we see as mercifulness is something created by man, and then only fitfully as when an inventor of machinery and light for mines eliminates blind pit ponies, or a Pasteur saves humans from the horrible death of hydrophobia. The special support of science by the more intelligent implies the belief that we must master nature if it is not to master us. Among men and women the surest labor of love is to work toward the increase of human knowledge and its farsighted application. Basic to that philosophy is the concept of the universe as an "indifferent" surrounding in which we have to work for what we get. The humanitarian "feeling liberal" backs up his politico-social position essentially with the belief in a benign, mankind-centered universe, and a being that will overlook all mankind's mistakes.

Benignness *within* human society has to square with the fact of a nonbenign universe from which what we borrow, as a loan, is what has to be fully repaid. The political problem we must always face is, "Can a society be both 'human' and 'functional'?" We may call the universe benign because it has produced mind, and we enjoy the possession of mind, but through what a history of unremitting cruelty has human intelligence been produced? The final effects may be benign, but the path to them has been one of endless suffering. The difference of Beyondism from indiscriminate humanitarianism is in seeing frustration and punishment as poignant necessities in evolution.

Elsewhere (1938,1972) I have suggested that one possible concretization we can give to the concept of God as it has been held over the centuries is as God-in-Man (the *Theopsyche* as I ventured to label it). The Theopsyche is the island of love, rationality, and protectiveness that an advanced society can produce. It is what Shaw called for when he said "Man must change himself into the political providence which he formerly considered as God" (1944). That is to say, we identify the particular "godlikeness" in the universe concretely with altruistic group mind as it emerges in the interactions and institutions of good men. Concretization is hardly the just word for so abstract a notion as a group mind but the character of a group, like the character of a person, or the nature of an electron, or the "strong force" of nuclear physicists, is nonetheless real for being invisible and having to be *inferred* from actual observations, rather than held in the hand. The factor analysis of human groups (as recently carried out on over 100 countries) shows measurable dimensions, on which each can be characterized by scores assignable by a social scientist. One of these dimensions of national groups comes close to this conception of a moral, merciful, and dependably conscientious quality emerging in the group.

However, it is presently not possible clearly to unify this quite acceptable scientific, measurable concept of the theopsyche with some notion of an emerging form of an ultimate creator such as most people will accept. The two do not come together by any insightful bond, as the theopsyche does not have any particular relation to the common basic concept of God as the original creator. What philosophers speak of as "Paley's argument (for the deity) from design" is questioned by some philosophers. The critics say that the human belief that a creation must have a creator is part of a habit of limited human reasoning.

It has been a sound act of discipline among scientists, at least since Francis Bacon, not to get inveigled into the verbal wild goose chases of speculative philosophers. It is true that a few fundamental philosophical positions, e.g., that of Berkeley, and some of Kant's, must be explicitly recognized by the scientist as standing as epistemological question marks at the very frontiers of science. And he recognizes the intellectual right of the philosophical tradition also to erect speculative houses of cards. But there is something even more important than raising the questions, namely, as Nietzsche said, "to have *sufficient discernment and humility to draw a line bounding what our intellects are really capable of handling*" (1930). For example, a scientist may bewilder a logical philosopher by saying that empirically determinism and free will can coexist, in ways our intellects cannot yet grasp. The scientist has had experiences in, say, recognizing the irrational value we call Planck's constant, or recognizing light as having both wave and corpuscle properties, incompatible with our experience of waves and projectiles, and yet needing to be accepted.

Any keen scientist is, naturally, prone to continue into philosophical thinking when he reaches the limits of hard scientific theory. Like a dog chasing a duck into a pond, he is unwilling to admit that he is at the limit of firm ground. Let us by all means enjoy a bit of epistemological verbal barking, but not be deceived thereby into thinking we are getting substantially nearer to our quarry. Instead, let us recognize that there are some questions that are best honestly and explicitly put on the shelf, until the human mind has *biologically* advanced beyond its present level. Scientific advance is not always possible merely by increased data gathering. The tool of investigation which is the human brain has to be fashioned further before certain theoretical constructions can be achieved. Outstanding among the questions that stand stonily in the wilderness where the scientific pavement ends are, "Does the existence of a universe imply a creator?" "Can we justify believing simultaneously in free will and determinism?" "How can we link the phenomenon of consciousness with the physico-chemical properties of neural action?"—and quite a number of others in response to which we can at present only run in verbal circles.

Recognizing these limits, and that operationally the most he can describe is an ongoing evolutionary process, the scientist cannot today focus any concept of God akin to abstractly continuing the qualities of the old man with a white beard in Michelangelo's painting on the Sistine Chapel. If a creation implies a creator, then the observable creation is so wonderful that we may well stand in complete awe of that creator. But what we actually see is an ongoing *process* of organic and inorganic evolution, and a variety of ultimate laws that gradually are mastered by our power to research and comprehend. The Beyondist (and probably, if we correctly interpret axioms for followers of other religions, as in Islam's accepting "the Will of Allah") accepts facts as other religions do, and additionally aims emotionally to be one with the evolutionary process.

Regarding the notion of a deity with benign personal attitudes to man, thinkers have found themselves throughout history in the position of Freud, who asked, in the *Future of an Illusion* (1928), what gain a human being has in setting up in his imagination a benevolent God, and then having to continue to face the slings and arrows of outrageous fortune by supposing God meanly wills the evils that man suffers. The philosophers have long expressed this in "God cannot be both omnipotent and benevolent." It is, of course, possible to argue that in the inscrutable purposes of God what seems to us hideous evil and injustice is not what it appears to be. This approaches the position of the Beyondist, who, however, has the simple and more intellectually honest theory that the universe (including a creator if it has one) *has not a special benevolence or mode of treatment for that particular genus among living things that we call homo sapiens.* The latest philosophical pursuit of the idea of God is that (Bennett, 1933), "The realization of deity is the realization of external form as opposed to accidence." This is actually precisely the view of the scientist, rejoicing in the discovery of dependable laws.

A conceivable argument for benevolence in the universe is that we exist, enjoy life, and are conscious of a seemingly important position in the scheme of things. For this we should be grateful; but to whom or what? And if the suffering exceeds the joy, where is the argument for benevolence? In any case, to say that we—mankind—are given guaranteed life and its enjoyment, unlike most beasts that end their lives in the savage jaws of some larger beast, is somewhat presumptuous about our own importance. Since it is true that all illusions are likely, in the end, to give more frustration than the acting on a correct perception, mankind would surely plan more wisely if it concluded that it stands in a universe that is neither benign nor malignant, and that there is no evidence for a man-loving deity who interferes in response to personal prayer and saves man from the consequences of blundering in dealing with nature.

By contrast to the acceptance of a false benevolence, the Beyondist can put his faith in the reality of an evolutionary process that has so far had a discernable direction—in spite of instances of stagnation and retreat—to "higher," more effective, living forms.

In search of significant idealism, if not merely of benevolence per se, we can perhaps point not only to recognizable ongoing "purpose," but to the emergence, as described above, of a benevolent guiding body in human organization—the theopsyche—to which the altruistic and conscientious individual can attach himself. Through the latter's development as "civilization," for instance, we can forestall the cruel death of overpopulating masses, from starvation or war, by foresighted population control; we can advance medicine to reduce human suffering; and, by eugenic control, we can eliminate the misery of individuals born defective relative to the demands of the society into which they would (one might say, unwillingly) have been born. Similarly we have already discussed in the natural selection process of groups as a whole, how we might avoid the otherwise catastrophic annihilations that usually occur, by, instead, monitoring relative survival, and recognizing customs and genetic deviations that are the morbid preludes to such ends.[17] But it remains true that it is "the business of the future" to be dangerous.

We must face here, as in later issues in this book, the fact that benevolence, as administered by human judgment, also has tremendous hidden dangers. Because compassion has usually been a scarce commodity, and self-interest has been dependably universal, the inspired religions have encouraged "compassion" with a boundless sanction for all kinds of expressions, many of which *from the perspective of Beyondism, seem positively evil*. Traditional religious ethics have rightly concentrated on the control—almost to virtual extinction—of two mammalian drives in man—pugnacity (aggression) and sex. St. Paul, to save the human species, admitted the second instinct could regretfully have expression at any rate in marriage—but only for procreation, not for sensuality per se.

The fact that the person melting with the warm glow of sympathy and commiseration for all unfortunates overlooks is that *any and all of the mammalian emotions can be exploited in our complex world and miss the real purposes they developed to serve*. The parental protective instinct is to be given unique invulnerability to criticism and control only at our grave peril. All inherited human, mammalian emotional impulses can go astray and fail of adaptation in some way. No drive is inherently, and completely, "good" or "bad" from an ethical standpoint.

It is necessary to be clear at this point that we are not arguing that because the universe is coldly realistic in its demands on human societies those societies must necessarily be without benign attitudes and compassions toward their members. On the contrary, there needs to be almost boundless compassion in the raising of its children, and care for the adult fallen by the wayside, if the coherence of the group and the growth of altruism toward it are to prevail. This is a caution on accepting all of what has been called "Humanism."[18]

We have next to raise the psychological question of how far the motivational roots of ethical strength and high morale in the population demand compassion and indulgence of error. It is naturally first raised in this chapter, in questionning the benignness of the outer universe. But though we survey the problem here a more specialized psychological analysis and appraisal is appropriate in Chapters 13 and 14 notably on the social operation of guilt and forgiveness.

Compassion in modern societies usually goes astray in religiously and socially "approved" ways. "The poor you have always with you" is true partly because religions have cherished poverty. They have done so partly for the good reasons that the services to society—especially the nonmaterial ones—have to be unpaid (because they are new and unwanted), and that, on the other hand, wanton luxury is a perversion of human interests and a social curse. But the evil of the boundless giving (charity) that the classical religions advocate probably more than offsets its obvious gains in less obvious losses. For, between groups, interference with economic aid may blunt and slow down the recipient group's own progress, as when a nation calls for help perennially on grounds of famine but does little to improve its agriculture, and nothing to stop a proliferating population. We are distinguishing between emotional *compassion* and planful *altruism* when we say that endless giving is not the answer.

Learning begins always with an unsatisfied need, and to remove the need by other means (outside the system) is to remove learning. Similarly, *within* groups, social psychological analysis based on measurement has to conclude that the *continually* unemployed, are maladapted to the culture, in some one or all of the qualities of competence, emotional stability, idealistic social values, good spending customs, and so on. Beyondism would first look a generation ahead, and restrict birth rates of the less adapted, and secondly institute post-school education programs not just in job skills but in values. In short, compassion would do better to extend itself to future generations than to act impulsively on every call to charity in this one. However, as Robert Whitaker well says (*A plague on both your houses*, 1976) "superficial goodness to the underprivileged is the stuff of which heart-rending stories and good publicity are made."

In considering habits of charity as in other habits, such as criminal negligence of citizenship duties, we should always return to the fact that the "final check," as we have called it, on non-adaptive within-group values, comes through the justice of inter-group natural selection. If, for example, a group expends unrealistically on welfare, or on luxuries, at the expense of education, defense, and research, an obvious consequence is that it is likely to lose the birthright of its own values by defeat in war. But, more subtly, it can collapse economically, or have a drug plague, or fail in other ways.

However, if the feeling liberals and the self-indulgent classes *seriously set themselves politically to avoid this test by survival*, it is at least a remote possibility that they could do so by avoiding all the intergroup competition pressures by the device I have elsewhere described as "the Hedonic Pact" among nations. This is a pact to abolish competition. It is true that abolition of competition among groups would not stop the second instrument in natural selection: the forces of nature. But at least for a time natural selection would be rendered less efficient, and much stimulation would vanish. (Consider American science education if there had been no beneficient challenge from Sputnik.) While the rise of intelligent international cooperation, for example in the sense of combined comparative research proposed by Beyondism, introduces the danger of real attempts at an Hedonic Pact, one may doubt, rivalry being a built-in need, that it would be a stable success. Moreover though such mutually indulgent agreement might be reached with other groups, nature is quite unwilling to sign such a pact. A nationwide earthquake would still call upon the more realistic values and disciplined action that an hedonic pact would have let fall into desuetude. It seems improbable in any case that such a pact could be stably maintained, but it needs facing because some modern internationalist ideas have this hedonism as an unspoken goal.

Although it is realistic and adjustive to look on the outer universe as neither benign nor hostile, in the course of history tribes and nations have had periods when the environment (plague, famine, drought) or inner problems (civil war, economic maladjustment) have pressed harder upon them than at other times. In his study of history Toynbee conveniently refers to Chinese description of a period of peace and stagnation as Yin, and of stress and movement of Yang. Let us precision these two terms here to mean the up and down levels of the pressure states.

Since the Middle Ages, and due to the continuous advance of science and order since the Renaissance, Europe has been in a prolonged phase of Yin, broken by only a few periods of Yang, as in World Wars I and II (incidentally, we find in more precise factor analytic studies of history [Cattell, 1953] a definition of this Yin-Yang dimension in such modern variables [in the Yang direction] as reduction of government expenditure in ministries, reduction of people in service occupations, an unfavorable balance of trade, heavier armament expenditures, and other signs of hardening and "tightening of social life").

Future social research may show that this cycle of tightening and loosening of life demand is not only inevitable in a changing world, but that it is an aid to progress. Perhaps the loosening in prosperity introduces more adventurous, liberal, diverse customs, among which larger variations and more far-reaching natural selection take place when the tightening follows. If so, this is difficult to document, and must apply to subtle values, for actually it is in war and stress that the biggest innovations have occurred, especially in science, legal customs, the arts, education, and so on. In the period of Yin, from 1950 to 1975, we saw mainly a relaxation of sex mores, a toleration of homosexuality, an increase in luxury expenditure, and a decay in the more disciplined areas of higher education. These are documentable.

We must suppose that reduction in the external pressure and challenge leads to *tolerance* (which may be in some ways as good a movement as some assume) and to expression of compassion and kindness on a larger scale, which includes a system of mutual indulgence. That is to say, it is the luxury satisfaction of the recipient individual rather than his real good that is produced or aimed at in Yin. Briefly, it is the attitudes that produce the spoiled child, carried into adult life, usually by well-to-do classes, in which it is tacitly mutually agreed that everyone has a right to self-indulgence and to avoidance of the discipline-demanding aspects of ethics. What objective personality structure research (Cattell & Child, 1975) has shown, since Freud, is that the chief opponent of superego growth is simply this narcissistic sinking into socially sanctioned self-indulgence. It is the equivalent of the group Hedonic Pact, but now worked out among individuals *within* a group, where the final check cannot operate as immediately and directly on an individual as it inevitably does on a group.

If a Beyondist sees it as desirable to avoid the worst excesses of Yin, we must ask two realistic questions: (1) If a group somehow tightens its standards, and if, in religion, it refuses to accept the *assumption* of a benign deity, will not the operation of the pleasure principle cause its members to leave it? and (2) Can one define an ideal of "optimum" balance between self-satisfactions and the demands of an evolutionary morality, or is the proper ideal a continual maximization of the pressure of planned evolutionary advance? As to the first, the basic proposition in group dynamics is that people (or lower animals) join and remain in groups so long as there is a positive balance of saitsfactions, e.g., to needs for security, the gregarious need, sex, the self-assertion satisfaction in status, and so on. Why then did Spartans not desert to the more lenient rules of Athens? Through most of history, despite any perceptible greater ease in another society, the average citizen was constrained both by acquired habits and external threats from such migration. Sparta successfully retained its exacting ethical laws and ways of life (and, incidentally, defeated Athens). Today, governments (seemingly due to politicians being always proud of gathering a larger population under them) have freely permitted appreciable immigration of people with different standards. There is apparently no awareness of the limits that a social scientist clearly sees to successful assimilation, or of the extent to which alien values are likely to replace those long cherished and proudly defended by the nation in question. In the modern world of relative high international mobility, it may therefore come about that groups offering a less demanding life style expand at the cost of others. (An American not wishing to pay taxes for education, defense, research, and whatever, can move to the Caribbean.)

It is probably church rather than national groups that have been most subject in the present generation to "emigration" of their people to avoid the more exacting standards of their religion. The gains from the moral restraints taught in churches are largely given to the community as a whole. (As we have seen, the medieval Christian church contributed habits of social cohesiveness which contributed, with some transfer of object, to the unity and strength of the main European nations.) However, this whole escape process from more demanding groups is only one of several mechanisms by which group morale can run down. This is not the place to gather the skimpy and scattered social psychological research on measured personality and attitude changes, but there seems little doubt that in societies long in relative security and luxury a gradual dissolving of mutually exacting values leads to tolerance of "mutual self-indulgence" in ethics, and in fields of intellectual discipline. The Beyondist derivation of values from anticipation of natural selection is the only sane shield against this.

The second question above asks if there is some optimum balance in the pressures that citizens are asked to bear, and how that level, in population density and other pressures, is to be determined. As to the comparison of Beyondism with the revealed religions and especially the modern relativistic, humanistic rehashes of those religions, there is little doubt that Beyondism makes more demands on individual self-sacrifice than would naturally occur in the absence of regard for its tenets. In war, a curtailment not only of luxury and indulgences but even an increased toleration of suffering is expected, and Beyondism is, in one aspect, a recognition that mankind is permanently at war with a natural world—an indifferent world—that can seem to us at time threatening, cruel and treacherous.

A scientific ethic such as Beyondism forbids the usual acceptance of *unchanging subsidiary* laws and attitudes. It asks the citizen to react more flexibly in ethical perceptions. It obviously calls for different within-group rules in peace and in war, for example. Realistic practice actually has always done this, but the rigid, detailed prescriptions of current religions have never explained this to the citizen—indeed, their priests have never explained it to themselves.

At some point of pressure societies begin to sacrifice not only their indulgent practices but their charity to whatever is a burden upon them. Thus, under extreme privation, Eskimos leave their old folk to die. With a shortage of heart transplants medical committees presently deny the life saving operation to patients above a certain age. In the extraordinary Exeter trial, half a dozen shipwrecked seamen at the point of death from starvation, voluntarily cast lots, and ate one of their number, and survived. The law went inflexibly through the motions of trying them for murder.

The simile of being all in one boat is a suitable one for following the derivation of interindividual ethics from group survival laws under different situations. As we shall discuss in the next chapter, the notion that "human rights," or any other ethical standards, are independent of the circumstances of the group is an instance of rigid, childish, subjective thinking, often aided by the absolute dogmas of revealed, subjective religious systems. When the ship sails from balmy seas into the teeth of a hurricane, the passengers lose their right to be on deck, and other freedoms, and sacrifices of life and limb are demanded of the crew that would not fit the more halcyon "humanitarian" ethical rules.

In societies today, the debates on what is "moral" and "just" often turn on how much should be given relatively to "welfare" schemes and the unemployed and how much to the national defense, (in times of threatened survival). (As well as to basic scientific research for the future, and to education.) As yet scarcely considered expressly in our society is the rivalry between the wants of the present generation and provision for the needs of the next. Often the alternatives to be considered are those between a tough-minded, realistic, position associated with foresight as to the magnitude of stresses to come, and on the other hand, a tender-minded, withful-thinking, emotional sensitivity, as when advocates of the latter deny capital punishment for repeating murderers, while the former point out that to imprison a criminal for life costs enough to give ten deserving young people a higher education.

However, especially at time of prosperity, when the phase of Yin looks as if it would last forever, the kindly person asks, "Why must we divert resources from ample gratification of human needs, e.g., free food for pets for everyone, to such adventurous ends as the activities of scientific research, e.g., space exploration, that seem remote from these personal 'needs'." Or "Why should we take measures, e.g., making eugenic control everyone's responsibility (as in China's new birth control laws) directly aimed at aiding evolution, rather than allow the freedom of unrestricted reproduction?"

Our inquiry on the consequences of accepting the necessary conclusion that the universe is—as far as human purposes are concerned—neither benign nor hostile, are, finally, four: (1) that the calls to make society anything from humane to indulgent have to be reconciled with keeping society functional, and at a survival level in relation to natural selection; (2) that external stresses come and go, through Yin and Yang, and cannot be avoided by attempts to reduce competition among nations, which is changeable in onset and in any case covers only part of the stress; (3) that what are appropriate ethics of "justice" and of human rights and relations are shaped as derivatives from basic Beyondist principles, fixed according to changing circumstances; and (4) pressure of evolution needs to be maintained, as far as we have control of it, at one level—the highest—and to this the ethics of human intercourse must be adapted, according to changing circumstances.

The reason for these laws in Beyondism is that humanity, at our lowly stage of command of nature, lives in ever present danger of unanticipated annihilation. Astronomers are aware that even the near approach of a large meteor could swamp our world, and biologists know of deadly viruses that might suddenly flourish. Whatever still-not-understood forces caused the great ice ages could, for example, again present us with a savage challenge to our intelligence. And biologists do not rule our the possibility of a microbial mutation and plague that all our resources of knowledge and intelligence would be strained to combat. The answer to "How fast is it desirable that the evolution of human intelligence should proceed?" is "As rapidly as the dedication to Beyondism can bring it about." The compromise with human comfort and pleasure—like that necessary in a liner's lifeboat in a rough sea—has to put survival first. These conclusions place Beyondism in an austere and Spartan tradition; but the truths of Nature as presently understood, certainly call for this basic value. The fact that Nature becomes benign only as our intelligence is able to master it, means that there are limits to the resulting "benignness" of society itself.

Chapter 10

How Can the Verdicts
of Probable Relative Survival of Groups
Be Reached?

The chances of survival of a group, as a gene pool, a culture, or both, depend on several determiners, such as natural resources, its geographical position among other countries, the genetic quality of its people, the fitness of its culture, and the ethical beliefs and moral standards of its citizens. Beyondism as an ethical system is concerned primarily with the last, but since, say, billions of barrels of oil beneath its land may compensate for a country's defective political and ethical values, there is no evaluating the intrinsic level of the latter without taking into account the former. In brief experimental terms, survival is the dependent variable and the diverse variables just mentioned are the independent variables contributing to the former, as in the equation (10.1).

The social science which Beyondism calls for needs (a) either to use "recorded nonsurvival" as "the criterion," or (b) to learn to measure the signs of health or sickness of a society so that a graduated "probable survival index" can be assigned to each society. Discovering such an index—thus eliminating the need to wait on complete collapse as the "criterion"—will appeal to humanitarian motives. Hopefully this substitution will not insidiously invalidate the calculating processes here, and certainly it will carry with it more scientific understanding of the "disease" (if such it be) of national decline. Or (c), if reaching an objective ethics is our primary goal, to discover how to allow for, and "partial out," the effect on survival of the other independent causes, so that we are left with a "survival contribution" value based *strictly for the ethics and morality* conditions themselves.

We are in this chapter taking the basic position reached in Chapters 4 and 5, reached by what we believe to be sound logic, and progressing to more refined experimental, quantitative, technical analysis for obtaining the desired guidance on the effect of ethics and all else in the group's profile.

We shall begin with the measurement of the criterion: the relative success of a country in terms of its signs of a healthy promise of survival. This measurement is important not only for the inhabitants of the particular country, but in extracting *general* genetic laws. These are needed in guiding the dependableness of adoption (imitation) of its cultural elements, and genetic strains, by other countries in the interests of the central task of finding the best diverse paths of evolution for mankind generally.

In the past (and, alas, probably, through slow acceptance of social science, for one or two more generations) we have had to depend on the verdict of irreversible, accomplished history to decide when a culture was moribund. Farseeing statesmen have more than once, by intuition, correctly judged a society to be in decline—a few years ahead of the catastrophe. To know that "all our pomp of yesterday is one with Nineveh and Tyre" comes too late for reform. We can roughly conclude that if a country finally expires, and the winds of the desert mourn around its fallen stone idols, there was a morbid condition that depopulated it or rendered it easy prey to a conqueror. *If a science of society could avoid leaning on so final and ineluctable a verdict, and substitute action on dependable prior signs of decline*, it could proceed with evolutionary guidance more rapidly and better suit the appeal of man for humane treatment by the universe. For the collapse of a culture, or the shrinkage toward extinction of a racial group, is generally accompanied by suffering. Suffering, one must recognize, has always been the price of trial and error progress and we must not expect, realistically, completely to eliminate it, without eliminating progress itself (as, for example, by the Hedonic Pact). But scientific ingenuity might lessen the ratio of pain to progress in intergroup competitive life, as it does, for example, by eugenics in interindividual natural selection.

This thought brings us to one of the major practical, political suggestions from Beyondism: that there be set up an International Cultural Research Center, the function of which shall be to gather data on the condition of each country and to extract by comparative study, scientific laws on ethical customs and other determiners of vitality and progress. Since a single world power—a monopoly in determining world affairs—is anathema to an evolutionist (except in policing against war) this power would need to be a *federation* in structure, and *advisory* in function. It is little realized by most citizens, incidentally, how many subtle international influences already have taken some control in the world, spiritually and economically. Barry Goldwater, in a statesman's autobiography (*With No Apologies*, 1979) indicates that "foreign aid" is out of control of the U.S. He states that the Trilateral Commission is taking on the control of poverty by "a world wide economic power superior to the political governments of the nations involved. They believe the abundant materialism they propose to create will overwhelm existing differences." Beyondism, by contrast, accepts the spiritual values in existing differences, and supplies only knowledge.

Such a world research institute will need a political basis—but hopefully as unpolitical as possible! The numerous writings, and the few practical steps, toward the need for a world organization have, it is unfortunately true, frequently taken the form of asking for a single world power. But the principles of Beyondism can by no means tolerate the concept of a world monopoly of general power, and the resulting spreading monotony of cultural style and racial homogeneity. This would have been the goal of a very different, cruder era—that of, say, Napoleon, of Hitler, and of the Roman Emperors. Many attempts have been made by the ambitions of one man or one country—for example by the brutal methods of a Genghis Khan—to reach the uniformity of one world. The same goal has been pursued, using combinations of war, superstition and insidious persuasion, by the various claimants to being *the* universal religion, perhaps most characteristically by Islam. The psychological difference between one world reached by a power struggle and an organized diversity reached by voluntary federation is very great, and so also are the evolutionary consequences. Stagnation lies in the first, and adventurous diversity, ever proceeding, in the second.

In Chapters 16 through 19 we shall come to the details of social, political, and research institution organizations that this evaluation of goals ultimately calls for. But here we are concerned purely with the question of quantitatively evaluating the "dependent variable"—the vitality and promise of a culture—in order to infer, from comparisons thereof, what ethical and other conditions contribute to its state. In so doing, a reminder comes to us from biology: (1) that success is always relative to a particular environment. How much have we to allow for the difficulty of environment of a particular nation at a particular time? (2) that since, even in one general environment, biology witnesses that many *different* genuses, and species may flourish side by side, the condition of survival can obviously be met by many different devices (as in the animal world) and diverse combinations of qualities. This does not *necessarily* make the dependent variable unmeasurable, if we have the right diagnostic signs. It only makes its contributing factors different in different settings. (3) that in the symbiosis of living forms—from true symbiosis to parasitism—the survival of one is to some extent tied up with the survival of certain others. The mathematics of this model is not simple, but the existence of complexity does not deny that the principles Beyondism has adopted are correct: They only make the analysis of connection of properties with survival somewhat more complex.

Regarding (2), the production of the same survival potential by different combinations, there is no problem to psychologists, who have already made considerable progress regarding *individuals*, in predicting which individuals will survive in advanced education or a particular job situation. Briefly, the psychologist takes measures on a number of distinct traits, such as intelligence, emotional stability, introversion, and so on, and finds by experiment what weight each needs to be given to each, in what is called the *behavioral equation*, in estimating success in a particular situation, as follows:

$$S_i = b1T1_i + b2T2_i + ... bnTn_i \qquad (10\text{-}1)$$

where S is success, $T1, T2 ... Tn$ are n traits measured for the given person (hence the subscript i, for individual) and $b1, b2 ... bn$ are the weights that have been found in the population for each trait for the given kind of success—which in this case would reside in the indicators of survival potential!

If one asks the typical good citizen, proud of, or at least concerned about, the "goodness" of his country, he will have difficulty in suggesting how to measure it. He may, as in reaching Thorndike's (1939) "goodness of living" index for cities, mention freedom from crime, goodness of educational opportunity, absence of excessive income tax, freedom to work where he will, high material standard of living, number of books read by the average person, freedom from riots, creativity in the sciences and the arts, and so on. And he would mention several intangibles, as the poet William Henley did (*England, my England*):

> Life is good and joy runs high.
> Between English earth and sky.

or Rupert Brooke in "hearts at peace, under an English heaven" or Shakespeare's "this happy breed of men." All of which could be matched by the poets of "la belle France" and many other countries in which citizens feel, if they cannot express, the special virtues of their countries.

Science has to begin with reliable measurement, but psychologists were told that since they dealt largely with intangibles they could not hope to measure! The rise of a refined science of *psychometry* has dispersed this pessimism. But it has demanded difficult statistical propositions. In the first place, the sheer number of diverse behavioral traits in a human personality is baffling, and it has only been through the development of a sophisticated use of the research method called factor analysis that the problem of understanding personality has been shifted to a relatively few significant broad traits underlying these innumerable manifestations. From the discovery of these source traits, personality science has proceeded to equations precisely analogous to (10-1) above, but in which S is *any* particular behavior response, the T's are a person's scores on the significant source traits and the b's fit (and describe) the situation in which he stands.

In the last 30 years a few researchers skilled in the same methods have applied them to a population sample of modern nations, correlating a lot of "social indicators" across some 120 countries to see "what goes with what." This approach is very different from the endless theorizing from armchairs about national characters and causes that used to go on (and still does with some historians, sociologists and even social psychologists). Recently a check on extended samples of countries has supported the patterns of at least eight among the 20 or more pattern-dimensions so far seen only more dimly.

One of the most stable dimensions has been called *Intelligent Affluence*, the theory being that countries high on the following social indicators (which we know correlate) are high because of better intelligence and education levels.

Intelligent Affluence

High expenditure on education
High real standard of living
High musical creativity
Minimum press censorship
High calorie (sugar) consumption
Low TB death rate

The sense of this is very clearly the reward in living standards, freedom from avoidable disease, and support of cultural activity that comes from application of intelligence and education to a country's management and ethics.

A second empirically found dimension has been called:

Vigorous Development-vs-Underdevelopment of Resources

It appears as a pattern affecting:-

High ratio industrial to agricultural workers
Many telephones per capita
Low birth rate
High energy consumption per capita
Low percentage of illiterates
High percent Nordid race in population
Higher percent population Protestant

This comes close to being the axis between developed and undeveloped countries. One notes with curiosity a connection of Protestantism with Nordid race, which we hypothesized from McDougall's research, and an illustration also of some slight interaction of race and type of culture, which we discussed in general terms in Chapter 6.

A third illustration of the larger dimensions is that which Gorsuch and the present writer called Morality and Morale, set out in Chapter 7 and in a new sample as follows:

Morality Level
Fewer deaths from venereal disease
Fewer deaths from alcoholism
Lower death rate generally
Fewer calories consumed per day per capita

The last item illustrates that a concrete variable can be the result of two or more factors. In this case we must assume that general affluence increases the amount of food available, and that superego morality, self-control attitudes tend to reduce the amount consumed. This factor also is concerned with the number of people constituting a healthy population.[19]

Just as a psychologist draws the profile of source traits for an individual economically to describe his *personality*, so the social psychologist draws the profile of a nation, by its score on a dozen or more traits, measured as above, to describe its *syntality*. When syntality *profiles* are compared together, and arranged objectively in groups according to patterns, they yield *types* such as Toynbee (1947) and others have called "civilizations," e.g., the old Mediterranean civilization countries; the North Atlantic countries (Britain, Sweden, Holland, Norway, Denmark); the Eastern Asia culture patterns; and so on. All this has brought the verbal handling of cultural concepts to the level of a more exact science, and one which is highly relevant to the developments anticipated in Beyondist thought.

What is defined by syntality is the behavior of *the group as an acting organism*—its frequency of involvement in war, its making of treaties with other autonomous syntalities, the style of its economy, the legislation which it creates, its liability to riots and insurrections, its relative expenditure on state education, and so on. It is important for research to make a distinction between *population* scores (which are averages of the personality scores of the people) and *syntality* scores, which are complex "emergents," in national behavior not simply predictable from the personality averages. In general terms we can explicitly state, at least as a very likely hypothesis, that the syntality patterns, S's, must be a function of the population traits, P's, and the structure within the group which we will write R, giving the general equation

$$S = (f) R * P \qquad (10\text{-}2)$$

Such an equation is of course at present only an indicator of where our ignorance needs to be remedied. It is not possible to pursue here the quite fascinating question of what all those syntality dimensions are and how nations gradually develop along them (though studies of the latter have begun with Adelson (1950), Gibb (1956), and others). But these illustrations will suffice to show that answers to the question "How good is your country?" are beginning to leave the dominion of glib journalism or vague historical terms and to become answerable in actual measures on basic traits. Of course the question will arise, "Which direction is 'good' on each of these traits?" This *can* be positively answered *with respect to a particular performance*—a particular S in the above national behavioral equation (10-1)—when the necessary research has been done. For example, the frequency of becoming involved in war is a variable to which preliminary research gives weights as follows:

$$F_w = .10T1 + .58T2 + .21T3 - .44T4 + .29T5 \qquad (10\text{-}3)$$

where the syntality dimensions, $T1$, $T2$, etc., are as defined in Cattell (1953). Actually $T1$ is what we have set out above as Affluence, and $T2$ is a dimension of Cultural Pressure, about which more is set out in Chapter 12 on cultural-genetic lag.

As a point of method, let us note a two-stage process. We have first to find the equation, as in (10-3), for estimating a particular form of group behavior in the estimation of *probability of survival-vs-non-survival*. In short, there will still remain a question of how important that S is in the final criterion of survival. There is thus a two-tiered calculation: from national characteristics to observable particular criteria, and from observable criteria to the final criterion of relative survival.

Although we have confessed there is not yet firm knowledge as to the signs diagnostic of general morbidity, there is some interesting speculation, mainly by historians, of whom Gibbon in his two-volume study of *The Decline and Fall of the Roman Empire* and Eisenstadt's *Decline of Empires* are worthy prototypes. Such writers point to a loss of belief in the values of the culture; doubt of government by the governing classes; the increase of poverty in a dispossessed proletariat class (the main plank in Marx's concept of decline); a reduction of population (failure to support the same size of population at an acceptable standard); the "return of the jungle" (the decay of a degree of control over the general environment previously gained, e.g., in the canal system of Sumeria); an increase of relatively pointless crime; in literate cultures an increase of illiteracy; a failure of military defense against encroaching neighbors; the spread of escapes such as drug addiction; and so on.

The systematic difficulties that a Beyondist international research compiling institution will face are, in method per se, of two kinds. First as some critics have rightly said, is it correct to take the nation as the true "organic" unit for unravelling the functionality of customs, gene pools, and ethical systems? Second, since we have distinguished between the properties that, on the one hand, are necessary to *any* form of group life, and, on the other, those peculiar to the cultural experiment of a *particular* group, do we not have two distinct indices of survival to deal with?

The answer to the second is clear enough: future research must develop health-vs-decline indices for both of these, though the first—the general decline syndrome—will always be the most important.

The doubts expressed in the first can be resolved only by going deeper into technicalities necessarily left elsewhere (Cattell, 1982). But the critics must recognize that the methods of analysis heed the fact that there are other living groups—religious and commercial—that overlap variously with one another and with nations. An important instance is the multinational business corporation, which spreads its tentacles across several countries. The ideal organization both for group evolution in itself and for accurate evaluation of the health of a group is one, as we have initially stated, in which the consequences of the group customs, ethics and international actions feed back undiluted to the health and success of the group itself. Anything else is an inefficiency in evolution and a blurring of the equations sought in relating customs to the criterion of health. A religion straddles several countries, but the living substrate that carries the consequences of its beliefs and customs is still a nation, or a group of nations. The analysis of variance design we set out in Fig. 6-1(a), primarily to get separate evaluations of culture and race, can also be used to evaluate elements of culture, such as style of religion. By more complex methods the social science of the future will be able to pull out the effects of multinational corporations and other groups straddling groups.

When we are told, in criticism, that factor analytic and similar analytic tools, though successful at getting at the dimensional personality structure of persons, cannot work so well on the characteristics of group syntality because groups are not so independent of one another, we are dealing with a misconceived assumption about persons. For the fact is that they also develop embedded in a network of relations with other people and the environmental circumstances. We can nevertheless deal logically with their traits and develop ways of measuring them.

Both the action of evolution in itself, and the means of evaluating the success or decline of cultures—leading to analysis of the promise of new cultural elements—demand the existence of organically self-contained groups, in natural interaction. If there were not nations, experiment would require other test tubes of merely a different size or style. As Hardin (1982) well says in his critique of Selah's (1980) horror story, nations are the most convenient large groups at which the value of cultural decisions can be made and tested, and "Eliminating nations would merely move the locus of the mistake-making down to the next largest political unit, the tribes (called "ethnic groups" in the U.S.). We do not need to imagine the consequences of enthroned tribalism, we can see them throughout central Africa."[20]

The present chapter necessarily leads to a view down a long vista of technical advances in social science that are not yet made. But the insufficiency of present ability to make the calculations does not affect the soundness of the Beyondist principle of comparative research. We shall pick up this need in a more immediately practical design in Chapters 16 through 19, in the form of work of a central, international, Beyondist research institute. But it is desirable to suggest initially here that its role be best conceived as an *advisory* one. What the actual power structure of the world will lead to when advice is not taken is another matter. In the past, inasmuch as historians generalize that "power abhors a vacuum," the degeneration and collapse of any society has been aided by outside military pressures and followed by dissolution of government and partition or absorption in another culture. It is unlikely that complete collapses will suddenly cease to take place, and we may expect that the final verdict of extinction—free from human error of evaluation in the more humane process here defined—may still give at times the last word.

The research institute we have foreshadowed will require a full integration of biological, social, and psychological sciences. And let us make no mistake by underestimating the challenges of this task. The integration of the human sciences will require a level of genius as great as, or greater than, any yet reached in the physical sciences, which have recently conquered space travel. Clearly it will require greater funding than any common undertaking—the building of the Panama Canal, the world meteorological service, the world health service, UNESCO and the U.N.—has yet attempted for a common service to humanity.

What is perhaps harder to grasp is that it will require a greater objectivity and detachment than has previously prevailed in international affairs and older sciences. For here there can be no adequate verdicts from experiments on rats, such as medicine can do. The extraction of laws and principles can come only from human beings and human cultures. This demands a willingness to stand and study a misconceived racio-cultural experiment as it demonstrates its failure. The ethics of Beyondism demand recognition of the tragic aspects of life.

Chapter 11

How Must Society Handle Individuality, Counter Cultures, Evolution, and Revolution?

We have explored the form of a dependable, ethical system based on the goal of human evolution, and adjusted to the essential nature of the given environment. Our next concern, through the following two chapters, has to do with how society should take its adjustive steps in the evolutionary process. For the evolutionary requirements must be not only the basis of ethics, but of the political and social organization and their changes, that proceed under those ethics.

In Chapter 6 we have seen the importance of individual thought and invention in modern social progress. But the often awkward question of individuality versus conformity to group goals is one that must be clarified at the outset of any discussion of socio-political systems. For thereon depends the style of group progress, between smooth change and cataclysmic convulsions, and much else in social action. There are several emotional misunderstandings of this individuality question, provided largely by man's capacity to rationalize exceeding his capacity to reason objectively. The first is a failure to distinguish between creative deviation and ethical shortcoming. There is no end to the forms of avoidance of ethical obligations, defended in the name of freedom and individuality; for as the Bible justly observes, man is "desperately wicked" and his paranoid ingenuity in attack and defense of his deviations is never lacking. One is reminded of the sheer bias in Marx's "dictum" that "all methods for raising the social productiveness of labor are brought about at the cost of the individual laborer"! The hopes for advance in making this distinction of rationalization from reasoning are that (1) Beyondism offers a more objective basis for calculating what is ethical deviation than do the subjective and mutually contradictory dogmatic revealed religions, and (2) Psychology is increasingly able to distinguish what cognitive attitudes originate in the unconscious, avoiding the reality principle.

A second comment on deviation that any psychologist must make is that the couplet due to the playwright John Dryden (*Absalom and Achitophel*):

> Great wits are sure to madness near allied
> And thin partitions do their bounds divide.

has misled a lot of people. *True* originality naturally leads to deviant ideas, but those ideas, except in bizarrely based tastes in art, are very different, when reality tested, from deviant ideas that spring from some degree of mental illness or revolt against ethics. As Kretschmer pointed out, schizophrenia occurs in geniuses with a frequency well *below* the average of the nongeniuses, and as Terman's more statistical examination of the highly gifted showed, they are above average in mental balance and emotional stability, as well as in intellect.

The Dryden illusion is that since creators and lunatics alike produce deviant products they must be similar people. Another source of comparison springs from the immense appeal to human vanity of the limelight gained, in a shallow press, by *being* deviant and noteworthy. For example, though the dynamic-biological roots of homosexuality are major, the personality profiles of hundreds of homosexuals (Cattell & Morony, 1962) contained on the average significantly more motivation purely to be "avant garde" and different. It is a very easy way to choose to be different.

Socially the problem of the ideal form of individuality of expression is tied up with politics of communism-socialism, democracy, and fascism. It has been pointed out by Chapter 9 that laws must be adaptable to group circumstance, restricting rights and freedoms during group stress, but encouraging in the long term a high degree of individuality.

What is not sufficiently perceived in political choices is that (in spite of the typically escapist, emotional slogan "Liberte, Egalite, Fraternite.") liberty and equality are actually incompatible, since people are naturally unequal, and are brought to equality of living style, earnings, influence, or whatever, only by interference and coercion. A recent survey of immigrants who got out of Russia to come to America revealed that they were chagrined to find that the freedom they had longed for included the freedom to be out of a job. (Apparently, without any personal effort they would have been provided, under Communism, with a job, regardless of its social usefulness.) A psychologically deeper observation which emerged was that they preferred socially a sense of herd solidarity and dependence, finding Americans too concerned with their privacy and independence. (This European culture of privacy, perhaps Protestant, with its greater restraint and aloofness, is epitomized in "Every Englishman is an island.") This is but one illustration of the fact that political abstractions, like communism, democracy, capitalism, etc., are tied to important patterns of temperamental emotional adjustment of individuals. The bee does not make a honeycomb out of square holes, and a bricklayer does not get accustomed to making the wall of a house out of hexagons. It is another example of the argument elsewhere in this book that racial temperament collectively acting through individuals *does* tend to decide the form of adopted religion, and, as Kretschmer, Oliver, and Spengler independently point out, of art.

It is in the intelligent adolescent university student that one commonly sees most clearly (and certainly hears most loudly!) the arguments for individual versus group values. He is more aware of these group restraints, as he struggles beyond childhood docility, and is at a stage of painful awareness of the antitheses of the individual (and sometimes new) idea and the conservative ethos. Although he commonly espouses some particular reforms that are right, yet he is clearly wrong in considering an unmitigated individuality to be desirable. Indeed, the whole antithesis of group and individual is philosophically in the same area as whether "the egg exists for the hen or the hen for the egg." In psychodynamics, i.e., drives and their satisfactions in the group, the group is basically an instrument for the satisfaction of the individual's needs. But unless the group controls the individual, as a means to its struggle for those ends and its survival, the individual will come to that frustration and futility which Hobbes described in the *Leviathan*.

The issues here cannot be fully examined without looking at the idea of the Group Mind which Hobbes, Hegel, McDougall and others entertained, and which I introduced with a more empirical social psychology in the concept of the "Theopsyche" (1938). If we take the analogy that an individual in a society is like a cell in the human body, then it is evident that we have just as much right to consider the organic *unity* of this "group emergent"—the body and soul—as to stress the individuality of the cell. It is true that at present we cannot predict and calculate how this self-directing *syntality* of the group derives from the personalities of the population and the structural pattern of their roles; but we have a beginning.[21] In fact, there is little doubt, from experiments with small groups, that the behavior of a group, as a group, can be inferred from its *syntality* profile and the situation, and by the same formula as individual behavior from the personality profile and the situation.

It is also clear that this group behavior is more than any simple sum of the behavioral contributions of the constituent individuals. Interactional "emergents" are very great, as equation (10-3) above suggests. The relation of an individual to the group is therefore something more than the description of his relation to the other individuals in it. We cannot, after these reflections, accept the view of the arch-individualist that he himself is the only reality and that the group is a mere intellectual abstraction. The group has a life of its own, with its drives and its integration of consciousness, and is bound on a life course voyage just as real as that of any individual. It has to consider, for example, its ethical obligations and rights among other groups, just as the individual does among other individuals.

The position that we have taken that the survival strength of a group is dependent on (among other things) its citizens' morality, *defined as conformity to ethical laws, which we have warned above must not be construed as support for conformity in other aspects of life.* Cultural advance, as Chapter 6 argues, is to quite a surprising degree the product of innovations, technical and social, by individuals. Cultural evolution, though partly shaped by material group and environmental pressures, especially in early historic and prehistoric times, has increasingly in the last two thousand years been the result of inventions by individuals capable of independent and realistic thought. Consider the automobile, the airplane, the elimination of infectious disease, the telephone, the computer, and the dynamo, and in each case you will find that the truly original idea was given by a generally economically relatively poor man, working in obscurity, but possessing the priceless gift of introverted independence and boundless curiosity. The rest of the developments as we actually see them—the enormous dynamos at Niagara, the supersonic jet passenger plane, the pocket computer, and so on—that revolutionize our life styles, are the product of competent but relatively unoriginal minds powered by commercial support, and following an almost inevitable series of small-step improvements. The importance for cultural evolution of the first free-thinking, governmentally, and institutionally unrestricted, and little supported, creative individual can scarcely be exaggerated. The Beyondist's starting point in regard to the survival and progress of a society as such thus leads him logically and in terms of social science to cherishing the creative individual (but distinguishing such nonconformity from ethical nonconformity).

Admittedly, there is likely to be *some* definable *optimum* level in society for encouragement and permissiveness of individuality, but that level is probably higher than most countries have ever reached, and creative individuality should therefore be much more fostered than restrained. Although Beyondist ethics therefore calls for a substantial defense and acceptance of individuality, it also requires conformity in ethics.

The basic instruments for diagnosis that society needs in this dilemma are those to distinguish between unethical deviation—crudely, in crime—and creative deviation. Techniques in psychological knowledge are needed to recognize the cases were moral deviation will masquerade as the right to individuality and "civil rights." The independence of a James Watt, John Stuart Mill, Edison, or Bernard Shaw is one thing; the sociopathic murderer or rapist who obstinately ridicules ethical norms of behavior is quite another. The intellectual moral-relativist who rationalizes the primrose path for himself and his cronies is certainly no less dangerous to society than the outright criminal.

Free thought is vital to the long-term chances of survival of a society, through the improved adaptations it ultimately brings about. But, as we have seen, rejection of conformity and loyalty may be fatal, especially in short interludes of high threat to a society. Even in times of lesser stress it is vital to have clear conceptions of what is a creative and what is a moral deviation, and what the rights of the individual are relative to the rights of society. Beyondism offers a basis to draw clearer and more rational conclusions here than those derived from the hash of past religions on which the laws of many countries are traditionally based (See today the Muslim grip on Iran). Today democracies part company from communist or fascist dictatorships on the question of civil liberties, and from dogmatic religions on the question of intellectual liberty, but, although true liberties are vital, we should ask where calls for civil liberties pass over into civil licentiousness, and for religious liberty into ethical license. We shall discuss below how the ethical division between conditions common to all group survival (System 1(a) in Figure 8-1) and ethical values peculiar to the adventure of a particular group (System 1(b)) affect the evolution of individual deviations.

The 17th and 18th centuries' intellectuals confidently pulled the "rights of man" out of thin air, or their own hats. Thomas Paine, Rousseau, Locke, Montesquieu, and the French encyclopedists did so. As several independent thinkers today point out (Ardrey, *The New Social Contract*, 1970) versus Jean Rousseau (*The Social Contract*), the latter in particular built a house of cards from his own capricious assumptions ("supremely silly" premises says Professor Oliver), e.g., on biological equality, the noble savage, the born virtuousness of man, and the like. One cannot pull the "natural rights of man" out of one's hat. They require a reference to the evolutionary conditions of societies.

It is reasonable to forgive these perfervid writers, considering the stresses of an age when wrongs were rife and the merest common sense sufficed to recognize the insufferableness of the ancient entrenched inequities. But less emotional thinkers of our later age should be able to recognize that there is no such thing as the "natural" rights of an individual. The sturdiest of early liberals, Jeremy Bentham, recognized this before others when he said, "Natural rights are simple nonsense; natural and imprescrible rights ... nonsense upon stilts" (1834). The rights that an individual has vis-a-vis his group depend upon the condition of the group. No man who joins a ship's company can demand "the right not to drown," nor can a man who invests in common stock in a corporation demand that his shares shall not decline in value on the stock exchange.

At the present moment such issues have come to the fore partly because "rights" are being used to trespass on the property of others and partly because a number of countries have denied their citizens rights which we take for granted in Western democracies. Regardless, however, of what the rights are, it should be recognized that anything that we can legally call a *right* has meaning only in regard to a *contract* and if, as in the possibility of a ship sinking, an "act of God" may be beyond the control of either party, a conditional clause enters into every contract. The problem in defining the individual's rights in a society by meaningful legal standards is that the individual has no chance to sign a contract before he consents to be born into that society. Only if he is an immigrant is the situation such that a contract with mutually accepted rights can be considered. However, if the right to emigrate were universal, a citizen coming of age could sign his contract or emigrate. Meanwhile, in various so-called "civil rights" movements, and expounders of personal, relativistic, subjective ethics, there is often an assumption that only the individual, and not the group, has rights. (The group is usually, by these writers, assigned only duties and obligations!)

Insofar as rights, and necessarily associated duties, are part of the ethical basis of social contracts, they derive firmly from the conditions of group survival. (As we have seen, these have a dual basis: conditions necessary in *any* group functioning, and values peculiar to the cultural adventure of the *given* group.) How this leads to universal rights and rights in a particular adopted society is a matter for legislators. In either case, the argument hidden in many "rights" claims, namely that "ethics is an individual matter" is a complete logical contradiction, since ethics deals with rules *among* individuals. An individual may sponsor a different system which he hopes others will adopt, but until more than one adopts it, it cannot prove itself to be a group-functional ethical system rather than a personal whim. Acting according to a personal whim is by no means always a right!

As we have seen, in working out the origins of ethical rules and individual rights the behavioral rules which emanate from the condition that the group must survive have two origins: (1) in the behaviors required in order that *any* group shall survive, and (2) the behaviors necessary for the survival of the particular racio-cultural experiment of that group. The former might be called *maintenance* values and the latter *adventure* values, respectively, in the common and the *specific* ethical basis in Systems 1(a) and 1(b) in Figure 8-1.

One may reasonably hope that the social science research institutes we envisage (Chapter 18) will soon be able to infer objectively what behaviors are the most ethical for the maintenance goal. But although the specific ethics needed within a group can theoretically also be inferred from the goals of its specific adventure as a group, that derivation may long have to remain relatively inaccurate, at an intuitive level. All that one perhaps can conclude is that these rights have to be open to higher degrees of the kind of individuality we have discussed. Since objective determination of appropriate limits is more difficult, and the *specific* set of values in a given group are heading in the direction of new trial and error values, one can afford to be more experimental regarding the specific group values.

Historically it has naturally turned out that the revealed religions, claiming universality, have settled on the values for maintaining *any* group, whereas the nationalisms have launched the group into specific cultural adventure values. It follows that despite some rivalry of general and specific, the nations adopting universal religions have benefitted in their general individual maintenance and strength. The encouragement of a strict Catholic Inquisition by Isabella and Ferdinand could be seen as an emphasis on common ethics, and its result was first to strengthen the society and then to leave it culturally, relatively infertile and bereft of new cultural trends. Similarly, the communist church (for such it is, in its belief in its universality, rather than in a specific, tentative, and national experiment) promises infertility. (Dean Inge [1929] conveniently labels these two—Catholic and Communist—authoritarian systems, respectively, as the "black" and the "red" totalitarianisms.)

The problem of conceiving a value system as universal is, scientifically, that it arranges for no experimental variations. Since the variations belong to independent groups, and universal communism or any other belief hopes to bring all groups within its fold, the universalist position (unless like Beyondist, uniquely recognizing divergence) tends to be inimical to special adventure values, and therefore also restrictive of innovation. We see this for example, in the end of genetic research under Communism as described in Zirkle's *Death of a Science* (1949), and the effect on agriculture of Lysenkoism, as well as the ejection of intelligence testing from the Russian schools. This authoritarian, imperialist type of political or religious value system illustrates the result of a conceptual failure to distinguish between the goal of basic survival, with its need for common ethics, and the need for specific group experiment ethics.

Let us next consider the connection between acceptance or denial of *individuality*, on the one hand, and, on the other hand, the style of *growth in societies* as a whole, varying from steadily continuous, and relatively smooth, to spasmodic and violent. Essentially, we point out that if no distinction is made between deviation and criminality, a society cannot grow. One is familiar in the biological world with the difference between vertebrates, which grow with steady continuity of form, and the crustaceans, which, as in the crab, go through a series of crises, putting on a burst of fast and furtive growth between one rigid, outgrown shell and the next larger. What happens analogously between two different types of society is illuminated by what we can study in this particular biological difference. Some countries, such as Britain, Sweden, and Holland, change cultural values and government by steady procedures and others (notably in South America and Russia) by a series of attempted revolutions. The former, like the mammals, sometimes have the defect of carrying vestiges (like the human appendix) in the form, for example, of continuing nominal kingship. But they "broaden down" in their history from precedent to precedent, with minimum economic loss and slaughter. Since we know that certain group properties are undoubtedly (Cattell & Stice, 1960) products as much of population temperament as of rules and regulations, the propensity of a group to revolutionary rather than evolutionary change may well prove to rest on temperament, the more phlegmatic, English and Scandinavian countries having a history of reasoned change. Dean Inge (1929) comments on this with perhaps a little too much English patriotism (and overlooking 1649 and 1775) when he says,

> Evolution without revolution is the great achievement of
> English history. Common sense is the central thread, one
> flower of which is the glorious gift of humor, from Chaucer
> to Dickens. England "developed the idea of the gentleman,
> and by this gave an ethical ideal of great though not unique
> value to the world."

The emergence of gentlemanly behavior and evolutionary politics
is a joint product of temperament and cultural events.

Cultural revolutions are major historical events that are usually
slow, whereas the overthrow of governments are culturally less important and trivial events, but hold attention by dramatic suddeness.
Within the range of revolutionary style between these extremes some
common psychological and ethical principles apply. It can be argued
from the standpoint of Beyondist ethics that a system that does not
have a built-in mechanism for the more continuous type of progress
is defective, since evolutionary progress is the law of life, and flouting
it may be the death of the social organism concerned. Yet, unless
explicit attention is given to evolving such a mechanism, it is almost
inevitable that societies will first stagnate, and then be forced to move
on by the wasteful, dangerous, and stereotyped procedure of the crab.

Psychologically we have to recognize that what we have called the
genetic lag, as studied more intensively in Chapter 12, means that
most of the population will always stand at some degree of frustration
of its psychological needs in its biological make-up, *by reason of the
complexities and long-circuiting restraints of a civilized culture.* Under
civilization one lives longer and better, but nevertheless with more
"bother," frustration, and demand on intelligence. And those of lower
intelligence, and capacity to sublimate ergs, have a tougher deal from
society because they enjoy less so many of the intellectual excitements
that civilization offers. All this has been well said, from different but
supplementary viewpoints, by Freud in *Civilization and its Discontents* (1930) and Stoddard in *The Revolt Against Civilization* (1922).

Let us first concentrate on what may be called "force" revolutions,
in which an establishment in power is pointedly attacked as the object
to be destroyed, as in the French and Russian revolutions. At the opposite end of the range are events like the industrial revolution and the
communications revolution now in progress in which, though the
changes are variously disturbing, there is little that can be (or, as most
think, should be) done to aid or stop the revolution by attacking some

particular organization. The study of the former shows (1) that typically they do not occur at times of extreme hardship, as stereotypes suggest, but more frequently when some better degree of well-being and spirit exists in the "downtrodden"; (2) that a "defection of the intellectuals" to new views has been going on for two or three generations against the established order (as in France before 1798 and Russia before 1917); (3) that national defeat or great natural disasters which government seemed too weak to avert must first have weakened severely the existing government (as in the Bolshevik and Nazi revolutions); and (4) that an alliance takes place, psychologically, between the reformers and those who, by genetic lag, are essentially continuously in revolt against the complexity of civilization.

The psychology of this type of revolution has become much better understood, to the point where, like typhoid epidemics, the future may see less thereof. In this condensation let us leave (1) and (3) to the historians and focus on the psychology of (2) and (4). What writers have covered in (2) is actually not quite correctly described as "the defection of the intellectuals" but only of a class of more verbal intellectuals and associated writers, who today we would call journalists. In the French Revolution, Lavoisier, and many scientists like him, were not with the revolution (whence Lavoisier was guillotined as the prosecutor declared "the revolution has no need of scientists"—which is also reminiscent of Hitler's Nazis). In the Russian revolution, Pavlov studiously ignored it, and some almost equally eminent scientists, e.g., in genetics and physics, did the same at their cost.

A careful study of the role of "intellectuals" would probably show, as in Terman's studies of genius(1926), that intelligence is equally high in geniuses in art and literature on the one hand, and those in science on the other, but that significantly higher emotional stability and maturity co-exists with higher intelligence in the scientists. As argued elsewhere, rationalism, even if not deceived by subjective verbal concepts, and untainted by rhetoric, cannot direct "reform," since the goals and means of progress are really matters for scientific, empirical elucidation.

In short, the intellectuals of what we have called the "feeling liberal" type, who operate more in literature and the arts, in contrast to "thinking liberals" more frequent in science, are as vulnerable to emotional distortions as the average man in the street. An unhappy result is that they communicate, by their emotionality, with the man in the street more than do thinking liberals, overbusy in their backroom laboratories.[22]

There are two major examples in history of the feeling liberal movement prevailing, with relatively simple emotional measures, over the thinking liberals' more complex realisms. They are Marxianism with its economic oversimplifications and distortion of the source of civilization's troubles, and its primarily emotional appeal against government hidden therein, and Christianity which swept around the Mediterranean under and past the fine thinking of the Greek philosophers and their more educated followers. In the case of Marx, the psychologically penetrating biography by Weyl can leave little doubt, in any one but a purblind devotee, that his personal twists of character shaped the form of his economic "interpretation" of history.

As "reading" mankind is becoming a little more sophisticated, the likelihood of false solutions to progress being successfully peddled by emotional intellectuals, bent on "revolution," becomes less, and critical examination of needs by scientific and statistical debate is likely to prevail so long as orderly procedures remain to sustain such examination. Evolution can be continuous revolution, as Trotsky argued, but we should nevertheless pause to see what has happened in violent revolutions of the past, if we are to avoid their mistakes and substitute the quality of evolution.

The unfortunate alliance of progressive deviates and regressive deviates will remain. The storming of the Bastille released not only political prisoners but ordinary criminals, e.g., the Count de Sade. The fact that the antisocial, the emotionally unstable, and those with personal allergies to authority supply the true reformers with much of the motive power needed for social change has systematic consequences. An alliance arises between those who are ahead of their time and those who lag far behind it. (See Stoddard's *The Revolt Against Civilization* (1922) for supporting detail on this.) It is not surprising, therefore, that many revolutions, by the crudity and barbarity which they quickly develop, astonish, and often disillusion the reformers. More than once a revolution has created a longing for law and order which has brought the new society almost to a re-adoption of outworn customs that the revolution was out to improve upon. If we compare the period of, say, 1789-1849 in France and in Britain, it is evident from the latter that social progress can be effected as readily without a revolution as with one. No psychologist can read Marx, or his biography, without realizing that the bloody revolution was more important to him than what was to come after (Weyl, 1979). Dissidents executed by the Czars were trifling in number compared to the millions sent to their deaths by Stalin. And the hatred for the bourgeoisie—or the planful "haves" in general—

remains an unmistakably powerful motive behind the elaborate and untenable facade of the economic arguments of those continuing as Marxists. In Marx's comment (which any good observer will support) that "The more a ruling class is able to assimilate the foremost minds of a ruled class, the more stable and dangerous becomes its rule" could well be applied to the small minority constituted by the Communist Party that now rules Russia. It is something, incidentally, that we must examine as a possible weakness in a "just" democratic meritocracy. Since proletariats are partially born and partly made, the solution to the proletariat problem is partly a eugenic birth rate, raising them to bourgeois intelligence and enterprise level and partly free cultural mobility, to enable proletariat and bourgeois to become a single nation.

Elements in the above discussion seem to imply that Beyondism indicates always an evolutionary rather than a revolutionary process; but this is a very tentative conclusion. It remains for a true social scientific investigation to ascertain the relative virtues of a flexible gradualness and a series of violent revolutions. At a glance it would seem that countries like Sweden, Norway, Holland, Britain, and Switzerland, steadily reforming this and that social tradition, have advanced *at least* as fast and well as, say, the South American, or African, republics with their right-left pendulum swings from extreme to extreme.

Revolutionary changes, whether bloody or civilized in their methods of transition, seem from time immemorial to have harped on the struggle of the haves and have-nots, or the power struggles of the higher and lower status incumbents, which has nothing to do with *progress* as such. This kind of right-left motivation tries to pick up bits of more *ideological* progress, to vary its monotonous intrusion of "cash," since history began, but the real direction of progress is in general on an axis *orthogonal* to right-left. The changes in the modes of production, in educational content, in inventions affecting domestic life, in the basis of ethics, and so on, constitute an ideological and life style revolution that could better proceed without the battle of greeds. Redistribution of wealth is sometimes vital, and may need "revolution" to produce it. But the serious call is for redistribution among *institutions,* not among classes; for equality of education and opportunity, class differences should diminish or remain transient or innocent.

The most obviously needed redistribution today is from the enormous wealth tied up in ancient religious institutions to scientific institutes, especially those that are taking over, by research and service, the services which dogmatic religions carried on, say, during medieval times. But alertness to redistribution is *always* needed in medicine, education, politics and elsewhere. One way that a Beyondist outlook could achieve this peaceably would be by legislation whereby all old foundations should become disendowed every couple of centuries, and to be re-endowed if that is still the will of the people. This experimental disestablishment is relevant to both religions and to political dictatorships, e.g., those that have nationalized industry and the like. For, unless it is introduced as standard legislation, it is unfortunately true that these establishments are unlikely to permit the gradual, rational, empirically indicated reappointment that avoids ultimate revolution. To argue that this should be done is not to say that it should ever be done suddenly. One is out to change the structure of a house while people have to live in it, which needs wise planning by the constructors.

Both revolutions and evolutions have frequently been based not on attempts to introduce new ideas and social structures as such (as, for example, in abolition of an unnecessary bureaucracy, of a reorganization of representative government) as upon a conviction by one group that it is being unjustly exploited by another. As we have seen in Chapter 9, the making of a distinction between symbiosis and parasitism needs sophisticated thinking and good sociometry. It was a combination of the upset by the advent of the industrial revolution, in a feudal distribution of land ownership and with a high proletarian birth rate, that gave some truth to the arguments of such as Proudhon, Kingsley, Marx, and Lenin that the unskilled worker was being exploited. But today it may well be that management, scientific workers, and inventors are being exploited by the proletariat. The productivity of the less intelligent is vastly increased, raising their standard of living greatly, through the direction by gifted technical management. Without this parasitism upon brains, the real earnings of the less gifted would be much lower. Yet democracy has put up with the perhaps fatal weakness of permitting robbery by the proletariat by the ballot box. If this reduces the birth rate, or the motivation, of intelligent management and inventor types, polling is an injustice and an unethical procedure in the sense of lessening the survival potential of the society as a whole.

Our desire to avoid tragic destruction and loss of life impels us to hope that social science will demonstrate that progress can be engineered by evolutionary procedures alone. Beyondism should, however, ask the question whether evolution can be substituted for revolution, not merely on grounds of the "convenience" of the former and our "distaste" for the latter, but on grounds of effective achievement of progress. In the biological side of human evolution we see that the brain does not abolish old systems, but tends rather to build new cortical systems above and controlling them. As we know from the attempt to reconstruct our city centers, this style is often forced upon the reconstructor by immovable necessities. And perhaps evolution *is* very slowly actually retracting older, instinctual brain remnants, but is faced by the same problems of combining a new addition *immediately* with the removal of an old system. The analogy of the brain suggests that endowment of older, superfluous social organs must very probably have to proceed quite slowly with coordination of the concomitant new structures with older structures.

The positive contribution to an evolutionary style that Beyondism would suggest is the introduction and monitoring of *experimental communities* within the main community. When we discuss ethnic and religious pluralism in the composition of a state, the question will come up whether, *when a nation has such pluralistic opportunities* to evaluate deliberate experiments within its control, more experiment will be done. If, through this or other opportunities, nations see their way to greater monitored social experiment than now, then we may expect continuous evolution more completely to replace revolution. Attempts to substitute relatively undisturbing continuous evolution for spasmodic revolution will, however, not succeed in bringing about the necessary adjustment, if the evolutionary style is interpreted as nothing more than simply "going slowly and comfortably." Experiment, on the other hand, might indicate quite radical desirable changes, which could then be performed, as the demonstrated future, deliberately, though with less violence than would occur in an unplanned revolution. Trotsky's "perpetual revolution" is not bad if it is evolution well oiled, and directed. In any case, it might be argued that social developments that go so far as to require a change of basic principles in a constitution are few and far between. To consider a simple case, it is just conceivable that a country would be more intelligently governed if the franchise were restricted to say, the 75% of the population who can read, and are over an I.Q. of 90. Presumably this would require some rather far-fetched psychological interpretations by lawyers in the Supreme Court to clear such a reform of a charge of being "unconstitutional." (Jefferson, however, called for revision of the constitution every 20 years.)

Inasmuch as a government is an elite, one would expect all intelligently progressive steps—short of perhaps a necessary abolition of government—to be more smoothly made by leaders and associated technicians within the government than by possibly violent movements and demonstrations outside it. In general, a democratic form of government, even if staffed more by lawyers than scientists, is surely the form more likely to move by evolution than revolution. The problem of envy to be met here is one we have already faced elsewhere. The verbal oversimplification of considering society as divided wholly into "rich" and "poor" aids the working of envy. There is no doubt that revolutionary solutions are favored by envy (Proudhon) which makes leaders the object of attack. The true expression of envy requires true information on *which* person is the parasite, which is extremely hard to get. Babeuf, in heartening his destructive followers, cried "Perish, if necessary, all of the arts, provided we are left with total equality." This is envy in its essence.

Talking to Russian students in Moscow, I met repeatedly the idea that the strife of parties in the U.S. must be due to the fact that the Americans do not trust their government. By the devices which Skinner described (*Beyond Freedom and Dignity*, 1971), the land which developed "conditioning" appropriately succeeded, by indoctrination from infancy, in begetting this Communist youth satisfaction with a monolithic political constitution. The vital difference between the communist system and the democratic system no longer lies in having or not having a written constitution (though the communist constitution is further tied to a vast economic theory). The interpretations which lawyers make in the U.S. Supreme Court, and the detection by Communist Party intellectuals of "revisionist deviations" allow little latitude in either case for unwitting deviation. It is the American democratic freedom to *amend the Constitution* which gives to democracy its almost ideal capacity to progress by evolution rather than revolution.

There is yet another aspect to this, connected with the principle we have stated that Beyondist ethics does not necessarily call for "the greatest happiness of the greatest number." Humans, except perhaps a small minority of very healthy, vigorous, and bold individuals, mainly avoid stress. To the psychotherapist, stress, anxiety, and insecurity are bad words. But when we look at the many steps in social progress, it has taken these very stress-facing motivators to bring about new adjustments. In short, many experimental and historical observations suggest that at least a moderate degree of social stress actually aids movement. It is everywhere admitted that various social advances underway in Britain were speeded up during World War I, and no one in scientific work during World War II can forget the surge of progress—in basic as well as applied science—that happened through stress persuading the public to spend more intelligently on research. And scientists have seen in the 60s how this "knowledge for knowledge sake" research steadily lost its support in a decade of return to stressless "peace and prosperity."

The position of Beyondism on rights, discussed above, is consistent with its position on evolution and revolution. A high regard for individuality requires sensitivity to the difference of creative individuality from unethical individuality, i.e., truly antisocial ethical deviation. Incidentally, it is a distinction which psychology, going beyond the lie detector, may increasingly be able objectively to draw. Individuality, and the survival of the state, are linked by contractual rights for each. Purely subjective positioning of divinely given right by either party, though prevalent, is expensive nonsense.

On evolution versus revolution, Beyondism indicates that a basis of democracy, on which there now needs to be erected an institution for scientific experiment and monitoring of social variations, is most likely to avoid the cost and evil side effects of revolution, and achieve a better result by evolution. However, as we are reminded by the history of science itself, being advanced by humans, error is still possible, so that revolution, like war, though reduced in frequency, may still be a last resort method of adjustment. One problem here is the "glamour" of revolution, especially to the young and inexperienced. The addict to revolution per se, like someone who seeks to cure by a violent drug some ill that might be cured by diet and exercise, may cure it, but at the cost of long lasting side effects. Frequently the revolutionary is an extreme environmentalist, who fails to realize that no revolution will change the fundamental nature of man, which will develop only as fast as evolution and eugenics will allow. The spuriousness of the glamour of revolution is akin to the spuriousness of the argument, again common in the immature, that because a thing is "modern" and "done" it must be right. An experienced dialectition generally recognizes at once that this appeal hides a bankruptcy of deeper arguments. However, human nature being what it is, revolution, though second best, must remain a possible last resort means of change.

Chapter 12

Culturo-Genetic Disparities: What can be done with genetic and cultural lag?

The first within-group problem that a Beyondist ethic has to bring within its value frame is that of the relative rights and functions of the individual and the group, and how these best operate in the inevitable movement of the group in revolution and evolution. To this, essential answers have been given in the preceding chapter. The second problem is to understand the general dynamics of personal adjustment to standards and changes in the population as a whole—alike for the conforming and the nonconforming. We need to examine the reactions of this average individual to the changing discrepancies between the cultural roles and his genetic inclinations.

The main phenomenon for study here is the stress that arises between the genetic nature of man, based on several million years of adaptation to a simpler environment, and the present nature of his culture, begotten in a mere five or six thousand years. We have encountered this tension in the preceding chapter, as an ingredient in revolutionary forces—one which, unrecognized by its pawns, is, in essence, always as much a retrograde hankering for return to the simplicity of the past as it is a genuine progressive call for rational cultural advances. We have encountered it also in the general principles of interaction of culture and genetics, in Chapter 6. There we recognized (1) that genetic endowments exercise a shaping influence on cultural creation and cultural borrowing, somewhat as the construction of a computer puts limits to the programs—the "software"—that can be used on it; and (2) that cultural patterns and standards in turn, by natural selection, shape genetic development. We further recognize that in recent times, with some alleviation occurring of the natural selection that normally operates within groups, this shaping action is probably blunted.

The course of events in genetic-cultural interaction is like the paths of a tennis ball in which the change produced by one player affects the change next produced by the other. Probably some genetic mutation gave to our ape ancestor the possibility of, to some extent, the opposing the thumb to the finger. The "cultural" experience of throwing sticks and stones, which then spread, gave advantages to mutations toward larger brain size. Thus these mutations in turn aided the growth of social intelligence, going beyond the original mere manipulative "thumb" gain.

However, we shall concentrate in the larger, first part of this chapter on the cultural and emotional, dynamic problems that arise when the cultural demands move ahead of the genetic endowments of much of the population. This we shall call the situation of *genetic lag*. But the general principles above remind us it is equally possible for the cultural level to lag behind the genetic potential of the people, in what would appropriately be called *cultural lag*. This seems so much harder to detect, define, and prove that we shall find few firm illustrations.[23]

It happens that we have an instructive example of both, however, in recent research on the advance of intelligence *in the individual*. Two general ability factors are now recognized: *fluid intelligence, g_f,* which represents in its growth curve the maturation of genetic potential, and *crystallized intelligence, g_c,* which represents the result of investment of the individual's fluid intelligence capacity in the particular richness of cultural concepts he happens to encounter. When measured over the life course, these show highly distinct courses: fluid climbs from birth to about 18 years and then begins (for psychological reasons which affect also hearing, metabolic rate, etc.) a slow decline to old age. Crystallized intelligence, representing accumulation of learnings *through* fluid intelligence, shows a slight steady growth throughout life, despite the feeder of the store, fluid intelligence, weakening.

In the life phases of the individual, there is first a stage where his fluid intelligence is ahead of the levels of complexity in culture that it has not yet had time to reach and absorb, and, secondly, another in later life when the cultural level of his crystallized intelligence is scarcely within full reach of his genetic capacity to handle it. We shall consider this as an epitome and a model for at least *some* types of group cultures in history—the *genetic retreat paradigm*.

Therein, as in crystallized intelligence in the individual, slowness of mutation and a reversed natural selection leave a culture under complex cultural demand without any longer having people with the higher fluid intelligence to sustain it. However, this is a rather special case of genetic lag, for what we study as the genetic gap or genetic lag probably arises more frequently from cultural borrowing, or imposition, wherein a primitive people comes under a more complex culture. Since the invention of new cultural elements is the product of, say, a hundred countries, and borrowing is now quite fast, any one cultural group is essentially in the position of a "primitive culture," having to handle more culturally innovative additions than its own genetic pool has produced—and perhaps more than it is genetically equipped to produce.

In general, in the biology of evolution, we see the more advanced forms developing new specializations and the older forms retaining a generality of functioning. In the genuses of the primates, something unusual happened in that the comparative lines, e.g., the gorilla, specialized in physique, where man relapsed in most physical features to a physically regressive neo type, except for the brain. As Ardrey points out (*African Genesis*, 1961), the appearance of man was peculiarly associated with the tremendous selection that went on when the great forests disappeared between the ice ages, and man appeared as "a break with primate orthodoxy in the name of what can only be described as adventure." This adventure is a central tenet of Beyondism, as we shall see, and promises to continue the upward human trend.

The sharpest new demands in culture nowadays come from the direct products and the indirect social side effects of the advance of science. (Currently, computers are changing all office procedures and thereby affecting the type of personnel demand.) But in exemplifying these, let us not overlook other sources, independent of science, e.g., in a change in sex customs consequent on the intellectual undermining of the theology of dogmatic religions.

A basic perspective to be kept in mind in this chapter is that the problems of adjustment to culture spring more from the persisting genetics of our drives and emotions, in the hypothalamus and the old brain, than from the cognitive genetic intelligence limitations, in the size of the cortex, to our cognitive grasp of culture—though both cognitive and emotional inadequacies have to be considered. The reason for some disproportionate concentration on the former in current discussions is simply that psychologists can more readily bring precise quantitative research results to bear. Since Jensen (1973), Vining (1982), Van Court (1986), the present writer (1937, 1974), Lentz (1927), Burt (1943), and many others have documented the distribution of native intelligence and the changes therein in relation to cultural demand, this matter can, however, be left to the sources indicated and to latter references here on the effect of dysgenic trends in intelligence on cultural events, while we concentrate here on the persistence of instinct.

In a recent popular broadcast, the astronomer Sagan correctly described the old brain as the seat of inherited drives, and the cortex as the receptacle for factual matters in our culture. But apparently wishing to cash in on the bias (popular since Rousseau, Helvetius, and Locke) toward the importance of environment, he made the old brain equal "heredity" and the new cortex, "environment." In support of the importance of environmental learning, he pointed out that the number of bits of information in the chromosomes is outnumbered, in the order of thousands to one, by the number of "bits" that can be stored in the cortex. Even so, we must point out, first, that the chromosome bits are so numerous as to make it highly improbable, for example, that any two people (twinning aside) in the billions on earth will be born genetically the same. The astronomists' fascination with numbers is grossly misleading in this case because (a) although what goes into the cortex is environment, the *magnitude* of individual differences in what our inadequate cortexes *can hold* is much more genetically decided; and (b) the argument neglects the major psychological conclusion of this century (clinically through Freud and Jung; experimentally in structured learning theory) that *the cortex is naturally the servant of the old brain*, concerned with finding means to the ends of the ergs (instincts, drives) which the old brain presents. The cortex is the bureaucracy concerned with effecting what the mid-brain members of congress define as goals. The fact that the bureaucracy may outnumber the legislators who state the wishes of the people, by thousands to one (or whatever number Dr. Sagan announces), does not mean that the bureaucracy is more important than the setters of goals.

The neural analogy, like most analogies used in instruction, is not completely, accurately, representative. The cortex has its role in instructive matters too. By its rational analysis it can set one drive against another and thus achieve some control over goals. We see this especially in the action of ego and superego in the frontal lobes. But what 20th-century psychology—beginning with Freud—learned, in contrast to the subjective reasoning of the 18th and 19th, was that the motive forces lie in the mid-brain, and command much of the cortex. The cortex is the home of the means-to-ends knowledge. But it is the instinctual equipment of the older brain that still directs—remarkably well on the whole—our balance of desires and goals. However, it is here that the genetic lag exists, in the adjustment of genetic impulse to cultural rules.

However, before we pass on here from the simpler issues of the total genetic magnitude (convolutions and transmitter efficiency) of the cortex, in determining limits of intelligence and memory, in the cognitive field of social behavior let us note that a useful *social* concept for calculation of the spread of cultural ideas is that of the social "percolation range" of a given idea. This is defined as a percentage for a given population, stating how far a given more complex social concept can percolate down from the inventors into the lower intelligence ranges. It is perhaps most easily illustrated by scientific examples. Although computers are now used by most of the literate public, perhaps only 10% could understand the translation of, say, 34 into the binary system that computers are based on. This illustrates the percolation range, but the computer example is not so socially important. However, it *is* important in the cognitive field if trade unions and employers cannot grasp the ultimate fate of protectionist measures as explained by Adam Smith.

As far as cognitive capacity lag is concerned, it could well be an optimistic estimate that perhaps one-tenth of the world's population understands the complexity of the mechanical, economic, legal, etc., underpinnings of our culture sufficiently to restore the culture if it were destroyed. And perhaps only 50% are well informed enough by reading to vote meaningfully on political issues. We can augment our limited memories by libraries, and to some extent the intelligence of decisions, as well as the memory involved, by computers. It seems likely, however, that the human brain will remain the only broad integrator and perceiver of new truths. Each new wall of a library creates a specialist; but only the super-Renaissance man can hold enough to see the emerging relations across specialities and live in the library as a whole.

Both genetic lag and genetic superfluity can exist in the cognitive world. The latter probably existed when Cro-Magnon man, with brain probably a little better than ours, had only to remember the names of his family, the forms of a few beasts, and the lie of the land, and no one asked him to record his income and expenditures for the preceding year or remember his way around in 20 large cities. His genetic cognitive ability had superfluous elements.

With this glance on some essentials in cognitive lag, let us turn to the far more complex, insufficiently researched, and more far-reaching problem of genetic lag in the *endowment of desires*—ergs (instincts)— relative to the requirements of a culture at a "civilized" level. *An erg is a genetic predisposition to attend more to some classes of object than others, e.g., for a young male to attend to girls rather than to logarithms; to experience a particular kind of emotion, e.g., fear, sex;*

and to be impelled toward a certain goal. Since in man the ways of getting to the goal are obviously learned, and differ therefore somewhat from culture to culture, the notion that there is probably even a predisposition (as Jung especially argued) to "racial memories" and archetypal response patterns is not easy to prove. A brief glance at technicalities of psychological theory is therefore necessary, if social consequences are to be clear.

The rewards necessary for cultural learning ("conditioning") are in reaching or approaching the innate ergic goals. In the departure from the most natural, innate sequence dimly laid down, two forms of strain must be taken into account: (1) what we may call *deflection strain*, D, proportional to the deviation demanded in the new, learned behavior from the most natural perceptions and responses; and (2) *long circuiting strain*, L, which depends on the number of successive steps and subgoals the individual has to learn, beyond instinct, before reaching the same goal, e.g., food or sex, culturally.

These constitute much of what the learning theorist meets in animal experiment, e.g., maze learning, but clinicians, as psychoanalysts, recognize a further form of learning—sublimation, S—in which the *goal itself* is set aside, in order that other goals may be reached. In sublimation the behavior departs considerably from the goal-seeking of the natural erg. For example, thwarted, repressed sex may motivate interest in art, religion, or even the elegant beauty of mathematics. The magnitude of the human cortex, relative to that of any other species, permits a greater flexibility of ergic expression. The lower mammals modify the innately suggested patterns more readily than insects, and man and the primates do so more readily than the rest of the mammals, but complete sublimation—which would be fatal in hunger, fear, and some other drives—is naturally rare.

The demands of the culture that enforce D, L, and S modifications are, of course frustration. (All learning begins with failure—or imaginal failure—of an existing approach.) And pugnacity (aggression) is an instinctive reaction to frustration of any erg. As we shall see below, the discovered syntality dimension in nations which we call "cultural pressure" shows, *simultaneously*, aggression and creativity, both arising in part from culturally, situationally enforced sublimations.

In surveying the sources of strain and aggression, we have to consider frustration not only of *ergs*, but also of *sentiments* (or *sems*, for short). These are demonstrated unitary factor patterns among attitudes and interests that correspond to networks that we are taught by our social institutions. Thus, we find a set of intercorrelated attitudes centered on attachment to the home, the religion, the recreational mode, and so on, of each individual. It is only when culture *changes* that frustration comes to sems. Toffler in *Future Shock* (1970) has looked closely at these strains and frustrations in any rapidly changing culture. Thus, theoretically, we shall expect the burden of D, L, and S, residing in the culture's regular frustration, to be augmented, as Toffler suggests, in times of rapid, revolutionary change. This means, incidently, that the dynamics of revolution we studied in Chapter 11 should show an initial *acceleration* of drive as the process goes on, due to the increased tragic frustrations from change.

Mainly by trial and error, societies have developed a number of institutions to give expression to the sublimations and frustrational by-products that the complexities of culture—initially begotten by necessary food-getting, defense, family order, raising of the young—demand. Among these are art, religion, drama, literature, sport, and the emotional rituals of the revealed religions. Some of these—notably religion, with its tiresome ethical demands—add to the need for further outlets. But many of these have motivation from the instinct of *play*, which cushions the demands.

In seeking to understand the institutions and activities of a culture, sociologists seem to the present writer to have given not nearly enough attention to the special properties of the particular erg of play. All mammals and many other animals possess some degree of the innate play tendency. Its characteristics are:

1. That it is innate and strongest in the young.
2. That it appears most readily when there is excess energy and no other erg is demanding attention.
3. That it functions as a learning device, as when the kitten prepares for hunting mice by clawing a ball of wool.
4. That it is specifically connected with phantasy, and capable of expressing all other ergs through that "defense." It may be that it is connected with the signal, in fighting between members of the same species, which saves life by saying, "I'm not serious." The underdog often gives the signal of "let's stop, I'm playing."

Play is, in any case, centrally concerned with opposing the not-serious to the serious and avoiding the stress of the life behavior it mimics. One knows the actor shot dead on the stage will get up when the curtain drops.

This analysis has its main relevance to understanding the function of the arts. An unfortunate obscurity in cultural anthropology comes from the anthropologist's use of "culture" for the totality of the group's acquired behavior, e.g., a hunting culture, a neolithic culture, whereas the intelligentsia use it in the much narrower sense of the higher culture of the arts and sciences (German "Kultur"). To distinguish, let us at once separate the latter and split it into two parts by designating the parts as *p-culture* and *r-culture.* By p-culture, we mean those developments that are based on play and phantasy, by r-culture, those technical cultural developments concerned with realistic manipulation of the environment in food getting, defense, organization, etc. As noted elsewhere, this has relation to Lord Snow's distinction, in his "Two Cultures" (1959), but that was a divison nominally between arts and sciences and based on social grouping in the university common room, whereas we are arguing for a basically psychological foundation in the play erg on the one hand and the Freudian "reality principle" in thought on the other. Thus art, music, drama, sport, fiction, and much else belong in p-culture, and science, engineering, business, and social administration are aspects of r-culture. A few activities, notably religion, partake of both p- and r-culture, and, of course, there are some mixed features in all institutions and activities. For example, theory development in science has imagination, and phantasy activities, while musical creation has to face the immutable laws of physical sound; for art is not a fully walled playground. Nor should we make the mistake of considering that esthetic values belong more to p- than r-culture. Much of the higher theoretical development in science is pursued with an esthetic pleasure.

The growth of r-culture development does not so strongly concern us in connection with genetic lag. The direct ergic satisfactions achieved for hunger, safety, and so on, proceed as far as the increasing innate intelligence permits, though sublimations from other drives may assist, as when Pascal advanced mathematics, seeing beauty in it that apparently derived from his sexual renunciations. *What a Beyondist finds hard to justify, at first glance, as assisting survival,* is the p-culture. It is often said, historically, that art and music begin only when the physical basis of life is assured, and that since they begin where the struggle for survival ends, they have no relevance to the latter. A not common view is that of Gimpel, "A decadent society loses its political grip and influence in the outside world and in a way of compensation turns toward art. Decadent societies lead the world in art and fashion" (1969).

The truth seems to be more subtle; though admittedly psychological investigation of this truth is still much needed. In the first place, at a quite obvious level, needing no discussion, national prestige, and therefore alliances and safety are raised by high p-cultural reputation. For example, many well-educated people, realizing the extremely high contribution of Germany in science, literature, and music were reluctant to go to war with Germany even when a gangster political group got in control. Secondly, in a deep and more pervasive sense, the p-culture provides survival value as an exercise ground for the more sensitive and complex thinking that can be turned to advantage in the r-culture. It must not be overlooked that the learning function, which we recognized as central in play, is carried out powerfully by the humanities. History is admittedly part p-, part r-, culture, but the classics of Greek and Roman life played a valuable part in the top British public schools in giving perspective to British political leaders. And the novel, if written by a master artist, teaches in phantasy trial and error much that the average person ultimately learns about human motives and social adjustments. A scientific psychology could admittedly teach more, but it scarcely exists yet, and in any case most people prefer the sugared pill of fiction. Thirdly, there is the safety-valve function of p-culture permitting the pressure behind r-culture to reach high levels without wrecking the social organism through aggressions, intoxications, and the like. (By intoxications, we mean the resort to drugs and excessive alcohol, which belongs in the same class as the p-culture, though the phantasy is—except in a Poe or a Coleridge—individual and unconstructive. In this category also we must include the role of humor and laughter which have precisely the same role of permitting emotional sensitivity to develop without the depression that might otherwise arise from the frustrations of life. Humor utilizes again the basic function of the play erg to switch from the serious to the nonserious.

In evaluating the role of p-culture, therefore, let us not overlook that in spite of the superb intellectual quality of the guidance and consolation offered by the greatest of literary figures—the Goethes and Tolstoys, Shakespeares—and many moderns, it would be a mistake to turn to them for answers to fundamental religious questions about the universe, ourselves, or what we should do. The arts have had to take their account of the universe from the scientist, annd increasingly they have taken their answer to "What am I?" from the psychologist—often a sophomoric misunderstanding of, say, Freudianism—but their greatest inadequacy has been in knowing what to do with the third question, "What ought I to do?"

The literary man himself asserts that "The arts hold up a mirror to man while probing deep beneath the surface to reveal the terrifying innards of man's soul." Those innards are better revealed, however, by a Freud or a Lorenz, though not all readers have the mental discipline to appreciate the difference. The greater part of the work of even literary "reformers" has been either purely a questioning of existing values as in Swift or Rousseau (values generally harking back to dogmatic religion), or a search intuitively after new values, as in Nietzsche and Shaw, or a beautiful restatement in less exact and dogmatic terms—and in effect in watered-down perceptions, of older religious values. One can search the length and breadth of literature for new values that are adequately logically and empirically sustained. This is not surprising when one reflects that literature requires no training in a discipline of investigatory method, as science does, but at best, a training in expression and style. Neither does it have the power arising in science from the result of a cumulative and precise building of each contributor upon the work of predecessors. Today's leading article is no advance on the Old Testament.

The institutionalized deviations that are in fact sublimations, and which occur as a result of unavoidable blocking of ergs in the complications of r-culture, and the increasing severity of ethics, can thus be regarded from a long-term genetic evolutionary viewpoint as p-culture splints around a broken limb, or a place of storage for energies and skills probably some day of practical use. The sublimations can make difficult cultural demands that cause a large genetic lag, endurable by most until the necessary genetic mutations strengthen the natural satisfaction in that culture. Parenthetically, one must observe that these sublimations will be easier for some than others. Although higher intelligence is not the only genetic source contributing to greater ergic flexibility, it is an important one, and whereas a gifted person might sublimate antisocial elements in sex and aggression into, say, drama, a borderline defective is more likely to commit rape (as the intelligence statistics show).

This useful p-culture cushioning function—this safety valve through which mental energy may unconsciously be stored in complex form to meet reality challenges yet to come—deserves intensive social psychological research. It deserves watching in part because sublimations often, in times of luxury, relaxation, and permissiveness, teeter on a knife edge between social contribution and perversion. The distinction between a sublimation from a natural ergic goal and a perversion is virtually impossible to make on psychological grounds alone, though a psychoanalyst might say there are more maturational regressions in the latter. But basically the distinction, as a Beyondist sees it, lies in whether a new behavior contributes to the progress and survival of society, i.e., is ethical, or not. Is keeping domestic pets *instead* of one's potential offspring a perversion, or is it a sublimation as it might be in an overpopulated world? (Julius Caesar is reported to have reproached patrician women who kept lap dogs and monkeys instead of children, and Napoleon has similar views in his diary.) These possible social outcomes of various deviations, especially of homosexuality, deserve social psychological study.

The possibility must be considered that the arts, and other institutionalized sublimations, can go astray also in the sense of developing a social activity to an excessive, deformed expression, since the usual reality checks rarely apply to such developments. Does it, for example, continue to use up energy in a storage circuit long after r-culture has opened a more direct realistic path to satisfaction of the ergs concerned? The Marxist claims that this is true of emotional and mythical religions, which pray for good crops rather than attend to fertilizers and plant hybridization. A beautiful example, in both senses, of how energy can be so tied up, lies in the island of Bali, where every item of daily communal activity is tied up with rites and festivals, and the mythical cosmology directs the ethical code, the form of town planning, and the individual's home life from birth to death.[24]

The animal workshop in ancient Egypt and in the Hindu religion similarly tied up large resources and interests. Here is a development absorbing life energy like a tumor. The special case of sublimation in religion deserves expanded discussion in Chapters 13 and 14, but let us note here other variants, in the arts and humanities, where survival value of the behavior looks questionable. For example, might fascination with opera be in part a substitute for raising a family? (Middle-class Vienna had a miserable birth rate!) As for sport, when Britain depended vitally on a volunteer army in the critical first year of World War I, Kipling was impelled to scorn "the flannelled fools at the wicket and the muddied oafs at the goal" (1940). In much of Europe and elsewhere, still stunned by the frustrations of World Wars I and II, the pride, the gregariousness, and the protective, succorant ergic satisfactions that went into patriotism now hang like a directionless cloud awaiting either a p-culture or a new realistic direction. One may point out that the controlled cooperative competition of Beyondism offers one promising return to reality for such suspended energies, in the concept of deliberate, distinct, and creative group cultural adventures.

The above concepts of p-culture as a splint to a growing limb, or as a domain of exercise for skills needed sometime in r-culture, as a safety valve at junctures of high frustration, and, finally, as possible obsolete encumbrances in the way of r-culture expression, need further, empirical evaluation. Certainly there is a perennial tendency, because poor verse, popular music, and fashionable plays are easier to follow than physics or biology, for an overpursuit and an overvaluation of p-culture, vis-a-vis r-culture, by the general public, viewing this p-culture as the essence of "culture." Some would assert that civilizations began when "arts for art's sake" appeared. To consider the greatness of a culture by how much p-culture it produces is, up to a point, like estimating the power of an engine by the noise it makes, for the p-culture is, in part, a by-product—an expression of conflict and escape.

Anderson (*The Drama Circle*, 1982) has recently questioned the authenticity of "modern art," saying that "culture is largely social bonding" and that "it is the classical conservative perspective that is important in defining moral art, and social bonding, whether the artist used traditional or original methods." He points out that much abstract, individualistic art misses the social function of art and quotes Carlyle, "We shall either learn to know a hero ... when we see him, or else go on forever governed by the unheroic." "Artists today should be in the forefront of restoring the heroic ethos as a cultural necessity," he adds. Which means that the arts should be interpreting the new visions of science, in Beyondism.

Our concern to this point has been to ask how the misfit occasioned by the genetic lag is in general handled. It is now time to scrutinize more closely where the genetic lag is strongest, once more in regard to the genetics of the mid-brain and the emotional goals, leaving the simpler issues of the shortages of cognitive capacity "as read." The conclusion of Freud, Darwin, Ardrey, Keith, Lorenz, McDougall, and Wilson, that all behavior is directed to biological goals, is distasteful to some "rational" members of the intelligentsia, who prefer the more gentlemanly views of Allport, Maslow, and many cultural anthropologists, that man chooses his own goals, or that at least there is "functional autonomy" of motive when something is done often enough. Our position is that man constantly chooses his *path* and *means* to *a goal* of sex, pugnacity, security, nutrition, curiosity, etc., and he invokes one erg to suppress another of which he (or the culture) disapproves, but his rational mind cannot make him satisfied with eating rubber or drinking gasoline. It was the excellent mammalian instinct of curiosity that led to the satisfactions of Aristotle or started Euclid in his purpose to "look on beauty bare"—though as the poet surmised some sublimated sex may have entered too; but the roles of such drives as innate curiosity, gregariousness, etc., must not be overlooked in socio-cultural adjustment.

As we turn to the particulars of genetic fit to our culture and ask *which* ergs are more maladapted to civilization, we are dealing with questions of ethics and of eugenics. In concentrating on dislocations, let us not overlook the basic fact that, on the whole, the primate ergic, emotional make-up is still pretty well suited to civilized behavior needed in raising the young, living with one's neighbor, begetting the next generation, and protecting the continuity of one's tribe or culture. It would be a great mistake to underestimate the wisdom, far beyond our conscious understanding, that resides in the ergic potentials built by millions of years of mammalian experience, extending into the same socio-sexual problems as face the insects. The genetic gap in its sharpest conflicts is a recent and changeable phenomenon.

The ethics of the great religions, and of social communities, have nevertheless seen the inheritances from some ergs as less desirable than others, and the sins, venial and mortal, systematically set out by the Catholic Church, and roughly present in Moses' Ten Commandments, in their vital parts, actually follow a psychologist's classification of ergs. It is, of course, specific situational behaviors that are good or bad rather than an erg per se, but nevertheless the total of specific behaviors from a given erg may differ in *average* ethical worth from those of another. And on this basis the commonly recognized culprit ergs are sex and pugnacity. For although pugnacity may support moral indignation, it is more likely, statistically, to issue in murder. And though the sex erg is the origin of procreation in marriage, it is also the origin outside of marriage of adultery, pornography, and rape.

There need be little doubt that we have a genetic lag in our endowment in these two drives relative to the need of a civilized culture. A desirable birth rate of two or three children per couple scarcely demands a sexual activity of perhaps 50 years. And although sexual pleasure may be a cement to hold couples together and stabilize a home, it can also de-stablize it, and is a less-effective long-term bond than congenial temperaments and common purposes. After the mastery of birth control by the "pill," we need a second chemical step creating an "antiaphrodisiac," contributing easier sublimation to culture. We have become, through the pill, sexually shameless, without becoming immune to what Brooke called "all the little emptiness of love" and Shakespeare's "expense of spirit in a waste of shame." Similarly, pugnacity and aggressiveness, especially in their group expression, have become, with modern weapons, a threat to humanity.

As culture travels on, much of the better adjustment of genetic make-up to culture will have to come from genetic breeding, rather than by a backward deforming of culture to genetics.[25] In Chapters 15 and 16 we shall consider, in a practical spirit, what can be done, but here we are at the stage of diagnosis. That a dislocation exists in the above two ergs, and perhaps in the gregarious erg (which piles people in cities beyond what is desirable in terms of physical and mental health and economic efficiency), and in one or two others, few will dispute. We shall therefore conclude this examination of ergs with a long analysis of a rebel drive which few people seem to be aware of, namely, the parental, protective, succorant, pitying erg, which is the root of disinterested charity, and has actually been lauded ethically by most religions, as in St. Paul's Epistle to the Corinthians.

Since mankind has entered a new style of life in the last few thousand years, relative to the few million before which shaped his instinctual mid-brain, *every* ergic pattern could be in need of control and re-formation in genetically more flexible tendencies. Nevertheless, we have recognized that, *on the whole*, we are impelled instinctually to goals that are still basically the most appropriate for survival. However, in the case of the parental, protecting erg, with its emotion of pity and kindness, people have unfortunately been taught by such religions as Christianity that it can *never* be wrong. The current ethical belief seems to be that its impulses can always be followed, and that one's indignation is a *moral* indignation when it is frustrated.

One can see in broad terms that a religion of evolution, requiring a steady disposal of extinct species and of failures within a species, is bound to have a confrontation with religions which make the succorance of failures one of their chief raisons détre. In broad terms this contradiction is real, though in the particular dealings with people en masse it is more humane, because its foresight in regard to the inevitable realities is greater.

Human beings who are failures are so, from either or both of (a) genetic defects or (b) environmental causes. In the environmental interactions, we can further recognize a distinction between (b1) accidental misfortunes and (b2) misfortunes brought on by the carelessness, laziness, egoism, defiance of control, and so on, that are with the individual realm of decision. A psychologist will recognize, e.g., in the Freudian "repetition compulsion," that a not negligible proportion of what look like accidental misfortunes to the layman are in fact due to the personality of the individual concerned.

No punishment or reward, pity or concern for individuals with genetic defects can remove these defects. But society has to watch that in making the conditions tolerable for the individuals affected it does not in indirect ways encourage their production and reproduction. If society, for example, took away the burden of sustaining each mental defective, as born to borderline defective parents, the probability is that more would go on being born than if the parents faced the burden of their lack of foresight. It is very likely, in the same connection, that the production of illegitimate children is taken more lightly by those likely to produce them, when it is known that adoption societies can find a ready market for them in childless wives. (Today a woman childless by reason of the husband's infertility can be artificially inseminated, e.g., by the Muller Germinal Repository, by sperm of fathers with eminent genetic gifts, e.g., contributors who are Nobel Prize winners.) In these circumstances, the resort to illegitimate children, or children from crowded countries abroad, is an instance of the parental succorant instinct working against the best interests of society.

Since boundless love, and mutual indulgence therefrom, is the slogan of powerful revealed religions, we need to analyze what is meant thereby—if indeed anything clearly definable is meant. Thoughtful observers, even before the biological analyses of Darwin and Lorenz, have always recognized however that the word "love" is a vague, cloudy one. (What is in common to "kids love candy," "John loves to consort with prostitutes," and "God loves humanity"?) Long ago the Greek philosophers at least distinguished *agape*, as an altruistic, pitying, parental love, from *eros* or lust. Psycho-biologically we have good evidence for tracing these emotions, respectively, to the succorant parental instinct and the mating instinct. Indeed, with today's dynamic calculus methods it is possible to take any behaviorally expressed form of "love" and trace it quantitatively to its various instinctual roots. There are indications that in addition to parental-protective and mating erg sources there are also sources of what would be called "love" in the gregarious (herd) instinct, security-seeking (fear), narcism, acquisitiveness, appeal, and self-abasement.

In behaviors alleged to spring from "charity" (St. Paul), love, or altruism, one has to consider both deliberate hypocrisy and also the difference between the emotional intention and the effect which ensues in the real world, with *all* short-sighted impulse. "Love" of an only child by an opulent family has not infrequently created a selfish monster, for whom the effect was far from being for his real good. This discrepancy of the impulsive emotion and its consequences is a possibility in all drives, but in modern society it is particularly dangerous in the pitying, succorant, expression of "love."

In the flotsam and jetsam of relativistic ethics and faddist religions floating from the intellectual torpedoing of the great revealed religions, it seems that humanistic love is one of the few values these new subjectivities agree upon, though it sometimes also takes the form of permissiveness for love of one's neighbor's wife. The sterner, more idealistic austere altruisms have not washed ashore, from the wreck of religions, along with this lighter humanistic permissiveness. All along the line we see today a public alleged compassion which has no regard for the necessities of evolution and the strength and happiness of the next generation. (Or even of the present, for parole boards have repeatedly out of pity released some criminally insane murderer, now "judged sane," who has then gone out and murdered three or four more people.) Modern governments have spent their substance to the immediate end of bequesting a false standard of living to the unemployed and unemployable, instead of removing unemployment. They have done so at the unseen cost of denying more distant gains to society from better education of the gifted, from scientific and medical research, and even from the military defense of the very existence of the given society and its own special values. A discussion in depth of the short-sighted misuses of the precious commodity we call compassion is given in Hardin's *The Limits of Altruism* (1977). The value issue was clearly stated also in Nietzsche's *Thus Spake Zarathustra* in "Higher than love of the neighbor is love of the furthest and the future."

Meanwhile the advertiser, in the name of "love," encourages everyone to overindulge himself, his wife, his children, his friends, and his dogs and cats. The entrepreneur of charity grows fat on adoptions of children from alien cultures, and government welfare agencies find jobs for ever more social workers who, it has recently been indubitably shown, succumb to all sorts of fake appeals and sly trickery in their "clients" (at the cost of the hard-workers' taxes). It is clear that there easily springs up in periods of release from evolutionary pressure ("Yin") what may be called a "lap dog compassion"—a widespread mutual indulgence which is very different from deep compassion truly applied to striving humanity.[26]

This perversion is not just a contemporary phenomenon. Rome knew it well and many a human being was butchered to provide a proletarian holiday, in the name of kindness to the masses. (One is reminded of the story of the child onlooker at the arena weeping in sympathy "because that poor lion over in the corner is not getting any!") Whenever humanity has enjoyed a respite from the stern demands of war and natural calamities, there comes an overwhelming wave of sentimental feeling essentially directed to mutual indulgence and ethical permissiveness in the name of "compassion."

Of course, what happens to the erg of compassion here is the same as what goes on with less popularly respectable motives; it is the usual emotional overreaction relative to the realities, followed by paying the price. But in this case the main religions favor the overindulgence, while the ultimate historical reactions to the stresses this produces are precisely the opposite to the goal of the emotion, which is, namely, an elimination of brutality. The overprocreation of the lemmings is followed by suicidal starvation marches. Much the same happens at the human level.

Instead of a realistic foresighted anticipation of stresses to come, and the transformation of barbarous stresses to steady pressures, which the planful Beyondist achieves, societies—especially mob societies— prefer to behave like a spendthrift, a staggering between overindulgence and acute distress. Every society that would eventually survive has to develop and possess a group of realists, in government and among the would-be *intellectual leaders*, who are self-disciplined to face the inexorable demands of the physical and economic world, and are prepared to stand up unpopularly against the perennial weedy growth of the instant pleasure principle in humanity. They have a difficult time, and democracy, when it has an ill-educated population, seems constructed to defeat them.

The question of the extent to which love of an individual for another individual not in his community should, ethically, prevail over other considerations, e.g., those of efficiency and group accomplishment, or group survival in catastrophe, is not to be decided by feelings or traditional religious authority. If we are to remain rigorously objective and as scientifically guided as is presently possible, it has to be decided by the *coordinated loyalties* calculus of Figure 8-1 (in Chapter 8). Chief among these is the loyalty which gives survival to the primary group— typically the nation. However, the analysis we are about to make applies equally to the other memberships—that of the primary group to the world group (1-5), and that of the individual to all humanity (2-5).

If we are to be entirely consistent with the scientific approach, we should examine this question of the role of love in society in clear separation from our existing emotional attachments and religious traditions.[27] We need to ask, in terms of sheer functionality of a group, if a group can persist and be progressive if it lowers the individual's expectation of love and care and demands more austere values. It seems likely at first glance that the individual will not give love to a society that does not give love to him. In the extreme case, what happens to a society that allows its defective infants to die, that makes sparse provision for the unemployed and the aged, and that kills off its young men in millions on the battlefield? Psychologically we would then expect less group cohesion, less self-sacrifice for the group, and less creativity. Maybe research will show this, but meantime, on historical evidence, the strange conclusion emerges that societies have held together despite a lack of love for their members—at least in the sense of indulgence. Before Elizabethan times in England, no systematic poorhouse provision for the unemployed existed; the Eskimos and some other societies have virtually killed off their old and decrepit; and modern world powers have sent their young to death by millions on the battlefield. There is no indication that the very stringent rules of Sparta on delayed marriage or valor in war (as at Thermopylae) begot any lack of morale as duty to the state. On the other hand, the industrialists studying Japan at the present time are concluding the Japanese worker works so well because his "parental" corporation looks after him as if he were a family member.

These irreconcilable observations from history seem to conflict with our basic research conclusion from group dynamics that a *group is a means to the satisfactions of individuals* and that it will be cohesive only so long as it provides those satisfactions. But the above observations do not really conflict: they only require recognition of more subtle mechanisms. Factor analytic study of small groups (10 men) (Cattell & Stice, 1960) shows two major factors in morale, and there is no reason to believe that the same would not be found in larger, culturally organized groups. They are (1) *Morale I*, that of leadership or group purpose. This depends, in level, on how far the individual is taught that the survival and well-being of the group (and his satisfaction in it) depend on certain behaviors on his part. If these behaviors are in fact well chosen for that purpose, the leadership explains (or "conditions") the connection of his responses to the group purpose, the morale factor is high. This is a morale from morality shaped on the group ethical values and goals. (2) *Morale II*, that of *congeniality and love among members.* This is a component in what is frequently labeled *group cohesiveness* that derives from trust, love, and congeniality with others in everyday living.

In accordance with the finding of factor analysis, one of these can be high without the other. Both literary observation (Remarque's *All Quiet on the Western Front*) and psychological studies in the Korean War show that there can be fairly complete disillusionment with the ideals and purpose of the group but still an effective level of morale from the mutual liking and kindliness of members in a congenial group. Conversely, one may see Morale I, in, say, the officers' mess of a crack flying corps, with much mutual personal friction, but a solid devotion to the reputation of the unit. As far as one can glean from Thucydides there was not much camaraderie among the Spartans, but a fierce enduring form of Morale I. Russia, in part, aims the same way.[28] As *Shogun* (Clavell, 1979) and the records of World War II show, we have a clear instance also in the Japanese culture of an ethical emphasis on duty and loyalty to group purpose (Morale I) accompanied by quite limited emphasis on what is regarded as a sentimental love.[29] The author there (p. 370) says, "Love" is a Christian word—anjin-san.... We have no word for 'love' as I understand you to mean it. Duty, loyalty, honor, respect, desire—those words and thoughts are what we have, all that we need." Incidentally, this deserves social psychological research in connection with the lack of headway of Christianity in Japan, in that high Morale I requires less assistance from Morale II, and indeed conflicts with Morale II in the sense that state patriotism on the one hand and universal religious brotherhood—a general extension of Morale II—on the other have been in conflict for two thousand years of European history.

There are psychological issues here too deep for chapter-length analysis, and too uninvestigated in social psychology, to permit new and reliable answers. Let us assume that an individual has a fixed sum total of what he can give to loves and loyalties. Althgough there are more competitors for the individual's loyalty (see Figure 8-1) than Systems I and II (national) on the one hand, and System III (world universal) on the other, it is clear that these are the two chief competitors. The duality of loyalty to a particular national culture on the one hand, and the "love to all mankind" of the universalistic religions—Christianity, Islam, Buddhism—on the other, is entirely identical with that in the duality of morale sources I and II that we introduced from small group dynamics experiments. For each universalistic religion has its special nonuniversal group values. But the Systems I and II versus System III, observed in the light of history, contributes to understanding the psychology of the problem of Morale I - Morale II action.

Granted that we define love in the sense of compassion, or *agape* rather than *eros*, we see, as in the arguments above, that this instinctive endowment needs control as much as does *any* inherited erg (and can indeed show genetic lag). The problems in its disposal and bestowal on others, as seen by Beyondism, are two. First, how far is it to be invested in the diverse available ethical loyalties of Figure 8-1, and secondly, within the ethical obligation of Systems I and II (national loyalties), how is charity (giving) to be divided among the competing claims within the group for defense, welfare of the poor, education of the young, material luxuries, and scientific research?

As to the first, though the attachment to every one of the systems and their objects of service should never fall to zero, the love of man should surely be highest for his own group and those who share its adventure with him. For these groups are the bricks forming the building, and without their concrete existence there can be no international building. The unusual "love of mankind" is justified by all cooperating in the great experiment of human evolution. (This is the "children of God" phrase of the preacher, though from a Beyondist's standpoint he draws the misleading conclusion from it that we should all be the same!)

Our pursuit of the genetic gap problem over love requires us to carry the meaning of the basic diagram (Figure 8-1) of ethical subsystems a stage further. For its basic importance is involved both here and later. If we consider the loves and loyalties and ethical obligations (all aspects of the same relation) of *individuals* in the hexagon, we find there are eight, as follows. (The obligations of groups turn on different organic entities than individuals.)

Obligations of an Individual who belongs to a Primary Group
1. The love and ethical obligation to another individual in the group
2. The love and ethical obligation to the government of the individual's own group
3. The love and ethical obligation to the government of other groups
4. The love and ethical obligation to members of other groups
5. The love and ethical obligation to the world organization of groups
6. The love and ethical obligation to other individuals per se (assuming no group affiliation)
7. The love and ethical obligation to other individuals explicity committed to Beyondist principles
8. The love and ethical obligation to the Evolutionary Principle in the universe itself (to "God" in some terms)

The derivation of these is regularly visible from the paths in Figure 8-1. It will be noted that it is vital to distinguish the *individual-in-a-role*, as an object, from the individual of unspecified role, the former distinguishing 1, 4, 6, and 7 above.

Not only will the ergic make-up (the qualitative emotional character) of these attachments alter throughout the eight ethical-object categories, but so also will the sheer strength. Indeed, as we have said, the human conflicts over rank order of obligations, with which law courts, religious analysis, and the soul searchings depicted by novelists, are concerned, are real, and in time psychologists may get around to incorporating the problems systematically in the quantitative Dynamic Calculus. This is no place for so ambitious an undertaking, but we have ventured to assert that 1 and 2 should, in a Beyondist ethic, be the strongest, followed by 8, which should outrank the next most important, 5, 6, and 7. An individual, whatever he says in words, has a sum total of energy, love, and ethical obligations such that greater investment in one causes less in another (the basis of jealousy in humans and gods). A quantitative dynamic calculus of the normal distribution fitting a Beyondist position is therefore an ultimate scientific objective, and we would expect that it would be significantly different from that now demanded by revealed religions.

One of the differences between the Beyondist and other people is that, whereas all are involved in triumphs and tragedies of the evolutionary process, only the former are tolerably aware of the process in which they are participating. This makes the emotional brotherhood of Beyondists a more keenly experienced relationship. It means that the human existence is heightened in those with a common tragic sense of life that pervades all sensitive Beyondist vistas. They are more keenly aware that all our human cultural experiments are, as it were, bound for ports whose very names we do not know, and on a voyage which, so far as we know, has no end. Here is the need for all the compassion we can summon—the compassion for the courage of those who strive, together, for more light in this darkness.

Particularly hard to grasp, among those who think hate is an inevitable concomitant of competition, is that since competition is an indispensable tool for progress, hate has to be seen by the Beyondist as ugly and misplaced, even when competition breaks down into war. If the healthy competition between groups deteriorates into war, then still, in the words of Sir Henry Newbolt (*Clifton Chapel*), the Beyondist learns, as we have stated:

> To honour, while you strike him down,
> The foe that comes with fearless eyes;

Often there is no alternative to a pragmatic testing of social theories, the values of which cannot be decided upon logically, and the world citizen who can rise above immature hates knows that both contenders are cooperating by the decision of experiment, by testing, by living, to evaluate the ethical power of alternative social systems. Incidently, it is realistic, in connection with the maintenance of a hardy universal love, to realize that even when destructive war is abolished there will still be "cold wars," i.e., all-out competition. The loyalty of each individual to the specific culturo-racial experiment of his own group calls, functionally, for his jealously guarding it from outside attempts at modifications inconsistent with its basic ideals, from economic collapse, from undesired immigrations, from loss of morale, and from environmental catastrophe.

If, as one would hope, a more consciously, evolutionary-directed, international organization is to develop out of the present United Nations organization, it will have to grow beyond "political action" to give far more attention to creating a great surge in the psychological and biological sciences, by the knowledge from which all contemporary problems and debates on relative progress can be illuminated. Beyondists need to give their efforts to shaping it in that way, and to developing the UNO ethic from its present mere maintenance of a legalistic status quo world, to an orientation to positive experiment in evolution.

Education and propraganda in this generation need to be directed to the concept of national federation. For, as far as patriotism is concerned, it still today seems capable of taking care of itself. Consequently, though the international center concerned with order and research may not finally rank higher in loyalties than that which people experience to the primary culture group, yet a beginning can be made in the development of a sense of loyalty to an international organization of groups in an order-preserving, and development-advising, world organization.

We have just pursued into some ethical areas the problem arising from popular thought not having focussed the nature of genetic lag in our instinctual make-up. What Beyondism has first to insist on is that though our genetic endowments in some ergs, such as sex and pugnacity, are more obviously excessive in regard to most civilized cultures, yet every erg is only a very approximate fit to the needs of social motive power and progress, and of the apt behavioral expressions of ergs needed in advanced cultures. As we have seen, a peculiar ergic case, in which the lag is not one of genetic excess but of cultural perversion by parasitic religions, is that of the primate parental, succorant erg. The condoning—and indeed worship—of boundless succorant expressions which, in an atmosphere of hypocrisy, prolong the duration of genetic and cultural failure and block a seemly, appropriate extinction of chronically misfitting types, is contrary to all Beyondist principles. A much more far-sighted expression of pity would reduce the cruelty of nature, notably by eugenic means. Insight on the ethics of the compassionate emotion could simultaneously aid evolution and reduce human misery. As Elmer Pendell analyzed the succorant behavior of our time, "Charity is a matter in which the immediate effects on persons directly concerned, and the ultimate consequences to the general good, are apt to be at complete war with one another" (1951).

Secondly, we see cultural developments from the deflection strain and sublimatory action arising from the culturo-genetic dislocation that are not so much positive adjustment as unavoidable by-products of the disparity. In particular, the arts and music, and some aspects of the humanities and religion, are the equivalent of adjustment by fantasy in the individual who is frustrated in his ergic expression. This perception throws a new light on the evaluation of cultural developments. However, these p-culture developments may have adjustive and evolutionary value in permitting sensitive psychological developments (the "splint support"), that later become useful in r-culture, in realistically adjustive developments.

The empirical evidence for the genetic and cultural habit lag behind cultural developments having a feverish disturbing effect on both types of culture, r- and p-, is found in what factor analysis of a majority of modern nations has revealed as the *cultural pressure factor*, with the pattern of loading on social indices and syntality measures shown in Figure 12-1.

In further discussion of this pattern, it is interpreted as showing (1) deflection strain and goal frustration through increasing complication of life, seen especially in larger percentages of the population being shifted to the complexities of urban living; (2) the first *psychological* reaction to this frustration, in the form of pugnacity and hostility, expressing itself (a) outwardly in wars and riots, and (b) inwardly in neuroses and suicides; and (3) sublimation into cultural productivity in both p- and r-cultural forms. Of the p-cultural responses it can be said, in the words of a famous writer, that "much is learnt of life through novels and plays." One must add that this refers to more than the writings of callow journalists. But the observation does illustrate the new interests that arise as a result of primary ergic frustration and the institutionalized developments that follow therefrom.

Since the clashes between genetic lag and cultural advance are inevitable in an evolutionary process, Beyondism evaluates these resulting behaviors of cultural pressure differently from the conventional reaction to conflict. It *accepts* them as part of an inevitable process but addresses itself to modifying genetic endowments toward the cultural demand. So little is presently known about the mid-brain (the

Figure 12-1

CONNOTATIONS OF THE FACTOR OF CULTURAL PRESSURE AS A DIMENSION OF NATIONAL CULTURES

Variable
High ratio of tertiary to primary occupations
High frequency of political clashes with other countries
High frequency of cities over 20,000 (per 1,000,000 inhabitants)
High number of Nobel prizes in Science, Literature, Peace (per 1,000,000 inhabitants)
High frequency of participation in wars (1837-1937)
High frequency of treaties and negotiations with other countries
High expansiveness (gain in area and resources)
Many ministries maintained by government
High creativity in science and philosophy
(High emotional complexity of life)
High musical creativity
High death rate from suicide
High incidence of mental disease (especially schizophrenia)
High horsepower available per worker
High percentage of population in urban areas
High cancer death rate
High divorce rate
More severe industrial depression in world depression
High total foreign trade per capita
Numerous patents for inventions per capita
Higher number of women employed out of home
More riots
Lower illegitimate birth rate

Variables are here arranged in declining order of loading, averaged over two or more researches, but for actual numerical loadings the original researches must be consulted. Thus the first listed variables are more closely connected with the action or genesis of cultural pressure than the last.

"old brain") and the limbic system in producing ergic behavior that their limits of flexibility will need to be explored by systematic research. How large are the tolerable limits in deflection strain and long circuiting? The role of sheer *cognitive* adaptation is clearer since we know of positive correlations between intelligence and cortical development, and of memory with neuro-hormonal actions. It is extremely likely that selection for higher intelligence would result in easier sublimation of drives into more complex intellectual activities, but that is clearly not the whole story, and the deeper issues of what can prove satisfying to ergic patterns remain.

Logically, as stated initially, the disparities of genetic endowments and culture can include both genetic lag and cultural lag. A simple nonhuman instance is seen in the various color signals we ignorantly give our dogs, though they are colorblind. We have likened the situation of cultural lag to that of the intelligent child in school whose intelligence fits him for studies that he will not be planned to encounter for another two or three years, but which may soon thereafter grow beyond his real grasp. If the evidence that the brain size of Neanderthal, Cro-Magnon, and Grimaldi man was, 10 to 15 thousand years ago, as good as our own, means that their intelligence was as good, then they could have handled modern problems in chemistry and physics as well, if these studies had been part of their culture, and some of them, sitting in their caves, could have understood Newton and Einstein.

It is not until culture reaches out into new areas and levels that we can know what genetic potential is "idly" waiting to be used, and so can be recognized as "cultural lag." If swimming underwater were demanded in school, it is just possible that some humans would be found endowed with a capacity to hold their breath almost as long as porpoises. Our culture would then lag behind their genetic capabilities. The fit of genetic supply to cultural demand is known to us only in part. But in many obvious activities the supply is short. In many matters, and especially in the genetic potential to meet cultural complexity, it is surely clear that nowadays *genetic* limitation predominates, and that we are typified by the middle-aged individual who has invested his fluid intelligence practically as far as it will go into the wide domain of crystallized intelligence skills. This situation—with its ensuing genetic decline of fluid intelligence—is almost certainly a factor in the decline or stagnation of cultures as a whole. The brilliant may, it is true, continue to lead, but except for using the *technical* gifts from the brilliant, the mass of the population cannot follow. And if our population studies are sound, the trend is toward the brilliant becoming genetically less frequent!

Elsewhere in this book we have argued that "harmless" genetic mutations should be deliberately brought about, instead of depending for advance purely on cultural lead and chance genetic adaptations. This would produce more *cultural* lag, reciprocal to genetic lag, and open up spaces into which radically new cultural mutations might follow. The first ape-man who found that a changed hand formation enabled him to use an animal's thigh bone as a weapon opened up a whole new domain of behavior, which, in its further demands, increased intelligence. Genetic and cultural innovations are *both* necessary, and there are consequently problems both of genetic lag and cultural lag.

Chapter 13

What Parallelisms and Differences Exist Between the Emotional Life of Beyondism and the Revealed Religions?

Beyondism begins with a scientific view of the universe and works back to the spiritual values appropriate and needed in man. Most religions have done the converse. Accepting the vague, ineffable longings and yearnings of man that arise as sublimations and compensations from his ergic frustrations, they have fashioned beliefs, rituals, and ethical values to fit them. The latter approach can unfortunately easily pass into an emotional masturbation in which, by hashish or peyote, music, incantations, states of starvation, dance, colorful ceremony, and the like, the mystical moods are elaborated into habitual religious attitudes with ethical values that can cease to have any rational connection with what ethics is really about. When Bertrand Russell gives his belief that "we should penetrate to the core of loneliness in each person, and speak to that" he is groping like any mystic. In short, we have to beware that what each feels to be "spiritual" is not an accidental personal perception that might well lead *away* from a true universal ethics.

Two main functions of religion have been: (1) to satisfy frustrated primary instinctual needs, and (2) to aid societies to reach some degree of internal ethical organization. Sometimes less emphasis has been placed on the second: that is to say, the introspective approach may lead to actions that are only tangentially related to the survival of society or the effective integration of the individual. By contrast, as Keith asserts, "The Darwinists' Bible is the great Book of Nature. Creeds will come and go, but this is the book that will endure as long as life lasts" (*The Religion of a Darwinist*).

Beyondism, on the other hand, asks first what our best understanding is of the framework of reality within which man's morality should be shaped as he aspires to progress. It then asks *"What forms of emotional life need to be encouraged and cherished to assist in that adjust-*

143

ment?" It is first a question for the physical and biological sciences, and then a challenge to psychology, to discover the possible emotional expressions best suited to the adjustment to evolution. In claiming that Beyondism is based on science and especially on socio-biology, we are not claiming that all scientists should be prepared to follow into the developments of inner values which are explored in this Chapter and the next. Through Chapter 10 we would argue that any comprehensive scientist *should* agree. But Chapters 11 and 12 are scientifically still poorly furnished and therefore more speculative, and Chapters 13 and 14 proceed into what may be called spiritual values that are perhaps not the only "church" that could be erected on the agreed scientific foundations. That is why the present development requires for its clear designation the special name of Beyondism: the call beyond the horizon.

The history of traditional religions building on Protean and transient primitive spiritual aspirations and effable emotions resulted in unavoidable, logical incongruities and conceptual expediences. Religious leaders were inevitably forced in their attempts to get some moral behavior to embrace motivating allegories, emotional cajolings, and briberies, such as death-dealing taboos, paradise and hell, a loving father in the sky, and the like. At the more detailed ergic accountancy, in buying some ethical restraint by these partly fictitious rewards, we can look more analytically in a moment. But even before this we should note as part of the natural history of religion that the "spiritual" experiences often broke down, under the psychological effects of excitement, into frenzied dancing and drugs, and into orgies of sex or cruelty, reverting to the simple ergic patterns of the undischarged drives that were the sources of the quasi-spiritual emotions.

Considering the dark jungle of violence, brutality, and despair out of which the great religions have had to coax mankind, we must not criticize them unduly for seeking to establish more civilized and spiritual behavior by a paraphernalia of parables and illusions, such as a loving God, an eternal life in heaven or hell, and the gregarious satisfactions of congregations.[30] At first sight, what the scientist considers a truer view of the situation of mankind brings only quite dangerously less robust motivations for devoted action toward good and against evil. The scientific explorer must recognize that after the intellectual acceptance of Beyondism the Beyondist has to face the major task of marshalling the emotional forces that are necessary and that sincerely belong in it.

Those good thinkers who have examined the earlier statements of Beyondism (1972) have pointed to two characteristics likely to slow

144

its growth as a new ethical foundation: (1) as just seen, it falls short of the emotional appeal of religions that have shaped themselves directly to human emotional archetypes (in Jung's sense); and (2) in contrast to religions which provide humans with the desired safe rock of unchanging values, Beyondism must necessarily *move* on, with scientific developments.

The English "thinking liberals," like Locke, Bentham, Huxley, and Mill, developed their attempt at a rational ethics with no more attention to emotional sustenance than in the assumption that all rational, well-behaved people like themselves would find altruistic satisfaction in working for "the greatest happiness of the greatest number." The Enlightenment in the French Revolution, on the other hand, saw more need for popular involvement, and went through an imitation of religious rituals and pageants so artificially stuck on top of their rationalist system as to seem comical today. They had several powerful sentimental and emotional writers, of whom we have taken Rousseau as a typical case, who sang lyrics to "self-evident truths," freedom of speech, and the perfectibility of all humans by education, while others arranged parades in which Liberty, Equality, and Fraternity were represented by attractive, bosomy women, not unlike our Statue of Liberty in New York harbor (Professor Oliver informs us that the new pageantry of the rationalists included a nude whore on the altar of Notre Dame).

The eighteenth century rationalists can be credited with useful demolitions, but science, needed for construction, is more than reason, and the panorama of facts and principles of evolution we have today did not exist for the rationalists' use. In this latter lies the possibility of an emotional appeal that is real and organically connected with the ethics which Beyondism demands. In passing, one should note that Beyondism differs also from rationalists' constructions in that it does not lead to permanent Utopias, with which rationalists have attempted to match the appeal of the paradises of religions. The rationalists, with whom one must classify also some religious thinkers with unusually independent minds, have hopefully presented us with such interesting products of the imagination as Plato's *Republic*, on through St. Augustine's *City of God*, and Moore's *Utopia*, and so to the modern versions in Robert Owen, Fourier, the Oneida communists, the concepts of Bellamy, the Marxian dictatorship of the proletariat, and the practical proposals for almost equally permanent utopias by H.G. Wells. Despite some differences, the utopias shared what the great religions had had—a paradise—but tangible and not too far away on the calendar, where everyone could be perfectly satisfied and happy. Actually, social science is not at a level fit to design a perfectly satisfying Utopia, even if that were the goal.

If we are intellectually honest, we have to accept the absence from Beyondism of any such permanent social paradise around the corner. Beyondism has progress as a goal (as its name implies) to a higher degree than any other ethical system (most religions being, on analysis, better adjusted to stagnation). But it sees and accepts a succession of steps into a greatness we cannot yet hope to grasp. It does have its tangible, occupiable utopias, but they are the camping places seen at the end of each day's journey. Thus its positive goal for the nearer future is that man's knowledge and his biological growth of intellectual capacity will so increase our understanding of evolution, both biological and astronomical, that goals will become more clear, and our serenity constantly greater. Meanwhile, presenting no terminal heaven, as in rationalist utopias, and possessing no array of comfortingly final dogmas on tablets of stone, it stands ultimately by one immutable truth: that we can be clear-eyed and adventurous participants in a vast ongoing process of evolution. And while—with due concentration of resources on the human sciences—it can shape for each generation some immediate targets of progress, it tells us that the specific ethical values we have to practice, and the goals we see on the next horizon, are "way stations" on a pilgrimage of indefinite duration.

The emphasis just placed on research for clearer vision, to which we shall turn in practical socio-political terms in Chapters 16 and 19, means, as just admitted, that there will be changing, temporary *instrumental* ethical values, consistent with discoveries in biology and advances in the social sciences. Emotionally, it means grasping a certainty in life that resides only in an abstract principle, rather that in dogmatically pronounced moral "axioms." In stating this, let us be careful to add that the ethical values gradually developing through Beyondism with each phase of research will be, at each period, no less firm than those of the revealed religions. Indeed, one of the primary virtues of the Beyondist system is that it abolishes the chaos and permissiveness of dependence on the relativistic, subjectivistic flotsam from the wreck of the great religions and establishes objective landmarks and beacons as precise as research can make them. No "modernist" should attach himself to Beyondism with the notion that he will thereby receive sanction for a personal "flexibility" of moral behavior. If the survival and progress of a society depends on sound ethical values, the sounder those values are, the happier the future of the society. The firmness of laws of an old religion is the firmness of a wooden cart, not too well

146

adapted to traversing rough country. The firmness of Beyondist ethics is that of well-fitting bearings and pistons in an efficient machine. The engine will give its finest performance when the fit is as close and smooth as is possible at the given technical stage. The construction must recognize what degrees of approximation the stage of science truly reaches; but apart from that free play in ethical laws—undeniable in our present level of social sciences—the position of Beyondism is that the clearer the ethics the better. How far morality will follow the ethics is another question, but at least a precision in what is right and what is wrong is a basic asset of the Beyondist position.

To hold faithfully to such a standard makes a greater demand both on the intellect and on emotional maturity than to remain with traditional religions—enriched with all the artifices of art, ritual, music, and social congregation. And amidst these aids to ethical obedience which traditional religions possess, the most important is probably the belief in God. It is extremely important for everyone with a sincere actual or potential religious belief to discover what happens to the concept of God in Beyondism. What we normally consider typical religions—Christianity, Islam, Hinduism, Buddhism, and others more tribally restricted—have, since monotheism replaced (through Akhenaten and Moses) a pantheon of gods, sought to define the nature of the one god. Confucianism, Shintoism, and Marxism show, however, that it is possible to have an ethical system without a single deity. In these and the rationalist Pantheon in Paris and elsewhere, reverence for great men, in whom godliness was seen, replaces the God concept. The street-wide portraits of Lenin and Marx in Russia and Mao in China replace God, and what Protestants regard as idols of hagiology in the Catholic church become acceptance of the worship of the godly man. God the Father and God the Son in Christianity is a compromise with that idea. In Marxism the replacement by dependable humans is complete, and God is pilloried as a bourgeois desire to keep the proletariat in its place.

The theologians recognize that the concept of God has changed, historically with the intellectual sophistication of the time, and socially with the education level of the populations. At first, anthropomorphic, like the grand old man with the white beard, extant in the art of Michelangelo, Blake and others, it moved, at the beginning of modern times and in intellectual circles, from theism to deism (through still possibly actively interceding in everyday life), and on to a First Cause, which set the universe to operate according to the laws given to it, and then "stood aside." Even this view, commonly considered best defined in Paley's "argument from design"—that a creation implies a creator—was attacked by philosophers. To identify God with the universe as a whole, as in pantheism, has appealed to some, but others deplore this as worshiping an inanimate machine, rather than its intelligent creator. A different form of this is what the present writer has tentatively called the *theopsyche* (1938)—the emerging group mind in man, with qualities of superindividual intelligence, universal love, and concern for human evolution.

This theopsyche concept could be developed further, but at present does not fit all requirements. Meanwhile, in the more conservative field of bibical-philosophical scholarship, the theologians surprised us by saying that in this generation "God is dead." The supreme court of professional theology, in Tillich, Jung, and others, reversed this judgment, by arguments that only a hair-splitting Supreme Court could discuss. Meanwhile, the scientists also can get to no firmer ground with the First Cause concept, since astrophysicists hesitate between two incompatible theories: the "Big Bang" and the "Endless Pulsation." Without the least intent to disparage or discourage either the philosophers' or the astrophysicists' researches, we must recognize that our minds are not yet fit to handle such questions as "What happened to time before time began?" Our position must remain as stated at the onset of this book, that we can grasp as a meaningful pattern little more than the evolutionary process, and that the best we can do is to follow this path until our minds become equal to asking such questions in a profitable form.

However, what we adopt in Beyondism as a contingent, approximate concept has much to do with the inner life of the individual in relation to the social ethics of Beyondism. The objection of the good and practical citizen to the atheist is, in one respect, sound. If it is true that the majority of mankind are kept in order by belief in a rewarding and punishing god, and that even the most intelligent draw emotional support in their frustrations as they strive for good works from leaning on this unseen support, then obviously its destruction is a social catastrophe. There have been trends in history, of crime and degeneration, which show that this connection operates.

If we consider the motivating ethical loyality systems in Figure 8-1, it will be evident that the superpersonal substitutes are largely patriotism and altruistic striving for a world society. (Dr. Johnson described the former as "the last refuge of a scoundrel" (1972), meaning that it can be insincerely simulated and is not necessarily tied to morality.) As to the second, the decline of belief in god is likely to correspond with increase in identification with a dictator, and with police expense. Thus a pragmatist will say that a common belief in god assures different people that they have ethical values in common, whereas what values an atheist believes in are open to doubt. Similarly, when it was understood that the meter is one 40-millionth of the circumference of the earth, engineers and surveyors could get together accurately in their work, though later the derivation was found to be approximate. Perhaps an approximate—or conceptually uncertain—concept of God is better than none at all.

In the Beyondist framework, we have said in Chapter 9 that our belief in the reality and aim of the evolutionary process can be used as a referent for what mankind gropes for in a definition of God. Analogously, in a semidesert climate, rain is real, and much desired, but no meteorologist can say exactly what produces it at a particular time. So here, the evolutionary process, in which we believe and to which we attach ourselves, will ultimately require some further abstraction, which at present we cannot define.

But we cannot agree with the sort of pragmatist who says something must be true because believing it has salutary results. If all persons planning murder believed they would end in the electric chair, it might well reduce such evil planning, but other considerations may check our belief in installing the electric chair, removing its restraint on murder. The belief that certain things exist must be based on a broad array of supporting evidence. The evolutionary process stands on firm facts, but it also happens that a belief in it and its possible origins does have a valuable ethical function.

What that function is, has, in its essence, been well discussed in the debates over whether love of man suffices or whether love of God is vital. The New Testament seems to identify love of God with love of one's neighbor, and in the last century the idea has been freely expressed by Leigh Hunt in the well-known poem Abou Ben Adhem. On a different interpretation of Christianity, Chesterton scorned this view, and for once we must agree with him. We are agreeing here also with St. Paul, for the equilibrium of distinct loyalties in Figure 8-1 implies the *precedence of love of the ultimate principle of evolution, over love of neighbor and loyalty to "principalities and powers."* The Beyondist principle stands especially as a safeguard against putting ultimate moral authority in a dictator or even a democratic totalitarian system governing by a committee. It is vital to bring this out clearly as a property of the Beyondist position because it sets Beyondism not only in contrast to some versions of Christianity, but especially to modern humanistic rehashes of Christianity and other products of "moral relativity." In Humanistic ethics, kindness to fellowman and effacement of the individual to ensure the satisfaction of the whole community (as in both Marxist and Maoist totalitarian dictatorship by the proletariat) are the ultimate goals. Beyondism, while placing the survival of the group as one subsystem goal within the ethical hierarchy (Figure 8-1), introduces the need of devotion to an evolutionary goal, with precedence over the immediate, presently existing community. Love of fellowman is probably more concerned with gaining freedom from stress than with the achievement of evolution. It has its place, but it is not the final love. As Sir Arthur Keith ventures to say, "Christ's mission in life was to break down tribal boundaries—the fences which nature had set up (for group evolution) with such infinite ingenuity and patience. His followers cannot succeed until they have smashed the machinery of evolution—the machinery which has made mankind" (1949). This is a true indictment; but as things have turned out, the substitution of large nations for numerous smaller competitive groups has already slowed down and transformed the evolutionary process.

The human lot is both a triumph and a tragedy, and cannot be the one without being the other. Among men, we should love especially the hero—the Icarus who flies too near the sun and falls to death, and the Prometheus who steals fire for mankind from the gods and lives in torment. But the tragedy in the triumph of evolution is shared by all mankind in evolution's requirement of mortality and reconciliation to the death of each beloved. This is the true love of mankind: to sympathize with and pity it in its burden of tragedy, while holding it to the course that begets both the triumph and tragedy of evolution.

The evolutionary loyalty, in any case, goes outside mankind, to other living things that just possibly, if man fails, will develop into biological leadership, and also to life on other planets. The assumption—or presumption—of revealed religions that God "made man in his own image" is misleading. Was this true when man was the low-browed Neanderthal man, or the earlier ape man? By contrast, our anchorage of one's emotional life to a majestic superhuman process in which we glimpse intelligence and miracles is important both for the independence of conscience in the individual—as in the saint and the martyr—and for society to avoid the hedonistic indulgence that could otherwise become its goal. At the present juncture in human history, there is a strong tendency to equate progress to material progress and to "raising the standard of living." The analysis we are making here provides principles for avoiding the notion that material charity to

150

one's neighbor is the goal of all ethics. (Parenthetically, a would-be translator of my earlier Beyondist book said that in his country it would not be sympathetically received unless social progress could be translated as "increased prosperity"!)

In analyzing the resemblances of the inner values of Beyondism to those of existing religions, to see more clearly what changes are taking place, we should turn next to the concepts of sin, of reward and punishment, of guilt and forgiveness, and even of the strange doctrine of vicarious absolution from guilt by sacrifice of the God. All these have roots going back into primitive religions, but their long functionality justifies seeing if they have modern Beyondist equivalents.

The word sin is not often heard today in the social sciences, and modernist "feeling liberals" declare it has a quaint, archaic sound. It remains, nevertheless, an important psychological reality for the social psychologist, and, as research in a Beyondist plan proceeds, it is likely to go beyond the Catholic division into mortal and venial sins and assign to each kind of behavior an index of the social and personal damage or good that it causes. These indices are likely to be useful in calculations of the effect of frequencies of various vices and delinquencies upon the survival of societies.

What the sterner religions have called "original sin" becomes perfectly understandable and definable as the genetic-cultural gap. A stronger ergic endowment in, say, sex and aggression, and a relatively poor level of ability to sublimate, would make such an individual stronger in original sin. The Calvinist notion of predestination and of an elite can be to some extent translated into the sociobiological reality of individuals being differently genetically endowed with respect to chances of adaptation to culture. While the findings in research on *Crime as Destiny* (Lange, 1931) are supported by further research, the degree of determination still leaves a major role to freewill. Even the seemingly fanciful religious concepts of "sin against the Holy Ghost" and the first commandment, against blasphemy, have a certain parallel in Beyondism. In the logical steps in basing ethics on evolution, there is, we have noted, the possibility of recognizing evolution but declining as an individual, with free will, to aid or participate in it. This is the equivalent of the religious concept of knowing what is goodness but blaspheming against it.

The question of guilt is one which has exercised both religion and the modern psychotherapist. To a remarkable extent, the latter has come to regard it as an evil, to be conjured out of the mind of the neurotic. Many psychiatrists can be accused of aiming at the simplistic

151

cure of neurosis by "whittling away" the superego to "harmless" levels. Indeed, a source of the mid-century social permissiveness that must be given major importance, because it seemed to come with the scientific authority of psychoanalysis, sprang from the alleged danger, in psychoanalysis, of experiencing repression based on guilt. A more balanced and scientific psychological view (less heeded however by the "liberal," from Bertrand Russell to the most callow journalist) was not that guilt needed to be reduced, but properly expressed by ego control as *suppression* rather than repression.

To delve in this chapter into the existing and the possible emotional life of religion, it is necessary to see what scientific, multivariate experimental psychology has made, since 1950, out of the rough-hewn concepts which clinical psychology, and particularly psychoanalysis, created in the first half of the century.

The patterns of the ego and the superego which Freud viewed as controlling man's instinctual, impulsive, foresightless, basic "id" inheritance have been confirmed, extended, and precisioned by psychometrics and factor analysis. But, in addition, source traits of almost equal importance have been brought into view, which are known as the self-sentiment and guilt proneness. The four have been symbolized, in the above order, as C, G, Q_3, and O. Obviously, any attempt to do justice here to what is fully set out in textbooks (Hall & Lindzey, 1970; Pervin, 1975; Smith & Vetter, 1982; Cartwright, et al., 1975) would be presumptuous and inadequate. We must be content with thumbnail sketches. The ego (C factor) is machinery for control of the ergic expressions in the interest of their highest long-term satisfaction. It shows in good emotional control, acceptance of reality as it is, and dependability in difficulties. The superego (G factor) acquired largely from introjection of a much-depended-upon parent, is essentially conscience, altruistic regard for others, and capacity to persevere on a basis of principles. Curiously, experimental psychologists have yet little to tell us about developing the superego. We have evidence that it develops best where there is both love and strictness in the parents. It is certainly an early product, depending much more on the family than the school or the church; though these can foster its later growth.

The self-sentiment (Q_3 factor) is a set of attitudes built around the self-concept, motivated by the need to maintain self-esteem and a good reputation in the eyes of society. The difference from G is that G has deeper, unconscious roots, acting as in Kant's "categorical imperative"

152

and generating *guilt*, whereas Q_3 is a later acquisition, oriented to social standing and leading, in its frustration, only to *shame*. The latter nevertheless subsidiates in part to G, since esteem by self and society usually requires some regard for a good conscience. The ego itself, C, regards *values* as only a part of the more extensive, awkward, reality with which it has to deal in arranging ergic satisfactions. The particular values adopted in G and Q_3 will vary with the society and culture in which they are acquired.

Guilt proneness, O, is a personality trait of easily experiencing a sense of unworthiness and dejection, and thus magnifying the effect of any transgression of the demands of the superego, G. It is a substantial component in anxiety, lack of self-esteem, and in neurosis. It is also a component in the inner experience of religion as an "oceanic" uniting, with forces altogether greater than oneself.

Comparative observations, as usual in science, help clarify the nature of action. Earlier we have looked at some social evidence that the emotional form of a religion and its beliefs will be partly dependent on racial temperament (and probably also the same with art). For example, as far as extraversion is concerned we know extraverts prefer brighter color masses (Eysenck, 1952) and according to McDougall's (1934) data, tend to take to Catholicism where the introvert takes to Protestantism). There is massive suggestive evidence (scarcely yet in measurement; see Christopher [1980], for example) that the mongoloid race, notably as in Japan, is more governed in control behavior by Q_3, as *shame*, than the Caucasian (especially the Mediterranean) whose ethics are more governed by *guilt*. The Japanese readiness for law-abiding conduct, for altruism and self-sacrifice, is no less powerful, under the need to stand well with his fellows, than the same readiness under the more detached and deeply emotional guilt of the superego. The self-sentiment, Q_3, in its control, is further along toward the purely rationalistic ethics of Confucianism and certain other oriental ethical systems. (In Shinto the onlooking population includes the ancestors.)

An argument could perhaps be made that the lesser role of an irrational, emotional guilt in maintaining ethics, and a greater regard for group observers (ultimately including the police) is a more evolved, because less emotional, system. The Beyondist regard for progress through individuals (Chapter 11), however (which here coincides with the Christian emphasis on the soul of the individual), sees considerable danger in a religio-ethical system in which the ultimate goodness is conformity with the group rather than standing by one's conscience.

For this conformity connotes the spasmodic (revolutionary) growth pattern of the Crustacean, rather than group change by an evolutionary process, aided by deviant individuals.

The differences in inner emphasis of control by Q_3, on the one hand, is, of course, a relative matter, the spurious use of distinct "types" being only a device of illustration. If we ask what religion has meant the world over, it has been some form of conscience, G, some emotion in O, and some social pressure in Q_3. Each, of course, has developmental stages, so that, for example, with small children, and the dog who would jump on the table for food, we see G going through developmental stages from immediate fear of punishment to a deeper control motivated by both love and fear.

There is an immense literature on the evolution of religious dynamics from primitive times, led by such classics as Fraser's *Golden Bough*, and Freud's *Totem and Taboo* (and the *Future of an Illusion*). Love and fear of the dead and awe of overwhelming natural forces combine to produce superstition, while the human thought habit of projection gives human dynamics to inanimate objects. The wiser tribal shamans and "medicine men" tie these superstitions to the necessary taboos and tribal ethics.

But now, woven out of these feelings, come some curious archetypal developments, of which the first serious attempt to understand the dynamics was in Freud's *Totem and Taboo* (1913). The phenomena here include the setting up as a tribal god, of some being normally taboo and remote. His favors are sought by propitiatory rites and sacrifices upon altars. But now comes the curious paradox that at the most important annual festival, the totem bird or animal is ceremoniously killed and eaten. One contributor here is the widespread notion (not entirely absent from modern faddist dieticians!) that in eating a tiger one gains something of his strength, or in swallowing a dispatched enemy, something of his unquestioned courage. With something of the abhorrence which Victorians felt for Darwin's idea of descent of humans from apes, we are compelled to recognize that this pattern is extremely widespread and that our own great revealed religions tend to conform to it. Thus Christ was crucified to save mankind, and in the wafer and the wine we partake of his flesh and blood. Incidently, this is no comment for or against the historical reality of Christ, but it recognizes that his life drama was selected as more significant than that of many other potential religious leaders.

Although these beliefs, rituals, and myths belong to superstition, one may gain some idea of necessary dynamic function in maintaining even a new ethic from studying them. One possible hypothesis is that the development of cultural stimuli and genetic sensitivities to reach a sufficiently sensitive conscience for the best social progress requires safeguards against overreaction. Instead of the model of an electrician inserting a fuse to prevent a dangerous overload, human evolution puts in an alternative circuit. Psychology seems to show this is the peculiarly human sense of humor, and laughter, an outlet virtually unknown in the less complexly developed midbrain of the primates. Its object is to function so that a strong sympathy in face of perceived suffering will not be a disabling pain. (As Wilfred Owen, a soldier poet of supreme sensitiveness, speaks of a point when soldiers "can laugh among the dying, unconcerned" [1919].)

The mechanism in the vicarious sacrifice of the god is surely that when guilt from offenses against conscience becomes to the individual intolerable, the responsibility can be shifted to the god who has come to share our transgressions and who must, logically, then suffer the punishment of being put to death. With that there comes individual "forgiveness of sins" that makes life tolerable again. All this is unnecessary to the psychopathic personality born with a defect of development of conscience. (His profile is quite abnormally low on G, almost normal on Q_3 and quite adequate on C (Cattell, Eber, & Tatsuoka, p. 279, 1970.) But society needs to breed out the psychopath and raise the level of conscience to the point where the cost of crime and police is decidedly lower than today. This requires a means of permitting high sensitivity of conscience to develop without eliminating its bearers by guilt and depression.

Surely, however, a less myth-ridden way of evolving and protecting higher sensitivity of conscience and social devices for forgiveness can be developed?

A psychologist today must seriously question religious tenets regarding forgiveness. A good deal is is now known about human learning by conditioning and the manipulation of reward and punishment. Social aspects have been authoritatively developed by B. F. Skinner in his *Beyond Freedom and Dignity*, 1971. As far as the efficiency of social learning, and learning vis-a-vis the physical environment, are concerned the more certain and immediate the reward and punishment the better. How then can a rational ethic justify the cancelation of punishment by forgiveness? In relation directly to learning in the physical world anything resembling forgiveness is an absurd reducer of learning. Even with consequences, as in Kipling's (1940) "Gods of the Copy Book Headings," it may still be true that "the burnt Fool's bandaged finger goes wobbling back to the fire." But if he is not given too soothing an anodyne, even the fool learns.

It is not given to Nature to forgive, but an individual and a society (and, of course, a deity) can forgive, and if, as some religions say, they should forgive "seventy times seven" times, it would seem that learning would be slow. However, in a well-organized religion, confession, repentance, and contrition are made a condition of forgiveness. (There is an interesting Protestant-Catholic difference here, in that the former reserves much of this easy forgiveness for children.) The psychological purpose here is clearly to retain the individual within the group. The man the driver ran over, when he had imbibed too much, let us say, is dead, and no restitution is possible. The social punishment (if he is, say, a minor or a first offender) is small, and the theory is that his punishment is the contrition under the impact of his own conscience. If he is severly punished, this presumably would not develop and he might be driven outside the group. The essence of the Christian-Judaic system is "To hate the sin, but love the sinner." This is often difficult to the point of impracticality, and one must register more support for the position here taken, which risks the loss of the individual from the community. One is reminded of Tennyson's "Move upward, working out the beast, and let the ape and tiger die" (1908) in the genetic part of this transaction. An outlaw can live in our society, but in primitive societies the breaker of an important taboo is so cast out that unless he flees to a "harbor of refuge" for the rest of his life he generally dies from psychological depression and starvation.

Although we can distinguish between "sins against nature," which normally have no possible forgiveness, and "sins against society," which can be forgiven, many of the former have social consequences which fall in the forgiveable. Gluttony and sloth will work their consequences unimpeded on a Robinson Crusoe; but medicaid and welfare will take some care of them in a society, and in the burden they put on others they become also an offense against society, which society forgives to a greater or lesser extent according as it is governed by revealed religion or a Beyondist ethic.

Legal systems for handling crime are partly based on religious feelings and partly on civil consequences. At the present moment, there is a strong call for ethical guidance on the distinction between intended crime and the crime committed in insanity. Punishment has three functions: to teach and reform the aggressor; to deter others; and, by expressing the outraged feelings of society, to reinforce the necessary convictions that the behavior is wrong and law and order are precious.

The last seems to be regarded by some feeling liberals as questionable, but probably without this reinforcement of standards in the normal citizen some weakening of his feelings about the importance of ethics would occur. In the case of the insane, function (1) above is believed no longer to hold, though psychological proof that punishment and reward no longer affect an insane person is lacking, and it is probable that this universal learning law is not entirely rescinded by distorted perceptions.

In this chapter, we have basically asked what similarities and differences exist between the inner emotional life when adjusting to Beyondism and to traditional religious beliefs. In summary, we can state:

(1) Beyondism calls for a greater degree of austerity and emotional maturity in leaning on belief in an evolutionary process, rather than on a personal deity, responsive to individual prayer.

(2) The rationalist breakaway from revealed religions called for emotional devotion and expectancy in regard to welfare of all in earthly Utopias. This is as remote from the Beyondist position as is that of traditional religions, for evolution involves, as far as our eyes can yet see, a continuous pilgrimage, in which Utopias are at most inns marking the target of a day's journey.

(3) The fact that the ethical laws in Beyondism alter with the evolutionary stage implies no alteration in the basic goals. Any expectation by "moral relativists" that this connotes looser ethics is quite wrong. On the contrary, the aim of Beyondism is to take the ethical values out of the realm of subjectivity and place directives on a firm scientific foundation.

(4) In this connection, the study of sin and virtue, over centuries, by religions, leading to such classifications as mortal sins (pride, wrath, envy, lust, gluttony, avarice, and sloth) and venial sins, could be carried further to quantitative indices of desirable and undesirable behaviors, as a guide to education.

(5) An analysis of the historical roots of religions reveals archetypal emotional needs, the catering to which has inevitably produced superstitions and values that in many cases are void or regressive from the standpoint of Beyondist ethics. The temperamental difference in the genetic pools (racial mixtures) in different populations also seems to have shaped peculiarities of religions.

(6) The instinctive, impulse-controlling personality structures are the ego (C), the superego (G), the self-sentiment (Q$_3$), and guilt proneness (O). Cultures differ in the role given to these, and the self-sentiment, being concerned with conforming to society and motivated by shame-

vs-self-esteem, fits better a totalitarian society, whereas the superego, using guilt, is more directed to a categorically imperative abstract goodness, democratically applicable.

(7) These structures are educated and maintained in different ways, and the sensitivity to guilt motivating the superego is perhaps fostered, genetically and culturally, by the religious emphasis on contrition and forgiveness and an elaborate mythology of vicarious absolution through the execution of a god. However, nature does not forgive, and in the division of offences against society and against nature, some of the former end as settling accounts in the latter. Consequently, Beyondism argues that a society cannot go as far in indulgence as some religions advocate without losing survival value. This has implications for the criminal laws. We face the same question here as in other areas of austerity versus indulgence, as to whether high standards will cause the individual to leave the group—in this case the religious group. The motivation in belonging to a group, as we have already glanced at it, can be diverse, and the morale of idealism—the leadership of an idea— we have claimed can be as potent as the numerous ergic satisfactions in what we have called Morale II—provided there is not too much genetic lag. Most will not leave a disciplining community.

(8) The pattern of conscience as a subjective motivation that Beyondism calls for must align itself with the responsibilities and loyalties that Beyondism objectively demands. The objectively required pattern, in Figure 8-1, describes duties to (1) the primary group, (2) its members, (3) the world organization, (4) individuals in the world at large, (5) the fellow Beyondist in the world at large, and (6) to the evolutionary principle itself.

The last plays the same role as God, the First Cause, the Laws of the Universe, or whatever form the *superpersonal* attachment takes in traditional religions. But although extant religions have included regard for various sets of the others, they have not precisely analyzed them or described what the special love and loyalty is in each. Perhaps the reason is that the average member of a congregation would have difficulty with the distinctions, even if expounded to him. Yet they represent realities needing to be grasped in vindicating any ethical choice.

The directing by conscience is, of course, a directing of loyalties, duties, responsibilities, and what would be covered by the word "love." For most people, love is toward living citizens—perhaps of the world— and toward God. Beyondism refines the qualities of love and the duties in (2), (4), and (5) above which cover "living men," and in (6) it calls for *love for remote future generations*—little noted in revealed, universalistic religions. Its love, we have noted, is also of a more ascetic quality, not catering for human narcism and mutual self-indulgence, and not requiring the belief that we are "the apple of God's eye," or simply returning the love of a loving personal deity. It requires, in regard to charity, Nietzsche's *Beyond Good and Evil*, warning that "One has not watched life very observantly if one has never seen the hand that—kills tenderly." Love and loyalty have to be directed by complex perceptions.

Chapter 14

What Are the Created Spiritual Values of Beyondism?

The term "spiritual" is one of the hardest to define in all psychology. It is first defined, by exclusion, as those interests beyond the practical, the commercial, the survival oriented, and the self-seeking. Their greatest association is with religion, and in William James's *The Varieties of Religious Experience* we have a first scholarly overview. However, what individuals call their spiritual values may be tied to their superstitions rather than the altruistic and ethical aspects of religion. The devotee contemplating his navel in an effort to dissolve his attachment to this world is concerned with a purely personal—one might say narcissistic—experience. In any case, the spiritual also finds expression in art and music, and in degenerate form in drugs.

The creation of spiritual values that last occurs by the action of sublimation sometimes beginning with the depression accompanying near-total frustration, and spoken of among the saints, such as St. Francis, St. Augustine, and Loyola, in some such terms as "the dark night of the soul," from which rebirth occurs. The initial sense of frustration may come from personal experiences or intellectual appreciation of the limitations of earthly existence. That appreciation may come as a reasoned perspective as in Plato's conclusion that "nothing in the affairs of men is worthy of much concern" (1946), or in the numerous thinkers like Pascal or Newton, who ultimately put spiritual values even above their mathematics, or as a religious belief such as the Buddhist's conviction that individuality is no more than the individuality of a billion raindrops falling into the ocean.

Psychologically, the basic reality is that spiritual values are ergic drives sublimated and transformed. The path of the transformation told in many a heart-rending biography of, for example, conversion, is part of what psychologists recognize in the *Adjustment Process Analysis Chart* (Cattell 1950c, 1980). It is "part of" because there are several alternative and socioethically very different sequelae to frustration. Two important inferences follow. First, that spiritual values are likely to be poorly developed in an individual or a society that receives easy, uninhibited satisfaction to most ergs. Second, through repression and associated defenses, spiritual interests are likely to be rooted in the unconscious. For that reason, they are likely to be inexplicable on rational grounds, and as shielded as a neurotic symptom from subsequent reward and punishment—as in the martyr who chooses to burn at the stake.

As to the first of these, our habit of looking down on the Middle Ages, before the fifteenth century onset of science's alleviation of poverty and suffering began, tells something about ourselves. For that was an age of highest spirituality (as Chesterton (1915) reminds us) when artists content to remain anonymous reared the great cathedral spires toward heaven. That it was also an age of endemic war, cruelty, and suffering is exactly what we would expect from the proportions of the Adjustment Process Analysis Chart. Light is thrown on this by modern data, by the factorial dimension discovered in existing national culture patterns which we call cultural pressure (Figure 12-1). There we see that civilized inhibitions, demanded by the increasing complexity of life, generate ergic frustrations, which, as in the APA analysis, lead to a trio of alternative expressions, namely, hostility and violence, creativity of a spiritual nature, and mental illness.

The modern world is given to assessing all progress in terms of prosperity. If a visitor from the Middle Ages or Greece or Rome were to come among us, he would look at our skyscrapers, rising in glittering majesty into the night, and at our flying ships and would think "verily these things are the work of a race of giants." But then he would talk with the people around, and watch T.V., and find neurotics, liars, drunkards, and criminals as abounding as in his own day. He might rightly conclude that these marvels are the work of an elite, or that the thinking that has gone into engineering has not been applied to the society of man. In any case, he will conclude we have made little or no progress spiritually.

Creativity and spirituality take both practical useful scientific (r-culture) outlets and sheer esthetic and religious forms (p-culture). And since sublimation and perversion have a common root, the spirituality may take perverse forms. Thus a Beyondist has to ask at once to what extent in each instance the spiritual values that emerge can be either an unguided consequence of outer circumstances—a random adjustment to the inevitable, in a form by no means understood by those involved—or the creation of a purposeful progressive ethics. As examples of the former, we may take Buddhist resignation in a world too complex to alter, or the values of humility, sexual restriction, and concern for the underdog, which were accepted from Christian teaching in the first three or four centuries of its growth in the Mediterranean. These early Christian values became established and incorporated in doctrine by a teacher because they fitted the lives of slaves and the downtrodden under the Roman Sword—as Nietzsche and many others have pointed out in detail. Whenever some socioeconomic or other environmental circumstances, and probably also a racial temperament, are common to most people, a common set of spiritual values is likely to emerge, and these are likely to be incorporated and given ritual decoration in a prevailing religion.

The expected result—in survival and evolution—of spiritual values that arise from a prior, allegedly insightful ethical and social system—as in French Rationalism, Bentham's Utilitarianism, Marxism, and the present derivation of Beyondism—is likely to be very different. For one thing, it is less likely to achieve emotional vitality and century-long endurance. Pythagoras founded a religious cult based on fascination with the beauty of numbers, but it had few followers and soon disappeared. Platonism, and the intellectual systems of the Stoics and Lucretian Epicureanism, held awhile in the educated classes, but were soon swept from the Mediterranean by the simple dogmas, the basic answers to emotional frustration, in the arresting, tragic story of Christ.

Before returning to the question of how spiritual values based on a scientist's view of the universe (not just on some rationalistic or economic theory) may reach functional power, it is desirable to look at the historical value systems in naturalistic terms and understand by psychological analysis what one may expect in the process of development of spiritual values.

There are, as we have recognized, spiritual value systems outside religion, in art and music for example, but the massive developments are in four or more great religions such as Buddhism, Christianity, Hinduism, Confucionism, and Islam. It would be possible by the dynamic calculus of modern psychology to discover the profile of origins in the several main instinctual (ergic) frustrations. But since social psychologists have not yet tackled this, we have to turn to the enormous, but subjective, literature on what the spiritual values and emotional outlets of these religions mean for their devotees. The Judaic-Christian branch, with which we are most concerned, has stressed charity, humility, low sexuality, a relative unconcern with this life in comparison with the kingdom of heaven, resignation, and love of all men.

As Weber's (1956) work on the Protestant ethic, and that of sociologists since, has emphasized, there is probably more difference between the Protestant and Catholic branches than perhaps these and Islam. Protestantism gives more individual, mature freedom, recognizes that forgiveness does not eliminate consequences, fits better into a scientific and business outlook of self-striving for betterment in this life, and is, of course, more liable to fragmentation into "heretical" sects.

No one can look at the diverse values of the great religions, free of prejudice, without recognizing, as we have earlier, that their boundaries tend to correspond to racial, and certainly ethnic, frontiers. In Asia, Buddhism has happily settled most stably in the Mongolian and part-Mongolian peoples. Islam, though pushed by conquest on some non-Semitic or Hamitic races, largely follows the boundaries of the Semitic people. In Europe, Protestantism has boundaries that cut through countries, e.g., Germany and France separating the Nordid from the Alpinid and Mediterranid areas, which latter tend to be largely Catholic. These value-belief conglomerates are nevertheless *partly* to be understood as based on genetic and *partly* historical-environmental causes.

If factor analytic research had been carried out on the half dozen great religions, it would doubtless yield meaningful dimensions on which they could best be differentiated. For example, it is clear that the teachings of Confucius (and of his equally influential contemporary, Lao Tzu) depart from other religions on a dimension of freedom from emotionality and myth, toward practical social ethics and an intellectual resignation to the facts of life. (I am reminded of my Unitarian minister friend who says "If you dislike religion come to our church; we have less of it than others.")

Among the conglomerates, we must recognize one that has slanted off into something more intangible than the others. In the early Greeks, and in the Northern Europeans as expressed in the Viking sagas, we have the worship of the hero and the free heroic life, which contrasts considerably with the Judaic-Christian pseudo-humility and apotheosis of the underdog. In the considered words of Disraeli, "No man will treat with indifference the principle of race. It is the key to history." The empire of Canute, extending over Scandinavia, Britain, Iceland, and points west, was the nearest approach to a community embodiment of this hero lifestyle; though since the Mediterranean had some thousands of years more to accumulate technical and military advantages, the Northern pattern eventually succumbed to Christianity imposed partly by the sword. Nevertheless, just as the Roman Empire lived on in shadowy form as the Holy Roman Empire, of Emperor and Pope, for several centuries, so one can still see the North Atlantic society (Canute's old empire) in Northern Europe, North America, and Australia. The NATO nations show the same spirit of individual enterprise, concern for the more heroic rather than the stall-fed proletarian life, and reference to reality, in science and exploration, rather than ritual-bound religious or political traditions of submission. (The sociologist will notice in this theory of a spirit outlasting a mere administrative or particular religious or political organization, a resemblance to Pareto's "residues.")

In a most condensed view, refusing to be lost in detail, we can reduce to three major presently existing "religious" value conglomerates: (1) the Buddhist religion, compatible with Confucian emphasis on social harmony and intelligent resignation to the inscrutable, in largely Mongolian countries; (2) the Judaic-Catholic-Christian complex derived from the Mediterranean (and having Islam as a tougher, still more ritual-bound offshoot); and (3) the "North Atlantic" conglomerate, partly Protestant Christian, partly rational skeptical (Russia), minimizing the resignation to things as they are, and the social dependence, which characterizes the other religions. Communism, considered as a religion, combines the rationalism brought by Russia's Scandinavian invaders (the Russ) with the denial of individuality fitted to the temper of its Mongolian masses. On such fringe areas we note the peculiarity of Japan, which combines much of Mongolian Buddhism with the worship of the hero, and Hinduism.

Beyondism breaks out into a new and unique spirit in relation to these old historical traditions of value and spirit. Its parentage, from the values of which it is a development, is clearly what we have called the North Atlantic conglomerate (to which, incidentally, the dissidents of Renaissance Italy, Spain, and Portugal once belonged in marked degree).

Among the six main values of this conglomerate, and of the matrix of Beyondism, we see: (1) The first value is that of individualism and the trail-breaking hero. Carlyle (1840) is the classical expressor of that viewpoint in his contention that human progress is the story of a few hundred cultural heros. (We would, however, not deny the Marxism or materialistic determinism view to the extent of recognizing that physical and economic impacts produced the tides which these leaders often intelligently embarked on at the flood.)

(2) This belief that creativity and progress arise in the minds of free individuals connotes first that the individual differences in intelligence and other genetic qualities must be treated with respect and hope rather than envy and the intention to level-down. As that inventive scientist, Roger Williams (1953) has well said, "Equality and Freedom are incompatible, since equality requires a forcible levelling." Here Beyondism sharply disagrees with many inferences from the Judaic-Christian values, where "equality before God" strangely becomes equality of income, compulsory redistribution of earnings, and the fostering of inadequacy.

(3) The commitment of Beyondism to harmony with the evolutionary process means an acceptance of the demise of cultures and races when nature's verdict overwhelmingly points to their incapability of survival. The record of the rocks has to go on to new pages.

(4) The spirit of community adventure is central in Beyondism, and since adventure is fraught with danger and death, the Beyondist philosophy must honor and comfort the hero and the heroic society in a way to make this lifestyle a tolerable one. There are various aspects to this. First, adventure is foredoomed if the society has to go out with a ball and chain on its leg. That ball and chain is most commonly a "welfare" program or a world of superfluous luxury expenditure incited by modern advertising which diverts the greater part of a society's resources from basic research in science, interplanetary exploration, higher education, and the like. Beyondism demands that luxury-living and charity of that kind should be regarded as shaming both him that receives and him that, in maudlin spirit, gives. As Elmer Pendell well says (*Why civilizations self destruct*, 1977), "There should only be charity when it does not increase the need for charity." It demands that luxury living and poverty be abolished by adjusting the ability birth rate to the changing demand for ability levels in an increasingly complex civilization. A society in which one half keeps the other in the dependent, helpless status of domesticated animals—stall-fed, T.V.-entertained, and doubtless quite content—is intolerable to a Beyondist philosophy of united group adventure.

(5) A second aspect of group adventure into new cultural and genetic experiment is that the *diversity* between groups must not only be tolerated, but respected, encouraged, and enhanced. If there is rivalry among groups, it must not be the rivalry of mutual grabbing, but of ships that explore in different domains and signal to one another as to

their progress.[31] If by extreme circumstances and low maturity, in terms of Beyondist ethics, war exerts its reality, it should still be war without hatred, in the spirit of fair play which England and America have done much to spread into world affairs. The spiritual balance involved in recognizing that all are involved in pursuing a common goal of evolutionary advance, but that each has initial loyalty to his own group experiment, is perhaps psychologically not easily acquired, but it is central in the spiritual values of Beyondism.

(6) Central also in Beyondism is the pursuit of truth and new knowledge. The task of the scientist-beyondist is to express truth in the best words and formulae available. The task of the "propagandist," on the other hand, is to have his will by rhetoric (and even the ways of poetry) but gained evilly and untruthfully. The latter succeeds to the extent that his listeners are uneducated and of low intelligence, but all of us are vulnerable to some extent, and the spirit of Beyondism is toward truth at all costs.

(7) We had admitted, earlier, that whereas people turn to religion as to a firm, unchanging rock in the stream of life, the ethical directions of Beyondism will change, in some degree, inasmuch as Beyondism is a part of science. Discoveries will demand change in social values. The Beyondist has clearly to recognize that the abiding value of commitment to evolution will require changing particular values in the light of discovery. The discovery of the "pill" makes possible—though it does not dictate—a change in sexual mores; and the possibility of keeping people alive to extreme old age may introduce new values to voluntary euthanasia. A clear awareness of what is *basic*, and what is an inferred value, in means to ends is vital here.

(8) Finally, we have to recognize, as stated at the beginning of this Chapter, that the ergs that go searching for spiritual satisfaction are those which are denied more direct satisfaction, and that sex and aggression (pugnacity) are prominent here. But others such as the parental-protective drive will also favor spiritual expressions close to the original goal of the erg.

Some division will always arise between these by-product spiritual interests that fit the evolutionary direction and those that do not. As we have seen, the ethics of the former variety of spiritual conviction is the ultimate rational expression of the Greek philosophers, and most recently of the French Enlightenment and the Utilitarianism of Bentham and Mill. Incidentally, this duality exists in revealed religions themselves in the Christian (notably Lutheran and Calvinist) distinction of giving value to what a man is, by grace, rather than to what he does, by works. A modern positivist psychologist, however, can scarcely accept this division of personality, for what a man's personality is, in all its conscious and unconscious complications, can only be inferred from his behavior. Of course, some of the most important behavior is written in that restraint which shows itself by doing nothing in the face of various stimuli. So, as a matter of degree, the distinction of what a man is and what he does *may* be said to exist in degree.

The spiritual values of different societies should and must vary—beyond the basic values of group life which *all* groups need. No illustration surely is necessary that a set of psychopaths will tend to create a gang, a set of docile individuals a dictatorship, and so on through various structual isomorphisms and derivatives that experiments on syntality (Cattell & Stice, 1960; Cattell, Woliver, & Graham, 1980) have revealed. By this view, the goodness of the inner spiritual state of the individual is to be understood and judged by the society it creates—and, conversely, the soundness of a society can be judged, if one can assess inner spiritual states, by the goodness of those states.

To accept this principle should not cause us to fall into the misunderstanding voiced by some readers of the first volume of Beyondism: that because it accepts the reality of an outer world indifferent to man's wishes and therefore more harsh than that which revealed religions choose to depict, there is any direct implication that human relations *must* be correspondingly harsh and unfeeling. The relations among a crew in a hurricane do not have automatically to become mutually hostile and threatening, though they may have to demand higher standards of performance from one another. Because it is inevitable in blind evolution that we shall repeatedly bump our heads on a brick wall, our heads do not have to be filled with brick! The "outer covering" of a society, like that of a living cell, permits the inner processes to be very different from those on the outer medium. It may well turn out, indeed, that as the outer environment becomes more harsh the need for kindness of man to man becomes greater. Our position on this has simply been that the expressions of compassion, like those of any other mammalian erg, need control and redirection in a complex culture.

An increased realism concerning the outer world, cleared of the superstitions of some religions, calls for more disciplined and adjusted expression of *all* drives. Furthermore, ethics, and the law itself, have come to recognize that "circumstances alter cases" and that, in periods where a society is fighting for its life, its interindividual ethical rules, adaptive to the same goal in a different setting, must adaptively alter. In the case of two shipwrecked men on a tiny raft who pushed away a third, because scrambling aboard would drown all three, the law recognized, (under Necessitas inducit privilegium privata) that they were not murderers, and this miniature simply brings home what happens in many ways in a larger society.

It helps perspective if we glance developmentally at broadly recognizable stages in the relation of ethical value to spiritual development in the empirical record of history. With some simplification we see four steps as follows:

(1) The appearance of revealed, intuitive religion begins with a spirituality primarily based on the substitute expressions of frustrated ergs. This corresponds to an ethic crudely and inefficiently adapted at the same time to group survival, and aided in acceptance by superstitious illusions giving falsely generated compensatory satisfactions.

(2) A rationalistic seeking for true perspectives about man and his environment, which, however, is *unlikely* to reach an integration of fact and emotion that is as robustly emotionally satisfactory as what is offered to credulous mankind in the "revealed religious truths" stage of ethics. This integration for a time is lacking. This bleak rationalist perspective, from, say, 1700 to the present day's "existentialism," humanitarianism, or disillusion, is one that is unstably held, and then mainly by a minority of literary intellectuals and casual halfbelievers. In its most vigorous, yet ultimately empty, form, we can see this epitomized in Voltaire in the eighteenth century and in Russell during recent times. It rests on a "sense of decency," logically lacking any further goal. It is to this existential philosophy that the deeply religious conventional person reacts when he criticizes that "men no longer acknowledge sin, or the need for divine mercy." The Beyondist cannot go along with the *cognitive* beliefs of this religious person, but, as we shall see, he clearly recognizes sin, and he builds up a social leadership that aims at mercy and forgiveness for error. For the path of evolution is *necessarily* paved with innocent error.

(3) Extension to biological realities, made possible by the advance of science, and resulting in ethical reconstructions, as in Ardrey, Bentham, Mill, Hardin, Haeckel, Huntington, Huxley, Keith, Lorenz, Nietzsche, Waddington, and Wilson. These, in Beyondism, faithfully portray the new realities—ignored by traditional religions. In Bentham and Mill, the goal of "the greatest happiness of the greatest number" was a sociological goal only, whereas especially in the more recent of the remainder, biological realities also entered. However, most of these have not attempted the final step we face in this chapter of adequately fitting the newly admitted truths to a radical *personal* re-adjustment of emotional adjustment and spiritual values. A seemingly brutal realization has to come to Christian countries that, as Sir Arthur Keith

dared to express it, "The law of Christ is incompatible with the law of evolution—as far as the law of evolution has worked hitherto" (*A New Theory of Human Evolution*). Nevertheless, as we shall see, even in intergroup ethics, there is a possibility of several values in Christian ethics persisting in Beyondism.

(4) The Beyondist integration takes on this house-cleaning, by concepts of natural science and the new evolutionary, biological perspectives, and undertakes the deeper psychological analysis required to fit the new perspective on the world and society to an appropriate religious emotional meaning in the life of the individual.

Without this last interpretation, most intelligent people today will be left in perplexity. It seems that in every age there have been sturdy independent critics of revealed religion, often in no sense "intellectual," who have struggled into the bleak realities of stage 2 above. A folk verse comes down to us:

> Johnny Jones, a bag of bones
> A belly full of fat.
> When he dies he shuts his eyes
> And what do you think of that?

Unfortunately, the initial price of this sincerity of thinking was the "quiet desperation" which Thoreau described as the state of many intelligent men. It is the result of honest demolition without equally fundamental reconstruction. From this honest but barren view of reality, too unrewarding to be either popular or stable, we can recognize three diverse attempts at an emotional solution. First, there is sheer retreat, with rationalizations, to the comfortable fold of the dogmatic religions. Secondly, there is some build-up, mainly among intellectuals, of mutual support in hardily enduring what is, under the banner of "existentialism," or some such dreary and nondynamic philosophy, a possible dark haven. Somewhere in this cul-de-sac of logical skepticism roam many intellectual liberals. What ultimately motivates them, when action has to take place, is a hash of humanistic and humanitarian inclinations that are relativistic reconstructions from fragments of such religions as Christianity, (which, in their statements, they have abandoned.) Incidentally, it is the short-sighted form of "compassion" in the existential feeling liberal circles that comes regularly into conflict with the more far-sighted concern for man in Beyondism and with any spirit of positive adventure and risk-taking.

No one can examine the second stage (above) of "adjustment" to human frustration (and to the bleak truths of an indifferent universe) without recognizing as belonging logically in this family of adjustments the massive developments present in some oriental religions, and, in particular, that of Gautama Buddha. If it is one's wants that hurt one, then peace and happiness may be sought by a process of denying and ignoring these wants. This is a more wholesale process of suppression than any Freudian repression in a particular area. This broader negation of human "wants" denies the importance of the individual and all his ambitions. It sees him as a ripple caused by one of a million similar and equal rain drops falling into the sea. It is a possible spiritual adjustment (though complicated in Buddhism by the belief in transmigration of souls). But it is radically different from the Beyondist emotional adjustment. (We may speculate that it arose as perhaps an outcome of the less dynamic temperament which psychologists are coming to document in the Mongolian people.)

The Beyondist position in spiritual adjustment which we are now studying, under the *fourth* form of emotional adjustment above, needs thorough examination of its spiritual form. We need to ask what emotional frustrations and controls are demanded and what is the ergic composition of the outlets and sublimations it offers. First, we recognize that Beyondism is stripped of the satisfactions of a superstitious and mythical character which, as Freud pointed out in *The Future of an Illusion*, will manifestly fail to materialize (except in taking advantage of the uncheckable reward of a paradise "from whose bourne no traveller returns"). Much prayer for rain does not alter the dying crops. Like any illusion or hallucination, such beliefs always have to be paid for in other ways. Frequently the losses will not be seen as connected, but the punishments will outweight the initial rewards. Here also, we may reiterate, is the short-sighted satisfaction of emotional religious compassion which favors the reproduction of the poor and creates still greater suffering in the next generation. In this complex, also, we encounter that apparent benignness in the religious praise of "love" which is actually, in many cases, a pact for mutual self-indulgence and escapism from necessary thought and discipline in face of reality. Thus one of the first spiritual values in Beyondism lies in the *self-discipline*, not only of such genetically lagging ergs as sex and pugnacity, but of the parental protective-succorant erg, and indeed of the unschooled expressions of any primitive drive. This is based on the internal spiritual value of self-respect.

As we have seen above, a recognition of the reality of the external dangers to a group—the massive meteorite, the powerful antagonistic nations, the new plague germ—and the inexorable demand to be ready for them, does not really call for less love in within-group interactions—

indeed it calls for more—but it does call for more readiness to self-sacrifice, self-discipline, and more stringent ethical laws. A readiness for this devotion is the first spiritual call on the Beyondist.

One aspect of this may have to be a different attitude to forgiveness of sins, the role of which in religious systems we have discussed in Chapter 13. If a reckless, alcoholic car driver is let off lightly—"forgiven"—it does not restore either the dead victim or his own broken vertebra. What does society do to the learning process when it intervenes between people and reality and acts "as if" the damage does not exist? In many ways, as stated in the preceding chapter, it makes social learning inefficient, but, as an example of the complexities that Beyondist social psychological research has to regard, we may note that the evolution of a truly sensitive sense of guilt may depend in part on society intervening with forgiveness where contrition is shown. We have to recognize that "to err is human," but that a being incapable of guilt will not learn, and perhaps affectionate forgiveness in contrition is a condition of sensitizing to guilt and to the evolution of gene pools free of psychopathic insensitiveness. (Parenthetically, our argument in intergroup natural selection for monitoring relative culture failure *before* natural genocide, i.e., the extinction of species and cultural death occurs, rests on the same reasoning.)

Additionally, one must keep in mind that obtaining forgiveness may psychologically become, perversely, a special end to itself. The dissolute Russian character Rasputin belonged to a sect, the Khlysty, whose motto was "Sin in order that you may obtain forgiveness," and whole societies have moved toward this perversion. In this confessional framework stand today the people who argue that the U.S. should be given back to the Indians.

Because of its austerity, Beyondism is unlikely to gain rapid converts among citizens immersed in the fanciful reward systems of revealed religions. It is a primary law of group dynamics (Cattell, 1980) that belonging to a group must bring a balance of greater positive total ergic satisfaction. Without that, people will abandon the group or migrate. A simple instance is that men and corporations automatically shift from a state in the U.S. with high state taxes to one with distinctly lower taxes. This can also happen with ethical demands, though in the long run that group with higher demands will alone survive. Pericles, in his speech to the Athenians during the war with Sparta (431 B.C.), asked who would possibly reject the permissiveness and opulence of Athens for the strictness of Sparta. He added that despite relaxed ways, the Athenians, when called upon, could turn to face the horrors of war with equal fortitude; but the reality was that after twenty years Sparta defeated Athens.

From a scientific point of view, one recognizes that an equal affiliative internal strength—desire to belong—in various societies can be based on a summation of contributions from a theoretically infinite variety of satisfactions from different political structures and ethical systems. Similarly, two men competing in a race may have equal performances based on different contributions of lung capacity, heart efficiency, and muscular build. But the final accountancy on the total is inexorable. Compared to the combinations that *do* succeed there are millions that would not. There is reason to believe that the ethical systems of those that *do* survive will in the first place have certain common, indispensable moral characteristics. It will be recalled that we discussed the division of the ethical system of any group into two parts—the *universal* rules that are necessary *for any* group life, and the *particular* ethical values necessary to sustaining the culturo-genetic experiment in the adventure of that particular group. Certain ethical values of Beyondism will consequently be common to all surviving groups, but on the basis of what we know about the possible advent of quite unforeseen catastrophes in the universe, beyond the capacity of present mankind to handle, new Beyondist values will arise on the premise that *the only acceptable goal in the pace of human evolution is the fastest pace.*

As recognized elsewhere, this premise does not imply any panic of haste, but only a devotion to the spiritual value of experiment, to the organization of a totally new international research center, to the support of research by money now thrown away in international strife, support of nonproductive activities at both ends of the social status axis, and much else.

The first spiritual property in the individual attachment to Beyondism has therefore just been defined as a capacity for self-discipline and far-seeing austerity of purpose. The second might be called an esthetic satisfaction—an unfaltering worship of truth (under (6) above) and the growth of human understanding that this pursuit of truth brings. Beyondism is not the intellectual content of science as such—otherwise every physicist or socio-biologist would necessarily be a Beyondist. Beyondism is science with passion. It is the enjoyment of a sense of wonder, and a state of praise of the boundless and intricate beauty of the universe, with a willingness to move forward with it. (Note that this still does not require, logically, the belief in a personal deity, benign to humans. The origins of the universe are presently beyond our comprehension.) But wonder at the marvelous construction of the universe —from the stars to the electron—is a vital part of the spirituality of Beyondism.

In recognizing that a major spiritual interest in Beyondism lies emotionally in this march of science, let us recognize at the same time that the coloring of science by emotions can mean misunderstandings. Beyondism's blending of science with poetry could easily lead to something very different, namely, to support for the devastating practice of reaching scientific conclusion from emotional beliefs. Karl Marx's scientific-economic house of cards gave expression in part to his violent emotional dislike of the middle class; Mary Eddy's Christian Science was more Christian than scientific, and a host of less known academic social scientists, as I have discussed elsewhere (1948) have mixed reasonable good science with the religious and social views inherited uncritically from their school days. The difference is that these try to make science a servant of their emotional prejudices, whereas Beyondism lets emotions become attached to new, prediscovered scientific-ethical truths. A clear analysis of relations, and a vigilance against the above kinds of abuse, are vital to the infusion of scientific discoveries with wonder, gratitude, worship, and delight.

As to the role of a desire for adventure ((1) above), it will perhaps be said that adventure is the religion of the young, and that the old, the tired, and the decrepit desire only a religion of serene conservatism. It is true that some forms of adventure—say colonization of space— require youth, but to understand and follow with fascination the inner culturo-genetic advance of a society requires maturity and the capacity to handle abstract ideas. And setting out on adventure also has its serenity of mind. It happens that today the adventurous young deplore that the earth is now all explored, that heroism is no longer to be found in modern war, and that only the artificial triviality of sport remains for the young to adventure in. But if educated wisely and well from early life, they will be able to follow week by week the vicissitudes in the multiple experiments of mankind—the real adventure of mankind on a grand scale.

One difference among social values that this aspect of Beyondism calls for concerns the attitude to risk. The worst kind of conservatism— the true devotion to stagnation—constantly rationalizes itself as either prudence, or as protective compassion for those who might get hurt in the adventures of human experiment. Columbus was balked by "prudence" into waiting weary years at the court of Isabella and Ferdinand; but at least no bureaucracy interfered, as one probably would today, in his taking a crew of sailors on so risky a voyage. Adventure implies, in order to begin the adventure itself, perennial conflict with the status quo. In any narrow, specialized domain, we see this, in medicine and psychology for example, in concern over the "risk/benefit ratio." There are conservatives who would permit no new medical experiment in which the searched-for benefit involves *any* human risk whatever.

The question of research either in a largely un-research-minded world of stagnating comfort, on the one hand, or in a world oriented to adventure and exploration on the other hand, bears on the general proposal we have made for an international research center monitoring culturo-genetic experiments. For the spirit of Beyondism requires that research conclusions shall be considered in the future, not only on the basis of the *certainties* of long-established science, but on the principle which we may call "probability research action." This means that in the future social action should be based on research in which the 50/50 likelihood of success is exceeded by some definable, significant probability. What this probability or risk/benefit ratio should be is for the given group democratically to decide. The important point here is that the conclusions in such a clearing house of research should be used for guidance to culturo-genetic experiments on a level of probability equivalent to that which, say, Prince Henry the Navigator generated in his castle at Chagres for the great ocean captains of the fifteenth century. We should be ready for social experiment on a risk/benefit ratio higher than that accepted, say, by the Food & Drug Commissioners, as posited in Chapters 15 through 19 below.

Meanwhile, let it not be thought that the above castigation of those clinging to a zero risk/benefit philosophy leaves us unaware that great adventure can lead to great tragedy. The Greeks, in their religion and their dramas, saw "hubris" as a frequent precursor of punishment from the gods. But this did not lead them to black sackcloth and ashes, or to a religion of resignation. Evolutionary advance is necessarily a process of knocking one's head against assorted obstacles, in the dark, to find a way through. And at the heart of evolution remains, in any case, the tragedy of the death of the individual—of each small universe that is a glimpse of the whole universe. This brevity of our lives, which is the mourning note in all poetry, is yet offset by the permanent importance of each life in its effect on what follows it. The nearest attitude to that demanded of the Beyondist we probably find in history in the Greek, not the Hebrew or the Buddhist philosophies. The classical Greek sense of adventure—of Icarus, Prometheus. and Ulysses— necessarily often ended in tragedy. But in the Greek sense of tragedy, we encounter not so much compassion, in the Hebrew-Christian sense, as the sense that all mankind is bound together in a common adventure —and must accept the mystery of intermittent total failure. As Crane Brinton wrote (*Ideas and Man*), "The Greek religion was not a very consoling religion. For the losers, for the perpetual failures, it offered nothing." It tells the adventurer, "I do not pity you; but I share with you our sense of the cost of adventure."

The follower of Beyondism who masters its proper spiritual perspective has a serenity different in kind from that which is bolstered by illusions. What he builds upon in place of the nursery school pantheons, authoritarian, and bright-painted, of traditional religions is centrally one conception, but a very firm one: that one belongs to an ongoing process, that has every promise of leading mankind to greater understanding, and that needs heros. In that process we fully recognize that our own society will not escape the vicissitudes of adventure or the uneven fate of all living things. As we see it, individuals, races, and cultures have their brief rendezvous with life, and must pass into history. The world is not intended to contain, and be a mere "compassionate" museum for, the almost endless accumulation of extinct forms. They are intermediate instruments, toward some greatness we cannot yet conceive. That individual rendezvous with life, however, because of its consequences, is an eternally significant event. The Beyondist will grieve on the transitoriness of each beloved, and even unloved, miraculous inner universe—the individual mind—that is lit up, as by the warm glow of a great lamp, by a vista of evolutionary progress. His emotions span a spectrum in vital ways different from those that most of the traditional religions have shared. He climbs to a maturity beyond the nursery need to believe in a personally protecting god, and faces the universe beside his fellows, with a sense of solidarity in an undertaking to set out to understand it. That understanding includes a reasonable hope and intention to save mankind from premature destruction, by external or internal happenings, by reaching sufficient understanding in time to master our environment.

The pattern of ergic satisfactions in each religion are to some extent specific as we have recognized earlier in this chapter. In psychology we are only just beginning to approach some accuracy and meaning in measuring motivational profiles central to each religion. If we were to estimate analytically, from preliminary factorial experiment, what drives commonly get involved and are in part satisfied by religion generally, we would list the erg of appeal (dependence), assuagement of loneliness, some eradication of fear, sublimation of sex, of narcissism, and of pugnacity, stimulation of pity (parental erg), and probably some satisfaction of self-assertion in moral superiority as the individual incorporates values in his self-sentiment. At least until recent times these have been a sufficient emotional bond to hold millions to religious affiliations. What we called stage two—skepticism and existentialism —above, though initially confined to the intelligentsia, has spread more widely and drained away much of these attachments, leaving us with the inevitable consequences of generally low morale: neglect of social responsibilities, increased pursuit of sensual pleasure, individual goals, crime, drug abuse, alcoholism, and pornography.

From this, the third step in growth above—the recognition of *biological* truths—first rescues us. That is only a first step of knowledge necessary to the emotional perception of the full Beyondist position in the fourth and last step above. But this fourth step is at the moment known and discussed by only a minority of intellectuals with time to read and think. How can it be brought to a *way of life* open to all mankind? There are two problems: (1) the limited education and intelligence of perhaps a half of all citizens, and (2) the immersion of the media—the roots of adult education—in the largely relativistic ethical values that have followed the breakup of dogmatic religions. Regarding the latter, an unbiased observer must recognise that in spite of a few glaring exceptions the journalists have moved in the past 50 years from the rubbish of large scale village gossip to acquainting their readers with the movements and impacts of discoveries in chemistry, physics, and medicine (and therewith some parts of biology). But the biology of the social sciences—particularly sociobiology and Beyondism—are still something too hot for the media to handle. T.V., for example, invariably conducts discussion of social questions with politicians, religious leaders, lawyers, and others belonging to the old guard of social authority. The discussions remain bereft of science, in a totally different atmosphere from the newer newspaper debates on physical science, engineering, medical discovery, astronautics, and the like.

A science which takes the social organism as its subject matter and looks objectively and quantitatively at human motives, inherited and acquired, in social life, definitely requires a new step, upsetting the habits of thought and feeling of the majority of people today. Beyond the larger vision required in this field there are also some technical, educational difficulties. The man in the street is beginning to think statistically, but these newer sciences require the ability to make statistical decisions that are inevitably complex—else "all statistics is lies." Whereas the citizen understands that if one connects up a battery to, say, an electroplating cell, the mass of silver deposited will depend on the ampere-hours, he is uncertain of the inference from a statement that 73% of the variance of fluid intelligence in a given society can be ascribed to heredity, while only 52% of crystallized intelligence can be. A glaringly simple example is that when Jensen (1973) said that blacks have lower score than whites on various intelligence tests, he was misunderstood to say that *any* black scores lower. Even the simple concepts of an average and a standard deviation cannot be assumed in newspaper readers. Because of this, I sadly anticipate that any well-intentioned journalist seeking to explain the social, psychological, and biological conclusions of Beyondism to popular audiences will have much greater difficulty than with the physical sciences, astronomy, and even medicine.

By contrast, the truths which existing revealed religions offer have been skillfully concocted over centuries of experience of propoganda, and are therefore well adapted to the mental age and social circumstances of the recipients of doctrine. God is a considerable abstraction in the pages of Spinoza or Kant, but a benign old gentleman, radiating light, in the paintings shown a child or placed on a Roman Catholic chapel ceiling. Similarly, the ethical standards are conveyed authoritatively from original tablets of stone, without the need to follow that complex chain of social scientific fact and calculation that a Beyondist would wish to understand as the basis of ethics.

The problem in Beyondism of enlisting the support of the less gifted members of society looks difficult, because of our appreciation of the limited "I.Q. percolation range" of each idea. The battle of life is exciting to the leading thinkers, but what does it mean to the equivalent of the social "infantry man"? We agree with Longfellow "that every human heart is human," but the red and the black—the Communist and the Catholic dictatorships—have long agreed that the *direction* must come from an elite. Democracy plays on a broader basis of influence, but it also depends, for movement, in the last resort, on "open" elites. As that shrewd observer of men, Somerset Maugham, wrote hopefully, "the less intelligent, the less competent, the less enterprising will no longer resent it if the more competent and the more intelligent enjoy advantages that are denied them" (*Le Rouge et le Noir*, Renier). Substitute "powers and responsibilities" for "advantages" and we have a desired religious viewpoint from a Beyondist position. Christianity, as we recognize, has contained, in the view that "all are born equal in the sight of God," the truth that since they are not *biologically* equal an acceptance of different status in life is sensible. The Terror of the

French Revolution ended with a present day acceptance of adjustment to occupational differences, which emotionally steadier Britain (and the Scandinavian countries, for example) had moved to without involvement in trying the inanities of a classless society of faceless molecules.

Actually, the differences of emphasis of an ethics based on evolution, from say, those based on Christianity—which might, a priori, be expected to be considerable—turn out for the majority of people to be small. They are real in some areas, e.g., in regard to tolerating illusions and myths, and the attitude to poverty (as seen in Chapter 15). Also much follows from the vitally important difference regarding many further inferences in the fact that one is "revealed," "inspired," and subjective, whereas the other is potentially on a foundation of research. For example, the fact that Christianity frowns on "free love" can be lightly dismissed by a modern relativist or existentialist. But if it can almost certainly be shown by social calculation that the results of obliterating marriage are damaging to cultural vigor and the probabilities of survival of a group, then Beyondism would take the "conservative" position.

Just as, in the Catholic religion, experts in the scriptures *interpret* ethical standards, and in Communism, exponents of the Marxian doctrine *fix* standards, so in Beyondism it will inevitably fall to experts in social and biological science to clarify and defend ethical decisions. Ideally, therefore, Beyondism will need a far more scientifically educated citizenry, if it is to be democratic, than we now have. This is particularly necessary in the case of understanding those features—such as the shaping of the ethical values of group adventure, competition, differential survival, and greater activity in the increase of organized knowledge—which in fact do differ from traditional religions, because they are devoted to a goal of evolution.

Just as those religions of the Red and the Black, and others, have their researchers in exegesis and their colleges to train skilled teachers for the layman, so, as described under Chapter 19 below, Beyondism must now begin to train its skilled interpreters. Let us admit that both in religion and in politics there will always be a quite substantial fraction of the population lacking emotional concern for ethics (except for some purely personal gains) no matter *what* the religious or political form of their country may be. The ship of state, it seems, will always have a busy crew alongside a set of nonparticipating passengers. To what extent the spiritual participation of all can be recruited by Beyondism, for them to follow intelligently the navigation of the ship, and to become excited at new horizons, remains to be discovered.

We have answered the question at the head of this chapter by clarifying the spiritual values of Beyondism and showing where they resemble or are distinct from others. Consistently, with a scientific empirical approach we must recognize that only experience, in a large group accepting its principles, can fully demonstrate how that spiritual balance will develop. But the development must not be left entirely to experiences of survival and functionality. It must be built up *directly* from the Beyondist aims. Those aims are the common adventure of the group, and the common purpose of the adventures of all groups. The central core in the spiritual values of Beyondism is group adventure —the willingness to reach out to meet new environmental demands. This involves the desire, in a broad sense, for colonization. As Gilfillan (*Migration to the Stars*, 1970) well observes, "For every species existing today more than a hundred have vanished, perhaps because they ceased to be colonists." "Imperialist expansion" is part of the ethos of a Beyondist society.

Chapter 15

What Are the Implications
for Genetic Social Policies:
I. As to goals?

Having thoroughly discussed the rise of ethics from evolutionary principles, and their meaning in the spiritual life of man, we turn in the remaining chapters to the practical social policies which follow. Thus, in two chapters—15 and 16—we shall look at the *genetic* consequences, and in 17 and 18, at the *cultural* policies needed. It has seemed best to deal in the first of each pair with the *aims* and in the second, with the *mechanisms*, though we recognize that this causes some overlap. The separation has some parallel in those countries which permit the separation of religions and political parties, inasmuch as politics often becomes the mechanism for reaching religiously approved values.

Although the Beyondist aim of (a) a specific genetic character for each nation, and (b) a centralized purpose of basic survival for all nations, expressed in genetic and cultural advice given to each, is clear, the particular direction in each will change somewhat with the stage of scientific research. But, in any case, the complete break with older systems—such as prebiological rationalism, the revealed religions, and Marxism—requires a complete reappraisal of movements now going on upon those bases.

Three main genetic goals exist: (1) to *adapt* the genetic pool toward the cultural directions of the particular group, (2) to *create* in each group, also, entirely new genetic variations that may in turn affect the culture, and (3) to *assist* and monitor the genetic evolution of *all* groups, through a central comparison of the consequences of genetic movements.

The immediate practical need—the keeping of research records within groups—we shall consider in the next chapter. The ensuing chapter also leads to mechanisms for international coordination in

181

deliberately avoiding duplication of patterns and encouraging deviations. The third goal above, however, runs into some obscurities of aim that demand general discussion here. The first of these obscurities lies in the charge that human evolution has ceased—or become gravely reduced—because man no longer adapts to environment, but shapes environment to his own needs. We are told that he is like the examination candidate who found the questions unanswerable, but wrote, "In order to show that I am competent in the area I will make up some questions myself and answer them here."

There are two possibilities of eugenic purposes being rendered null and void in this respect: (1) within one cultural group, where the genetics can become, as we have said earlier, "adapted stably to the cocoon of one's culture," and (2) among groups, by a cessation of competition, such as we have envisaged in "the Hedonic Pact."

Let us look more closely at the first in terms of actual examples. The problem arises in such areas as the provision of spectacles for poor eyesight, which brings to a halt the evolution of eyes better adapted to the needs of cultural occupations. Again, we see it in the provision of automobiles, which (except for a few joggers) make a clean-limbed growth superfluous. Again, we see it in the provision of hearing aids, which reduce the disadvantages of poor hearing. And so on.[32] But what is overlooked in the "adaptation to the cultural cocoon" is that, in creating the sheltering cocoon, man inevitably creates *new* demands for adaptation. The spectacles connote microscopes and telescopes, enlarging a demand for adaptation. The automobile brings in demands for a whole new class of adaptations, to speed, complexity, and police laws. Probably only in the early stages of culture—the long-lasting introduction of man to agriculture, for example—does one see some regressions comparable to the advances.

Admittedly, we need to do something about the regressions which, for example, the advances of medical science sometimes tend to bring about. But on a broad front, the statement that "man adapts environment to his genetics" instead of the converse is simply not a widely defensible proposition. Environmental adaptation will always bring its unforeseen by-products, throwing the present adjustment aside and requiring new genetic change. The recent statement of Gould (1970) that man has reached the end of his biological adaptation and the rest is only cultural advance is nonsense.

Incidentally, we shall need, through the advance of behavior genetics, to become far more aware of presently unrealized genetic tendencies and their cultural consequences. It has been surmised (Weyl, 1973) that

182

the need for privacy and a large "personal space" is much greater in Caucasian and American Indian people than in Mongolians and Blacks. In the case of Indians, this produces occupational choices that are less easily obtained, and in Caucasians, probably a greater demand for National Parks and unused countryside. There are probably hundreds—indeed, thousands—of gene-affected behavioral tendencies of this unspecified and unnoticed kind which have long-term effects on survival. We may expect advances soon in knowledge of their effects on culture. Always a mutation will not be a *single* effect but a "permission" toward a wide range of different cultural adjustments, for all genes are pleiotropic.

As to the second change: that of a world without mutual rivalry and competition among groups, it might advantageously be reached in the near future to the point of outlawing war. But the deep genetic nature of dominance, territoriality, and dislike of the strange (ethnocentrism) in man is such, as Ardrey (1970) has well argued, that no political concoction of the next ten thousand years is likely to force us into anything beyond a competitive federation. A federation nevertheless introduces the possibility of bringing about a "noncompetitive" world in which all agree on common sloth and noncompetition. As in our discussion elsewhere, we doubt that such a world organization of an "Hedonic Pact" would remain inherently stable.

We seem, in both within- and between-group demands for adaptation, to have entered upon a phase in which human individualistic invention and exploration guarantee a continually rapidly changing world—after millenia of slow change. (Toffler brings this fact home to this generation in his book on "Future Shock.") This acceleration of change is a fact to be taken into account in any realistic practical prediction today.

The possibility must nevertheless be entertained that in some sense we still operate, for national cultures, each within a cocoon, but without being able to discern its boundaries. In any case, nature has by no means come to the end of *its external* challenges! The origin of the four great Ice Ages (the last two of which produced the enormous changes in human brain size) is *still* conjectural. No one can tell us there may not be a fifth around the corner. In any case, either Nature or man could easily produce an entirely new catastrophe, cutting off perhaps a third of the human race and producing a corresponding great change in the genetic pool. Or a change in the upper atmosphere could let in so much radiation as to multiply a hundred-fold the rate of genetic mutation, producing, with stress, new human strains.

Meanwhile, the ordinary course of cultural invention causes the tug on human genetic selection to veer like a kite in the wind, so that too close a following, i.e., too "well-shaped" a within-group eugenic movement, must be kept open to constant reshaping.

As for the second approach above—"para-eugenics," as we may call the blind creation of viable but unknown genetic variants (mutations), without any preperceived relation to environmental demands—we stand on the verge of entirely new horizons. Para-eugenics (which includes genetic engineering) will surely proceed—but cautiously—to bring about mutations that, on the best socio-biological evidence, are *likely* to give new powers and sensitivities. The social impact of these new propensities will not be understood immediately, and it is, in any case, the social effects of *several* individuals of the new type that we shall need to know before proceeding further. The big fallacy in present thought about chromasomal transfer, for example, is that we are dealing with a single clear-cut additive action whose effects are fully known. But, as every geneticist knows, every mutation brings not one effect but several, and every change results from several gene mutations. Add to this the fact that we are dealing, not with the effect of one individual on his society, but a whole class of individuals, capable of producing an unforeseen social emergent, and one recognizes the extreme complication of this branch of engineering behavior genetics. (One recognizes also the special "emergent" action in genetics described by Lykken.)

Nevertheless, controlled and measured para-eugenics needs to go on. In any case, it *is* going on—uncontrolled and unmeasured—all the time. The aim of a full program of conscious para-eugenic advance must be to ascertain its power to produce larger effects, and to keep close track of what those social effects are. The path of para-eugenics is like that of a runner, who produces a lack of balance which is caught up by each next step. Here, this means immediate cultural testing, and, if the behavioral direction is sound, it must be continued to further "losses of balance." The difference is that many viable mutations may, despite their individual biological viability, *not* produce a better *survival* adjustment for the group. Para-eugenics, aided by the devices we now have for producing mutations, is a novelty about which much needs to be learned if we are to get the highest benefit/risk ratio.

Probably the third eugenic aim—that of deliberate genetic diversifying of groups, with comparative study of their diversity—will cause most debate, in a world presently apparently careless of the issues. Let us recognize that plant and animal breeding has typically alternated *inbreeding* for comparatively pure lines with *hybridization*. Nature has called a distinct halt to the second step by putting a ban on *hybridi-zation across species*—with occasional exceptions such as the mule. But *within* a species it has, on the one hand, segregated lines— "subspecies" or races or breeds—and, on the other, crossed the lines again. The ice ages succeeded in segregating out, with the help of mountain ranges and seas, the races of mankind, as we now recognize them. But modern travel and migration bring about some degree of hybridization, and from certain of these, much as the Japanese-Euro-pean, some valuable new types may well emerge. Incidentally, we tend, especially in "liberal" circles, to think of this hybridization as more common than it actually is. Even in the happy "Aloha" spirit of the Hawaiian islands, the total result, as Table 15-1 shows, is still a rela-tively small hybridization, although Japanese sansei females marry Caucasians more extensively. Elsewhere, religion and many other cul-tural associations militate against hybridization (Jewish Rabbis, for example, tend to advocate within-group marriages). As made clear ear-lier, through migration and conquests, especially, it would be true today that at least half of all countries are racially mixed, though frequently social class, e.g., in South America, still preserves some division, but *marked "genetic pool" differences nevertheless exist among these mixed groups.*

Table 15-1

MARRIAGE CHOICE AND RACIOETHNIC ORIGIN:[a]
Limits of Hybridization

	Mother				
Father	Caucasian	Japanese	Filipino	Chinese	Hawaiian
Caucasian	41,939	2,877	1,002	688	558
Japanese	692	45,976	182	417	101
Filipino	697	962	12,033	209	658
Chinese	344	1,002	71	6,579	71
Hawaiian	219	179	53	78	1,176

[a]Taken from a total of 179,327 children born in Hawaii 1948-1959 (Morton *et al.*, 1967).

The goal of a distinct gene pool for each group is therefore well maintained through most modern nations, and in a few cases, such as Spain (Mediterranid), Sweden (Nordid), China (Mongoloid), the group corresponds also to a particular Pleistocene race. The majority of countries are today creating new gene pools from the mixture of Pleistocene races that have occupied them, and it is these developments of new gene pools that principally concern the goal of creating new racial diversification.

The question of what to construct in its gene pool is one to be democratically handled in those countries that are democratic. The main obstacle to a similar democratic handling of the immigration that mostly changes the make-up of a country has been commercialism. The hand of the employer can be seen in the battle over Mexican immigration into the U.S.A., West Indian into Britain, and Arabic into France. Regarding black immigration, Stoddard has well said (*The Rising Tide of Color*), "While no white community can gain by colored immigration, white *individuals*—employers of labor—may be great gainers, and put private interest above racial duty." Many more aspects —social and genetic—should have entered into these decisions than the call for cheaper labor alone. Japan dealt with the problem of cheaper labor without immigration (Reubens, 1981).

Since we have rejected all a priori, *subjective* assertions of the "rights of man," and the like, it may well be asked how these two standards in goals derive from an evolutionary goal. The first—equality of opportunity—derives simply from the goal of efficient survival of the group, which is harder to reach if those of better ability and character do not get to more leading positions. The second derives from the ethical system, based on necessary loyalty to all fellow humanity, aiming at the common evolutionary goal, despite diversity among groups in their particular individual experiments. Man as a natural object is a wonderful creature so far beyond our understanding that it deserves reverence—which is what we mean by spiritual equality. Everything beyond the analysis of our mental horizon is equal.

Meanwhile, however, in the practical ordering of societies, the six ethical relationship systems we delineated (Chapter 8, Figure 8-1) need to be clearly distinguished in their application. Here as elsewhere, as Weyl (1973) reminds us, "What may be moral conduct to one man or group of men may be immoral then to a different individual or group."

A practical and perhaps urgent case here concerns the genetic and cultural change of a nation by the kind of immigration it permits.[33] Parenthetically, politicians love control of ever-larger populations, and are always deaf to good reasons for qualitatively controlled immigrations. (See Hardin, 1977.) Once an individual becomes a citizen, the ordinary in-group ethics applies, and he must be treated as an individual regardless of cultural or racial origin. But when a country is opening its doors to immigration from diverse countries, it is like a farmer who buys his seeds from different sources by the sack, with sacks of different average quality of contents.

The whole problem of the desired gene pool, in regard both to influencing immigration and eugenic birth rates, needs to be handled by an altogether more complex scientific-comparative method. As we have insisted, the aim of eugenics is not production of a single "type." A complex modern society needs a great variety of gifts, but this, nevertheless, does not mean an ill-balanced excess of this and a deficiency of that. At least in the area of measured intelligence we are already aware that the demands of a modern society are calling out for an increase in the supply of (educated) intelligence and a reduction in the immigration or birth rates of those who join the permanently unemployed. If we knew more, we should undoubtedly see also roots of insanity and crime that need elimination from the desired gene pool. Meanwhile, it is certain that the genetic lag discussed in Chapter 12 can, in part, be designated by deficiencies in a number of ability and personality factors of known degrees of heritability, and readily subject to *within-group* natural selection.

The raising of the average population level on a number of definable traits within a group is a task that could already be undertaken. The changes that would be desirable in distribution is a matter for further research than we yet have—except in regard to intelligence, where the deficiency is clear. To anticipate—planning the question of mechanisms, in the next chapter—we need to discuss more fully here the question of aims. Principally, the question arises immediately concerning the distribution of intelligence. That the bulge in the distribution curve badly needs reduction below an I.Q. of, say, 90 or 100 is evident from the unemployed statistics in the U.S.A. and Britain. That numbers of people could advantageously be increased above I.Q. 125 is implied by every consideration of survival in peace and war. A method of bringing this latter area of increase about *without* any increase in the total positive genes in the pool is to have a society with assortive mating, i.e., one in which the more intelligent tend to marry the more intelligent. This example brings us to the "mechanics" of the next Chapter, where assortive mating needs discussion in the light of other consequences.

Meanwhile, let us keep in mind that one reason for starting here in Chapter 15 with implications from *genetic* relations is that, in present ethical and political concepts, they are far more dangerously neglected and repressed than the indications based on *cultural* evolutionary laws. The reason lies largely in the deadly sin of envy, preventing recognition of the biological inequality of men. To this situation the avante garde has responded that "injustice is the equal treatment of unequals," which is true in some connections, but leaves untouched the Beyondist position that within a group all citizens should have equal opportunity, and that, both there and across groups, love calls for accepting the spiritual equality of all human beings. But this still leaves us with actual biological inequality. In dealing with the American and Soviet reluctance to definite eugenic action, we have already examined some of the irrational roots. It is good to recall the comment of a free and wide-ranging "left wing" mind in opposition to this reluctance. Said H.G. Wells, in advanced age, "It seemed to me [when young] that to discourage the multiplication of exceptionally superior people, eugenics was the only real and permanent way of mending the ills of the world. *I think that still*" (1940).

The first application of Beyondist genetic principles is to the group. Except that the intergroup ethics requires that a nation shall not breed individuals who are tigers to other groups, each group is autonomous in its own genetic direction. It is free to control that direction by whatever form of political control takes charge of its other directions, e.g., educational and economic, and in Anglo-Saxon countries, for example, it will tend to be democratic. In Chapters 6 and 7, the Beyondist position has been stated that it is ethically desirable and practically important for a group to direct its *genetic* direction by similar principles to those in its *educational* shaping of its children. Opposition to this is pernicious nonsense, which succeeds in holding adherents mainly because of the great practical difficulty that genetic policies meet. For example, our argument that mankind should consider variation, even into distinct species, will meet opposition from all who are intoxicated with man's performance as he stands. Further obstruction springs from the political fact that we seem just now to be reaching a single world consciousness which could apparently be threatened by talk of segregation. Yet, how biologically fragile man is, standing as a one-species genus! There are slightly more than 200 species of primates! Man has put all his eggs in one basket, and seems unaware of the danger. It must perhaps be accepted that segregation into species can hope to reach effectiveness only after some generations of human socio-biological education, increases in emotional maturity, and acceptance of Beyondism.

Meanwhile, regardless of its evolutionary desirability in terms of safety and progress of the genus, today's academic population genetic experts mostly declare that full speciation of humans would be virtually impossible to bring about, and, except for the Nobelist Muller, they mostly even tend to declare that it would be undesirable. At first it might seem that the only chance of sufficient segregation to develop species no longer cross-fertile would be through success in colonization in the solar system followed by deliberate or accidental cutting off of migration and communications. (We speak of too long and slow a process to have been entertained in dramatic science fiction!) For humans presently to think of several human species is practically about as real a possibility as spatial colonization itself.

Yet, actually, we do not have to depend on such fanciful extraterrestrial journeys to create distinct species. Innumerable species have been created on earth by comparatively simple combinations of circumstances. Although man's intelligence gives him the capacity to interact with all mankind, his will gives him the capacity to isolate his own kind and to develop his own cultures if he is sufficiently serious about it. The chief protectors of segregation in man have been—apart from physical sources in oceans and mountain ranges—the existence of languages, religions, nationalities, social classes, and physical differences that reach the point of creating aversion. The flux of historical events has been such that none of these has succeeded in creating ethnic differences of a species magnitude. However, we lack gynecological records and research that might well show that *relative sterility*—the forerunner of interspecies infertility—exists in mating between the presently most distant racial types.

Language communality, which is mainly national communality, seems already to have operated on mixture of the old, geographically developed races (Mongolian, Negro, Nordid, Alpinid, and Mediterranid-Caucasian) to have produced a slight indication of physical typing by *national cultures*—as in the differences of Japanese and Chinese. A striking example of genetic characters associated with religious segregation is seen in the Jews, with an unequalled record in time (possibly roughly 5,000 years) of guarded inbreeding despite every kind of interfering circumstance. It is conceivable, therefore, that if greater diversity, toward actual speciation, were urgently desired, it could be achieved without interplanetary segregation and by strong, diverse, sociobiological cultural ideals alone.

In a book of this scope of enquiry, this speciation question has to be briefly considered, but it is a less practical, probable, and important issue than the goals of genetic action within our existing societies. Let us therefore turn to consider the processes, the customs, and the ethical values that affect the raising of a society to its greatest intergroup-outer-environment survival potential, in terms of its genetic component. What happens within the group, in short, calls for wise guidance in "genetic navigation."

If we consider for a moment the well-researched matter of intelligence, we see that a eugenic differential birthrate could well raise the average. Granted the usual normal distribution, this will also raise the level (or numbers) of the brighter group at the same time. But if a group fails to raise its average, should it not, in the name of intelligent management and national safety, set out specifically to raise the level and number of its highly intelligent subgroup (of, say, 5% with I.Q.s of 120 and above)? This simple aim actually introduces a social dilemma. If we do foster this subgroup, we are in danger of producing a rift in democratic habits and social structures, since these people will tend to form an "elite" subculture which, by exciting envy and manifesting values incomprehensible to the majority, may excite hostility and mistrust. On the other hand, if we do not attempt to provide such a gifted subgroup, the main group, through mediocre management, may survive poorly or meet disaster. (Of course, if we accept the basic aim of having natural selection effectively act on the average goodness of groups, then to save a low group by a high leadership is "cheating" the purpose. However, it is to be expected that the survival of a high leadership group will in time lead to raising the cultural and genetic level of the whole group. If this expectation is false, then natural selection among democratic, little-stratified groups is more efficient than among groups led by able oligarchs or even dictators.)

In the present "permissive" generational atmosphere, the label "elite" has, for the time being, become a bad word, and to dissect out the prejudices or real values that may be involved in an elite can arise from recognition of a segregation both biological and cultural. In its cultural aspects particularly, an elite has rarely escaped developing vanity and complacency in those within and envy and malice in those without. Many ill-founded, self-styled exclusive elites of fashion and ostentatious wealth have cropped up today and in history, and fairly often, as in the French Revolution and the court of Charles I, they have met their desserts. To distinguish from these what might be called elites of merit—medical doctors, Nobel Laureates, Ph.D.s, authentic saints, military heroes, cardinals, great inventors, and artists, and others who have earned rank by performance—let us call the latter "choice groups" in that they are *chosen* for outstanding abilities, whereas elites generally need not be.

It is unfortunately a fact of history, and of the shabbier side of human nature, that such genuine "choice groups," open to all who can qualify and greatly needed by society for their contributions and their managerial expertise, encounter almost as much hostility from the "sub men" below the average as do parasitic elites. Weyl (1973 and elsewhere) has given us a view of some adverse effects of resulting "aristocracies" and the reaction to them, on the history of culture and government, as, for example, in the assassination of presidents in the U.S.A. Darlington (1969) similarly sees failures of group survival by the envious or uncomprehending laying of punishing burdens on leaders. Plato's guardians, chosen for complete disinterest in power and position, have not escaped conceptual criticism by academics. Catholicism ranks envy among the "deadly sins"; probably a Beyondist evaluation would have to give it a still more egregious and dangerous standing.

If Beyondist societies plan to evolve at the best possible pace, as is likely, it is almost inevitable that they will set out to create an advance guard of the highest possible ability—the best that can be constructed from the available gene pool with superior education. Since these experts will tend to get culturally separated, also, as indicated by home and school education and backgrounds, they are likely to form either an almost distinct "choice group" or, more naturally, at least a far-out, skewed segment of the population distribution curve. So long as democratic ideals prevail it will be necessary to take strong steps to bring up the rear, for an untroubled democracy depends on there being not too great a spread in *genetic* as well as in *educational* levels in its members.

The upshot of these social realities, in terms of needed Beyondist ethical values, is that, regardless of whether the problem is met among individuals or among subgroups, the ethical values must encompass charitable and cooperative adjustment to certain forms of inequality, eliminating self-destruction and group destructive hostility, envy and distrust.

Here and in the earlier chapters (Numbers 5 and 8) in this book, we have discussed and accepted the principle that natural selection requires the *precondition of a genetic diversity* (what, on each single trait, is inequality). It behooves us, therefore, at this point, to confront the whole problem of the *real* and the *political* use of "equality." The man in the street is himself usually under no illusion about men being born genetically different in capacity—tall or short, keen or poor in eyesight, variously resistant to diseases (malaria is a standard example), and more or less intelligent. The values humanly given to these are a different matter; for example, tallness is favored, e.g., in sexual selection, but physiological engineering would indicate why beyond a certain point it brings reduced survival, so that over half a million years mankind has kept to about the same stature. Moreover, beyond the uncertainity of human evaluation of these differences stands the uncertainty in regard to environment; for the gene advantageous in one environment may be disadvantageous in another.

However, in a given culture a given trait can be evaluated (see below), and on a probability basis, *all* conceivable human cultures and environments are likely to find certain genetic endowments universally inadequate. And it is inconceivable that *any* environment could be put together that would make all traits equally desirable. The most common rhetorical reaction to inequality is that it is "unjust." Indeed, in much of the popular media one could easily conclude that the terms *inequality* and *injustice* are synonymous! Here we run again on to the confusion over "rights" discussed elsewhere. Our society today declares that all have a right to equal opportunity, while our religions, including Beyondism, declare that all have equal spiritual worth and rights, i.e., the rights to the dignity of an unknown potential. Rights have to be contracts, and so far as an individual signs himself into a state or church, his rights are to the equalities just indicated. But biologically he has no contract to equality, and, if we suppose some supreme being to have designed the universe, it would seem that such rights were never intended. One has then only the right to variation and adventure on the course of evolutionary advance.

As for the relation of inequality to injustice, some common-sense citizens have, as we have seen, added the viewpoint that "injustice is the equal treatment of unequals." It is clear that if we take off from the premise that the group has, if possible, to survive, then equal treatment of unequals is unethical. One would not spend large resources of physical education funds to train a man of diminutive physique for the Olympic shot-put competition, or endow university scholarships for individuals of, say, I.Q. 80 or less.

Confusion over the meanings of equality, justice, and freedom have caused much bloodshed, and threaten all real social progress. We have paused here to recognize clearly the four forms of equality and inequality that individuals can encounter in society.

1) In biological endowment.
2) In social and political opportunity.
3) In the level of actual effectiveness, and use to their fellows, that they have reached from the interaction of 1) and 2).
4) In the spiritual sense of respect for the individual, based on the individual's potential relevance, in ways inscrutable to us, to the process of evolution.

Opponents of recognizing and accepting inequality in any form, if forced to open their eyes to facts about the first above, have two possible arguments against its having any substantial meaning: (a) that the number of possible endowments (e.g., traits of intelligence, emotional stability, etc.) is so great that there is a high likelihood that people will be equal in "desirability" *when averaged over all traits;* and (b) that genetic traits desirable in one environment and culture are different from those needed in another so that no "absolute" goodness can be assigned to any biological trait. The latter must immediately be accepted, unless one can show that certain traits are inherently advantageous (or disadvantageous) in *any* known culture. But in accepting it, we recognize that people can still be unequal from the standpoint of desirability in a *particular* culture. A colorblind man is subnormal in a hunting culture, but equal to others in, say, a computer culture.

The "total effectiveness" argument has been seriously put forward by respected writers, who argue that though in, say, a technocratic meritocracy, intelligence, mathematical ability, perseverance, etc., are clearly desirable, yet generosity, friendliness, altruism, etc., are probably equally important, though no scholarship examination measures them. The fact that the latter are not measured, or able to be appreciated in, say, a school scholarship or college entrance examination, does not mean that they do not count in life. However, in regard to the hypothesis that individual trait endowments, as finally reached through the interaction of inheritance and learning, "even up" in social usefulness through their diversity, *the facts are against it.*

Psychological studies show that, if we rate traits on estimates of their general desirability, such traits are not *randomly* related in the population as the "evening-up" hypothesis would require, but are somewhat positively correlated. Fisher (1930) speculated that the free promotion process would tend to bring desirable traits into positive correlation, and the work of Chassell, Terman, and the present writer shows this to be true. For example, Chassell found intelligence and altruism positively correlated. Terman found intelligence and emotional stability correlated, and the present writer found ego strength, superego strength, and the development of the ideal self correlated (about $+.20$, $+.55$, and $+.50$ for the sides of this triangular relation (Cattell, Eber, & Tatsuoka, 1970). It is true that this is for a particular culture (Western) and may not apply to those features of group survival common to all groups. But at least, just as we can find what traits have positive weights for successful performance of a particular job, so we can in principle sum across job and citizen contributions to a particular culture and discover the weights of traits—or the genetic parts of such traits—that best contribute to that culture as a whole. On the other hand, if we imagine all the possibilities in the whole wide universe, we cannot know what the weights would be for each of these, and, in our ignorance, the best conclusion is a nihilistic one: that all traits are possibly equal in importance. But in any real cultural situation, the fact that weights are unequal, together with the fact that traits are not chance-related, but systematically related by desirability, means that the undoubted biological inequality implies also an inequality in fitness to contribute to the given culture.

The second proposition above—equality of opportunity and political influence—also requires closer scrutiny. Equal educational opportunity actually increases, with age, whatever differences exist genetically, just as a willow, a Scotch pine, and a sequoia tree, properly attended to, will show increasing differences of height with time. Christ's parable of the talents also describes how equal opportunity to unequals quickly leads to unequal performance and station. Here we encounter an absurdity in those who simultaneously call for Equality and Liberty, showing this to be an ill-thought-out slogan. Our second principle above—equal opportunity—is essentially *freedom*. If such liberty exists along with the first principle, that biological inequality does and should exist, then inequality in later life will unquestionably arise. The only way to gain equality is then to enforce it artificially, i.e., to abandon freedom in favor of dictatorship. By that course, as doctrinaire socialists like Proudhon and Bakunin insisted, all persons should then have the same social access to the most beautiful women (provided by the State), and presumably wear the same state uniforms! One must declare a different conclusion: that liberty means inequality, and that injustice is the equal treatment of unequals—*in certain circumstances*.

On the one hand, one does not need to disagree with *practical* "socialism," e.g., the community ownership of its water supplies, its military defenses, etc., and, on the other, one needs to avoid also broad equality slogans that ignore circumstances. In ethical values and laws, unequals must commonly be treated equally. But at the heart of the Beyondist ideal of maximum evolution is the requirement that individuals should be different in their genetic endowment, and, as we have seen, in any *given* culture this implies that they are unequal as well as different, and that this must be accepted as realistic in social arrangements. The social arrangements concern particularly the various services which society has developed to take care of those who lag. Considerable inefficiency and waste has recently been brought to light in such social services. But the root psychological cause, residing in the overblown parental instinct in the practitioners, has escaped public notice. In Sheldon's investigation of young delinquents he states, "Nearly every well-case-worked youth had developed a stage presence calculated to 'bring out the mother' in the usually personally frustrated social worker." Such systematic psychological perversion tendencies must be watched.

In the present chapter we are concerned with Beyondism's social policies in the genetic area. The need for eugenic steps, as mentioned above, is quite obvious, but other requirements are more subtle. The issue of equality we have argued leads to equality of opportunity and political rights. These are necessary because, not knowing beforehand what is best for a new adventure, it is important to give opportunity for all kinds of innovations to develop. But, as will be pointed out when we come (Chapters 19 and 20) to effects of present individual principles on social structures, democracy, which is one expression of "equality," will work poorly if the range of ability and emotional maturity is too great. In the U.S.A. today, for example, more exact records are beginning to show a decline in school achievement records and that about a fifth of the school population is functionally illiterate as well as amazingly ignorant and misinformed on matters relevant to intelligent voting. It is true that there could be an argument, from the standpoint of population genetics (but not from any cultural standpoint) that natural selection operates more efficiently with a larger genetic range. This we do know, but we also know that an attachment to democracy will be more natural and stable when greater genetic and cultural equality actually prevails. Jefferson wrote that "Whenever the people are well informed they can be trusted with their own government" (1961). Unfortunately, surveys show that three quarters of our high school leavers are far from being well informed. An important quality of a democracy is what might be called the people's "coefficient of rationality and knowledge." We have to admit elites; but can we save them from the sin of pride and the arrows of envy? Chaucer called envy "the worst of the seven deadly sins." It often arises from the failure to develop gratitude to the leader. People need to direct more of their pity to struggling leaders. Instead, as Johnson said of picayune criticisms, "Mankind expects from genius a uniformity of greatness, and watches its degradation with malicious enjoyment" (1972). To this one may add Macaulay's comment on Francis Bacon, "No reports are more readily believed than those which disparage genius and soothe the envy of conscious mediocrits" (1897). Lincoln's comment shows his usual wisdom: "You cannot strengthen the weak by weakening the strong." Yet *entrenched* elitism in government is unsupportable. The genius of World War II, Jones (1978), tells us, "If I'd relied on the British Government there'd have been no radar and no Spitfire," and in more general terms Freud warns us that scientific elites can be and often need to be as ruthless as those of old religions. Yet inequalities of authority must exist and humanity must deal with them wisely.

Society on Beyondist principles will cut out inequalities inconsistent with the primary needed inequality, but has to find what range is optimum. It has then to teach ethical values consistent therewith, and this involves clearly separating in people's minds the different forms and meanings of inequality above. We must forever abandon the grey mirage of a completely classless society and the accompanying note of an equal wage for skilled and unskilled work. In discussing evolution and revolution, we conclude that, though both have their place, much that was done by revolution could have been done by evolution. There is also good reason to believe that intolerance of inequality is one of the "gut" causes of revolution and revolutionary doctrines. (It is difficult for a clinical psychologist to read the biography of Marx [Weyl, 1977] without concluding that envy of the British middle class, who ignored him, produced his greater interest in the bloody revolution, rather than in the needed analysis of what social developments were to *follow*.) Beyondists, seeing the distinctiveness of much unreasonable social envy, therefore, need to study carefully legitimate and illegitimate envy and their social outcomes. (Legitimate envy may be a necessary trial of leadership's capacity.) The psychologist should study, for example, how the emotional drives concerned came about in mammalian and especially primate evolution. It is clear that the self-assertive drive, which functions in all jockeying for leadership, has had the useful function of testing leadership, to ensure the best. Like any other erg, it tends also to overshoot its function. But to make mammalian societies workable, the erg of self-abasement—the root of admiration and reverence—also evolved. It eliminated group loss by substituting an innate ritual of surrender and cooperation for fights to the death, still preserved in our political party rituals. The answer to the problem of destructive envy is thus such just and objective promotional procedures as permit, with good discrimination by the individual, of admiration and identification instead of frustration.

In a recent poll in Japan, 9 out of 10 respondees placed themselves as members of the middle class. This is what a nation needs, and what it should aim for, eugenically and therefore economically. This easy kind of equality can exist still with the irrationality of some envy and the emotional pull that "All the world loves a loser (or an underdog)." Yet, as we have seen, a certain range is desirable and, as an educational specialist (Bereiter, 1966) says, "Enabling each child to realize his fullest potential" allows greater final differences when inherited differences reach full flower." The opposite to this adjustment is what forced Coriolanus to leave Rome "Where gentry, title, and wisdom conclude but by the yes and no of general ignorance." What Winston Churchill wrote with unusual foresight in 1908, "Dimly . . . I see the outline of a policy of social safeguards . . . which I call the 'minimum standard'." When two years later he set up Labor Exchanges and relief, he set society on a path which has unfortunately provided a net in which an eighth of the population is not comfortably caught and by which education and national defense are impoverished.

The crash "elimination of elites" reached a more than Russian equality in the Chinese "cultural revolution." A visiting top scientist (Nobelist Bardeen) observed "elimination of a cultural elite was one of the goals of the 'Cultural Revolution' . . . now they are not trying to do research. They're trying to catch up with what's been done in (Western) technology but they are not doing anything original."

To give us some idea of who does what, we may look at the statistical biography of 10,000 children born in one year in the U.S. (Compiled by Harry Latshaw, Division of Special Education, Baltimore Public Schools, Baltimore, Maryland).

STATISTICAL BIOGRAPHY OF TEN THOUSAND CHILDREN BORN IN ANY ONE YEAR

Those Who Die

1323   Die before the age of twenty.

Those Who Live

34	Are crippled.
15	Are deaf or hard of hearing.
5	Are blind.
17	Are visually handicapped.
86	Have tuberculosis or are malnourished.
260	Have defective speech.
86	Are so emotionally unstable or delinquent that substituted care is needed.
8	Are so mentally defective, dependent, or delinquent that institutionalization is needed.

78   Are mentally deficient and in need of special classes.

347   Are mentally handicapped and in need of opportunity classes. (Vocational level - manual labor)

1214   Are dull normal, and in need of occupational classes. (Vocational level - semi-skilled trades)

5206   Are normal, and fit into regular grades. (Vocational level - Skilled trades and small businesses)

1301   Are bright, making a college education usually desirable. (Vocational level - larger business enterprises and professions)

20   Are sufficiently gifted to make professional and research education highly desirable.

In terms of effect on progress, much depends on the elite of 20. Here we meet again the problem of "love of mankind" as seen by a Beyondist. A forthright extirpation of the influence of this beloved mediocre is cited by Xenophon alleging that Socrates frequently quoted Homer's description of Odysseus's restoring of order in the Achaen assembly, by striking the common men with his staff and telling them to sit and listen to their betters. "For you are unwarlike and without valor and count for nothing either in battle or in council." (I.A. Anderson, *Xenophon*, Scribner, 1974). The expression is one with which the Constitution writer Hamilton would have agreed, but which few today have the courage to make. We must recall, in support, that mankind would never get anywhere with leaders who love it as it is, but only those who are benevolent to the coming man. As Rowse says, "The cult of the common man is the greatest enemy of incentive, quality, and achievement. In itself it is a lie. The age of Shakespeare was not afraid to face the truth about human nature and the human condition." Today we are.

Chapter 16

What Are Beyondism's Implications for Genetic Social Action: II. As to mechanisms?

The preceding chapter has evaluated the genetic goals of a Beyondist society, both in terms of within-group selection and of diversifying, from existing races, the genetic pools generated in different groups. As we shift attention here to the methods needed there will inevitably be some repetition, but from a new angle.

The practice of eugenics has always been its weakest, most vulnerable aspect. In part, we shall look at the suggestions of the eugenics of Darwin, Huxley, Galton (especially 1883), Pearson, Wells, Fisher, Shaw, and other trail-breakers. Their efforts met the historical accident of being propounded just before Hitler's lunacy, which, to the minds of the undiscerning, led to eugenics acquiring, among other undesirable features, the tang of inhumanity. Actually, in the history of human movements, it takes second place in humanitarian movements in the last 2,000 years, only to Christianity and Islam. Anyone with a biological education—or even simply knowledge of nature—must be appalled by the endless cruelty of Tennyson's "nature red in tooth and claw" and dismayed by the terrible cost in suffering by which each small gain in human or animal sensitivity is mastered.

By contrast, eugenics, exercising all the knowledge of genetics that we now possess, permits us to mold human nature—or the domestic plants and animals that we handle—without those demoralizing costs. In a given society it aims, simply by control of birth rates, to reduce the proportion of severely handicapped and miserable, and to increase the presence of those citizens happily adjusted to advancing culture.

In classic eugenics it is customary to speak of "negative eugenics" as the avoidance of the birth of the physically and mentally handicapped. It constitutes a generally "bringing up the rear guard," to reduce the genetic lag behind any kind of functional society. By contrast, *positive eugenics* is conceived as arising as an overall advance in both the average and the leading minds of and physiques of society. Love, as we have seen in Chapter 8, has its distinctive hierarchy of objects. As Santayana tells us (*The Sense of Beauty*), "that which is common to all men is the least part of their natural endowment." Human nature directs our love; but perhaps it directs too much. Positive eugenics is where concern is most needed.

The obstacle put in the way of eugenics in this century, since its proposal 90 years ago by Galton, have sprung from every imaginable misunderstanding and special interest: from employers fearing a dearth of low level labor, to denyers of the natural "restriction" of heredity, to the aggrandisement and defensiveness of racial groups, and to soft-nosed "feeling liberals" who think that "love" of life should be uncontrolled.

Any investigator soon comes to see the terrible cost which society pays for listening to these and ignoring the need for foresight. Mankind prefers to alternate sentimental indulgence with ruthless cruelty, as the results of following the former close in with the latter. Even on simple issues of overpopulation, there are those who, in India for example, object to the foresight of surgical action (voluntary sterilization) while simultaneously complaining bitterly about the epidemic disease of starvation such action would eliminate. It remains to be seen whether democracies will accept leaders with disciplined thinking, and whether there will be leaders willing to be reproached for mediating between reality and the "I want" of the improvident mob id, by respecting the new findings on human heredity.

In practical eugenics against a standard of group survival we have to consider both the *average* competence and the *standard deviation*. The problem that presents itself to group selection direction is "Are the improvements in society due to the intelligence of the leaders or that of the average population members" and "Should eugenics aim at one or the other?" Clearly it is possible for one group to succeed relative to others, largely from the wisdom of a few outstanding leaders—so few that they mean very little in terms of the genetic average level of their group. One may guess that intergroup success is more tied up with the *average* population intelligence in a democratic society than in a dictatorship. Consequently, if natural selection is to raise group averages, it might be well to have competition operate *only* among democracies! Actually, it is only an elite, persisting across generations, e.g., as in ancient Egypt, with a dull mass below, that this "unfairness" of competition due to elite eugenics exists. For in serious war, democracies quickly cancel democratic rights and assume the structure of a government dictatorship, with the allegedly most able directing. The issue is real, in that Britain was probably saved in the second World War by generations of eugenic inbreeding among its leaders. But cultivating a high group mean versus a high elite mean is a quite secondary issue within eugenics.

Some thoughtful, insightful criticisms of eugenics certainly exist to be discussed, and let us deal at the outset with three main queries as follows:

(1) Does society have the right, the duty, and the technical knowledge to shape in any way the next generation?

(2) If advances in education, in medicine, and in genetic engineering can take care of the defects eugenics, in part, sets out to eliminate, is it necessary to influence birth rates?

(3) If concepts can be reached of what is desirable in the distribution of intelligence, resistances to disease, etc., is it possible to set up acceptable social procedures for reaching them?

Our answers to the first of these has already been given: that societies *already* shape the next generation, by schooling and home influence, in an approved direction, and that since culture to some extent shapes genetics, control of the genetics of the next generation is not new. A democratic society can decide democratically where it wants to go genetically just as it does educationally. If one accepts the Beyondist position of deliberate participation in diverse adventures of evolution, then it is not only society's right but its *duty*, in eugenics as in education, to give direction.

As to the second question, it is possible , as we have been reminded, in some defects, e.g., poor vision, readily to correct by environmental means. But in others, indeed the majority, e.g., mental defect, diabetes, kidney disorders, etc., the conditions can only be palliated, and, frequently, remain a heavy lifelong expense. School education of the borderline defective now costs over twice as much per child as for the normal child, and the end result is still significantly below what is needed in a self-sufficient, voting citizen. The social burden (consider, for example, the cost of kidney dialysis) of palliating genetic defects of a major kind would increase with time (unless reproduction is denied), and a point could be reached when survival of society is threatened through a burden causing inability to attend to normal necessities.[34] The number of children that society can support is essentially fixed, and every support of a person with extremely low intelligence means the loss of three or four normal children. This point is brought out in recent eugenic surveys in China.

Genetic engineering for humans is at this moment overplayed by the media (in the spirit of scientific fiction). Its real role, either as the intervention between parental sperm or ova and the child, as negative eugenics, is to prevent defects. Its use as positive eugenics, to create superior qualities, is a long, long way in the future. However, as seen in the preceding chapter, it may well have an important role eventually in what we have called for above as genetic adventure—the call for the balancing of cultural sources of innovation with new *biological* sources.[35] It is in para-eugenics, in search of tentative, new advances, rather than the removal of a specific known defect in an individual offspring, that genetic engineering has a great future role. Let the scientist not overlook that until the person with a novel mutation has lived his life its value cannot be known, and since important social emergents can arise from the interaction of many individuals with specific genetic qualities, the effect on *a whole society* needs ultimately to be studied before such creative genetic engineering can be adopted. Genetic engineering is limited by our ignorance of the more subtle social "pay offs."

The third influence affecting the genetic pool, and one open to manipulation (after the birth/death rate balances and the approaches to genetic engineering), is that of hybridization, involving immigration. Obviously remarkable creations have been made in plant and animal breeding by these means, and a psychiatrist like Kretschmer (*The Psychology of Men of Genius*, 1931) and many historians claim to have seen cultural spurts through *gifted* peoples hybridising from migrations and interbreeding. The real source of gain in these instances seems to be more the initial selection for giftedness than the hybridization as such. In the U.S.A., praises are traditionally sung to the Melting Pot, but the first requirement in successful plant hybridization is a rejection of perhaps 90% of the hybrids as unsuccessful. As in the case of the foundry, the scoria produced must be removed from the melting pot if the remaining produce is to be above the average of the contributors. The appearance of unfortunate combinations goes on naturally, and this, rather than the sociologists' wild western frontier, is very likely partly responsible for the higher crime and insanity rates in the U.S.A. than in the parent countries. It is probable that *some* elimination of unfortunate combinations does, even under present haphazard circumstances, slowly go on. Nevertheless, the average citizen seems to be mistaught that the melting pot is good per se, in the first step, regardless of whether selection is made, in the indispensible follow-up, to bring out the more effective combinations.[36]

With most traits, whose genetic parts are due to many genes, such as intelligence or stature, a hybrid typically falls (dominance aside) half-way between the two parents. The same holds for hybrids of racial groups, so that virtually all studies of intelligence on white-colored crosses show the intelligence on a sufficient sample to fall halfway between the two groups. This polygenic action is characteristic of the majority of normal traits.

The first concern in planning immigration for absorption into the nation's gene pool must be the long lasting *genetic* effect, and the second, the social, ethnic effect. For this latter the psychological evidence is that family attitudes, religious values, etc., respond only very slowly to the formal school education of the new nation and many attitudes have an almost genetic permanence. As George Washington reminded his contemporaries on immigration (Congress, Nov.19, 1794), "they retain the language, habits and principles . . . which they bring with them." (Our plan of analysis handles this effect in the next chapter.) As far as genetics is concerned, an *average* of the two blending races is the main consequence in all polygenic traits. When a wise democratic choice on immigrants—rather than some quick search for cheaper labor—is made, it is surely necessary to ascertain that a fair deal in exchange of good qualities with the existing population is being made. The hardships which effectively selected among the Jews, the Pilgrims, the Vikings of Britain, Normandy, and Iceland, and in Huntington's (1927) study of the migrants who established Angkor Vat, as well as probably the recent migrations of some Koreans and Vietnamese to the U.S., have been lacking in regard to most world migrations of recent years. That is to say, the selective effect of migration upon the average in the migrations is uncommon and neglected. Positive surveys and evaluations have in fact been lacking in the larger immigrations to Britain, the U.S.A., France, and elsewhere for some hundreds of years. As Sheldon well says (*Prometheus Revisited*, 1975), "In the face of promiscuous miscegenation the potentially valuable new genetic combinations are lost in the shuffle." Advantageous hybridization is a great genetic art. Herrnstein (1971) has found himself having to disassociate the prestige of intelligence testing from the now much attacked U.S. immigration act of 1923, which sought to guide immigration according to the I.Q. levels of countries of origin. That this act was soon repudiated was no loss considering the level of intelligence tests and sampling at that time. But *in principle*, and if it included all manner of traits, it would have been an *advance* on anything else—certainly on what *followed* it, as the new rule that anyone *in* the country could arrange to have as many relatives as he wished put on the quota.

Invasion by organized parties, such as in the Spanish invasion of South America, the Israeli occupation of the West Bank, or the Anglo-Saxon invasion of Australia, almost certainly supplanted a less advanced race and culture. But immigration guided only by the whims of "feeling liberals" will almost certainly be shown to have lowered the standards of a number of modern countries. This is where the expressions—"race-crossing" and "miscegenation"—derive their separate distinct meanings. A recent analysis shows that over *one-half* of the population increase in the U.S.A. in the last few years has been constituted by legal and largely illegal immigration and only one-half from the reproduction of the pre-existing core of two hundred million natives.[37]

Having introduced the major influences of eugenic and migrational change, let us pause to put them together in the perspective of all influences in a nation's genetic change, which are:

(1) in and out migration,
(2) differential birth rates,
(3) differential death rates,
(4) differential marriage rates (regardless of illegitimate births!)
(5) differential lengths of generations,
(6) sexual selection,
(7) assortiveness of mating, and
(8) mutation changes,

to name the most important. (Genetic engineering, presently at virtually zero action, might become a real influence later.)

Regarding in and out migration, the matter has been discussed above so that little need be said. A group needs to adjust economics, for example, to avoid, in immigration, for instance, a "brain drain," and its immigration policies need adjusting to reduce entries of those who have not shown themselves capable at home of reaching a good level of civilization (see Hardin, 1977, *The Limits of Altruism*). There is also the question of retaining a socially effective degree of homogeneity. Especially we need to keep in mind Sir Arthur Keith's summary: "A social pyramid which is to endure must be made of individuals, preferably of common racial origin, who are conscious of a common evolutionary destiny and work together to attain it. The Roman Empire is an example of a failure to observe this" (1949). An evaluation of the "melting pot" theory is undertaken elsewhere, but let us note re ethnic plurality the thoughtful words of Matthew Arnold, that "The mixture of persons of different race in the same commonwealth, unless one race has a complete ascendency, tends to confuse all the relations of human life, and all men's notions of right and wrong."

Regarding differential birth, health, and death rates, enough has been said. As societies become "domesticated," selection is shifted from death to birth rates. That change that never today becomes sufficiently consciously realized when we speak of "selection." Incidentally, the present realitivistic ethics often leads the young to attribute—on a misconception of Freud—all their faults to their parents. The counter argument to this particular side-stepping of responsibility is that they should have chosen their parents more carefully. The only possibility here is eugenically to choose better the parents of the next generation.

Sexual selection has interesting but probably trivial effects. The handsome man may be more able to choose the more beautiful woman, but this does not prevent the plain marrying the plain and having at least as many children. If there is some overall greater ousting from reproduction of the less sexually attractive, that is not necessarily a eugenic advance; for it is a judgment of man, not of nature. Indeed, the notion that eugenics calls for interference with marriage choice, in the sense of enforcing homogeneity is one of the standard misunderstandings.[38] Students of evolution evaluate sexual selection as frequently a move in a biologically questionable direction. The stag laboring under the weight of a too ornate set of antlers, and the Hottentot woman so protuberant in the rear (by preference of her men folk for a biological bustle) that she can scarcely sit comfortably in an ordinary chair, are victims of the whims of sexual selection.

On the other hand, *assortive mating* (sometimes called "assortative")—No. 7 above—has some group survival worth. In the intelligence area its action has meant that the above average intelligent person tends to marry another above average, while below average persons also come together. (Vandenberg [1965] and Jensen agree in putting the correlation around +0.4, but Johnson considers it lower in the U.S.A, relative to Europe.) Its effect is to leave the average unchanged (if there is no birth rate differential) but to produce notable results as we shall discuss.

Setting aside from the above list No. (1) immigration, and No.'s (3), (4), (5), death and marriage rates, etc., we recognize that the humane process—that of birthrate differentials—by which genetic changes can be shaped need to aim at (1) a high community average in each measurable *desirable* trait or genetic component, (2) a diversity and distribution of endowments—at least away from complete homogeneity and toward a distribution fitted to society's occupational and cultural needs, and (3) regardless of the *mean* level, a sufficiency of individuals *really high* on such valuable qualities as intelligence and character, for the sake of improved leadership, in areas from science and invention to government.

The question of whether natural selection is still operating toward group survival is answered primarily by a comparison of birth and death rates for desirable qualities. Except perhaps for death rates from such factors as smoking, alcoholism, automobile accidents, and life style, socio-medical intervention has probably wiped out most of the survival differentials based on death rates rather then birth rates. When birth rate differentials remain the decisive factor, and are allowed to operate dysgenically, without social control of births as well as deaths, "fitness" takes on a new and sinister meaning. Many an academic population specialist today calmly admits, with an almost cynical detachment, that the unemployed, with large families, are the "fittest." That civilization would probably reverse the ordinary definition of "survival of the fitter," and lose its beneficial action, has long been recognized. As Carleton Putnam (*Race & Reason*) has well said, "the taxation of success, enterprise and thrift to support failure, indolence and improvidence is (now) institutionalized." Outside Beyondist thinking, however, the supreme importance of society recognizing its ethical duty to the next generation and to the evolutionary principle has scarcely been recognized, and when it has, a shrug of the shoulders at the concept of enforcing legal responsibility, or even economic encouragement of eugenics, has left open the possibility that we are due for a lingering decadence.

Here is a domain where Beyondism definitely demands ethical values neglected or avoided by most traditional ethical systems. Granted an extremely simple method of birth control, aided by social work, the socially unfit who have previously had large families of neglected and illegitimate children will be glad to avoid the burdens they have suffered.

Let it be recognized the we are not arguing from an oversimple relation of social fitness to genetic fitness, and that we recognize many exceptional individual cases. That is to say, we have to think statistically—which the average high school graduate today apparently finds difficult. With the various other factors and intermediate links, the correlation of social fitness and genetic desirability might be only, say, +0.4. But so long as it can be kept statistically significant it is our best guide to a general policy, free of interference with personal sexual life (such as has had to be instituted in China).

If we had in education a training to think statistically and biologically, we would not have eugenic arguments confused by such issues as sterilization of the mentally defective, which concerns only perhaps 1% of the population. A little recognized problem in the social judgments of citizens is that, as McConnell points out (*A Legislator's Listening Guide to the I.Q. Controversy*), "Most persons have little intimate social interaction with others whose I.Q. differs from their own by more than 20 points. As a result, most Americans seriously mistake the life styles of other population segments." (The present writer from being once a school psychologist in a big industrial city can strongly witness to this.) The need for definite handling of the span of borderline mentally defective individuals becomes clearer with first hand experience.

It happens, as we have seen in the previous chapter, that assortive mating tends fairly strongly (compared to random mating) to increase the number of persons above, say an I.Q. of 130, who would be leaders. This goal can, of course, alternately be achieved by encouraging a high birth rate in brighter parents. Assortive mating has the defect of increasing also the number *below* an I.Q. of say, 80, but there again birth control could reduce that class's birth rate. In any case, people's personal proclivity for assortive mating is an adjustive procedure that the state neither can nor should control. The evidence of Cattell and Nesselroade (1967) and others is that marriages are more stable when like marries like—on virtually all traits. Assortiveness in mating—on esthetic, social, sexually attractiveness, and economic grounds—will continue to play its part despite some interruptions by greater travelling facilities and learning of foreign languages (languages are one of the greatest forces in maintaining separate national gene pools). It operates in the widest sense, in any case, regardless of whether the chosen traits— esthetically, socially, and even, to some degree, sexually—are natural or acquired. That part, at least, is natural is surely indicated by the fact that positive sexual selection is absolutely widespread in the animal and insect world, and is a powerful agent in the progress toward distinct species from distinct breeds. There is even an analogue at the physiological level in the body's rejection of grafts and transplants in proportion to the genetic distance from its own chromosomal make-up. This cultural side-effect puts limits to genetic hybridization plans that go too far.

Both in human history and in animal and plant breeding there has been, as noted in the preceding chapter, a rhythm in which relatively pure lines are first established and then, often, hybridized. The spectacular effects of such processes with breeds of plants and animals, when particular crosses can be organized for use in one generation, has tended to bring to our attention the need in human evolution for attention to segregation, as in racial histories, to stablize unique, relatively inbred lines. (Of course, new mutations can occur just as well in hybrids as in diverging isolates. However, there is a sense in which cultivating new mutations in isolates corresponds to a productive undertaking, testing new patterns, contrasted with a business of taking in one another's washing, as in hybridization.)

Regarding mutation, one should distinguish between what geneticists quantify as normal "mutation pressure"—essentially the readiness with which a gene "clicks" from one allelomorph to a generally previously known alternate—and a radically new mutation not previously present in the gene pool. It is surely likely that in a society seriously pursuing a Beyondist goal, *there will be very great attention to provoking and evaluating entirely new mutations, by natural processes or genetic engineering.*

Normal rates of occurrence of mutations in man have been worked out, and it is recognized also that perhaps only one in a hundred or more can be considered advantageous, as would be the case if one made a hundred *random* alterations in, say, the shape of a bicycle. That slowness and chanciness is why the course of evolution has been cruelly and boundlessly costly of life. It is also why the current concern about mutation pressure from medical x-rays, nuclear power, and nuclear warfare has mounted so high. Yet if there *were* ways—such as amniocentesis is demonstrating—of detecting deleterious mutations, in order to abort before the infant is formed and born, this dread of increased mutation rates might give way to speeding them up, to advance the evolutionary process. For it is only a eugenic compassion for the increase of individuals whom natural selection would eliminate miserably after birth that causes our fear of increased mutation rates. At present, the possibilities of actively pursuing increased mutation rates stand only at the level of science fiction. Yet if evolution is the goal, then some humane method of increasing the mutations among which to choose will probably come in time to be seriously sought.

In the preceding issue of what the *aims* of Beyondism should be in the *genetic* domain we made an argument for developing the one species-genes of man into a number of *distinct species*. We did so from a survey of the biological world which suggested the improvidence and danger of putting all one's eggs in one basket. This multiple deviation of mankind is a long-term, but vital, objective, and we have admitted that some leading biologists think this development would be difficult or impossible. Earlier we have pointed out that Beyondism is little concerned with existing races, but sees the future races, in any case, with which its principles have to deal, as genetic fashioning by *distinct cultures*. This will happen naturally and unconsciously through the selection peculiar to cultural values—the "cocoon" or the "old shoe" effect. But progress could also proceed through a deliberate genetic intervention based on what each culture considers important for mastery of the environment.

The difficulties which cause some scientists to see this branching of the tree into new species to be impossible are not arguments against its desirability, but only against the probability of man's overcoming its difficulties. As man's capacity for intellectual understanding of the mechanisms of society has increased, it has so far led to division into ever larger numbers of countries and religious aggregates. Presumably, it would readily be possible soon, in the opposite direction, to make the earth a single community, in the sense of a single nation or primary group. As we have seen, from an evolutionary standpoint this would be the final catastrophe and the ultimate extinction of human progress. What is actually needed is a far more subtle unity, a federation of nations, each nation as free as necessary laws of order permit, and all united in supporting a central research institute to sustain the common goal of differential evolution. That is to say, we need to reach the achievement of a *spiritual unity with bio-cultural diversity*. And if we have confidence in man as a species, we should want to see him multiply his species into a whole genus of species.

The privacy walls that have so far aided segregation of cultures, and their special blends of archetypal geographical races, have been not only distance, geographical barriers, the immigration offices, and the family ties of the language barrier, as just mentioned. For biologically we must recognize, as seen in Chapter 17, both some *psychological aversion to binding with too remote physical types*, and probably also some actual biological reduction of fertility (spontaneous abortion, largely) in less mutually internally consistent zygotes. Difference of religion has also aided segregation, and also those roots of marked differences occurring in other cultural values, as shown in the comparative instability of marriage of dissimilar cultural types compared to similar partners. The Jews and the Mormons, for example, give us some idea of how effective, over generations, the development of seriously considered cultural divergences could be in evolutionary forms, if practiced as an ideal over sufficient periods.

Although the notion of socio-cultural segregations proceeding to the point where distinct species begin to appear may seem improbable—with the immense counter forces from increase in communication, travel, and mutual imitation going on in this generation—it *could* yet occur. It could occur also through more dramatic happenings, like solar system "space" colonies being cut off by natural events for some centuries. But it could also occur, with a heightening of Beyondist ideals and its new morale, *by voluntary and mutually agreed autonomy of cultural-genetic groups* pursuing, with special affection and devotion, their own chosen experimental paths under common federal world government.

The reader will recognize that, in dealing as compactly as is necessary here with so vast a science as population genetics, many complex and fascinating concepts must be treated in an approximate style, and many question marks left to be answered by its now rapid development. Such a classic as Sir Arthur Keith's *A New Theory of Human Evolution* (1949) and many fine, more recent, writings filled with appreciably advanced information, of which Roberts's *Natural Selection in Human Populations* (1959) and Lumsden & Wilson's *Genes, Mind and Culture* (1981) are excellent examples of complexity handled with clarity, can introduce one to these new vistas. An instance of the simplifications we have seemed to adopt—but without major error—is the expectation that the level in one quality arises largely from one gene, whereas in fact most trait levels are usually due to additions of gene effects (polygenic action) plus emergents from interactions of genes in different positions (epistasis). Reciprocally, one gene has several effects. Further, those effects may appear only in *some* environments. When we spoke of the advantages to a society of having a diversity of genes in reserve, against sudden environmental changes, we referred, in fact, to this phenomenon of one and the same gene having unsuspected qualities "up its sleeve." A good empirical instance occurred when certain insects developed resistance to insecticides. As Dobzhansky aptly asks, "What was the gene for DDT resistance doing in the house flies during the aeons of time before DDT was discovered?"

A group positively planning well for its future will employ all three of the above: (1) differential birth/death ratio rates, (2) rhythms of segregation and well-chosen hybridization, and (3) creation of mutations along with genetic engineering. It will also, as Jensen (1973) points out, seek to increase its supply of high I.Q. (and other desired qualities) by favoring assortive (similarity in pairs) mating. He estimates that we presently have about 20 times as many leaders above an I.Q. of 160 as we would have with random, nonassortive mating (*Genetics and Education*, 1972). These methods we need to use toward group goals to bring about by a collective movement of its citizens (a) *survival* of the group, and (b) launching out on its own unique evolutionary adventure.

As far as sheer brain capacity is concerned, the judgment of most physical anthropologists is that no discernable progress has occurred in the last 12,000 years—or, say, since Cro-Magnon times. Probably there have been local instances of higher development, as in the aristocracies of Mycenae, of Rome, of Greece, and of Israel. If we survive the present world-wide "immediate welfare," pure charity, philosophy, future anthropologists may well declare the 20th century—the science-pampered century—the worst backslide in human quality in ten thousand years. Selection did not just stop; it went into reverse gear, multiplying, by false handling of the problem of the incompetent, the nonproductive, and the casually hedonistic, the incidence of lower capacity (Van Court, 1986; Vining, 1982).

So whether we will be able to pull out of this dive before "hitting the ground" is a moot question. The fact seems to be that humanitarian-hedonistic policies are now world wide, and there are no hardy barbarians outside the walls to step in, as in 400 A.D. The numerous existing equivalents of the Roman proletariat's "bread and circuses"—in food stamps, TV, etc.—will act as the originals did before. What a contrast to today is the fierce selection of the late medieval years that begot the Elizabethan flowering in England and strengthened the social, imperial, and scientific innovation of the eighteenth century!

In principle we see that within-group and between-group natural selection operate necessarily in mutual supporting action. We need to look at this again. The gross fact is that in the face of within-group degeneration of values the between-group selection is the final "safety catch" operating when the within-group selection fails. It is the electric fuse that blows when the house circuit is badly used, i.e., when dysgenic trends take over. It is like the bankruptcy procedure that finally charges corporations whose internal expenditures exceed their incomes through poor organization.[39]

That the downfall of whole societies has occurred historically through principally their failure to abide by internal eugenic requirements and other systematic processes is a claim made by many historians and social scientists of broad vision—Toynbee, Spengler, Gibbon, McDougall, Huntington, and others. Each of these puts his principal emphasis on a different explanation, respectively, for example, a severe challenge not met, a loss of morale, the enervating effect of Christianity, the sterility of the elite, the upset of a academic system, and environmental effects, such as a change to a desert rainfall level, or malaria or lead poisoning, and so on to even more specialized and trivial causes.[40] But a dysgenic trend is commonly recognized in all.

The present writer's (*Fight for our National Intelligence*, 1937a) with Elmer Pendell's (*Why Civilizations Self-Destruct*) and the researches of Van Court, Fisher, Vining, and several others, have put most emphasis in this decline on a genetic effect of *differential birth rates* in regard to intelligence. (In the next Chapter I shall point to perhaps equally important environmental, cultural, sources of possible cultural decline.) What is certain is that cultures and their associated race mixtures *do* fail, in many cases after a period of impressive cultural productivity. They "go down the drain of history" in unmistakable fashion. Just as with individuals, they seem to have died of many different diseases, but a dysgenic trend is always visible. There *are* also instances—perhaps Egypt with its three thousand years—of death by the analogue in the group organism of sheer old age in the individual organism.

Old age may be a meaningful concept, yet most of these diseases of whole societies certainly seem in retrospect to have been remediable. Far-reaching social, psychological, and genetic research is needed if we are to answer the question, in the first place, whether death or old age in groups is inevitable. The beginning of such analysis is the gathering of reliable quantitative records on social and psychological indices, as instanced above. Several pioneers—Buj, with his inquiry on national ability resources, Lerner with data on declining school standards (Cattell, 1982b), the Educational Test Service with its yearly nation-wide attainment surveys, Young and Herrnstein with their examination of the structure of a meritocracy, Adelson, Gibb, Rummel, and Cattell with their longitudinal studies of nations such as Australia, Britain, and the U.S.A.—have alerted us to some of the diagnostic signs and possibilities.

Our present chapter concerns genetic aspects, and we need to concentrate on the genetic evidence regarding the inheritable trait of intelligence, which has been most researched. In the first place, while we cannot safely conclude that the recent fall off in scholastic standards comes in the main from genetic changes, there is good reason to believe that downward genetic changes are occurring in the intelligence distribution, and badly need social awareness and counteractive efforts. From the time of the present writer's early (1937a) survey and those of Lentz (1927) and others, up to the recent checking by Vining (1982) and Van Court (1986), one must conclude that in Britain and in the U.S.A. (and presumably in most similar cultures)—results suggest that the birth rate is see-sawing between a normal and a dysgenic trend as to intelligence, and tending to the latter. These studies mainly offer inference on intelligence trend from intelligence test results and birth rates.[41] (Incidentally, the members of Mensa, the highest 2% by I.Q. of the population, have a birth rate well below replacement level.) But since the evidence is also clear that birth rate is inversely related to social status, it could be that the same dysgenic state is presently true of other qualities than intelligence. (For, except for some qualities of rapacity, there is a positive correlation, weak but significant, of most other desirable, effective psychological traits with social status (Cattell, 1941; Chassell, 1935; Stricker, 1981.)

Those who think up obstacles to eugenics ask, "How do we know what is desirable?" and "Who has the right and the means to control births with respect to these qualities?" With respect to the latter, we have already replied, "The democratic will of the people, exercised just as it is in its educational ideals (and as it should be in its immigration ideals)." As to what is desirable, there are a great number of traits about which one must be neutral, for lack of knowledge, and also because an optimum diversity is needed for a complex society. But there are qualities such as intelligence, emotional stability, conscience (altruism, superego), and especially size of memory, in our complex society—all of them with an appreciable heredity contribution (except conscience, where it is comparatively small), about the desirability of which, in a modern society, there can be no doubt. And on the physical, medical side, good health and energy, good sensory organs, and especially longevity are important. The targets of negative eugenics have long been discussed, and genetic consultation centers on avoidance of defects have become informed and ever more widely heeded in recent years.[42]

One may ask why so much trouble has been taken to find out what specifically is happening in regard to intelligence, when it is possible to argue that other traits are equally socially important. The reason is that one must begin with something, and something indeed validly measurable and of obvious importance to the group. However, there are hundreds of other psychological and physiological attributes that need improving, and which doubtless will soon be better understood eugenically. In this connection, one can recognize from clinical and educational psychology two distinct types of traits in relation to natural selection: (1) traits like surgency (F), affectia (A), premsia (I), which, like stature, constantly are adjusted a little by natural selection to maintain an ideal *central* value, and (2) traits such as some intelligence (B), ego strength (C), and superego strength (G) for some *increase* in which there is *always* demand, and which increase slowly under effective selection. It is perhaps noteworthy that the within-family genothreptic correlation for crystallized intelligence, ego strength and especially superego strength tends to be positive (Cattell, 1982), suggesting that the family presently does all that is possible to increase the child's level in these by education.

In the 180 years since Malthus (1976) called attention to problems of excessive *size* of population, the politicians and the media have at least caught up with free discussion of the issue, and considerable action on "population policies" is now forthcoming. The problem of quality of population, however, has been very gingerly touched—if at all—by politicians. We have to thank reformers like Ms. Sanger and scientists like Colton and Pincus who mastered the chemistry of "the pill" for the possibility of a eugenic national solution. It will require for success a spread both of biological, scientific education and of Beyondist ethics. With these we may expect economic and other encouragements to eugenics and deterrents to dysgenic life styles to be inaugurated, as discussed in the next chapter.[43]

If regard for the "human capital" of a society is to be morally in the forefront of public thought, the deterrents to wastage must soon be brought under the control of law; for genetic delinquency is actually more damaging to society and unjust to the individual born than are many crimes now regarded with marked repugnance. It is true that at present the sterilization of the genetically unfit, who continue to disregard social standards and pressures, is out of fashion, and laws once on the books in several states of the U.S. are now often disregarded. This is partly due to the flagrant abuse of sterilization by dictators and partly to the backward swing that can occur when a permissive society prefers to avoid immediate difficulties at the cost of graver ones ahead. Incidentally, one would estimate that voluntary self-sterilization has considerably increased in the past thirty years—mainly among the intelligentsia! Clearly, a wise society needs to find ways of handling *genetic* delinquency, along with its measures to inaugurate positive eugenics, through the full range of the population.[44]

The first need today is *research* on the nature of the genetic problem and on the efficacy of the proposed solutions. First, we need a thorough check on the findings of Cattell, Van Court, Vining, and others on the outcome of birth rate in relation to intelligence. Second, we need a check on Sir Ronald Fisher's (1930) proposition that it is in the competitive middle range of society that the birth rate relates most negatively to desirable traits. ("He travels fastest who travels alone.") Thirdly, we need investigation of the particular case of conscience (superego). Sir Francis Bacon made the sound observation that "There is rarely any social rising but by a mixture of good and evil arts" (which he realized most fully after his impeachment). The "good life" is eagerly, knavishly depicted by the advertisers as an excess of material possessions. The present day move to fuller employment of married women raised the question of whether this will mean the recession of the more able from motherhood (compared at least with the large families of many on relief.) If these influences were more even, we could expect some positive relation of conscience to birth rate—at least among those with a Beyondist view of life.

Another approach is to reward the more able citizens by giving scholarships to their children of above average ability. Or, as Leonard Darwin advocated (see Cattell, 1937), adjusting income tax more powerfully by child allowances, which would encourage those to have children who have a higher probability of more gifted children. This we can look at in the next chapter, concerning income tax.

The leading question, that can be answered only by far more research than society has yet dreamt of applying, is whether the above suggestion of leaving birth rate to direction by social status will work. Cattell (1937) and others have shown that even *within* one occupational group (postmen, for example), there is at present a negative relation of intelligence to family size *in culture fair intelligence tests*.

As to social status itself (Cattell, 1942; Sims, 1928; Stricker, 1978), the correlation with intelligence is only about 0.2 to 0.3, but this is partly because other positive qualities, with inheritable parts, such as energy, emotional stability, etc., enter into determining status. It is possible that valuable "advice" on fertility could be given even today by doctors and psychologists on the basis of measurements, and this technical approach should be developed. But as society advances in ethical sense, there should be little need for such aid, if birth rates are *adjusted to social competence, and parents' ability properly to support the young*. Elmer Pendell well sizes up the counter influences to this ethic when he says (*Why Civilizations Self-Destruct*), "The goals of our most capable people focus on an expensive car, a diploma, writing a best seller . . . .Bringing children into the world receives no status points . . . . In fact children now get into the way of activities that win social recognition." This is the cost of having free social mobility.

There seems little doubt that if this were recognized as a desirable ethical norm, all but the incorrigible lowermost tenth would voluntarily conform. For "noblesse oblige" and belief in the value of their culture and stock would lead to more than "replacement" families in the better endowed, while those of poorer earning capacity are really not eager to lose a modest standard of living. Even by that standard, however, since no society has ever existed that is free of delinquency, some decision will need to be made for dealing with genetic delinquency.

Finally, if we are to give attention not only to the selection of persons best fitted to *any* society, but also to the ideals of a *particular* society, attention must sooner or later be given to that problem also. Darlington (1969) has given us a glimpse of the reality of genetic shaping even to hereditary *occupations* and social subgroups. The extent of such genetic adaptation may still be speculative. But there is no doubt that it operates on the broader field of nations, segregated by language barriers, migration restrictions, and devotion to a particular culture pattern. As suggested earlier, direct genetic creativity and fostering of mutations is needed to avoid such a merely stagnant adjustment of gene pool to a fixed culture pattern, desirable though that is. The progressive movement by within-group natural selection toward highest survival potential for the group in comparative group selection is thus a two-handed manipulation (a) to follow the group cultural demands, and (b) to create new genetic mutations, in the spirit of experiment, of initially unknown potential.

Again we encounter the problem of evolving within "a cultural cocoon." It is widely said that man does not learn to adapt to his environment, but adapts his environment to himself, and that this could lead to his "persistence in a cleft in the environment," i.e., to an "eco-niche." No less a person than Thomas Huxley declared that "The history of civilization details the steps by which men have succeeded in building up an artificial world within the cosmos" (1901). That this increasingly happens cannot be questioned, but it does not place human evolution in any totally different category from all previous mammalian laws of evolution. The belief that it would easily happen overlooks the fact that man's constructions have to fit the laws of the environment. He still has to address himself finally to the environmental demands, as he builds his "eco-niches." He defends himself more effectively from gross and inconvenient environmental demands; but he still has to deal with those demands and face the ever-changing face of nature. Environment has the last word.

Chapter 17

What Are Beyondism's Implications
for Cultural Aims: I. As general goals?

As with the genetic problems of society, so here, we attack in two steps: (1) general goals, and (2) mechanisms for achieving those goals.

The general goals are implicit in the ethical and spiritual analyses of earlier chapters. They express themselves in specific educational, economic, military, research, social, and artistic areas whose mechanisms are discussed in the next chapter. Here we look at the general goals in terms of (1) propagation of Beyondist viewpoints and the acceptance of change, with high morale; (2) the institution of social research as a guide, on an unprecedented scale, in economic, social, educational, and other decisions of society; (3) the organization of cultural differentiation in nations, in a comparative research framework; and (4) the effecting of a change from dependence on revealed religions to guidance by an international scientific study of evolution and the spirit of Beyondism.

As to the first, the need for change is currently very great. There has been a constant accumulation of scientific contributions to our society on a *mechanical* level, without any parallel development of broader moral vision. There is consequently a spreading malaise, expressing the ancient cry, "without vision the people will perish." Innumerable special causes are named for the current problems, but at their root is the lack of perception of the evolutionary process and its consequences for man. It needs great men, in science and in statesmanship, to perceive this, for, as Burke inscribed on the memorial to Chatham, "The means by which Providence raises a nation to greatness are the virtues infused into great men." Do we create and possess them today?

We need vision and guiding hands on *change*. The first difficulty is that change becomes every day more rapid, without any conscious adjustment in most people to this fact. As Bury (1920) points out, in most periods of history—throughout classical and medieval times—the idea of a continuous progress had not entered people's minds. People expected the next generation to have to live essentially the same life as themselves.

A suspicion of change is well justified, for the now widespread idea that all change must be progress is quite wrong. The media—and various movements—today speak of all change as "reform." But, as Darwin well observed biologically (1871, 1917, p. 140), "Progress is no invariable rule." Greek philosophers, like Plato and Aristotle, expected city states to go through a *cycle* of democracy, oligarchy, and dictatorship—with no straight line of progress. The security and civility of the Roman Empire obviously regressed to the age of the medieval robber barons. In the biological field, it is estimated that 99 out of 100 mutations are for the worse, and have to be painfully removed. And there may be losses through shifts to a more restricted environment, as in the cave-dwelling animals that lost their eyes. The position of conservatives, questioning change, is thus not without statistical real-life support, though it cannot be fully supported because it lacks the vital, adventurous spirit of Beyondism.

We see a little further before our faces in cultural than genetic matters, but basically we are in the same trial and error position. Let us recognize that both the movement springing from revealed religious values, and the moral, emotional indignations of "feeling liberals," lead to mistaken steps much of the time. The adventurous spiritual quality of Beyondism does not avoid tragedy, but the scientific bases of its movements makes tragedy less likely. Sir Francis Bacon spoke as Lord Chancellor to his King: "Innovations are dangerous, beyond foresight" (1893), but he added that those knee-jerk conservatives who used his observation "as a commonplace against all noble reformations" are even more in darkness.

What Beyondism sets up, in conscious, recognized research, as a safeguard against the comparatively heavy losses of existing methods, we shall soon see. It concerns examining all the channels of the *new* which we have previously considered, and need to consider again, namely: (1) conceptual invention, social and material; (2) cultural borrowing, by imitativeness or enforcement;[45] (3) change, by no means always good, produced by pressures of human demand released by some other change, e.g., the demand for expensive recreations and unneeded travel created by advances in applied science, e.g., jets; (4) pressures of the natural environment—drought, plague, ice ages; (5) pressures of other competing groups; (6) genetic mutations making new adjustment possible and necessary. These are, exhaustively, the origins of change, which the Beyondist position has to integrate.

We see hopefully in several current movements some of the necessary elements in a Beyondist orientation to studied change. There is today a considerable interest in "foretelling" the future of mankind, much of it is spectacular, pseudo-scientific, "science fiction" language. But beyond this lies a broad spectrum of scientifically planned synoptic writing, as in de Chardin, Sagan, Jaspers, Rummel, Toffler, Williams, Waddington, and others and such technical writings as in Bell's "Toward the Year 2000" (1970). They concern nuclear war, pollution, decline in energy sources, overgrowth of population, and similar vexations more obvious to the educated. Meanwhile, however, we have the writings more basic to Beyondism, such as Wilson's *Sociobiology*, Graham's *The Future of Man*, Salk's *Anatomy of Reality*, Darlington's *The Evolution of Man and Society*, Herrnstein's *I.Q. in the Meritocracy*, Jensen's *Genetics and Education*, and earlier but still highly relevant books like Fisher's *Genetic Theory of National Selection*, McDougall's *Is America Safe for Democracy*, and Keith's *Essays on Human Evolution*.

In spite of "leadership" of the average man being in the hands more of the former types, of apocalyptic, sophistic, journalistic, writing, from a morass of revealed religious values and "instant satisfaction," fads, and fashions, *some* progress in serious thinking has been made in the past fifty years. It comes through the steady rise of science, percolating through top writers into all fields of thought, for example, from energy to abortion, to population, to nuclear warfare, and to national education, checking, appraising, and informing.

Meanwhile, however, Beyondism faces a solid obstacle from quite a different direction than those possibly partly educated confusions, namely, the fact that about an 80% majority of members of Congress and Parliaments come from a legal, not a scientific background. Law is obviously a *first* step in the right direction, away from "might is right." But in the U.S.A., the great liberal analytical minds do an immense business of re-interperting a 200-year-old Constitution. In Britain and other less stylized and documented constitutions, they interpret series of precedents. The incisive mind of a good lawyer is valuable in government; but are not the new and biological problems such that at least half the congress should be scientists? The practical answer at the moment is that no truly leading scientists are willing to give up their hot pursuit of truth to be bothered with mediating on largely banal causes with banal people. But as the social sciences advance toward having something definite to say in social problems, this must alter. Indeed, if we are correct in what we envisage below as the growth of national and international research centers, investigating social trends, the role of the advanced social scientist must become prominent in government. Such a change will bring about a new atmosphere also in the concept of democratic exchanges as presently practiced. For whereas the lawyer politician hedges every recorded statement, to tie him down as little as possible, and often to convey promises he has no hope of fulfilling, the aim of the scientist is to use language and figures to say as pointedly and exactly as possible what he believes the truth to be.

The charge of the "Hush! Let's be diplomatic" group is a very old one in politics. Safe reception of such a change in speech to freer style requires a more educated voting group. Quite obviously, a necessary first step in beyondist "propaganda" is a re-orienting of the general school teaching toward a higher scientific and, specifically, *sociobiological* educational presentation. The *practical* modification of education, government, and economics which follows from the rise of Beyondism is studied in the next chapter; but here we have still to deal with engineering the rise of *the values themselves*. No important movement—political or religious—has risen without what the French call a "chapel"—a group in which ideas are shaped and their propagation instituted. Clearly, the complex truths of Beyondism will have to come from a higher institution, moving downwards in its influence. These truths are of such a different, less dramatic, more complexly informed set of values from, say, those of Christianity or Zen Buddhism, that they can only move from an informal group downward into the mass of the population. The *decisions* on values and their propagation belong to advanced university level institutions, which now need to be created and brought to scientific discipline.

Let us face the fact that the main problem in public thought today is that the journalists—the syndicated columnists—who write on matters of ethics, education, economics, and *any specialty whatever*, are not graduated professionals. (Justice Fein, in a decision for the N.Y. Supreme Court, recently ruled that journalists are not "professionals!") We see this in, for example, some of their recent attacks (including sheer ignoring) of Young's and Herrnstein's drafts on the meritocracy. They react to meritocracy mainly as persons whom *no* attempts at justice will satisfy, and on other questions they equally voice the views

222

of a neurotic, ill-educated public. Admittedly, we are asking journalists to get away from the voices of the street parade and the town meeting to voicing the views of a more trained, intelligent subgroup. Is this an opposition to "democracy"? Not really, as we shall see, for we have to admit the demonstrated defects of professional groups, and segregated, pluralistic social structures that lose touch with common sense. Meanwhile, as the following paragraphs bring out, the important new principle in democracy is that subgroups, guiding by technocratic expertise, should operate in a wider democratic setting. They should not, in the first place, pose as exceeding the real levels of predictive accuracy in their special fields (Vide the psychiatrists and treatment of crime!).

It must be realistically recognized that the *ordinary* process of democratic elections creates a governing *elite*. In the primaries, those active enough to want to be in a given party first choose "competent" people. This happens also in Communist Russia where only a keen minority trouble to be members of the party. Regardless of whether subsequent voting (by that section of the population that takes the trouble to register) is one party of only two parties, the successful candidates will *tend* to be well above average intelligence. It would be additionally desirable, however, that they pass exams in economics, sociology, biology, etc., relevant to their tasks, as Bernard Shaw (1944) seriously suggested.

Let us come to an illustration of basic facts in the form of two personal acquaintances. "A" is a classics professor—famous for his researches, with a deep grasp of the political and social wisdom of the ages. "B" is an ordinary person who does some gardening for me. He has been in jail for petty theft; he can barely read the newspaper. Yet in democracy as now practiced, the wishes of B in public affairs can completely cancel A's long-sighted contribution to the community. Of course, people will say, "But A has more influence in other ways on public opinion, by reason of his greater ability to express himself." This is scarcely true, for outside his speciality he is an ordinary citizen, deeply occupied with his art and science; he has no more role in politics *as such* than B.

A society under any real pressure cannot survive if it gives equal voting powers to individuals so disparate. The most democratic and liberal English thinkers at the turn of the century—the Fabians—who included such as Shaw and Wells—were almost the first—and in present causalness almost the last—to give this problem the attention it needs. Shaw (1944) proposed an obvious solution of requiring a citizen to pass a test of general knowledge (which would have been partly of intelligence) before being enfranchised. A public opinion still belatedly moving from the practice of requiring a minimum property qualification to vote apparently confused the two ideas, and Shaw's arguments fell on deaf ears. There are, of course, other requirements than intelligence levels if the present theoretical concept of democracy is to work. The Greek cities themselves switched from democracy to tyranny; and oligarchy knew them, too. The decisions of democracy require surely many years of experience—and from this conclusion the cheap politics of dropping the voting age from 21 to 18 is a regression. But there should also be tests of sanity and freedom from crime.

As suggested below, it is probable that the real development of democracy, inevitably demanding consultation with experts in an increasingly complex world, will in any case move further away from the "town meeting" with its decision by a simple addition of votes. But it is still likely that these developments will call basically for *selection* of a healthy, intelligent voting core, perhaps trimmed to about 60% of all potential adult voters.

But in any case, the idea that democracy or communism are *not* examples of "government by an elite" is sheer nonsense. And having to report back to the electorate every few years does not prevent their decision at a given moment being contrary to (and usually wiser than) that of the general population. The selection process has usually meant that the representative is not only more intelligent but that he or she cares more and is more energetic.

The newly designed Beyondist universities for both research and teaching, referred to above, we shall soon examine; but the topic of research brings us here naturally to the second of the main goals initially mentioned—that of an unprecedented installation of social psychological and economic research centers in every country, as well as a central international organization for their intercommunication. The undeniable fact at the moment is that we do not possess the actual power, inherent in the Beyondist position, to decide many ethical issues more reliably and objectively than can the revealed religions. *All* questions— in economics, social behavior, education, and military matters—are, in the last resort, ethical ones.

To these questions, and these hundreds of practical associated issues, e.g., "Do we want more employment or more arrest of inflation?" requires research on a positively gigantic scale, relative to the sprinkling of small-scale, inconclusive papers in academic journals by academic sociologists, economists, and others today. It needs a thorough searching of available sources by first-rate research leaders. It means that they be installed *full time*—like researchers in a wartime project—with all necessary support and opportunity. It means an increased rapidity of intercommunication, such as, again, characterized the several war-time research units we set up for research on radar, on faster planes, on officer selection, and on nuclear power during the war. In short, it means that the general public must prepare itself to sustain national research centers in social psychology, sociology, and economics on an unprecedented major scale. A nation can, in most countries, well afford this, with trimming of the fat of countless excesses, from drink to yachts.[46]

The informed reader will appropriately have doubts as to whether even the most generous support of science will succeed, with a continuation of present research practices, especially in that breaking open of the new problems of derivation of ethics, and prediction and guidance of social change, which Beyondism must do. At the present juncture in public discussion, the literary and journalistic intelligentsia, and the vested religious organizations of the past, feel alienated and alarmed by the rapid growth of intelligence-demanding scientific findings in all fields. They spawn ingenious doubts about what science can do, and magnify every temporary failure. Doubts, of a testable kind, are, it is true, essential to science, and there are real reasons to wonder whether science can succeed as it has in the past when it encounters the special nature of issues in this new complex, mathematical domain of social and biological science.

Stripped of the uniforms of those glib philosophical issues ("reductionism," "positivism," "dialectic materialism," etc., with which the journalist "intelligentsia" often hide the real anatomy of thought), there are essentially three problems in this research, two in the material itself, and one in man the investigator, that we must clear up. The two problems in social research admit of clean logical and mathematic statement, as follows:

(1) *Understanding the Action of a System of Elements Requires Regard for the Emergents from the Interaction of Elements.* That is to say, one cannot start with knowledge only of the properties of elements, available before the interaction, and predict the group-emergents. To know the full properties of the elements, we must know also the emergents. (In chemistry we do not know everything about chlorine and sodium till we know that one combination emergent is the taste of salt.) It is implicit in this statement that causal action also has circular and other "path coefficient" structures, so, in a human group for example, the character and performance of the individual is shaped by the

group syntality and the syntality character of the group structure (Cattell, 1948, 1961, 1980; McArdle, 1984).

(2) *The Data Base is Eternally Incomplete.* We have recognized from the beginning that evolution is not just biological evolution as Darwin studied it, but evolution of a universe by physical laws of change also, e.g., radioactive transformation, entropy, etc. Nevertheless, the physicist of everyday phenomenon on earth can get along with little concern for physical evolution in our galaxies. In psychology and the social sciences, on the other hand, there is such a difference of degree in this respect that we can no longer ignore the fact that we are involved with a one-way process. That is to say, in chemistry we can dissolve iron in acid and redeposit it, but in human affairs, as Omar Khayyam (*The Rubaiyat, LXXI*) observed:

The Moving Finger writes; and, having writ, moves on;

nor all your Piety nor Wit shall lure it back to cancel half a Line....
This means, in the first place, that the few years or centuries of past historical observations that will ever be open to us in quantitative forms do not permit quantification of the full population of elements (events) in earliest history necessary for a complete prediction or precisioning of a scientific law affecting future history.

These technical issues of the scientific analysis I have expanded on elsewhere (Cattell, 1980) in drawing up a person-society-environment systems model that represents perhaps an advance but still not the full evolution of a solution. Meanwhile, in the genetic-cultural area, there is a promising development of really precise models by Lumsden and Wilson (1981) (whose bibliography gives several others), and this genetic-cultural interaction is the most important of all in long-term calculations.

Looking at the problems, from our present position, in development of the human sciences, we have at least a good array of needed instruments of measurement, in personality, ability, and interest (dynamic attitude) structures; a broad list of social indices, carefully gathered for many countries; and a structuring of those group measures in syntality dimensions (Rummel, 1972; Cattell, et al., 1949, 1953, 1969, 1973, 1980, 1982). The handling of such data I suspect will now advance first through confactor, factor-analytic methods conjointly by R- and P-technique attacks, followed by the testing of the resultant hypotheses in structural equations. It is presently full of promise, but desperately short on research support.

(3) *Limitations of the Investigator's Mind.* As to the third problem —that inherent in man, the investigator, himself—it has two main

aspects. The first resides in his emotional limitations; the second in those of his cognitive powers. Intellectual discipline such as I have discussed elsewhere (1938, 1980), with external checks and balances, and idealistic dedication to science, can do much to halt the intrusion of personal, political, and sectarian emotional distortions. "Science as truth" is a deeply held belief of most scientists.

The second problem is more intractable. It is customary to think that support for gathering more and more data observations, for building bigger computers and more potent instruments, etc., can continue indefinitely the advance of science. But in fact, there is unquestionably a limit to progress eventually set by *the mental capacity of the individual and the species*. Science has been lucky, there has been no problem in recruiting the best existing intelligences, who in general know better than to divert such intelligence to political, military, and commercial activities actually less relevant to human welfare. My cat rests its head at the moment on one of my manuscript pages dealing with diagrams and formulae in connection with a systems theory of personality. I don't know what it thinks, if it thinks at all, about what these diagrams mean. But it is quite certain that by no means of discipline training could the cat be brought to understand them. Similarly, the best scientific training cannot augment our present upper genetic limits of intelligence to the point of understanding much in the universe that remains to be understood. The computer scientist's aim of "artificial intelligence" can by no means guarantee transcending our own powers in essentials. That is why Beyondism puts emphasis on social programs of breeding for higher intelligence and particularly on experimenting with mutations affecting higher levels of imagination. It also, as stated earlier, pursues evolutionary ethics on the gamble that when the more intelligent, insightful understanding is reached the philosophy of Beyondism will be vindicated.

Progress of that kind is for the future, but the sensible tactic meanwhile is to recognize where we are—and where we are not—able to use our present intelligence effectively. Is our intelligence sufficient with hard scientific work to answer a given question, or do we waste effort beating our heads against a wall? As examples of the latter, I have cited trying to answer the question of moral responsibility in relation to the paradox of having both determinism and free will, and of the beginning and end of time, and of whether an existent structure indubitably implies a creator, and of how consciousness comes out of basic chemistry, and so on. By all means, let us speculate on natural mechanisms, for boundless curiosity has to be encouraged. I believe for the present in determinism; but I find it hard to believe that in today's rainstorm the exact spot that each drop will fall on the pavement was already predetermined millions of years ago. But many philosophers are obsessional neurotics, unable to leave a picked bone alone, and ready to brew some rather pompous and opaque verbal stew to hide their failure. The scientist needs to have a good judgment of the firmness of the ground from which he jumps and the analytical instruments by which he perceives. Far too many "literary and journalistic" nonquantitatives attacks on social problems remind one of those military blunders in World War I in Flanders that cost half a million lives, when attacks premised on firm ground for men and artillery were not cancelled when the ground transformed itself to a sea of mud.

Let us not, therefore, deny guidance in social direction because our present firm ground in science does not immediately yield the advances that some perfectionist philosopher of science demands. Estimating as precisely as possible this margin of error in a scientific social recommendation will always be important in Beyondist ethics to adventure when the risk/gain ratio is adequate. Regarding the apparent end of determinism in physics, we shall agree with Planck that "It may be due to lack of knowledge of all the factors that we have no idea which way an atom is set to go."

This is perhaps not the place to enter in detail into the organization of the research institutes that Beyondism demands (see Chapter 19). But we may mention the general design—that of "free lancers" in universities (functioning partly also as a ground for younger men to show whether they can win their spurs as creative researchers) accompanied by *institutions of pure research* on the Max Planck model, interchanging personnel with the best universities. In both, but especially this latter, small teams with a democratic leader, gifted in smelling out the problems and shaping attacks, seems best. And here we face the problem that society has very limited resources of first-class brains. Science is in competition for them with industry, the military, politics, and the various other professions. Most scientific journals today, reflecting the distribution of scientific personnel, are filled with pot-boiling, career-demanded, mediocre but "correct" papers, or with the valuable, but not trail-breaking work of those who carefully check well-known hypotheses. Some way has to be found, in view of the boundless complexity and the strong mathematical demands of the bio-social sciences in Beyondism, to bring the exceptionally talented and creative individual's influence to bear. Science "has many mansions" and work for all dedicated individuals, but it has to give more attention to seeing that its geniuses are born, educated, recognized early, and put in positions of strategic leadership. We want no more of an Einstein having to earn his living in the patent office or a Faraday by packing books in a print shop.

There is, however, more to this large-scale development of social research than marshalling talent. A new type has to be worked out from a hybrid of the scientist and the politician (hopefully the statesman). After nearly a century of social thinkers like Wells and Graham Wallas, asking for scientists to take a part in government, scientists are still extremely rare in the government of, for example, the U.K and the U.S. Unfortunately, this outcome is undoubtly due less to public conservatism than to the unwillingness of scientists to suffer the irrationalities and stupidity that the present immovable organization of politics and public education makes unavoidable. Quite apart from the social compromises that make a travesty of truth in the application of scientific results, the scientist balks at the lack of more control over the subject matter in his research design—people—than with present values he can possibly have. He needs, for example, first, all sorts of data on psychological tests, personal attitudes, incomes, life styles, sexual habits, etc., than he can possibly get on account of privacy laws. Fortunately, provided he can get his information, he does not need to manipulate, by asking a group to go on a special diet, or practice sexual abstinence, since sophisticated statistical analysis methods will generally make up for the absence of manipulation.

However, let us not forget that research depends, in the last resort, beyond disciplined thinking and strategies, on the sheer intelligence of the researcher. To a cat a closed door is something that a human miraculously opens, and all the drawings of the handle mechanism placed before the cat will still leave it puzzled. It will be increasingly the case—unless we turn to breeding intelligence—that our top scientists, with all the data gathering in the world, will stand bemused at a closed door. But we can do a great deal yet before that day arrives.

In Beyondist cultural planning, a very different domain of concern has been skirted from time to time. We recognize that the main social experiment must depend on comparisons of independent and highly integrated social groups, such as nations. But in view of the fact that conquest and migration have led to many nations' being pluralistic, in the sense of containing easily recognizable distinct ethnic subgroups, one wonders (a) if these differences *within* the larger group could be used for research, and, (b) whether this pluralising in itself strengthens or weakens the group survival of diverse ethnic and other values.

One need spend little time over *class* diversity, because it is bound to arise in a meritocracy of freely promotable individuals. Some stratification will continue to arise genetically, economically, in recreational and social tastes, and in networks of congenial association. As when all strata meet in an English pub or a religious congregation, this has nothing to do with man-to-man intrinsic worth, respect, and political weight, but it is real in the more developed human areas indicated, and remains as a basis for research on the effect of customs.

Furthermore, one must note that a democratic organization of society is *born* as well as made. There is an optimum spread in, for example, ability which, if exceeded, makes a democratic structure hard to maintain. It is less clear, but possible, that too great a spread also in temperament could cause difficulties in democratic action. The spread in ability and education that we count necessary, for occupational reasons—including the high levels necessary for national defense and industrial efficiency—may nevertheless favor the emergence of elites and oligarchies ill-fitting a political democracy. However, properly to assemble and discuss the measures and the correlations depicting the functioning of social strata would require a book, and here we must pass on with an acceptance of "open" elites.

The question of optimum variety of ethics (racial and cultural) in religious and other subgroups has two aspects: that of assisting comparative research, as just seen, and that of national functionality. Subgroups may be used—but the main research designs here envisaged as necessary would begin by comparing the groups that show the *most* functional unity—in language, economics, intermarriage, and special ideals—namely, nations. But one must raise the research question whether there might not be an advantage—in getting quicker answers to comparative life style questions—in having a variety of relatively segregated ethic and religious subgroups within a nation? The answer is not clear, for we cannot easily allow in assessment of practices for the effect of embedding the subculture in a more dominant national culture. India, with its numerous language, racial, and religious subgroups (its perennial mutual riots and massacres) is sometimes cited as an example of the *obstructive* effect of subgroups on uniform progress, and even on steady economic reform and defense. (The ease of British conquest by Clive and Hasting sprang largely from this pluralism.) Recently in the U.S., observant writers have described the cost, chaos, and educational deterioration occasioned by minorities demanding their own language and customs in all public affairs. The verdict of most discussants seems to be well summarized in Nietzsche's "The best of their powers have a blocking effect on one another" (*Beyond Good and Evil*, CCVII). Nevertheless, the ethical position of Beyondism concerning pluralism awaits considerable research.

With this rather intensive study of the research needs in a Beyondist state, we come next to our third proposition: that Beyondism needs to cultivate and monitor *interstate* differences. This in practice may not seem to call for more than what is now done; but it has conditions and goals very different from what UNESCO and other "modern" international action groups tend to demand. For it supports the need for basic *independence* of countries as the basis of its data, and calls for the concentration on and mutual interest in their *differences*. It calls, in fact, for a spirit of responsibility for maintenance of individual differences in race and culture, for approving of them, and, what is more new, for extracting general laws and conclusions, for common use, from the outcome of their differences. It corresponds in ethical nature to the obligation to the competition of groups and to the evolutionary principle itself (4 and 7 in Figure 8-1).

The delicate difference in the Beyondist use of state of national differences is that it invokes both a "hands off" and a "hands on" action. It is "hands on" as regards concern for each group and the exchange of analyzed data with it, as well as, in special cases, exchange of population and cultural elements. It is "hands off" as regards illegal immigration, demands for special grants and "foreign aid," and anything but alliances for recorded cultural and economic exchange.

A positive new interaction becomes incumbent on Beyondist countries calling for the free exchange of all kinds of information, from a comparative study. From such studies (as in the syntality studies mentioned in Chapter 10), laws dealing with the consequences of various cultures and racial compositions can be made by the international scientists concerned and handed out as "advice" to the participants. Here the difficulty will naturally arise that some nations will regard even nonmilitary information as private, and subject only to espionage. To this there is perhaps no more subtle answer than that nations which do not contribute data should not receive advice. This same problem arises even in the privacy demands among clinical cases in psychological research, and the problem of effective sampling of psychotherapeutic results is currently still unsolved.[47] UNESCO currently comes closest to an international research organization, though this excellent institution is still burdened by early "social work" values, e.g., on free food distribution and other acts that need revision by Beyondist principles.

Finally, we come to the general aim of supplanting revealed religions and their tangled and frequently obstructive creeds by the general rationality of an evolutionary religion. This is a matter of teaching, and obviously, as stated above, it requires biologically well-informed pupils. As Jung and others have pointed out, there is some kind of innate need for believing in the occult, the mysterious, and the supernatural. Our study of the genetic gap has also brought out that the form of "spirituality" will differ according to the area of the ergs in which expression is most frustrated by the pattern of the present culture. Some expressions, notably of sex and pugnacity, are bound to be curtailed in our modern society. The search for the magical and the transcendental will therefore always continue.

As pointed out earlier, the pattern of ethical values to which we can best expect Beyondist influence to lead will come fairly close to what is common to Christian, Confucian, and Islamic values—but without the surrounding legends. There is every hope, therefore, that, as in Russia and China, most of the people educated without regard to the stories and superstitions, will accept essentially the same ethical values. In Russia and China, as communist countries, they will also need to accept the equally difficult proposition that Marxism does not spell out final values, which on a Beyondism foundation will alter with circumstance. (In particular, they will face the considerable task of accepting the role and purpose of biological inequalities, which are central in an evolutionary ethic.) Beyondism thus faces, once again, the task of transcending both the red and the black dictatorships. Only an open and unrestricted education can achieve this.

Through all these purposes runs the most vital one of deciding what elements of interindividual and intergroup behavior work out as most ethical, at a given place and time, and to this we turn in the next chapter. Let us frankly recognize, however, that though Beyondism naturally turns away from the intellectual nihilism of dope, perversion, idleness, and pornography, which are plainly antisocial, it cannot *yet* claim to a scientific research basis for its newer values. One must presently act on ethical probabilities and some standards of established religions while the foundations are being worked out.

Society is moving, at the moment, from the production-oriented industrial revolution to what has variously been called the "informational" or "communication" revolution. With that change goes a movement from production to service occupations, and a change, if conditions remain calm, to increased leisure. We have seen, however, how little we can predict the future and how little we can insightfully plan it. Over the great stretch of evolution, how far could a fish foresee and conceive mankind? We have just discussed the limitations to the success of a major shift to research institutions. Fortunately, these restrictions do not limit social experimental groups, and they only limit the firmness of the steps we take in social adventure and our capacity to evaluate success versus failure. But with the right spirit, experiment and diversity of design can go on. Some goals of idealists of the last generation—such as the mirage of the classless society and the abolition of competition among nations—will need to be seen in a broader perspective of values. The violent idealism of the young will need to be better informed. There must be a recognition that evolution means stepping out in the dark, and that failure is part of instruction about obstacles. In these cultural experiments we can restore a glimpse of the glory that formerly adhered to war and physical exploration. There is much to do, and really no need to cater for leisure by introducing trivialities. Culturally, we can "leap as swimmers into cleanness leaping" and leave "the sick hearts whom honor could not move" (Rupert Brooke, 1943). An undying fire of effort lies in guided and evaluated cultural diversity.

Chapter 18

What Are Beyondism's Cultural Implications:
II. Regarding political, economic, and other steps?

Let us recognize that in this final chapter on practical cultural steps, we enter, as the concluding words of the last chapter indicate, without the basic research which Beyondism requires. We have to proceed partly on hunches from general principles.

A perennial topic, on which some fundamentals have already been stated, concern "equality," as a practical political "ideal." We have seen it to be biologically, fortunately, not true. However, in the interests of group survival, social equality must be strongly maintained in terms of equality of opportunity. It is in the interests of group survival, because we do not know in any final sense what traits are most desirable, and we want to use all.

Equality of opportunity goes with democracy, but democracy is something more than that, and it is something that has to grow in meaning with Beyondism. Its variants are many. For example, we have commented that in Britain it is viewed largely as a political arrangement, whereas in the U.S. it has an almost religious meaning. To substitute a voting booth for a battlefield is its basic *raison détre*, on the grounds that normally a larger following would win the battle, and the odd case where it would not does not justify the costs of battle on each issue. Democracy's present-day problem is that, as Plato foresaw, it becomes legalized robbery of the haves by the have nots. Its second weakness is that it substitutes judgment by an ill-informed multitude for that of a selected intelligent elite. Elsewhere (Chapter 17), we have asked how Beyondism would modify these weaknesses in democracy, and have argued particularly of separation of judgment on what is *wanted* by the majority from judgment by democracy's elites on *how* to get it.

Genetically, we must have an aim presently not included in democratic ideas. We are reasonably certain that health, energy, intelligence, and capacity to reach emotional maturity, (C) factor, are important, and that most groups will want to enhance them. Here we can follow the same principles as in education of a meritocracy, cleared of some false interpretations. Different cultures will have different merits—up to a point. Some will especially cherish, say, musical creativity, others art, and others science. For the first, a good sense of auditory pitch (a heritable quality) is important, but, say, excellent vision, if flying is what is primary. Genetic emphases can be consciously guided.

Efficiency of a group requires in education the meritocratic principle: that longest and most intensive education be given in a given field to those more genetically gifted in it. It is a great waste and a great frustration to the individual to force years of education in violin playing on a child of I.Q. 80. (We do educate intensively at more than twice the cost to the community of the normal child, the borderline defective; but that is an attempt to avoid complete social and occupational incapacity. It belongs under the different principle of hospital care.) Incidentally, the failure in some countries to make streams of education according to general mental capacity is a great waste. The gifted are slowed down and bored; the less bright are "lost" and made unduly aware, in classroom interactions, of their disability.

Beyondism calls, in the areas where intelligence is primary—mathematics, classics, science—for special care, in different streams of classroom education. To this, certain people object on grounds of "justice"—a slippery concept when its real meaning is sought. It happens that in this era of increasing complexity, in the arts of peace and of war, intelligence is in short supply. It follows that more care needs to be given to begetting and training higher intelligence, and, if the open market principle prevails, there will be higher pay for an hour's work by, say, a surgeon of I.Q.140 than a taxi driver of, say, I.Q. 100.

How does this square with our principle above that society should accept biological inequality but insist on equality of opportunity? All horses at the start of a race begin with equal opportunity. Within a minute their opportunities, as chance of winning, are unequal. The equal opportunity to persons of different genetic make-up begins to alter from the moment of birth by (a) the effect of their own actions (A carpenter doing well and a carpenter sacked for alcoholism no longer have equal opportunity.), and (b) the needs of society in relation to the individual's gifts.

236

What do we say now about the meaning of justice and injustice? There are those who consider being born biologically different an injustice. Like being born to die in some four score years or sooner, it is a necessary price of evolution and though both belong to the tragic and heroic life of man, to call them an injustice, in a temper tantrum, is on a par, in Beyondism, with an utterance of "blasphemy" in a "revealed" religion. That society offers greater rewards to those born better able to help it is thus an unavoidable "injustice" if we would have societies survive. But surely there is no injustice in rewarding more, among those of equal natural gifts, those who work harder and suffer more stress, for the good of society?

The notion that society should share wealth quite equally among its citizens, which seemed so brilliantly original to socialist writers of the late nineteenth century, has been faulted on the common-sense grounds that differences of, say, extravagance, would make men who are equal today unequal tomorrow. If, as suggested in Chapter 16, a eugenic action with greatest individual freedom is to be achieved by allowing birth rate to adjust to income, the internal genetic movement of society toward better group survival would be arrested by equal income. It does not matter that those individuals happy in their jobs would often be ready to work for less, and that in certain small, definite segments of society, e.g., clergymen, artists, boxers, embezzlers, and rogues, so long as a positive relation exists *generally* in society between social contribution and the level of means to support a family.

From the standpoint of discussions about equality, therefore, we make sense of the words of Jefferson, Franklin, and others that "all men are created equal" to mean equal before the law, equal in initial opportunity, and equal in some spiritual sense that is not easy operationally to define.[48] But clearly there is no equality on (1) the various biological dimensions, (2) the various cultural dimensions, e.g., education, after personal history unfolds, and (3) on the genetic potential itself, before birth, if relative contribution to the survival of a particular culture is the arbitrator.

These truths thus affect also the inferences from Beyondism about what is to be done *culturally* about differences. In the first place, these facts lead to conclusions in economics contrary to what is commonly held up as an injunction of Christianity and other religions. Societies like those of the early Christians and early Communists, which started with the equal wage and sharing of wealth, finished later by paying bishops and commissars more than lower ranks. This could be a power phenomenon: that the leaders are nearer the decisions on use of resources. But one can see that at least some other factors enter. When, in Russia, and to a lesser degree in Britain, salaries were bestowed on abler young students to induce them to pursue higher learning to which their abilities suited them, an appreciable fraction still preferred to avoid the stress of study and gravitated to lower earning positions.

Since money can be exchanged for most—though not all—primary satisfactions—it is natural to make it the *primary* social motivator—though status, medals, social approval, and security play some independent part. Most thinking men, and especially the creative, are nevertheless haunted by Wordsworth's observation that "getting and spending we lay waste our powers." This is everywhere obvious in haggling and miserliness, and particularly evident in people trying to retain what they have gotten in the great annual income tax hunt. The tremendous waste of professional level intelligences in this bureaucratic income tax circus is, incidently, one more powerful argument for an equal percentage uniform tax—accomplished by a simple separate *family* allowance, *positively* correlated with income.

The effect of a free consumer market in regard to services and rates of earnings should, if normally operative, assist the eugenic process within society, the necessary supply of goods, and the cultural process of being willing to pay for and apply oneself to a higher education suited to one's abilities and occupational aspirations. The open market works without modification only where people appreciate more remote needs, e.g., those of the next generation, and of personal education. Basically, it is the commonly present dislocation of the distribution curve of human genetic *supply* (and the education that is properly geared to it) from the distribution curve of social *demand* that produces a wide range of earning levels. It is difficult for the nonsocialist rationally to defend this uneven earning, as well as the painful existence of a permanent pool of unemployed and the need for the various crutches, such as a complex differential income tax, to bolster a fundamentally poor supply design. This raises the question whether there are desirable objective bases for fixing the differentials of income. *Simple* application of supply and demand laws will not do, because demand is often irrational. A favorite film star or athlete often earns a hundred times as much as a scientist working on human health, or the discovery of, say, a basic antibiotic. Demand is only as good as the discipline of the average citizen extends. On the supply side, the birth rate of intelligence levels in an ethically undisciplined society again affects the supply-and-demand determined earnings, by a greater supply of lower intelligence levels than are needed. *With fewer lower level abilities and many more higher than now*, the garbage collector and the postman should command the same earnings as the lawyer and the architect. Over and above adjustment of income to the skilled market, earnings should, of course, also be adjusted to stress and risk and similar factors in the attractiveness of the occupation.

Granted that the first principle in the allocation of earnings should, in the name of survival of society, be that of a free market,—capitalism—we nevertheless evidently face the need for secondary principles. First, as regards eugenic values, the interplay of heredity (regression to the mean) between high and moderately high ability is such that better earnings need to be assigned to the moderately high as part and parcel of the *production* of really high ability. That is to say, supply-demand laws must include the demands of the unborn generation. This calls for a readjustment, by actual earnings or tax, that respects the second rank of high ability as essentially *part* of the first. Secondly, among adjustments of the supply-demand laws, there is, in a completely open consumer market determining earning, one correcting the basic weakness that the buyers' market determines what a person is paid. That demand extends all the way from preposterous earnings for the film stars, boxers, etc., cited to equally improper earnings by criminals. In short, in demand the tastes of the average (or subaverage!) buyer, rather than the needs of society seen by the wise, prevail.

Dictatorships, communist or right wing, have tended to overrule the consumer economy. Communism, for example, is said to do better by its scientists. Some interference with the consumer market has existed since history began. We see, for example, special help applied to science and arts by King Alfred, the Medicis, and many others. But so also have there been developments in democracy which, by heavy taxation, seek to correct, in, e.g., liquor, smoking, prize fights, and the like, the "consumer economy." Without any endorsement of dictatorships, one may note that Mussolini built a fine University of Rome for which a democracy had been unable to collect enough money, and that communist Russia spends a larger fraction of the national income on science than do the majority of democracies. It also, without haggling, spends more on national defense, by economizing on luxury expenditures throughout society. Again, it can be said here, as in genetic matters, that in intergroup competition a democracy more quickly and accurately gets the survival verdict that its level of thinking and acting deserves—though at a disadvantage relative to a population led against its wishes by an elite. The weakness of the consumer-ruled free market is epitomized in the millions spent on prize fighters, drink, film stars, horse race betting, and the like. It would be interesting to know what the average salary from 20 to 65 was for the discoverer of penicillin, of the transistor, and of the means to make the first successful open heart operation. From the biographies it is evident that all of these latter had a far more stressful time than a moderate income could have saved them from, and earned well below the caterers for narcissistic pleasures.

Let us recognize that each group's world philosophy has its own special economic recommendations. Indeed, with Marxism the philosophy *began* in economic dogmas. In Beyondism we see a free market as the basic definer of economic values, modified in three ways: (1) taxation for the services, such as health and military and public services, *which only the group can* provide; (2) an adjustment of earning differences by a eugenic rationale additional to sheer market values; and (3) the introduction of economic eugenic support for providing the next generation. Recently, there has been a demand also for progressive capitalism to become more "participatory"—that is to say, to direct society more by charities, educational innovations, political guidance, and organizational change. The need for diversion of power and influence—outside the monolithic power of a single government—has always been part of a democratic "warning," to preserve freedom and growth. We seem to be moving in the direction of this new unselfish capitalism of large concern. It is at least an experiment worth watching.

The need for (1) above is a commonplace; but one must add that government services, e.g., in postal and telephone, are often taken as necessarily a government monopoly when, in fact, private enterprise can handle them more efficiently.

The need for (2) is often discussed—notably by those who call for a single earning rate for *all*. The primary emphasis upon experimental variation and natural selection among groups argues for all individual and corporation competition being denied monopolies and for each being allowed to sink or swim according to its efficiency in the widest sense. It argues similarly on the worker's side, for an open market for the worker's wage—which to most feeling liberals will be anathema. Most capitalist countries accept trade union bargaining, but the result is that the extra wage gained is charged to the customer and sets off the round of continuous inflations—so unfair to the substantial fraction of the population not in trade unions. The liberal needs to be reminded that with the high birth rate at the beginning of the industrial revolution we have lived through times when the wage of a substantial group of people would have been negligible, and trade unions were a necessary temporary anticatastrophe organization. Continuous inflation, however, has been a feature of this period in which trade unions triumphed. We are now entering a different distribution of births, supply fewer at the unskilled intelligence level, when the trade union will become superfluous to raise wages to their good natural level, and when the garbage collector may command as good a wage as the teacher. Most capitalistic societies have met the excess in the lower distribution of ability, character, and education by fixing a minimum wage and supplying artificial support and welfare to the unemployed. It is obviously a burden on the employed, and needs removing by adjusting birth rates to social success and usefulness.

The differential earning rate should ideally both handle much of the eugenic need and the inducement to individuals to study and produce in higher skilled jobs. Its shortcoming, as we have seen, is that giving the customer what he wants creates a lot of worthless occupations—from sheer luxury suppliers to various degrees of crime. An equal wage for all—imposed by government—is, incidentally, not a Communist ideal. Khrushchev (1970) "I've never been in favor of reducing everybody to the same level" but "the wage situation in our country is all messed up." It is messed up because no clear principles for differentiation have been worked out, once tradition breaks down, in the light of ultimate Beyondist goals and the supply-demand laws. If we let the market rule apply to people, as Adam Smith and all argue it should for goods, then we have a basic self-adjusting scheme, requiring a touch of control only to curb absurd customers (to eliminate, for example, drug peddlers) and to provide services, e.g., police and teachers, that people are not far-sighted enough, usually, to provide for themselves. Insofar as the state has to fix certain wage differences, it needs clear principles and among these are the amount of training the job calls for, the amount of daily stress it occasions, and so forth. It is our contention that, although the birth rate should be higher for higher earning people, as the basic eugenic process, yet economics has to enter with an additional system. It costs, in today's dollars, between 150 and 250 thousand to raise one child to independence. This is a contribution to the state—there would otherwise be no state in the next generation—and those citizens who have families deserve to receive this amount, relative to those who do not bother with children. The lack of a eugenic economics is a staggering omission of attention to an obvious need.

The so-called "capitalist system" contains natural adjustive mechanisms that we dismiss only at great peril. It avoids even Marx's dispossessed proletariat if eugenics prevails; for a proletariat is born, not made, by economics. *Within* a country it meets to a high degree both the cultural and the genetic needs, but it requires some control of public taste and a periodic "disestablishment" of vested capital, both in individual families and in institutions, to prevent capital being tied up in obsolete institutions and "obsolete" talent in families.

One wonders also whether private enterprise cannot find a way of disposing of products without charging the consumer roughly 25% of the price of advertising. It is a colorful art, which children watching T.V. often enjoy as much as their parents deplore the interruptions, senseless as far as the main play or documentary is concerned. Would not one-tenth of the time spent on these parades suffice, if the point and character of the goods in one field were simply presented *factually* side by side? It happens to be true that in nature, advertising, in roses and the peacock's tail, plays a substantial part; but so also does constant death by predators and other activities dropped from civilization as far as possible.

Finally, in capitalist economics we come to the laws of inheritance of wealth, by individuals and institutions. Saving is desirable, and inasmuch as it is undertaken partly from concern for the next generation, it results in the inheritance problem. The inheritance of wealth is today justified on three main grounds: (1) that hard-working individuals save for a secure old age and that many die before achieving it and will it to the children; (2) that the proposition that higher ability deserves more assistance (mainly educational) is met by the fact that offspring resemble the ability of their parents, genetically, to the extent of a correlation of 0.5; (3) the more able tend to be better provided for educationally, to the extent that, except for a rapacious government, it would be hard for many to see to what institution the inherited property should be given. Although with its emphasis on the desirability of higher birth rates in the more able, some energetic and imaginative Beyondist argument favors retaining some connection of monetary inheritance with biological inheritance, it nevertheless recognizes that with one or two genetic steps the psychological connection falls low (e.g., 0.25 of uncle with an inheriting niece) enough to justify appreciable death duties on wills.[49]

While this reduction of financial inheritance has probably (under other motives) gone as far as it should, it is quite remarkable that virtually no nation has ventured to interfere with the maintenance of *complete* financial continuity in *institutions*. Yet it is perfectly obvious that many institutions continue "in business" long after the period when money was aptly contributed to them.

In the first place, the tying-up of increasing sums in institutions that do not actually produce useful goods or essential services is one of the several factors in inflation. But what is far more important is that these unchanging, locked-up endowments continue to hold religious propaganda, political patterns, and educational practices in original channels long after they have ceased to be appropriate. The two first are so gross as to need no illustration. The educational effect can be seen in England in the persistence of Latin and Greek in the public schools and the provincial Universities of Oxford and Cambridge long after it would have been more valuable for cultural vitality, prosperity of the population generally, and national defense to have spent at least half of those endowments on the broad scientific education that reformers called for in vain. Clearly, a Beyondist ethic would call for *progressive partial disendowment* of old institutions—slow enough to cause no hardship to existent incumbents—and managed along with reinvestment in institutions for which contemporary need could be demonstrated. That this could be a powerful stimulus to social scientific advance cannot be doubted when one sees, in actual historical revolutions, how much wealth has sometimes been untied from ancient hiding places, e.g., in Henry VIII's disestablishment of the monasteries. This redirection of capital is, of course, a central plank in Marxian arguments, which we can accept without accepting the rest. Any church, school, or business that rests on endowments made long ago may be holding up the transfer to new ends and compelling the worker to work at a disadvantage in his bargaining, because the redistribution of wealth is beyond his power or that of his representatives to alter.

This brings us to the fuller discussion of income tax we approached earlier. Each society has tasks to perform—defense, education, internal order, welfare—which can be done only by taxing all. There are, of course, different boundaries to what society believes can best be done by society and what by private enterprise. In free market societies, defense, internal order, and the provision of water, garbage collection, and other inherently group-health-dominated purposes, are given to the tax community, whereas education, industrial production, health insurance, and much else, is allocated *partly* to private enterprise.

Here we encounter a quite staggering paradox that seems never to enter public discussion. It is that, whereas a man contracts for services from, say, an insurance company, choosing a company to his liking and paying a fair rate regardless of his income, his obtaining of the *community* services are met by charges *according to his income*. It is surely questionable that there are any essential differences in the community services received by a man earning $15,000 a year and another earning $30,000. Both get national defense, police services, and all other community required services, but the latter pays perhaps three times the income tax of the former.

Where is the logic and justice of this widely, passively accepted ruling? There appear to be only two possible arguments: (1) That it is compulsory charity, fixed in the ballot box, from the haves to the have nots. Being compulsory it loses any of the spiritual benefit that might (by non-Beyondist ethics) occur to the giver and remains a form of theft. (2) That, cynically, the tax collectors know they cannot collect due contributions from people who do not possess a surplus. The latter, as the history of taxation shows, is the main argument.[50]

The effects of this uneven taxation are mainly two. (1) It shifts the burden of taxation from those below average to those above. The genetic effect of this extra burden on the latter is unmistakable, conspiring to reduce to a subnormal figure the birth rate of those who aim at more expensive education for their, generally, above average children. (2) Environmentally, it limits the real charity of the above average, and affects the direction of the "consumer economy" toward lower tastes in recreation and life style. Both of these—the genetic and the environmental—reduce the progress of society. And the effect of the genetic burden, as we know from species cases studied in biology, is very powerful over even a few generations in eliminating the variant carrying the slight extra burden.[51]

The remedy that Beyondism would seriously advocate is a *common tax*, fixed at a level that will produce the present national tax income, and terminating (among able-bodied men and women over 21 and under 70) at an income of, say, $7,000. Since the role of democratic voting has departed in several ways from any discernible right-left philosophy and increasingly acquired the secondary vice of being a means of "transferring" money from the haves to the have nots, it would be a necessary consequence that persons over 21 should have a vote only if they paid tax. This might eliminate from the vote some 10% of the population that can presently swing an important vote in a self-seeking direction.

A not-to-be-despised gain from the common tax would be the turning to productive work of the considerable number of professional assistants in tax evaluation and evasion now operating, whose abilities could add vigor to many activities valuable to society. This gain in the GNP would not be negligible. The problem in gaining social acceptance for a common tax is partly the encouraged habit of the man in the street of thinking in terms of "rich" and "poor," where, in fact, 80%

of the population are neither. The 10% of individuals with high earnings, who demonstrably (except for the Mafia) do not spend unduly on themselves, would be freer to contribute to charities that they esteem. And it is questionable whether elected governments have contributed as much to higher education, medicine, and more speculative adventures of society than the Carnegies, the Grahams, the Mellons, and the Rockefellers. The issue of having expenditures directed more by first-rate individual bodies, rather than elected political committees comes to the fore in this taxation, but we cannot pursue it here.

So much for the economic system needed *within* groups to meet the need of group survival. We need to discuss also economics *between* groups. There free trade is surely the proven solution. Contrary to this, there now arises the practice of "foreign aid" and the action of the world bank. As discussed elsewhere here, this for most citizens is a prime piece of hypocrisy, in which political manipulation hides itself as Christian charity. So long as it really remains politico-economic manipulation in favor of imitation of an alliance with the more successful "giving" powers, it is, however, entirely beneficial. But the giving to get a certain country "out of a hole," either that it can buy goods from corporations in the giving country, or truly as charity, is against the intergroup Beyondist ethic we clarified in Chapter 8. It reduces the growth of foresight and morality in the "beggar" country.

Let us consider next the mechanisms to aid Beyondist goals, those in the area of education. We have already sufficiently studied the meritocratic ideal (Young, 1958; Herrnstein, 1971) of providing the longer and further available education to those selected by performance and psychological tests. To avoid the mandarin culture of bureaucratic examinations, we have made it clear that personality and temperament tests should be included, as shown effective by Cattell and Butcher (1968), and that the margin of predictive error should always be calculated. At the present juncture, the schools are not availing themselves of more than one-tenth of the sensitive guidance that the resources of psychometry can now provide (Cattell & Brennan, 1984).

However, we need to consider education in a broader context than that of the schools, even with their new emphasis on biological science and their installing of separate streams guided by the capacities of the children. We need now to look at the whole problem of how to deal with what we have called "the genetic lag."

The discovery of the syntality dimension in a hundred or more modern nations that we have called *cultural pressure* (Chapter 10)—with its combination of frustration, internal and externalized aggression, and its outbreak in cultural creativity in science, art, and music—is a dynamic pattern that is at the center of the genetic lag. Let us next recognize, from the plots of cultural pressure for Britain and the U.S., and from the more generalized view of Toynbee, that the level of cultural pressure changes, in a given country, with circumstance. Toynbee relates the changing pressures to the age-long Chinese concept of Yin and Yang. Now the advent of substantial scientific growth, especially in the North Atlantic countries, in the last five centuries has brought about a fairly steep increase in humanitarian attitudes, especially in the last century. It can truthfully be said that the material support and standard of living even of our unemployed equals that of princes in the Middle Ages, and the amount of human leisure is perhaps ten times that of men working a 60-hour week at the turn of the century. It is Yin indeed . . . .

Now one of the consequences of this easier life style is an arrest visible in the otherwise mounting curve of cultural pressures. Relative, for example, to the expenditure on science, we cannot point to an increase in the numbers of great men and their basic discoveries. However, more important from the standpoint of the majority, in everyday life, is an increase of ease, a concomitant increase in toleration of deviation, and a proliferation of new fads and fashions. One aspect of this has been the shift over the past 50 years toward relaxation of moral standards—of the "ancient, outworn, Puritanic traditions of right and wrong." It has appeared notably in the sexual area, but also in the work ethic and in the loss of devotion to superpersonal goals in life.

The phase of relaxation, which occurs in times of luxury, in the reaction after wars, and also through sheer passage of time, has its useful as well as its dangerous aspects. It permits unnecessarily "stiff" traditions and habits to liquidate themselves, e.g., as brought about by Professor Flugel's "Men's Dress Reform" movement. But the major event of the past 50 years has been the dissolution of sexual restrictions. It is true that we await the required broad social psychological research on this that a Beyondist research institute would bring about; but we must take a position on the probable outcome. Freud's finding, used as the liberal's chief argument for the dangers of sexual inhibition, is totally misunderstood and misquoted. He dealt with the neurotic, low ego strength subgroup in which repression of sex played its part. But the evidence in the normal range—of lesser anxiety and greater happiness in those exhibiting a strong superego—tells a totally different story for the majority. One of Freud's misguided followers, Bertrand Russell (1957), probably saw as much as any psychologist when he said that sexual abstinence bred bigotry, fanaticism, violent recreations, etc.—except that there is probably two-way causation here. For him this was grounds for condemnation of sexual abstinence, but a social psychologist might see in the sublimatory products, and even the associated officious intolerance, forces that have moved society forward. Since so large a segment of human behavior is here involved, a truly scientific study of the social impact of sexual restraint is one of the major researches that Beyondism would initiate. But on the general basis of psychology as now understood, Beyondism would stand for monogamous marriage and a sense of guilt regarding flagrant sexual play.

It is evident that whereas societies in the past foundered more frequently from inability to handle external problems—starvation, war, plagues, and changes of climate—the emphasis today points more to internal problems—drug abuse, loss of educational competitive standards, expenditures on luxuries, and general cynicism. These are the disorders of a relaxation period, and we see them in such times as came to Sodom and Gomorrah, and Sybaris, and in the decline of the Roman Empire, and probably the Incas. External attacks may be seen in some cases of decline, but they are late and lesser impacts, normally withstood, which, falling on a hollow shell of the former culture, become overpowering. In our society today, the quasi-liberal movements that float on the relativistic fragments of decayed revealed religions almost all point in the direction of toleration of everything from homosexuality, through rejection of the military draft, to universal fornication, and general cynicism on the ideals that have made our countries and taken them out of chaos, or, at least, mediocrity. The same drift could end in the attempt, internationally, at a Hedonistic Pact, which we have seen to be destructive of attainment.

These downfalls are henceforth unlikely to happen because, as in the past, a more sharpened group will arise to command the decaying groups, though which group that will be cannot presently be clearly seen. All that we can be certain of is that it will be a group with greater devotion to superpersonal goals throughout society.[52]

The maintenance of moral values within a Beyondist society demands, as we have constantly seen, research toward more precise evaluation of the consequences of each change of custom that an adventurous society introduces. In the preceding chapter we have indicated, indeed, the need for institutions and mechanisms for providing both within- and between-group comparisons of outcomes, and to the inauguration of these we must now come as a practical matter. The creation of a

Beyondist research center, with both national and international branches, requires imagination and boldness. We need first frankly to recognize that the paucity of the required evidence from existing academic and other research in the social sciences is such that a totally new and greater research and development organization is needed. There are springing up, it is true, quite small research organizations endowed for special problems (in the U.S., the Heritage and the Brookings, for example), mainly political, but also more general, such as environmental protection, utilization of land, the societies working on birth control, and the Institute for Research on Morality. The Planck Centers in Germany and in America the Rockefeller, the Salk, the Mellon, the Battelle, the Stanford, the National Science Foundation, and similar university-related research centers have approached the concept we need, but are presently centered more on medical and similar research. Since some findings of a social research institute are likely to be taken up by one political party and others by other parties, the political control of such a national institute is a real danger to be avoided. Where then will the funds come from for such an organization?[53] This question we take up in the next chapter; but meanwhile we can talk of the general functions and structure of the needed within-group and among-group socio-biological research centers.

The universities must, in the main, be regarded as the training centers in which, up to the age of about 30-35, the younger faculty are free to demonstrate their research capacity. What I will henceforth call the National Social-biological Research Center (NSRC) will draw its full-time research leaders from that pool. In an article—"The organization of independent basic research institutes symbiotic with universities" (1973)—I contrasted the life of the teacher and the effective researcher. The latter is, by psychological tests (Cattell & Drevdahl, 1955), a different type, and needs a different life style. Admittedly, however, he needs to interact with university graduate students, but otherwise does far better without entanglement in undergraduate teaching and numerous teaching committees.

Furthermore, as touched on earlier, the multivariate realms of socio-biology will call increasingly for sophisticated multivariate research methods, applied on a scale too vast for individual faculty management. Men and women will be needed for this work who possess in addition to thorough training, the most powerful imagination. Science becomes increasingly an expanding domain in which the mediocre, though usefully employed, can become completely lost in terms of well-directed total effect. The problem was foreseen by that great leader of medical research, Sir William Osler, when he declared (Oxford address, 1918), "The extraordinary development of modern science may be her undoing. Specialism . . . has fragmented the specialities themselves. The workers lose all sense of proportion in a maze of minutiae." This is a major problem to avoid in the development of Beyondism in social science. For that science will eclipse what we now put into words. Let us clearly recognize that we are admittedly in this new area approaching the limits of human performance, where the genius of a generation will be vital in each generation. An altogether greater effort to discover these geniuses and their collaborators will be necessary, in a path from high school to the institution. The national socio-biological research institute must have a working personnel of perhaps 10,000. We must at least recognize that we are speaking of "forces" at least as great as the "brain" group accorded to the army or the United Nations Organization. How soon will the general public be prepared to sustain such a "labor force" that it so urgently needs in its culturo-genetic growth?

The basis of the *international* research institute must obviously be international—in the sense of drawing its scientist members from the national research organizations. These should be no difficulty—judging by the typical temper of the scientist today—in forming from national laboratories a group of individuals truly attached to a world Beyondist viewpoint, and capable of rising superior to their home attachments—as did, for example, the Roman legionnaires from all countries maintaining the Pax Romana in times past.

The ultimate problem to be solved for both national institute and comparative international institute scientists is the relation of their knowledge to power. Assuming a majority of countries to be democratic or aspiring to democracy, we surely have increasingly to consider a new form to democracy itself—at least as we leave the small town level. It has been suggested (in Chapter 18) that with the increasingly technical methods needed in reaching any goal we must get used to fixing the goals—the needs—of the people by a regular democratic vote, but to transferring decisions of *means* of reaching the goal to technical elites. For example, a town might vote for expenditure on increasing its water supply, but have to hand the decision on "how" to a committee of geologists.

The problem of the interaction of democracy with technical elites is a growing difficulty which our civilization has not yet worked out. Trotsky changed the phrase "dictatorship of the proletariat" to what it actually became: "dictatorship over the proletariat." Plato thought similarly. In some areas goal and mechanism are clear enough, and the elite sufficiently numerous and well-professionally selected for the democratic outlook to feel able to trust the elite. Probably the term "selected body" would avoid the suggestion of fashionable detachment in the word "elite." The difficulty lies in cases where goal and method overlap and the political views of some members of a small elite bias the ultimate decision. For example, the public presently puts up with a decision guilty or not guilty by elite psychiatrists on a murderer claiming insanity. It frets also on the decision by physicists of how near a nuclear power plant can be built to a city. Somehow a democratic society has to lose its seeming present bias against judgments by technical selected bodies in a complex society and develop new machinery to embrace such elite decisions.

Another basis of resentment against elites is that they have genetic as well as social reality, as happened with aristocracies. Any selected group, e.g., university graduates or medical doctors, will be found generally to have more than the chance-expected degree in genetic interrelationships. This, however, despite the trend of Darlington's data (1969), is usually relatively small, but it exists alike in a capitalist and a communist society. It will occur and need adjustment of that envy which arises when differences become partly hereditary. As Weyl (1969) has documented from history, this envy, and fear of domination by a selected group, has led to revolutionary massacres, often to the manifest disadvantage of the community as a whole. Granted general education in school in biology, an objective "meritocratic" selection of the select, a free movement in and out of such groups, and a due modesty in the elite (as in the religious elite of the saints), a good society should be able to accept guidance from its selected groups.

The handling of selected groups is much tied up with questions of the future development of democracy, with its roots in spiritual equality and maximum freedom of the individual. As argued elsewhere in this book, democracy, as politics, has to develop (a) in separation of ends from means in democratic choice, as occurs in the human nervous system, where manifestations of hunger and other desires are in the old mid-brain, and the means of satisfaction develop in the cortex; and (b) possibly in some more explicit weighting of the votes of individuals, according to their intelligence, sanity, and education. This latter introduces the fact found in small group experiment that too great a difference of intelligence between leader and led can cause trouble, even though the wisdom of the leader reaches a point where everything is better managed for the group. Here lies the nemesis of the concept of the elite. In my experience with military, industrial, and educational concerns, I have found the selected group often to be presented by the general group with questions of need for solution that are the wrong question in the first place! Thus the separation of voting on *ends* (needs) and expert advice on *means* is not the *whole* answer.

The Beyondist suggestions for the growth of democracy as a political form are therefore tentative. Any political system tends to become encrusted with bureaucracy, and one can admit truth in Dean Inge's assertion that "Liberalism, democracy, socialism, and communism are . . . out of date" and that "the bureaucratization of democracy could destroy individualism as much as does communist or fascist despotism." The need to reduce bureaucratization is very real.

In short, democracy, though it has been the valuable tool of freedom, in a chaotic, primitive phase of history, needs serious examination as to radical improvements now needed. The basic advantage is that it holds open the paths of discussion, orderly progress, and recognition of the importance of individuality. Nevertheless, within democratic countries, and especially America, the expression "democracy" has become an almost intellectually vacant shibboleth. As Graham Sumner (*Folkways*) asserted, "Democracy is bad American mores . . . . It is almost impossible to criticize it. It is glorified for popularity and is a subject of dithyrambic rhetoric. No one treats it with complete candor and sincerity." And as Sheldon adds (*Varieties of Delinquent Youth*, 1947a), "A 'good living' is obtained by giving people not what is good for them but what they want. I am told that to question this is to question democracy." As stated elsewhere, democracy is not to be considered beyond improvement. Jefferson said our Constitution is not to be considered "Holy Writ" (subject only to exegesis by a group of lawyers) but something to be revised every 20 years. (Eight possible occasions of review have been largely passed up!) Democracy needs today to be analyzed, as a prelude to its improvement. Its historical collapses need to be studied. Its interpretation of "equality" needs to be sharpened. Its maladaptations to a more complex scientific society need to be ironed out. It needs to cease to be a term of rhetoric and to become incorporated in a Beyondist set of evolutionary values.

A glance over cultural mechanisms is not complete without looking at "freedom of the press." The press has improved enormously over the past 50 years in its attention to serious matters, science, and deeper social issues generally. The need for "free speech" is basic, but a scientist has to remind writers that *figures* are as much a part of free speech as *words*. We are entering an "information-communication" revolution. It must be objected that the average journalist is literary-trained and that, in consequence, the reporting of science is still inadequate. Editors need to be educated. Their silences amount to a selection of what is news. For example, the last 20 years of growth of socio-biology and human genetics has been grossly underreported. The information revolution will demand an educated public partly dependent, after school years, on an enterprising education of journalists.

In summary, the technical cultural tasks of Beyondism remain: (1) To spread socio-biological education as a basis for all political and religious decisions. (2) To promote group freedom of each group to diverge from other groups in racio-cultural goals. This requires social courage and as Solzhenitsyn says, "A loss of courage [is] the most striking feature which an outside observer notices in the west in our days" (1976). (3) To maintain rules permitting group growth and retraction (including self-genocide) in the process of *cooperative* competition. (4) To avoid, by preanalysis, the total genocide of a culture whenever possible. The normal processes of intergroup competition must deny a "revolutionary" step of this kind. (5) To avoid, on the opposite side, an overindulgent humanism and any step toward a Hedonic Pact. Here we encounter, if we do not succeed in reducing the essentially unemployable bulge in the population, the problem that the ethic of work contribution and the rejection of the "temporarily modern" hedonism of life style, creates a conflict for all who cannot find significant work. The advent of the computer revolution may mean that substantial sections of the unemployed population are left, by the charity of the remainder, to find ways of amusing themselves. They must come to the conclusion that nothing is wrong in following an unproductive life. This conclusion that we must abandon the "work ethic" can be argued for in the light of current trends. But "Nature abhors a vacuum" and we shall conclude that Beyondism cannot tolerate an ethic of pointlessness. (6) To accept the principle that evolution should be allowed to proceed at its fastest rate. (7) To set up powerful research institutions which, by comparative study of the effect of measures adopted in various countries, will offer evolutionary guidance to all.

As we have admitted, Beyondism does not yet have the research to rebut the false doctrines of moral relativism, but as Herbert Spencer said, "Ethical truth is (in fact) as exact and peremptory as physical truth" (*Social Status*). Nietzsche foresaw this research goal in his *Genealogy of Morals*, where he wrote, "All sciences are now under the obligation to prepare the ground for the future task of the philosopher, which is to solve the problem of value, to determine the true hierarchy of values." These pioneers foresaw the goal; but here we have progressed also to methods and sustaining institutions.

Chapter 19

How Must Beyondism Organize?

We have explored thoroughly the foundations of a new ethical system. It remains to ask what steps to its social development are presently *practicable*.

Among the intelligent people who have read and understood the previous writing thereon, I find different emphasis. One points to the large number of educated people who have abandoned revealed religions and are ripe for a new solution. Another stresses that Beyondism has a special problem because it is too complex for many. In the past, vast movements such as Islam, Christianity, and Communism (rightly considered a religion) have begun by the actions of a select few. But they have had an emotional starting point, whereas Beyondism, sui generis, arises from a complex scientific discussion. It follows the discussions of Darwin, Comte, Voltaire, Huxley, Spencer, and Mill as eighteenth- and nineteenth-century liberals and, more recently, of Ardrey, Bronowski, Darlington, de Chardin, Eysenck, Hardin, Jencks, Keith, Lindzey, Lorenz, Weyl, Williams, Wilson, and many others.

Like the Encyclopedists before the French Revolution, however, it has no financial status! As a power, in that sense, it is utterly dwarfed by Islam, Buddhism, and Catholicism, for example. Yet what it contemplates in, for example, research institutes demands an organization, a catechism, and a powerful congregation.

It has to *grow* with such a congregation, evaluating its central values and warding off heresies. And as Comte set up "saints" for Positivism, such as Darwin, Mill, and others, or Communism its icons in Marx and Lenin, it will develop its congregation of leaders best expressing its latest discoveries and values. This is what a living social organism means.

Although science is not simply sanity, it becomes one with sanity in debates on its sphere of application. The absence of a single leader makes Beyondism more difficult to follow than revealed religions, but its root in science guarantees its sanity. Its planned multiplicity offers a difficulty to the first formation of a Beyondist group. Different national groups must differ at a level of practical action, while serving the common goal of evolution. As in most organizations, it may best begin at a national level, or, for example, through action of those in the English-speaking world. It will probably make most headway in Protestant countries.

Beyondism, like any ethical system, has political implications, but it can honestly make no contact for support from existing right or left political parties. They are basically concerned with the have-vs-have not groups, which are equally irrelevant to basic progress. This aloofness may basically define Beyondism as a religion rather than a party. De Toqueville (1945) saw the roots of progress in "What the few have today, the many will want tomorrow," but this is materialist progress, (to which Beyondism subscribes—short of luxuries). Beyondism is thus a religious movement, without the dogmas and rituals which make both political parties and religions unacceptable to the more intelligent. What de Toqueville describes applies, but at the level of spread of *values*.[54]

Probably the nearest existing structure to that needed in Beyondism is a university, providing both teaching and research. Yet Beyondism still differs, for its teaching is wide and social—that of a people's university—and its research is more intensively into the social sciences. Perhaps the closest model, therefore, is a Max Planck, or Rockefeller institute, devoted to research, and symbiotic with a university. It must be symbiotic in being in the same city, to share facilities, in putting great leaders at the disposal of graduate researchers, and in exchanging faculty.

It may seem that, despite our expression "a people's university," this suggested growing point for Beyondism does not give the propagandist interaction needed in a value system aimed ultimately for the general population. It does mean, however, that the teaching must be a popularization of the basic principles of Beyondism, and of the research results, well founded in science. The findings on social experiment and health need to be fully publicly expressed. Actually, there are numerous activist organizations today that could be jointly organized with, and informed by, the Beyondist institutions. There are world population centers, geneonomic institutes, and countless educational groups seeking the solutions which the Beyondist institutes could increasingly offer.

In the preceding Chapter I have looked at the much larger "grand design" of an International Research Center, in interaction with national centers, all being devoted to the goal of an understanding of group life that must far exceed our present development of the social sciences. With data gathering systems and technical research methods that a truly adequately endowed institute could develop, these institutes would address themselves to the comparative studies, and the advice on results to different countries, that we see as one essential result of Beyondism. Such institutes can scarcely hope to be financed by a voluntary Beyondist Society, but must be nationally supported, as, say, UNESCO now is.[55] This will take some years of development of Beyondist values in various countries.

However, every movement must begin somewhere, and I have willed my small means, and organized a fine group of technical leading social psychologists in a Trust for the Advancement of Beyondism. What it will accomplish will depend on how far wise and well-to-do men now rally to its support and extension. Those interested in this development should write to the following:

> Dr. Raymond B. Cattell
> Dr. Heather Cattell
> Professor Richard Gorsuch
> Dr. Robert Graham
> Professor John L. Horn
> Professor John R. Nesselroade

These may all be reached via the Cattell Institute, 1702, Century Square, 1188 Bishop St. Honolulu, Hawaii, 96813.

The first task of TAB (Trust for Advancement of Beyondism) is to spread an appreciation of the principles of Beyondism among social scientists and educated people. Its second is to thrash out, in annual meetings, the tangible principles in everyday life and politics that follow from its basic principles. The political steps will not fit any existing political party and will therefore, in due time, call for a new political party. Politics and religion have hitherto, with a few exceptions, been considered separate, and the constitution of the U.S.A. explicitly calls for the restriction of religions from participation in politics. This makes temporary practical sense in a religiously pluralistic society. It is nonfunctional, however, in regard to the reality that political values must follow from religious values. It is an appropriate distinction only so long as religions rest on revealed intuitive beliefs. The advent of Beyondism brings the derivation of political steps from religion within the control of social and general science. There may be disagreements in the derivation, as there are disagreements always in the growing edge of science. But individuals can face these as they face scientific disagreements—by investigation and reasoning. These become the business of the research organs of Beyondism.

With good fortune we shall before long see the revealed religions fading out of the more advanced countries. The great cathedrals will become spiritual landmarks of the past, though one suspects that the abscession of the mosques will trail behind longer. Out of the superstition-ridden night of the past two thousand years will gradually dawn the light of science-based evolutionary religion. It is to this new structuring of life that the present believers in Beyondism must apply themselves.

Chapter 20

A Concise Beyondist Catechism

Let us sum up concisely the principles discussed in this book, in logical order.

1. That evolution is the prime process visible in the universe, to which we have to conform, and should do so in good will.

2. That human evolution proceeds ultimately by natural selection *among groups*, which determines and is determined by natural selection among individuals, genetically and culturally.

3. That natural selection among groups and individuals requires as a precondition *adequate variation* among groups and individuals, genetically and culturally.

4. That one important factor in group survival resides in the laws that govern its internal structure and the desirable mutual behavior of individuals. The evolution of the best interindividual ethical values is therefore based finally on the processes of intergroup differential survival, the competitive conditions for which must be maintained. The ethics of a particular group are fixed, additionally, by aiming to survive in relation to its particular aspirations and circumstances.

5. Historically, "revealed" religions are attempts to congeal the naturally, evolution-derived ethical systems and to aid their practice by priesthoods, rituals, and imaginary after-life rewards, etc. Historically, they made the imperialist mistake, however, of extending the within group derived values of any single group to universal values among men, thus conflicting with (2) above.

6. The spiritual life of Beyondism arises, in part, like that of the other religions, from genetic urges unsatisfied in everyday life, unavoidably in any culture with genetic lag. Beyondism differs in

257

shaping those desires explicitly to logically indicated evolutionary needs rather than, as in revealed religions, inventing subjective beliefs to meet and fit the accidental frustrations.

7. Beyondism necessarily regards many beliefs and practices of revealed religion as inadequate or misleading. For the notion of a loving father God, it substitutes faith in the purpose of evolution. It regards mankind as no "apple of God's eye," but as one species among millions, in a universe that is neither favorably nor unfavorably disposed to us. Our individual immortality is also restricted to what we pass on to the life of our group. This greater emotional austerity of Beyondism will slow down its universal acceptance, but develop a new sense of spirituality.

8. There are six main entities to which an individual's ethical values can be functionally oriented: fellow group members, the group government, other group governments, members of other groups, individuals committed to a Beyondist Ethic, and, above all, the Evolutionary Purpose. Each of these objects calls for precise alignment of its loyalties, in a situational hierarchy among them. For example, a man's ethical loyalty to his own group exceeds that to members of "mankind" generally. However (a) the injunctions of the different "object" ethics are different, mostly, in kind, and (b) circumstances put emphasis on the primary survival of *all* groups, if the total existence of man is threatened. The rose diagram of ethical values (Figure 8-1) should answer many ethical questions now troubling teachers and religious-political parties.

9. The only ultimate test of the fitness and progress of a group's culture-genetic make-up is whether it survives, historically. However, just as individual eugenics avoids the cruelty of in-life selection of failures, so the disasters of cultural death and genocide among groups can be lessened by foresighted changes based on objective health measures understanding the comparative morbidity of cultures and races, akin to a medical watch on individuals.

10. The cultural and genetic evolution of groups are alike in that variation—largely inaccessible directly as to evolution of desirability— must occur in *both*, followed by natural selection. The process is well understood in genetics, but has new, as yet unorganized, principles in the evolution of cultural elements. Culture changes by the mechanical and social inventions of leading persons, and by borrowing (willing or forced) from other cultures. As Graubard (1986) points out, "exceptionally radical inventions are the work of exceptionally gifted individuals." In addition to the direct mold-

ing effect of inventions, there are side effects from their interactions with economic, population, meteorological, etc., material pressures. Cultural elements survive on their own merits, independently of the genetic group using them, and show continual elaboration, though there is interaction of survival with the genetic suitability of the group, and the group's situation.

11. Being the work of superior intelligences, culture, as a whole, is likely to demand more complex adjustments from the general population than they are genetically suited to make. This discrepancy we call *genetic lag*. It has some correspondence to the difference between the instinctual reactions of the old brain and the adjustments made possible by the cortex. Genetic lag is the cause of many social problems.

12. The saying that "man adapts his environment to himself instead of suffering selection from environment," is a half-truth since his cultural adaptations are to *environment*. His cultural developments, however, are of two kinds: "p-culture" which adapts as outlets for his frustrations, as in poetry, music, and drama, and "r-culture" which actually fits him to environment, as in engineering, medicine, and science. The convolutions of p-culture may be training for r-culture, as well as for temporary emotional adjustment; but it is primarily by r-culture that he survives.

13. Eugenic measures seek to reduce the genetic lag; but the adjustment sought is partly to the universe generally and partly to a particular culture and its situation. The discrepancy of genetics and culture arises largely from the movement of culture by "inventions" (mutations). An adventurous society will deliberately create genetic mutations to see what they will do toward creating a new culture. Evolution is thus an interaction of genetic and cultural mutations, each shaping, by survival contributions, the other. Genetic advance on a broad front is dependent on man's adventuring beyond horizons. The spirit of adventure is therefore a central value in Beyondist ethics, and contrary to many "universalist" revealed religions.

14. Beyondism calls for an examination of the internal rules of progress, and concludes first that a substantial freedom for individuality is required. In revolution, advanced and atavistic groups (detesting culture) operate together. In reaching the same "revolutionary" changes by *evolution*, lesser genetic lag is probably a a precondition. When ethical rules are scientifically derived from social research, egoistic, antisocial individualism can be treated in distinction from creative individualism. The id constantly chafes for "human

rights" rather than duties, and rights are not "God given," but, truly, contractual and situationally fixed by the conditions of group survival.

15. Beyondism calls practically for a vast increase in social research, with such objectives as making national comparisons, defining ethical systems, clarifying the ethical and cultural values of each group, and so on. For each group should follow its own divergent adventure, racially and culturally, in cooperative competition with a world federation of groups, each with its own sociobiological research institutes.

16. The spirit of Beyondism is one of common human adventure, of risk taking, and of an austere acceptance of nonsentimental values, and the constant existence of tragedy. Our situation in the universe is more precarious than we commonly accept, and it behooves us to evolve in intelligence, and secure command of *possible* environments *at the fastest possible pace.* With every gain of security, from science, much of the gain has been socially lost to further support of science by expenditures in sentimental support of trivial id demands. We have to control succorant behavior, just as *every* instinct needs control, away from unbounded "social welfare" into knowledge-producing support. If survival is the final test of ethics, our ethical values, and the political practices resulting, need serious re-education, e.g., toward a simple even income tax, and the acceptance of direction by qualified elites, democratically watched.

17. Since Beyondism sees survival to be as dependent on genetic as cultural bases, one change of present values indicated is in an altogether more enthusiastic pursuit of eugenics. This involves the acceptance of genetic individual differences, without envy or malicious obstruction, and of better education for the gifted. Probably a positive eugenic condition could be most simply established by an ethic of more children from the socially more successful. The mechanics would require some economic laws, since a bright child, going to college, is decidedly more of a family economic burden than one of average intelligence. The particular goals of eugenic selection can be democratically set by the needs of each society and its ideals. One of the main sources of antieugenic thinking and dysgenic practice is the absence of school education of the voting body particularly in biology and statistics.

18. Races formed in the past, due largely to geographical isolation, are of only transient and esthetic particularity and importance. The genetic groupings (races) of the future will arise from self-conscious

selection by each cultural group. Their development requires regard for the efficiency of language barriers and for migration control considerations. In a long term view, the genus homo sapiens would be wise to split, by conscious segregation of ideals, into more than one species. This may involve "genetic engineering" or become achieved as a side result of solar system colonization.

19. The main cultural development that Beyondism requires is a quite unprecedented increase in support of socio-biological research. Many ideas in this book are "promises" of advance, and it is hard, for example, to substantiate such views as that the advance of culture occurs through restriction of sexual activities, by any indubitable present evidence of relation. The research institutes that need to be set up are both national in roots—attending to the particular national adventure—and international, obtaining laws of social effects by cross comparison of national cultures. The issues to be investigated are as mind-boggling as the most sophisticated problems in, for example, modern physics. Scientists in sociobiology will only rarely, with special selection for truly genius level of talent, be able to make the needed progress.

20. Beyondism is a coherent system of beliefs that scientists can be expected to understand and, in the main, support. At this point in history there has been a startling increase of interest in the bearing of psycho-biological discoveries on human organization. If a sufficient body of scientists and others can be brought together, in sufficient accord, the time has come for the development of an actual Beyondist *organization* to begin affecting political, educational. and economic decisions. An appeal is accordingly here made for Beyondists to get together in a fellowship of discussion.

1. Chap. 3. Since we recognize that each individual belongs simultaneously to several groups, the reader will ask whether the reference to a group throughout this discussion applies to a *national group*. The laws of group life, e.g., that the survival and success of a group depend on the group devotion and interindividual morality of its members, seem to apply to all groups—religious, recreational, family, industrial, corporate, and so on. However, there is a hierarchy, and most persons on earth today accommodate in loyalties, expenditures, and much else to the embracing national group, through cross-national religious groups, for some people outdo the national loyalty, while common markets, area alliances, and the like split loyalties.

The intricacy of interaction of loyalties and feedback of results in overlapping groups presents a mathematically beautiful but still only partly understood set of mechanisms studied by the dynamic psychologist. An examination of these would rapidly expand out of all proportion to the objectives of this book. Although the role of the individual in the symbiosis of groups is complex, there is no reason to see it as denying the basic relation to the containing national group or religious group. In the Middle Ages in Europe, the church or the Holy Roman Empire may have been the primary loyalty. Since the rise of national sovereignties, particular cultures, language barriers, and commercial frontiers at the Renaissance, the life and death of the individual are determined by the nation more than any other group. Like any bounding influence, this has not been without allergic protests, notably in attempts to substitute classes for countries. Hence, although much that is said here about group effects probably applies to other groups, the reader may assume that at present the primary reference is to national groups.

It is interesting to note that most historians and sociologists who are considered to belittle racial, genetic differences in unguarded moments show actually that they recognize the importance of such differences. Thus Marx, as Weyl records, considered the Slavic race as inferior to the German, and in his personal life referred to his rival Lasalle by "It is now quite clear to me as shown by the shape of his head and the (stiff, bristling) hair that he is descended from the Negroes who joined the flight of Moses." These unabsorbed irregularities in Marx remind one of some visitor's account of his house as "tattered and torn, with half an inch of dust over everything, and the greatest disorder everywhere."

2. Chap. 3. Because its dramatic and grim qualities cause the degenerate form of competition we call war to be always in frantic discussion, some enlargement of the Beyondist perspective that, realistically, war remains a risk, must be undertaken here. Obviously, international policing such as has appeared since World War I—in the League of Nations, at first with infant feebleness—is the solution, since all ethical law has to be backed by force in an imperfectly evolved mankind. In this connection one has to consider regulation of war itself (as in the Hague conventions) should it break out. The substitution of an ordered game of chess (or even physical combat of champions, as sometimes in history) is no satisfactory alternative since it denies use of that imagination and endurance which natural selection is out to improve. Probably, if a sufficient international force to outlaw war is not achieved, we shall see war becoming increasing total—economic, psychological (false propaganda), and scientific.

The problem of avoidance of war is complex, and involves, among other things, the introduction of international machinery to weigh the survival potential of all groups, and to bring about readjustments of territory, etc., that respect these differences of potential (for example, predicting more dependably to all concerned the outcome of a war without it being necessary for it to occur). Mere antiwar demonstrations are relatively pointless. Peace is more than the absence of war. It is illogical to create a power vacuum in the hope of controlling power. And it would be pleasant to be spared the air of moral superiority in all who participate in antiwar demonstrations, since *every* sane person wishes to avoid the horrible waste and cruelty of war. The occasion for a great demonstration would be if someone discovered the yet undiscovered way to avoid war.

The reaction of European intellectuals, liberals and establishment alike, in World Wars I and II, was one of indignation at the upset of the gracious mode of life—comfort, content, delight—that generations of peace had brought about, and a superior air that the whole thing was childish and deliberately wicked. Einstein called young men to defy the draft. Journalists have not been sufficiently psychologically shrewd to separate Einstein's preeminence in intelligence from his merely average emotional stability and practical realism. Within a year he was writing, (August, 1939) to Roosevelt to urge construction of an atomic bomb. The preservation of more civilized against less civilized cultural values often requires force, as in a policeman arresting a criminal. Criminals are likely to be with us for a long time. Dislike of the stranger is a natural reaction. It is a manifestation of Spencer's "law of enmity" contrasted with his "law of amity" which binds members of the tribe. It is a valuable ingredient in the keeping of separation among groups that is necessary for their independent pacing of national selection. There is, in the individual, however, more devotion to his group than antipathy to other groups. William James sought a "moral equivalent of war" in which that devotion could be directed more constructively than in war. Some people find this, but probably most find the excitement of war more appealing than any "civilized" devotion. War may last so long as the majority fail to find equivalent self-transcendence in civilized tasks.

Perspective requires awareness of facts such as the following: (1) Involvement in war, as our correlations show (Cattell, 1950a), is probably in part a function of the level of aggression in a population, as begotten by *cultural pressure*. (This syntality factor concerned loads simultaneously the acceleration of complexity and the begetting of war and riots.) (2) There is a high correlation between victory in war and what is normally called the level of civilization of the parties. Nations most developed in organization, science, medical services, general educational level, gross national product indices, etc., are also the most formidable in war. (3) The mortality from automobile accidents (60,000 annually in the U.S. alone) has, up to the present time, exceeded that from wars (50 million in 30 years). Can one expect a population willing to accept this auto risk, for convenience, refusing to face a lower risk for the sake of its cultural birthright? (4) The deaths from lung cancer are no less cruel than those from war. Can we hope for the personal discipline necessary in obviating war in a population unable to exercise the control necessary to stop smoking, etc? (5) In view of the apparent indifference of populations to future consequences, it is perhaps politically correct to call upon the aid of terror, by claiming that nuclear war will kill everyone and be the end of mankind. But technical opinion does not agree that either mankind or civilization would be destroyed by a war between nuclear powers.

Substantial areas of the earth are likely to be untouched, libraries would return the wisdom and knowledge we have, and a sufficient proportion of skilled professionals would remain to reconstitute our technical services. In absolute terms, the loss of life would be appalling. But relative to the earth's enormously expanded population, it would be a proportional loss no greater than appears to take place in tribal wars through which social organization and "civilization," as culture, endured. Every war in historical times has produced a momentary loosening of conservative and traditional rigidities, in which rationally sound but socially stymied ideas have had a chance to realize themselves. If, for example, the institution of social genetic control does not come about soon, with the ensuing increases of intelligence that would suffice to abolish war, the probability is that the substantial upset of a nuclear war would release the rational attitudes necessary to construct a more eugenic world. But the answer to the problem is a police force in a community of nations as we have a police force against violence in a community of individuals.

In considering natural selection among groups, it is important to recognize from the beginning that success in the total environment has two arenas, (1) in relations to other groups, and (2) in relation to the physical environment. The first involves commercial, diplomatic, and military action. It has distasteful features and features that balk the purposes of evolution, though these are not necessarily the same. Clausewitz correctly said that war is an extension of political action. Certainly, to be even passively militarily formidable (T. Roosevelt's "carry a big stick") aids political and commercial maneuvering.

From an evolutionary standpoint, the drawback of war is certainly not that its outcomes are correlated with success against nature. Again and again it has been shown that the most civilized countries (and, incidentally, often the most Christian), in terms of victories over nature, in technical matters, and advanced social organization, tend to win wars. The survival judgment in the two arenas is by no means so different as "feeling liberals" in their wishful thinking constantly assert. It is true that victories of man against nature are unalloyed contributions to evolution, whereas those of man against man have certain functional defects, besides the suffering they bring. (Incidentally, victories against nature also have their human costs, as in, say, the many thousands dying of fever in building the Panama Canal, and the astronauts who have died in the conquest of space.) Moreover, as pointed out above, the point is that surviving nations in "man against man" correlate in order closely with those in "man against nature."

The defects of the former method of selection are (a) that the countries which bear the cost and have the brains for scientific creativity almost immediately have their gains stolen by countries that may go to war with them, thus reducing the contribution of the more ethically desirable "man against nature" component of performance, (b) that in war sheer size and natural resources, somewhat dependent on foresight but largely accidental, tend to determine the outcome. By decided cultural superiority Greece survived against the Persian hosts and wealth; but, more typically, Finland had no realistic choice but to succumb to Russian threats, and in World War II Germany and its allies were greatly outnumbered in men and resources by the opposing cultures.

The second drawback is that a sudden onslaught, like that of a thug upon an unsuspecting child, might wipe out forever some promising new variant not yet showing its real powers. It may be objected that unlike the wars of, say, biblical times, extermination of a genetic pool (complete genocide) rarely occurs today. On the cultural side, however, complete extermination of a cultural feature often follows war (as in the imposition of democracy on Japan and of communism on Hungary, Lithuania, etc.). Other interactions than war can be equally a risk to evolution. One country's insertion of its culture as a rebel group in another, like a virus taking over a healthy cell, is now quite common. "Foreign aid" and commercial penetrations strengthen one group and undermine another. It would take a book to study these, but the enormous array of ingenious and successful parasitisms and symbioses known to the biologist give us at once a good model. The question arises, though there is yet no answer, whether Beyondist ethics directed to maximizing evolution, should require the coming international organization to rule out insidious penetrations of government, war, and various parasitisms, while encouraging a "fair" international competition.

Nevertheless, in any accurate sense, the relative potency of competition "against" other nations (actually better vis-a-vis other nations) and "against" nature (actually the struggle to control the environment) is unknown. A guess would be that, increasingly, conquest of nature distinguishes the group with better survival. (The Romans were aided against, say, the Britons, by a higher level of metallurgical knowledge. Bronze enriched art but also made better spears; but mainly survival in those days rested on morale and social organization.) More and more, survival goes to the nation with a genetic and cultural advantage in its dealings with the environment. Greater success and increased survival, as measured, for example, by a greater population at a higher standard of living, goes to the nation that conquers more of nature. The first to discover agriculture survived, with the same land areas, better than the less planful hunters. The initiators of the steam engine and the industrial revolution survived at a higher level than the agriculturalists, and so on. The rocket is today a weapon in war but may prove to be more important, to those who possess it, as a source of colonial expansion. Both expansion into greater realms of nature and expansion vis-a-vis neighbors are part of natural selection, but one would surely conclude—though quantitative evidence is yet hard to come by—that assertion to control nature is more rewarding and less costly competition. Incidentally, one of the roots of war today is lack of assimilation of the Beyondist principle of cooperative competition, i.e., recognition that relative expansion and retraction must go on in relative survival in natural selection. Blocking this principle of adjustment calls for explosions. National expansions must be allowed, but regulated by evaluations.

One thing is certain: that the evolution of mankind requires the construction and action of genetically and culturally diverse groups. It is, nevertheless, an observation of biologists that the struggle for survival is commonly greater within a species than between species. The reason is that all members of a species tend to have the same feeding habits, nest requirements, etc. With a shortage, overpopulation quickly leads, as most dramatically in the lemmings, to death—even though some potentially usable "unconventional" food source is avaiable. Each species finds its niche, often not directly competitive with that of another species, because of relative isolation, but is still competitive with nature in the sense of having to be "economic." This suggests that different national groups, embarking on different experiments almost as different species do, could virtually cease to be in direct intergroup competition, and be weighed largely by their success vis-a-vis the environment of the universe.

As we shall increasingly recognize, the aim of a Beyondist ethic is to recognize that groups, though in "competition" for survival, mutually and "against" nature, must be wholly in cooperation in the evolutionary purpose. They are engaged in a joint exploration of the environmental space. Each group, with its own cultural and genetic experiment, is reconnoitering to find more successful modes of human life. To be willingly subject to competition is the first ethical law in group interaction, but it is cooperative competition to a goal beyond any one group, best designated *joint exploration*. In this contest, it is a mistake to assert that war is necessary, or that it will be the end of humanity. Although it may be a desirable tactic to halt the stupid, bellicosity of masses by saying modern war will end mankind, objective examination suggests that though it would be horrible beyond all imagination, it would not be the end of mankind. In the first place, every new weapon has brought sooner or later a new defense, e.g., the new laser destruction of incoming warheads. A period elapsed between the invention of the machine gun and the defense in the form of the tank, in which casualties were greater than ever known before. Scholars of warfare tell us, however, that, relative to the size of populations, ancient wars like the Peloponnesians, or wars in which half a tribe were killed, were as deadly as nuclear war threatens to be. If we believe, as we surely must, that any illusion or untruth is dangerous, then, however much we detest war, we should not adopt scare tactics of calling nuclear war the end of mankind or even of civilization. Vast areas of Africa, Malaysia, Austrialia, New Zealand, and so on would probably be untouched. The folly of war has suddenly, after centuries, become evident to noncombatant city dwellers, because soldiers, sailors, and airmen, selected for fitness and courage, will no longer be the sole sufferers.

The answer surely is that intergroup ethics should do all possible to set up machinery that will outlaw war, and people put pressures on their governments to avoid it. That is to say, if we are to have force, let it be the force of an international consortium, truly well armed. The need of nations for their freedom leads to defensive armaments. Defensive armaments in one are rightly perceived as possible aggressive armaments in another. The arms race cycle is psychologically simpler than most group interactions: it is fear begetting fear, and the cycle has generally ended in war, unless the imbalance is great enough (as with Britain or America in relation to most nations during the nineteenth century) to make it absurd. If social psychology and the social sciences generally could become scientific enough to predict pretty reliably the outcome of a war, when the differences in power, as now, are much smaller, this would be an aid to peace, in the sense just cited for the comparatively peaceful nineteenth century. But, as with individual strife, the remedy is clearly a gun law supplemented by a police force strong enough to cover either opponent. Police forces have their own developments, but they are a first step to law and order.

Suppression of war can essentially be undertaken without fear that it might be curtailing evolution, for surely we can say that human evolution is about to reach a level where all competition can be naturally carried out without recourse to war. As in the earlier approach to the issue of war above, one must open-mindedly raise the question whether *any* restriction of mode of competition among groups endangers their development of the full spectrum of needed adjustments to the universe. If rocketry had been outlawed at the end of World War II, there would have been no men on the moon. This is quite a difficult issue, and perhaps the answer is that war is a legitimate test of power of group survival only at a lower level of the evolutionary process. Perhaps nations can exert all their powers at a higher level. If they slip back to a lower level, war will automatically recur. Like a shipwrecked mariner climbing a cliff, when the surge of water around tells him he has climbed enough, he will stop.

If it is untruthful to talk about wiping out the human species, or even civilization, what are the chances of a second dark age? (A thousand years?) No, I think that in the event of a war a small group of intelligent leaders will find each other, and, in isolation from other remnants, will build a small but better society.

3. Chap. 5. A good overview exists in Eisenstadt S. N., *The Decline of Empires*, New York, Prentice Hall, 1967. The phenomenon is a very old one with features that come up again and again. Polybius (Book XXXVI, Chapter 7), writing in the second century B.C., speaks of the once prosperous Greek province of Boetia especially, and Greece in general, "the whole of Hellas has been afflicted with a low birth rate . . . through which the states have been emptied of inhabitants and with an accompanying fall of productivity . . . . The fact is that the people entered upon the false path of ostentation, avarice and laziness . . . becoming unwilling to marry or . . . to bring up the children born to them, in order to leave them wealthy and to spoil them in their childhood" (After A. J. Toynbee's translation in *Greek Civilization and Charac-*

ter, New York, Mentor, 1952). This could make a good description of birth rates and customs in the middle class today.

When Napoleon had time to reflect broadly on history, at St. Helena, he dictated "Nations like men have their various ages—infancy, maturity, old age . . . . They also have their diseases like individuals, and their case histories would be interesting." This fits our concept of "physicians of societies."

We can see in our times instances of relative loss of morale. In Britain, the terrible losses of war and the disappearance of identity with empire produced on a small scale something of the same despair of values as occurred in Russia in 1917. In the U.S., we are told that the end of the frontier put a stop to the romance of self-realization—a setback to some ideas of self-realization. In France, the confusion in morale began before World War II, and showed its results concretely then. There are countless writings on such "local" symptoms in the 20th-century trend of nations.

4. Chap. 6. The remarkably large role of the individual inventor, relative to the recurring standard environmental, materialistic pressures—famine, disease, overpopulation, climate change, war—in producing really noteworthy change, needs full recognition. There may be a degree of truth in "necessity is the mother of invention," but if so, this mother can be around thousands of years to no effect until the inventing father appears. The invention, of course, can be in any field, e.g., in religion as with Christ, Buddha, or Mohammed, in architecture as with the Roman arch, in war, as when the musket put an end to chivalry, in travel as with Trevithick's and Stephenson's locomotive, and so on. In each case, like waves from a stone dropped in a pond, a widening circle of social readjustments and changes of custom follow.

5. Chap. 6. Intellectual honesty and scientific fact compel any educated man today squarely to confront the miserable practice of self-seeking minorities who try to make race a dirty word. We take our stand on solid scientific investigations such as those of Baker (1974), Hooton (1946), Jensen (1973), Loehlin, Lindzey, and Spuhler (1975), yet any traveler, shrewdly observing, recognizes that the difference in social life of the passionate Italian, the practical, empirical Englishman, and the patient Chinese, for example, is partly to be understood through their average differences of temperament.

Their differences of ability are more readily documented. In the U.S.A., for example, in the area of higher scientific contribution, the Jews, the Chinese, and, to some extent, the Scots predominate way beyond their proportions in the population. (Conceivably in opera and music, tho' I know of no data, those of Italian racial extraction predominate.) Now where—as in the U.S.A., India, Russia, and prewar Germany—there are well-defined ethnic subgroups—the problem will arise that the more competent will shape the development of the less competent. They may tend to crystallize out at different social status levels—as with Jews and Negroes in the U.S.—and this can, incidentally, be interpreted by the more led group as parasitism. Certainly it involves the imposition of values on the subordinate group that are likely to be different from their natural tempermental inclination. Incidentally, the fact that group A is more competent in competition than group B by no means implies that the temperamental values of A are superior, in eventual survival value, to those of group B.

The story of antisemitism in Germany and the U.S. is essentially just this. It is part of that general migration, and culture borrowing and imposition, studied as biological and cultural evolution in Chapter 6. Whether this form of "capture" is the most effective in evolutionary movement remains to be researched. It is typified by the stone-and-iron castles by which the Normans modified the good natured but rough temperament of the Saxon English. When such relations cease to be didactic and become parasitic is a complex matter that needs to be answered. Meanwhile, the best assumption, in racial terms, is that the imposition of the culture of a racial group that is superior in control, but different in temperament in itself. Africa, in colonial times, would offer many instances of imposed life styles clashing with native temperament in art and religion. If the degree of cultural selection of genes is what we have speculated it to be, one result will be a molding of the gene pool of the dependent group toward that of the controlling race.

The essential position here is that the racial belonging of *an individual* has very little predictive value, but that the cumulative effect of racial types in a whole population can, by "interactional emergents," significantly affect the behavior of the group as a group. Moreover, as Byram Campbell has well said, "Nature has so constituted us that race is a realm in which we find some of life's most cherished values. Therefore egalitarian propaganda has often assumed aspects offensive to the majority . . . :" It is regrettable that in a presentation aimed at maximum compactness for the reader one should need this rather extensive note to deal with use of race throughout the text. By race, I mean a gene pool which may represent either a relatively pure race as commonly defined or, more commonly, some particular mixture of races constituting the genetic pool of a particular country.

The problems are only in the misunderstandings, mainly from prejudice. It still happens that anyone referring to racial difference is met by the vulgar shout of "racist." Incidentally, and to the disgust of any modern scientist, even some supposedly educated persons join in, as in the recent vituperation by some professors on the work of Wilson in sociobiology, Herrnstein on intelligence inheritance, and Jensen and Lynn on race differences. Let us disentangle the problem first by clearer definitions. A *raciologist* (physical anthropologist or behavior geneticist) is one who, from natural scientific curiosity, studies race differences, applying the usual rules from species recognition to subspecies and races. Naturally, the raciologist will expect that genes will affect both the physical and the psychological features that develop in a defined environment. (The present writer, with Bolz and Korth [1973], has shown that breeds of dogs can be classified on behavioral measures alone, physique unseen, and Lorenz's studies show the same inheritance of behavior proneness in other species and breeds.)

What critics call a *racist* is defined by a set of attitudes, notably (1) not a hope but unsupported *belief* that his own race has superior survival value to others, (2) the passing of judgments on individual humans by their racial affiliation, and (3) a lack of interest or concern about the fate of other races than his own. The first at least has the virtue of a superpersonal loyalty, but cannot be supported, since no one knows what qualities unquestionably have superior survival value. Natural selection has yet to decide. The second is poor statistics, since differences within a race decidedly exceed mean differences between races (Lewontin, 1968). There is good reason to believe, however, that preference for one's own kind (notably in mating, Cattell & Nesselroade, 1967) exists and, as in other species, is largely innate, so that initial reaction to an individual by his race is understandable, though regrettable when occurring in a common citizenry. The third racist feature is directly contrary to a Beyondist ethic, which enjoins goodwill to every diverse racial and cultural experiment in the pursuit of evolution.

A third and last type to be pulled out of this confusion is the opposite of a racist, namely an *ignoracist*, who is so brought up that he finds it necessary categorically to refuse to recognize that there can be any innate racial differences in average behavioral potential. Sometimes this position is held despite a recognition that individuals differ in innate capacities. Yet a race is only a collection of individuals and if, in some migration, individuals of I.Q. over 100 tended to move and those under 100 to stay, we should immediately have two subgroups differing in their mean and sigma of I.Q. Our thesis here is that natural selection among groups will operate partly on gene predominances and deficiencies among the diverse racial mixtures.

Even the ignoracist cannot, unless blind, deny the physical types of races. Pattern similarity coefficients would reveal the broad existing types—at simplest (Baker, 1974) Europids (Caucasian), Mongolids, and Negrids, and in more detail, Nordids, Alpinids, Mediterranids, Sunids (Bushmen), and Austrolids. These are largely the products of inbreeding within geographically, climatically (and sometimes culturally) isolated sections of humanity. Our use of race is more concerned with races of the future than those—races that will be formed more by adherence to culture, language, religion, etc., and very soon by genetic engineering. Those will be, as in animal and plant breeding, a target, approached by hybridization and inbreeding phases, with dropping off of maladapted combinations. And although within-group ethics calls for individuals to be treated regardless of race, between-group ethics will more and more put a stop to the abortion of an experiment through permitting *massive* immigration of types different from the democratically chosen target.

As the racial ideas of particular group experiments become more explicit, and probably more directly shaped by genetic engineering, attention will be given, not only to the average level of the population, but to patterns of distribution suited to the culture, e.g., the distribution of intelligence at various levels in relation to job needs. Not that the culture is to be taken as the sole die, to stamp out a desired adjustive genetic pattern, but, as argued elsewhere, culture needs to be given a jolt by experimental genetic mutations for which no cultural use is presently foreseen (or, at least, precisely assessable). And variety of genetic resources in the pool is also needed to help survival in the event of rapid environmental change. The concept of the racial substrate in an experimental group is therefore more complex than at first appears. So also is that of the interaction (revealed in analyses of variance; explored and explained by later dynamic experiment) of races and cultures. Instances are discussed above in Chapter 6.

The attempt of certain ignoracists to argue that since the differences of means between populations are small compared to the differences of individuals within a race, the former are unimportant, ignores some principles applicable to groups. In the first place, there are the familiar statistico-biological facts that:

(1) Regression to the mean is always to the mean of the particular intermarrying social group. Thus the child of a parent of I.Q. 110 will tend to be 105 in a group of mean 100, but 100 in a group averaging 90. (However, let us note that if, in the former case, we take the level of the *mid* parent and the *mid* child, i.e., average of *all* born to the family, then the regression to the mean will be much less.) There is every reason to believe, from the *law of coercion to the bio-social mean*, that the same regression occurs culturally. A medium like TV, pitched at the quality of the mean of the population, is likely to raise the vocabulary level of the below average. What happens to an individual will therefore depend on the mean of the society in which he lives.

(2) With the normal distribution that occurs in such groups, a small difference of mean I.Q. (or acquired trait, also) brings about a far larger difference in the number of people above some high I.Q. (say 124 or 130) (see Figure 6-2). Consequently, from the racial and national small mean differences which Eysenck, Jensen, Lynn, and others have established, one is entitled to infer that there will be substantial differences in the levels of leadership types. Less investigated, but readily supportable by general observations and some group dynamics experiments, is the concept that there are *emergents*—forms of group behavior from the interaction of individuals—that differ greatly between groups with relatively small difference in population means or types. The observations of Cattell and Stice on performances of 100 groups of 10 men each, indicated that small differences in average emotional stability in the "populations" made considerable difference in the stability in the group itself, as if by an "emergent" action. As to the latter, one can build a honeycomb out of hexagons but not pentagons, and one cannot make a geodesic dome out of squares. That in a team activity or any demanding intercommunication, small mean population differences produce large group performance difference is understandable. *Within a group*, Beyondist ethics requires that each individual be treated on personal merits. "Group dynamics" experiments with small groups need to be vigorously pursued especially to give us at least an inkling of the relative duration of effects from more and less heritable traits.

6. Chap. 6. Oliver, R., *America's Decline*, notes that "the Japanese fashioned sixty or more varieties of Buddhism out of the Ch'an, which was itself a Chinese revision—a travesty of Gauthama the Buddha." He notes further that the Rinzai sect (a form of Zen Buddhism) is officially the basis of *bushido*, the admirable code of honor of the Japanese warrior. Now, if one reads the sacred documents of Rinzai (I unfortunately must rely on translations.), one can no more find in them a suggestion of *bushido* than one could find in the "New Testament" an authorization of the heroism and chivalric code of Roland, Oliver, King Arthur and his Round Table, Godfrey, Bayard, et al. In both cases, the code of honor was something that racial instinct imposed on the religion in clear violation of its tenets.

7. Chap. 6. An instance of necessary debate over their relative influence is whether the greater exploration by sea of the Europeans relative to that of the Chinese was environmental or genetic in origin. The coast of Europe is essentially concave; that of China a great convexity. In the former, one gets from place to place more easily by sea than land; in the latter, the sea journey

is an outer instead of an inner circle. Besides, finding islands close at hand is a good seaman's call to going further, and Europe abounds in western islands. The environmentalist argument here deserves weight.

8.   Chap. 6. One thinks of Housman's *The Welsh Marches*, where the young man deplores his ruined heredity:

>None will part us, none undo
>The knot that makes one flesh of two,
>Sick with hatred, sick with pain
>Strangling—When shall we be slain?

9.   Chap. 6. It is interesting to note how much the reward depends on circumstances. The jet had but a few months—insufficient to turn the tide in World War II. The ocean-going sailing ships of da Gama and Columbus, and Henry the Navigator associated technology, on the other hand, had an enormous effect in peopling sections of the world by European stock. The steam engine put Britain perhaps a century ahead of its European competitors in world trade, sustenance of a larger population, standard of living, etc.

10.   Chap. 7. Our theory that, among the primary causes of group decline, low morale is very high in importance awaits checking. It is beyond our space here to document quantitatively, in a variance analysis. However, to take a fairly obvious and superficial problem, specialists have calculated that the cost of alcoholism, in the U.S.A. alone, due to absenteeism, treatment expenses, automobile accidents, and social work in wrecked homes, runs currently at $14 billion a year. Comparable or higher figures are found for cost of prisons, police service, courts, and so on, and beyond gross law-breaking there is a hinterland of corruption and parasitisms that come to light episodically in Mafia investigations. Beyond these blacker regions is a grey belt of antisocial but legal behaviors in, for example, conspicuous consumption of luxuries and egotistic indulgences, pornography, and parasitisms. As discussed elsewhere, the distinction between symbiosis and parasitism can be drawn only by calculations, and the Marxian charge that the renter is a parasite would be a case in point.

However, long before the grey is reached, the grosser costs mentioned above are enough to gnaw away a nation's vitality, and, for example, to deny it necessary expenditures on self-defense, research, etc. Incidentally, the whole Beyondist notion that it is *group* survival that is vital to ethics is not reached in Social Darwinism, which perhaps thus merits the criticism it receives. As Darlington (1969, p. 343) says, "Spencer's *Survival of the Fittest* and Malthus's *Struggle for Existence*, equally ignore the stock and the race, the group and the community as entities (in selection)."

11.   Chap. 7. The reasons that within-group genetic selection, even if organized so as to be positive for improved conscience and altruism (as Muller, for example (*Out of the Night*), believes could be done) is so slow are (1) that by present research (Cattell, 1982) the superego, G factor, has only quite low heritability, and (2) that certain traits in criminals, such as self-sufficiency, Q_2, autia, M, and (in psychopaths) E, dominance, are valuable also in trailbreak-

ing scientists, inventors, creative artists, and so on. Thus we have to tolerate the criminal outcome.

12.   Chap. 7. The evidence (Cattell, 1982, p. 349) is that C, ego strength, and Q_2, self-sufficiency, reach a heritability of about 0.40, whereas G stands at 0.12, O at 0.34, and E at 0.18. These are total population heritabilities.

13.   Chap. 8. Since I have not hitherto sufficiently distinguished the meaning of "feeling liberals" and "thinking liberals," let it be said here that the former is a liberal guided by feelings, largely of a protective and even sentimental nature, who automatically backs whatever is said to be liberal. By contrast, the *thinking liberal* is one who disdains sheer conservatism and thinks his way into every current problem. He is the continuer of the line of such nineteenth century liberals as Comte, Darwin, Huxley, Ingersol, Mill, and Bentham. Unfortunately, perhaps 80% of modern liberals have no basic connection with that line, but simply ask for pie-in-the-skym regardless of means of producing it.

Rousseau may be regarded as the archetype of the feeling liberal, whom Professor Oliver, a leading classicist, designates as "a crack-brained vagabond who was given to snivelling ecstatically on the Virtue that filled his Pure Heart, and to denouncing the corruption of the Christian Churches that maintained the orphan asylums at which his bastards were surreptitiously abandoned. Rousseau, unfortunately for us, had the ability to write an emotional prose that gave spice to his balderdash." (This the feeling liberal always has.)

"The real gravamen of guilt falls on the educated, sceptical, intellectual society that did not laugh at his fantasies about the innate Virtue of hearts uncorrupted by civilization, the Noble Savage, the Equality of all human beings, who can become unequal only through the wickedness of civilized society . . . . You can grit your teeth and read all of it—and you really should, for otherwise you will not believe that books so widely read and rhapsodically admired can be so supremely silly and so exruciatingly tedious." (R. P. Oliver, *Christianity and the Survival of the West*, 1973.)

The wishful-thinking, reality-denying, indulgent young liberal (who in the past included Rousseau, Shelley, Whitman—and maybe Marx) I am suggesting we designate *feeling liberals*, while those who aim at progress based on full recognition of scientific facts and methods, we may contrast as *thinking liberals*. The restricted thinking of feeling liberals has a recent illustration in Arnold Toynbee's solution to international conflict by encouraging such wholesale intermarriage of races as would eliminate any differences of types among national gene pools. The broader vision of Beyondism sees this running down into entropy as about the worst calamity that could happen to the hopes of evolution. Most feeling-liberal movements have the same short-sighted, instant-satisfaction, self-defensive quality, even when the feeling is a benevolent one. The distinction made here has some alignment with Lord Snow's picture of "the two cultures"—literature-art and science-engineering as we might call them. Seeing this from a university faculty common room, Snow gave it a slightly different slant from that which we give it here and in Chapter 12, in connection with "genetic lag." At a deeper psychological level than the social developments in the arts and the sciences, we see the former as instinctually rooted in play and fantasy and the latter in curiosity and reality testing. The suggestion therefore is that *some* correlation and overlap exists between the literary intellectual and the feeling liberal, and the scientific intellectual and the thinking liberal.

14.   Chap. 8. Additional loyalty-ethic relations, bringing the total to 10, are possible if one splits categories. A national group is a combination of a genetic (racial mixture) and a cultural pattern. The alliances between groups— and therefore the sentiments of citizens—are largely determined by strategic self-interest, as in the European linkages in World Wars I and II. But probably, with increasing strength in an educated world, they are secondarily affected by similarity of cultural and racial goals, but rationally and gregariously grounded.

On the cultural side this is obvious. A common language, for example, is very potent, as in bringing the U.S. and the U.K. together in World Wars I and II. The ignoracist will deny affiliation by race, but whether it is desirable or undesirable it is an incontestable fact. In World War II, Japanese, but not German and Italian, aliens were segregated because, a protester said, "of the different color of their skin." The author of *The Good Earth* (Pearl Buck), with her Asian experience, predicted that Japan, Burma, and Southeast Asian countries would ally on the basis of racial similarity. And when Ba Mow was made first Prime Minister of newly independent Burma, the "official slogan of the new nation was 'One blood, one voice'. . ." (Toland, J., *The Rising Sun*, p. 517). A common voice has often been expressed by the blacks in Africa and in the U.S. In Malaya, on the other hand, the problem has been to get some unity between the Chinese and the racially conscious Malayans.

That these links of cultural and racial sympathy, cutting across the more highly organized national unities, have some evolutionary functional action would be hard to deny. And if they have, it is logical to assign an ethical status to such loyalties. However, the more powerful loyalties, and the interpenetrating ethical values that go with them, are covered in the eight above.

15. Chap. 8. As G. K. Chesterton brought out so clearly in his poem on Leigh Hunt's *Abou ben Adhem*

> And love not God, since men alone are dear.
> Only fear God; for you have cause to fear.

16.   Chap. 8. But not false, sentimental appeals to what society can do. Roosevelt's four freedoms have seldom been excelled in the realm of political claptrap, at least as regard freedom from wants and from fears. The first surrenders the ego to the id, since one's wants can include luxurious cars and film stars. Freedom from fear, since foresight is substantially fearsight, would end the use of the frontal lobes, and mankind's progress.

17.   Chap. 9. The nature of the "society" in which an individual lives and with which he is supposed to have a "social contract" (Rousseau, 1913; Ardrey, 1970) of rights and ethical obligations is regrettably loose and intangible in the philosophical discussions thereof that have prevailed up to this generation. Social psychology now sees an organic entity permitting the prediction of

actions of an organized group by a behavioral specification equation on the same model as for an organized individual, namely:

FORMULA

$$a_{hijk} = b_{hjk1}T_{1i} + b_{hjk2}T_{2i} + \ldots b_{hjkn}T_{ni} \quad ,$$

when there are n traits (T's), scored for the given individual i, in any act, a, responding by behavior, j, to focal stimulus, h, in ambient situation, k. The b's are thus the *behavioral indices* saying how much each trait (T_1 through T_n) is involved in determining the magnitude of the behavior a.

In describing the personality of an individual we have recourse to a profile (vector) of trait scores, T_{1i} through T_{ni}. In describing the *syntality* of an organized group we have recourse similarly to scores on the traits of a group. The delay in revealing laws in this area has resulted largely from anthropologists and political scientists making up these dimensions a priori, instead of finding them by factor analysis of social indices on a hundred or so countries, as has since been done by Brennan, Cattell, Breul, Hartman, Rummel, Woliver, and others. The meaningful nature of these national dimensions, such as *morale*, *cultural pressure*, and *enlightened affluence* is discussed in Chapters 5, 10, and 17. Here we wish only to consider this theoretical model as offering a firmer basis for discussion of the general problem of the relation of the individual to society.

If the characteristics of the population of individuals as such are represented by P (such values as means, standard deviations, on traits like intelligence, emotional stability, etc.) and the role structure in the group by R (social classes, form of government, and economics), then the essence of the relationship to syntality is:

$$(f)S = (f)P \cdot R \quad ,$$

where (f) is an unspecified function and it is understood that there is two-way causal action. The last means that syntality emerges from an interaction of the individual traits and the structure, and that this emergent in turn operates on the traits and structures among individuals. The implication, as discussed in the text above, is that the rights and duties of the individual to the state and the rights and duties of the state to the individual cannot be (a) defined a priori from some abstract principle, but only from the properties of a particular P, R, and S, and (b) defined in separation one from the other, i.e., one cannot talk about the civil rights of the individual without knowing the rights of the state over the individual. The latter will be defined by the conditions of survival of the state in the circumstances of the time.

18. Chap. 9. "Humanism" is a term of a dozen meanings. Matthew Arnold's biographer calls it "the attitude of those men who think it an advantage to live in society, and, at that, in a complex and highly developed society, and who believe that man fulfills his nature and reaches his proper stature in this circumstance." Far from being the "humanist-liberal" antipathy to Beyondist austerity that is rampant today, Arnold's definition is all of a piece with our insistence that natural selection of societies, *as* societies, is the first ethical requirement in Beyondism.

19. Chap. 10. At the present juncture of high birth rates in third-world countries, the simple index of "population per square mile" cannot be taken as a positive index of progress. But over long periods of unmitigated, independent evolution it was so. The population per square mile distinguished, for example, the agricultural revolution from the previous hunting phase. Anthropologist Gordon Childe points out that the most successful, culturally, of the North West Indian tribes reached a density of 1.7 per square mile, against 0.26 for the rest, and that Australian aboriginies were never able to exceed 0.03. In reaching high densities with health and contentment, the Mongolian race leads the Caucasian. *Granted an equal standard of living*, the population size per square mile counts as a measure of racio-cultural success. And its decline has normally been an aspect of general decline. As Moorhead points out regarding the Sudan in a period of poor government management (*The White Nile*), "of the original 9 million inhabitants about 75% were exterminated during the Khalifa's reign. The continual wars and the slave trade destroyed many thousands each year, diseases such as smallpox and syphilis were endemic, and now, in 1889 the country was overwhelmed by famine," p. 355. A true growth of self-supporting population is, of course, very different from what would be produced by such measures as Moynihan's attempt to supply a guaranteed state income to the poor according to family size. This (Rather, D. & Gates, G.P., *The Palace Guard*, Harper, 1974) is held up as a "model" that has been "successful in Europe and Canada," but what is this meaning of successful?

20. Chap. 10. In this review of Schell in the *Unitarian Universalist World*, 13(7):14, 15th July 1982, it fits the description of political tact before truth in universalist religions, given in various places here, that the last sentence above, on enthroned tribalism, in Dr. Hardin's MS review was cut out of publication!

21. (see also note 17) Chap. 11. As must be evident to everyone, I am drawing checks here on a scientific bank of the future. But not with the expectation that there will be money to spend here and now. Intuition, the mores of some existing religions, the best guesses of the shrewdest scientists will have to do for a while in lieu of checkable scientific principles and findings. The theoretical basis of the social sciences has for a century been a series of "schools," the very word implying loyalty and faith rather than logic and fact. We have had Hegelianism, Utilitarianism and economic theories, Boas's "Particularism," Spencerian Social Darwinism, Carlyle's leadership by "heroes," River's and Smith's diffusionism, Spengler Schmidt's Kulturkreise, Radcliffe-Brown's structural functionalism, Marxian and other cultural materialism, and Malinowski and Mead's psychological functionalism. The last of these got nearer the mark, but, from the standpoint of the standards of method a *multivariate experimental social psychology* embraces, they all have a touch of the Dark Ages. (For example, psychological functionalism among cultural anthropologists built with simple faith on Freudian psychology and completely neglected the new psychology of measurement and mathematical models.)

Although I have labored for four decades to bring quantitatively psychodynamic concepts and findings into the study of group structure, group behavior, and group learning, I have to confess that the fragile outlines that have emerged are far short of offering the blueprints that a Beyondist guidance of groups on the above lines requires. Nevertheless, the reader may wish to glance at the various contributions (see the bibliography for Chapter 7, in Vol. 2, of *Personality and Learning Theory*, Cattell, 1980) to recognize how different the foundation is from that of schools on which the understanding of societies has rested—with some contempt from the practical public and the politician—for the last century.

Incidentally, if we consider our individual immortality to lie in the spreading waves of consequences of our actions, such as the effects of our good example, the usefulness of our savings for charity, usefulness of our creations, and so on, we must also accept the corollary of that theorem. That corollary is that our sense of individuality is in part an illusion. We are the product of all that our teachers, parents, and friends—in short the cultural elements—have taught us. The principle is just the same as that which we have accepted for cultural natural selection, namely, that cultural elements can transfer to and live upon different biological substrates. The individual retains his claim to complete individuality, for he is, first, a unique combination of the ambient elements, and secondly, he is free to rearrange them, as a racial make-up in a group interacts with the cultural elements to give them new shape.

Our emotional difficulty lies in accepting this individuality as temporary. Many religions, and still more totalitarian political systems, have treated this individuality as unethical. (The Christian concept of "being born again" and the Buddhist notion of Nirvana seem to be in part not only a call to reduce the genetic lag, i.e., the necessary appeal to abandon instinctual behavior inappropriate to a more advanced culture, but also to reduce the degree of individuality.) Here, Beyondism produces different values; for it recognizes that an important fraction of social progress arises from thought processes which reach their greatest originality in an individual. It is one thing to purge individuality of vanity and "original sin" (failure to escape from inappropriate instinctual impulsive demands), and quite another to suppress ethically directed individuality.

Even when this is accepted as the best status of individuality, there remains an emotional problem. Nature endows us with an obsessive concern with our individuality, necessary while it endures.

22. Chap. 11. The world of the literate, as, e.g., in the *New York Times Book Review*, is curiously like a closed hothouse, in which for lack of outside perspective the vegetation is viewed as larger than reality. The capacity of writers to write about writers who write about writers is remarkable. When Shakespeare's Hamlet asked, "What's Hecuba to him, or he to Hecuba?" he was aware of this artificiality of emotion in the literate, that can overcome any array of cold facts and sense of proportion.

Oswald Spengler saw this force (*The Hour of Decision*, 1934), "The idea of the class struggle . . . was the creation of men who had aspired to a higher social class. Marx was a frustrated bourgeois. And the same applies to all the other jurists, literati, professors, and priests. This (misplacement) is the psychological prerequisite for professional revolutionaries."

23. Chap. 12. The concept of a genetic lag necessarily implies the possible existence of a population genetic pool ideally related, i.e., with zero deflection

strain, to a given culture. For reasons given later under the concept of the "productive imbalance," this degree of fit is not desirable in human society, though it is virtually realized in those complex and effective insect societies in which all essential behaviors are genetically programmed.

As a mathematical concept, a given degree of deflection strain, occasioned by genetic lag, could be reached by an infinite variety of genetic pools, any one of which could, by education, yield some degree of functionning of the culture. (It is necessary to counter the misrepresentation that our analysis says that the X racial gene pool is absolutely unable to acquire the Y culture. The question is always one of *relative* cost and frustration.) However even within the human ranges of, say, intelligence, it comes near to being an absolute impossibility to teach high school children of I.Q. 70 or less how to use partial differential equations. If anyone doubts the limits that genetics puts on learning, it is only necessary to refer him to differences of species. Within mammals, despite the long association of man and dog, no one has yet taught a dog to speak. Reference here is to cognitive genetic lag, but actually there are limits imposed also by innate emotional control (as demonstrated in ego strength, Cattell, 1982b) such that high impulsivity and incapacity to concentrate cause a poor fit to a complex culture, and a strain which is involved in substantially genetically determined psychotic breakdowns.

24. Chap. 12. It would be interesting to compare the contributions of the 2 million Balinese to physics, chemistry, medicine, and psychology with that of the same number of, say, white South Africans equally remote from stimulation of nearby cultures. The discrepancy in contributions to medicine, for example, by Barnard and the like in the latter culture would be especially great.

25. Chap. 12. We have accepted the general position that in a society that endures, and does not destroy itself by dysgenic processes, there will be genetic molding toward reduction of the genetic lag and a better natural fit. At present, sociobiology can present only circumstantial evidence for this, and anyone who wishes hotly to contest it can put up a good show. What we are claiming is a genetic change in two areas: (1) in the sheer strength of certain ergic needs, probably partly neural and partly endocrine (It is said that adaptation to high density of population has led to smaller adrenal glands in the Chinese, and apparently the glands governing fear and pugnacity are larger in wild than domesticated animals species.); and (2) in preferred paths of behavior toward a given goal. Here we encounter Jung's argument that not only instinctive (ergic) goals are innate, but also "archetypal" attitudes and behaviors of a more specific kind, e.g., connected with intrafamilial behavior. No sociologist can contest that in insects even the most specific behavioral reflexes are inherited. It would be strange if within the animal world there were an *absolute* difference in neural functioning between genera and classes, and it fits careful observation best to suppose that there are also differences in mean *dispositions*, making some *modes of behavioral expression* easy to learn and others harder to learn. The furious two year old will run open mouthed to bite: but he has to be taught to express his attack verbally.

Perhaps the nearest evidence for culture modifying the genetic behavioral inclinations themselves is available in the domestication of animals. It is possible to teach the sheep dog to round up sheep rather than to attack them like his wolfish ancestors. But the advance is gradual, and every now and then some dogs run in packs and eat sheep.

Granted that the long circuiting from more tempting behavioral forms, and the sublimatory deflections from ergic goal satisfactions, after being maintained for centuries with difficulty, will begin to breed a type of human who innately finds the adjustment less difficult. One can imagine that adjustment to complexity will take the form of higher flexibility—largely by cortical increase of intelligence, but there will also be specific changes in emotional need. For example, the uselessness in a society with, say, 95% of survival to middle age of all children born of a strong sexual disposition will lead, by the economy of nature, to reduction of sex drive by elimination of the highly sexed. It is very difficult to foresee what the particular makeup of emotional needs will be in the average person after some period of natural selection by culture. Freedom, political power, and independence, a desire for longer life, an immense curiosity, intellectually expressed, in the vast field of knowledge that will become available, and mastery of the physical world, would seem to be permanent in the future emotional basis.

26. Chap. 12. See cases discussed in *U.S. News*, June 27, 1983. The superficiality of the arguments put forward, for example, in discussing the death penalty for premeditated murder is another expression of the uncertainty about the expression of love. In these cases, the expression of love for some innocent but unknown individuals who will be murdered stands little chance against pity for the concretely described unfortunate who may be executed. Economics is a small part of the argument for capital punishment, but it may be noted that the cost of keeping alive in a safe custody the criminally insane person is now over $100,000 a year. Probably ten normal, healthy children could be raised on that—who will not be raised because the gross national produce of society is a fixed amount where expenditure one way forbids expenditure in another. In short, the "feeling liberal's" compassion for the criminal ends by murdering the as yet unborn. This is a real right-to-life issue. In several recent instances, convicted murders have themselves asked for the dignity of death and surcease from living in prison with their guilt. The paradox is that those capable of such profound remorse are the ones society might do best to leave alive.

Among all the possible misunderstandings of a Beyondist position, I expect the above call for what Hardin has well called "discriminating altruism" will encounter most. The psycho-social research indicating that the "poor" are not necessarily the "downtrodden," but occupy a level reached by inherent properties, as an oil level separates out from a shaken mixture of oil and water, is necessary for true action to remedy the problem. A typical feeling liberal writes, "The moral worth of any society may be judged by the standard of living it sets for the unemployed, the elderly, etc." The hypocrisy in this position is the trick of not mentioning that society has limited resources and that greater expenditure here means less on education, scientific research, and national defense. For example, in the U.S.A. (and elsewhere) in the 1980s the arguments ran round in an endless boring, dizzying, nauseating circle over relative expenditure on welfare or defense. Nations that win wars nowadays impose their values on the defeated!

Maintaining the very existence of society must take precedence over alleviating internal discomfort or suffering. Is it more moral to let the parental protective instinct have unmitigated expression in bettering the poor or to consider it well placed in succoring the values of freedom for which the nation stands? The second is a paramount value which all nations must maintain, or collapse. To allow the proponents of the former to pre-empt the luxury of public moral indignation (as they now tend to do) is to accept a confused ethic inferior to Beyondism.

27. Chap. 12. When social scientists begin seriously and scientifically to study what ergic modifications are perversions, from the standpoint of group and individual survival, they will probably come up with some conclusions infuriating to many in a "modern" permissive society. For example, the parental, protective, succorant propensity, intended for maximum care and attention to human offspring, presently sustains about 80 million well-fed dogs in the U.S.A. And the sexual drive, intended for procreation is, we are told by psychologists with vast, enthusiastic followings, intended really as a recreation between the sexes. Here the genetic lag is really great, for the urge to sexual activity is completely out of relation to the need for population growth, and some major adjustment is called for (as Christianity well recognized, but with no solution but repression). The question is whether this gap is to be met by great increases in the arts of pornography or by such attempts at control and sublimation as most religions have advocated, or perhaps by some scientific advance in physiology, following "the pill" which, by antiaphrodisiac action, will permit the energy of the sex drive to be spread into new realms. In general, looking at the problem of the genetic lag, one is surely forced to the conclusion that the nonreligious adjustments to it—to be precise, especially the non-Beyondist adjustment to it—in art, sport, luxuries, and perversions, play only a makeshift, unintegrated response to the Beyondist need.

28. Chap. 12. To give credit where credit is due, we must note that the modern value-forming literature of communist Russia has aimed to build up this sense of excitement in a group adventure. At the same time the government has (a) used "adventurism" as a bad word, as indeed any new exploration would be in a dogmatic, rigid Marxian religion, and (b) agreed on its imperialist, expansive adventures not in ideas but in the simple extension of economic-political forms. One is reminded also that in Lenin's speech to comsomols he asserted "morality is entirely subordinate to the interests of the class war."

29. Chap. 12. What is meant here, above, by sentimental—a word with numerous meanings—can be succinctly indicated by the contrast of the writings of, say, Dickens and Chesterton with those of Hardy, Flaubert, or Dostoevsky. We all love Dickens and the hearty absolutes of Chesterton; but there is a sense on which these tear-jerking writers are a bottle of alcohol (which Chesterton explicitly called for) in danger of turning a moment of relaxation of common sense into an addiction to crass emotionalism. (By which, above, I have distinguished today's "feeling liberals" from the great progressive liberals of the nineteenth century, and, more rarely, of the present.)
In a lifetime of work in social science I have several times written demanding in the name of science that social scientists clearly present their actual

scientific findings with a separate statement of any ethical or political values before they venture to combine them in social recommendations. There is no abandonment of that essential position in the above statement. The "purist" scientist rightly detests those quasi-scientists who cheat the lay public in this matter. Unfortunately, this purist ideal often leads to the equally mistaken view that a scientist should never—even with explicit explanation that he is combining these findings with such and such values—get excited or passionate about urgent social matters. I personally experienced these prejudices when I wrote, in 1937, *The Fight for our National Intelligence*. It happens that (a) few studies (see Van Court, 1986) before or since have used such adequate rural and urban samples relating birth rate to intelligence, and (b) no study has approached the separation of environmental and genetic factors by the unique use there made of culture-fair intelligence. The strong "emotional" appeal I made for facing this social problem (epitomized by "fight" in the title) automatically evoked entirely indefensible derogation of the scientific work itself, by shocked "academic" scientists. Since evolutionary values were clearly stated in the final integration of the findings, on the one hand, and the social recommendations on the other, I have no hesitation in standing by that book as an instance of the proper emotional vitality for an ethical position based on science.

30. Chap. 13. The reasons why Beyondism, unlike all the religions claiming to be universalistic, refuses to give complete carte blanche to all expressions of the succorant, pitying erg, as a higher spiritual and noble impulse beyond all reproach are three. Two of these are inherent in the logic of Beyondism and one is merely historical. Although Nietzsche goes beyond our considered position into rhetorical absolutes, yet he gets at the first difficulty when he says "Pity thwarts the whole law of evolution, which is the law of natural selection. It has been called *the* virtue, [but] by maintaining life in so many of the botched of all kinds, it gives life itself a gloomy and dubious aspect." Beyondist eugenics is clear in kindness to the botched living, but severe in its insistence on the crime of bringing such life into existence. Secondly, in a cultural domain, unbridled kindness, tolerance, and permissiveness breeds all kinds of mutual indulgence, waste, and sloppy thinking. Only the scientist is brought up sharp, by sheer failure, when he indulges in the last. One indicator that we are, incidentally, suffering presently from the adoration of toleration, is the inability to get the needed proportion of students into the hard sciences, compared to literature and the performing arts, less objective in recognizing poor performance, and giving more immediate expression to emotional impulse. If this is not cured by internal change of values, it will, according to the law of group check, be cured by results of Russia's greater success in co-opting students of the hard sciences. The historical reason for the Christian doctrine of pity and resignation (or the Greek fate and the Islamic Kismet) prevailing, as a spirit different from the boundless delight in scientific adventure which now informs the Beyondist, is the high level of frustration which prevailed in the Eastern Mediterranean. With sufficient unreasonablness (as still seems to prevail there today), hysteric emotionalism (of which New Testament times are full), crowding, defeat, and enslavement of peoples, the only emotions that could fit circumstances were those of pity and resignation. For what may

be only a brief vacation from such conditions (as Bernard Darwin suggests) begotten by science, its reasoning and its gifts of plenty, since the Renaissance, Europe entered on the spirit of adventure and control to which Beyondism gives explicit expression. Among other things, that spirit calls for not making a virtue of poverty, misery, and the false compassion which prolongs them.

31. Chap. 14. One reason for greater attention to genetic innovation and experiment per se is that, for historical reasons, experiment and natural selection in terms of cultural pressures might slow down and cease. And it is a general principle that the less severe and efficient a nation gets in its ethics of internal selection, cultural and genetic, the more it must expect to face the discipline of between-group selection. The activity levels in these two parts of the total system are inverse. However, both selections could presumably be made to slow down if the citizens everywhere put comfort, ease, and lack of risk ahead of adventure, and if nations attempted to establish what we called the Hedonic Pact.

However, if such collusion in simultaneously reducing both internal and external competition prevailed, there would still be the challenge of natural catastrophies in the physical environment itself. One of the dangers of reducing international competition is that it is likely to reduce simultaneously the capacity of groups to handle these inevitable challenges of nature. Environmental natural selection would safely take charge again after a period of hedonistically produced degeneration, but this might mean the loss forever of a potentially promising incipient direction of evolution. Fortunately, at present there seems little danger of such completely adjustive stagnation, for more people are concerned that "future shock" will lead, by its byproducts, to an overwhelming "chain reaction." However, the wide range of possibilities in the system calls for recognizing the important role of mutational, genetic engineering innovations undertaken at an acceptable risk level.

32. Chap. 15. Although quite a variety of genetic defects can be patched up (as by a kidney dialysis machine), the burden on society of handling a large number of such defects would bring the society to defeat. Intensive education, for example, may get children of I.Q. 75 to read and write, but it would be better for everyone to have the same number of children born of average I.Q., able to acquire reading and writing far more easily. One ethical evil here is the perverted parental protective erg which satisfied itself by having a sufficiency of dependent, subnormal, and handicapped children and would not admit consciously that it is deprived in the absence thereof. From the standpoint of the nation's genetic pool, the patching could lead to a dangerous accumulation of deleterious genes—a debt which might be hard to pay off later.

33. Chap. 15. It is documented that sheer greed—the business owner lobby—is the principal force sustaining unabated immigration of unskilled worker aliens into the U.S. (*The Environmental Fund*, March, 1983). A Gallup poll shows that one in four of the population of Latin America would like to move into the U.S. (presumably rather than attack the deteriorated economic conditions and social habits in their own countries). A very curious quota law has prevailed in the U.S. since the last immigration law, namely, that anyone

in under the quota can then have all his relatives brought in. This favors uncontrolled families and all the associations thereof. At present, moreover, an "amnesty" is being considered for the millions who entered illegally.

At present growth rates, the bursting Caribbean population will change in 50 years from 53 million to 141 million, and the Mexican from 70 million to 184 million (op.cit., p.2). With such pressures only the firmest measures can stop the flood of illegal immigration.

In this area a sincerely applied Beyondist ethic says that the nation is entitled to consider the differences of averages in the sources in fixing its quotas. Insurance companies, which have to be realistic or become bankrupt, make precise discriminations of this kind among age groups, the sexes, occupational groups, and so on, in what is recognized as actuarial *risk discrimination*. Inasmuch as statistically significant differences in longevity exist for different groups and their ways of life, it is a matter of justice that the individual shall pay lower premiums if he belongs to a lower risk group. Of course, in terms of long-term prospects of absorption of subcultures in relation to national survival, traits that are relatively more genetic become important in these decisions. Even with good genes in each contributing group, the geneticist has to recognize the existence of a few "by-falls" or "fringe products" due to oddly assorted combinations from rather neurotic types. As an instance of this complete lack of far-sighted responsibility, let us consider the fact in the *Honolulu Advertiser* (13 August 1983), "Nearly a third of Los Angeles County is now Hispanic (Versus in 1960), as are almost two-thirds of Los Angeles kindergartners (due to the higher birth rate)." Whereas Americans are willing to fight to the death for the values of their country against imposition of foreign cultures by war, they accede in bewilderment to the supplanting of these values in this fashion. For let us make no mistake, the educational culture makes little impact on the familial, religious, and racial values that immigrants bring with them. This spineless bewilderment of the American majority in the face of media-supported "feeling liberals" and the greed of commerce for lower wages, reminds one of the moral flabbiness of those Germans who disagreed with Nazism and whose concerted, alert action could have stopped its beginnings.

34. Chap. 16. I have presented the argument for dislocation of curves of supply and demand of intelligence in detail in "Inflation and Business Cycles from the Standpoint of Psychology and Sociology" in *The Journal of Social, Political and Economic Studies*, 1982, 7, 35-54. Briefly, it compares the distribution of *demand* for intelligence (duly educated) in our evolving society with the birth rate supply. The discrepancy of these two curves indicates the natural reward level at each. This shows why low pay and unemployment are highest at the lower levels.

If the discrepancy is allowed to continue, it could lead to a situation in which not 10% but perhaps 60% of the population is technologically unemployable. As Ryabov argues, this could lead to a new "third estate" of "superfluous human beings left to vegetate and to plan mischief directed against society." We have suggested that the measure in unemployed can be borne, at a cost to positive developments, by welfare, and that by careful supply of service occupation, harmless amusements may prevail over "mischief." The dislocation problem, heightened by rapid increase in robotry, may well prove to be the biggest social problem of the 21st century.

35. Chap. 16. A prominent public obstacle to nuclear energy at the moment is the justifiable conclusion that even small increases in radiation will significantly increase the mutation rate to which we, with all living things, are subject. Because such uncontrolled impacts are less desirable, it is likely that an increase of mutation rate by controlled means will be instituted by some more adventurous cultures. A faster rate of progress in an envisioned direction would be made possible by a higher mutation rate, provided the more numerous mutations unsuitable to that direction are eliminated. Success in such measures supposes (a) that choking of the gene pool by the more numerous unfit mutations is avoided, and (b) that a higher reproduction rate be instituted among the fewer desirable mutations to keep the population to size. A eugenic program would handle both humanely, the first by medical advances in detecting abnormalities and terminating such pregnancies very early. But even the incidence of moderate accidental (nuclear) production of new gene forms is not regarded as simply undesirable.

36. Chap. 16. The question of whether a genetic diversity is better achieved by aiming at a broad range in an otherwise homogeneous group or by a plurality of ethnic groups is one that has to be considered both here, in the genetic field, and later in the cultural field. The answer may unfortunately be different in the two domains in that although some sociologists make an argument for cultural pluralism, the broad verdict of history scarcely supports such a theory empirically.

For example, the Chinese and the Jews exhibit great stability and good performance over long periods on a culture of high uniformity, as also does Japan. The high point in Spanish world empire was at a time when the expulsion of the Moors and the slogan "One people, one king, one religion" was uppermost. On the effect of plurality of culture and race, such countries as India, Malaya, and some South American and North African countries present illustrations of the problem. A well-informed student of India says that it is still "seen these days as a land of poverty, famines, disease, squalor, untouchability, separation, and chaos—a reputation exaggerated but not altogether undeserved." (*Sun. N.Y. Times Book Review*, 1983). The hope that the ethnic subgroups can be used as experiments within a larger nation and as sources of hybrid variation, for some reason, does not seem to work, and deserves careful investigation.

The British population is largely a mixture of Nordid and Celtic (Mediterranid-Alpinid, in Baker's [1974] classification). Some first-rate geneticists, e.g., Haldane, have suggested that this hybridization is the origin of Shakespeare's "happy breed of men." However, as in most countries, the genetic hybridization of the constituent races remains, after many centuries, in any case, still only partial. So if there are indeed happy results of this combination, it may arise more from the cultural result of both types being active in the population, rather than to any genetic fusion.

37. Chap. 16. With regard to the desirable function of relative group success in advancing the level of group averages, this is, of course, unfortunate. The efficiency of leadership is more tied up with the *average* population intelligence in a democratic society than in a dictatorship. Consequently, if natural selection

is to raise averages, it would be well to have competition only among democracies. Actually, it is *only* an elite persisting across generations, e.g., as in ancient Egypt, with a dull mass below, that this "unfairness" of competitions exists, since in serious war democracies quickly cancel democratic rights and assume the structure of a government dictatorship.

38. Chap. 16. In the technical field we must note that Darwin and others first gave a large role in evolution to sexual selection, impressed by mating advertising. But in humans, though the handsome prince is chosen by and chooses the beautiful princess, this does not contribute to the increase of beauty unless they have more children than the fat slob who has to settle for a slatternly wench. There is little evidence that those rejected at one level do not get accepted at some lower level. However, this circumstance leads to what we know to exist; an assortive marriage of like with like, reaching on into correlation of about plus 0.4 for intelligence (Vandenburg, 1965; Cattell, 1982b), which is a special outcome of sexual selection. This degree of inbreeding in nonexplicit "castes" produces a larger spread (standard deviation) of trait levels than would occur by random "pan-mixed" marriages. Insofar as a group wishes to have more high level persons (at cost also of more low levels), for defense creativity or its cultural laurels, it has to encourage assortive mating. This is not a method of raising the average capacity in this or that trait, but it is relevant to any rise of unconscious elite structure, and it permits a differential birth rate to be more powerfully eugenicallyt applied.

39. Chap. 16. In terms of "work," Kipling (*The Gods of the Copy-book Headings*) expressed the issue squarely thus:

> In the Carboniferous Epoch we were promised abundance for all,
> By robbing selected Peter to pay for collective Paul;
> But, though we had plenty of money, there was nothing our money could buy
> And the Gods of the Copy-book Headings said: *If you don't work you die.*"

40. Chap. 16. The inheritability of longevity is well established. Its desirability needs discussion. In an evolving society, "scrapping" of those holding too long to earlier adjustments is inevitable, and indeed we are dealing with an aspect of the necessity of individual death. However, with the increasing complexity of society, training periods get longer and longer. Indeed, as a realist in education summarized, "Graduation ten years too late and death on time." For doctors, psychologists, and many professional persons it is not unusual to get into effective practice only after 30, so that roughly half the life is spent in preparation for life. There can surely be no doubt that longevity, with health, is one of the most needed eugenic goals. It is perhaps a disturbing thought, but fathering more of the population from men who have remained free of disease into their seventies would be one effective procedure!

Shaw brings his own waggish comment on this situation: "Civilization failed because the citizens and statesmen died of old age . . . before they had grown out of schoolboy games and savage sports and cigars and champagne. The signs of the end are always the same: Democracy, Socialism, and Votes for Women." G.B. Shaw, *Back to Methusaleh, II.*

41. Chap. 16. As stated above, the available researches, often carried out on a shoestring, are of very uneven quality. But the recent studies (1983) of Van Court (1986) and Vining (1982) confirm the present writer's early study (1937) on an adequate sample and with culture-fair intelligence tests, namely, that the trend in this century is dysgenic as far as intelligence is concerned.

42. Chap. 16. In the science of genetics we know enough to guide *negative* eugenics, i.e., the reduction of generally undesirable inheritances, and the pulling up of the social "rearguard" toward the central movement. Here, even the most cautious on the risk/benefit ratio would probably agree to reducing birth rates of mental defectives and borderline uneducable, schizophrenics, and a large number of clearly inheritable major physical diseases. Positive eugenics involves faith in the direction in which a special culture is moving, and therefore more hesitation. The inheritable bases of altruism and conscience (superego) has proved less than expected, but still one can argue for encouragement of higher levels of these along with intelligence. Indeed, Nobelist Muller made much of these.

43. Chap. 16. Two approaches to rectification of the dysgenic birth rate by economic aids can be considered: (1) by scholarship allowances relieving the parent from the greater educational cost of having a more able child, and (2) reform of income tax. Socialists have greeted the former as a complete solution, but obviously it is not, because the relief occurs perhaps 18 years after the planned conception. The only predictor at the time of conception of whether the child will be intelligent is the intelligence of the parents, which argues for an encouragement of the more intelligent parent, which is likely to be gauged by the parental income. To motivate the production of brighter children, therefore, requires a child allowance, by tax or other means, geared to the existing parental income. (Note that in, for example, the U.S.A. today the childless middle class couple is at an enormous advantage in material standard of living compared to a neighbor with, say, just three children. To raise a child over 22 years able enough to go four years to college (omitting graduate study) involves an expenditure in current dollars of about $150,000, i.e., $450,000 for three. Consider the interest which the childless gets on this money saved over 22 years, roughly $800,000, and it is evident that the child tax allowance, in the U.S.A. and, one may add, most Western culture nations, is laughable as a plan to keep the population at replacement value in the 80% middle group. (With deaths, celibacy, etc., mere replacement, without expansion, requires close to three children per family.)

The possibility must be seriously considered—and investigated—that in the twentieth century we have been in a phase of negative selection and retreat from genetic advance, even while we think we are advancing in social measures and cultural invention.

The question of whether natural selection is still operating toward group survival is answered primarily by a comparison of birth and death rates for desirable qualities. Except perhaps for death rates from such factors as smoking, alcoholism, and automobile accidents, socio-medical intervention has probably wiped out most of the survival differentials based on death rates rather than birth rates. When birth rate differentials remain the decisive factor, and are allowed to operate dysgenically, without social control of births as well as deaths, "fitness" takes on a new and sinister meaning. Many an academic population specialist today calmly admits, with an almost cynical detachment, that the unemployed with large families are the "fittest." That civilization would probably reverse the ordinary definition of "survival of the fitter" and lose its beneficial action, has long been recognized. Outside Beyondist thinking, however, the supreme importance of society's recognizing its ethical duty to the next generation and to the evolutionary principle has scarcely been recognized and when it has, a shrug of the shoulders at the concept of enforcing legal responsibility, or even economic encouragement, has left open the possibility that we are due for a lingering decadence. Here is a domain where Beyondism definitely demands ethical values neglected or avoided by most traditional ethical systems. Granted an extremely simple method of birth control aided by social work, the socially unfit who have previously had large familes of neglected and illegitimate children will be glad to avoid the burdens they have suffered.

Let it be recognized that we are not arguing from an over-simple relation of social fitness to genetic fitness, and that we recognize many exceptional individual cases. That is to say, we have to think statistically—which the average high school graduate today apparently finds difficult. With the various other factors and intermediate links, the correlation of social fitness and genetic desirability might be only, say, $+0.4$. But so long as it is statistically significant it is our best guide to a general policy.

If we had in education a training to think statistically and biologically, we would not have eugenic arguments confused by such issues as sterilization of the mentally defective, which concerns perhaps 1% of the population.

44. Chap. 16. There are some more technical and statistical points to be discussed also in relation to our above argument for income tax allowances to encourage larger families in the more socially fit. We have argued that it is hard to find more arguments for a differential income tax percentage than (a) charity (actually prevented), and, (b) the impossibility of collecting from those who do not earn. However, there would be arguments for child income tax allowances in the absence, in a given society, of (a) freedom to obtain an education proportional to one's abilities, (b) a free market fitting a person's earnings to society's need of him, and (c) a buying public that is not biased in its buying by inherited wealth or desires for what is not in its best interests, e.g., luxury feeding, or pornography, versus education. Failing these, a literal equality of taxation would not be appropriate.

In any discussion of economics and eugenics, one meets the same distortion from lack of statistical thinking as we described in note 43. We would not have to clarify, for example, the misunderstanding of this and other questions that arises when plans for using income tax as an eugenic aid based on untrue stereotypes under the rhetorical labels "rich," "poor." If these were properly used, they would refer only to the top 10% and bottom 10% at most. We are talking about measures applicable to the middle 80% of the earning range, for what happens genetically is decided by differential birth and death rates, etc., *across this large majority.* While on statistics, let us also point out that the genetic variance of children within families comes close to being equal to that between the family averages for the children. That is to say, it is almost as important to know one's genetic rank in the family as to know what family one comes from. This means that encouraging birth rates according to competence of the parents is far from fully efficient; but it is also far better, in raising population levels, than doing nothing, and it permits economic aid to eugenics because that aid needs to operate at the level of the parents who will decide their family size. In connection with eugenics and income tax, let us also raise the possible question that the unequal tax might be justified as enlightened altruism, on the argument that the lower ability group is for some reason performing more services than its earning power in the open market indicates.

The justification of some social altruisms, in the biological world, is that individual X is sacrificed, in the relative reproduction level, because his behavior benefits Y, where Y is largely carrying the same genes as X. The classical case in the insect world is the symbiosis of drones and workers in the bee community. If the lower ability and earning group were a reservoir of a larger gene variety than the upper, there would be some justification for not reducing its numbers.

But apart from arguments from biological co-function, as above, it seems that no Beyondist functional reason can be found for unequal income taxes. This, however, is a big econo-biological question that needs fuller discussion in the following chapter.

45. Chap. 17. In regard to borrowing, let us note again that: (a) What is *seen* by other countries as a desirable cultural innovation is what gets willingly spontaneously spread. The feature may not be *really* desirable, and (b) When spread is by pressure, at least the fact that one nation is in a position to exert pressures betokens some great cultural success of the habits.

One must recognize, however, flaws and mistakes in both of the above arguments for the desirability of imitation. First, it permits the borrowing culture to gain probable survival increase without any of the expense and sweat of creation, so that natural selection for *creativity* is rendered inefficient. Furthermore, it hinders the unique development of cultures entered upon sufficiently different trajectories. However, the pride and independence of nations and religions are likely successfully to resist wholesale imitation, as does also the indigestibility of certain imitated elements into certain functional patterns. As to the (b) process, there is again some tendency to reduce diversity, as when U.S.A and the U.S.S.R. bring pressure to get satellites conforming respectively to democratic and communist political systems.

46. Chap. 17. By present standards of research support as known to individual academic researchers and their grants committees, what I am sketching here may seem beyond all expectation, even though sober calculation shows that a few economies in numerous luxury advertiser-created expenditures could *easily* bring it to reality.

Where matters become visibly serious—which is in war and national security—the expenditures on research of any one country (and potentially of an international research center) expand to handle the most complex problems. For example, the U.S. National Security Agency at Fort Meade (concerned substantially with gathering international intelligence data, and, especially, code breaking) occupies 1.9 million square feet of space, more than 5.5 acres of computer machinery, and has employed as many as 95,000 people. (Thomas Powers in *The New York Review of Books*, February 3, 1983). An academic evaluator (Eysenck) of my MAVA design for obtaining more accurate and far-reaching results on the inheritance of personality and ability (Cattell, 1982) than the twin method, has told us best to forget it, because it would require the full time of three scientists for four years and a possible expenditure that might reach $500,000. The problem of human mental heritability, and a hundred others equally socially important, could be solved by a tenth of the NSA annual expenditure—not that the latter is unnecessary.

47. Chap. 17. The question of the right to privacy of the individual is currently being discussed in press discussions that a longer view would see as biased toward privacy. Criminal and antisocial, parasitic behavior is greatly aided by restrictions on government's right to know, to which one would imagine well-disposed, innocent, and altruistic persons would not object. The possible arguments for privacy are (1) that government is a particular set of people, on whose benevolence and morality one cannot depend (The U.S. citizen, in particular, as the Bill of Rights indicates, has a memory of British redcoats!); and (2) that if "all is discovered" were put in every mailbox, an appreciable number of people would leave town. The fully innocent and altruistic person scarcely exists; but surely degrees of trust must exist, and the citizen need not fear that the IRS gets informed that he has affairs with the parlor maid.

Whatever the determiners of an unwillingness to make personal information available to public institutions, there can be no doubt that it is a major source of loss to scientific research and to control of antisocial elements. Our concern is with the former. It is especially medical and social research that are hampered, since they depend a good deal on statistical analysis of intimate test and biographical data obtained from truly representative population samples. Any researcher in these fields knows that his hardest task is to obtain simple cooperation on these matters. The problem is likely to be more complicated and difficult in the area of statistical comparisons across cultures, unless Beyondist values are more widely adopted.

Incidentally, one of the most impudent recent arguments for privacy— notably in the sexual field—is that morality and ethical value are private matters. But it is the very essence and meaning of ethics that it concerns how one's behavior affects others. It is contrary to all psychological observation that an affair of sex or of hostility between two people affects only the two involved.

48. Chap. 18. In the satisfactions open to a human being in a world society, the awareness of the difficult-to-define spiritual equality may be more important than the unobtainable biological equality (in face of demands of a given culture), or the *defacto* cultural-legal equality. Presumably, by spiritual equality one means the self-respect that comes from what religions have called being "children of God," i.e., being given a genetic endowment of unknown potential. This means—given any new cultural development—being equally important for the great experiment. This does not presume on the existence of a benevolent deity, for whom mankind is more important than any other creation, but grants

self-respect and spiritual meaning in the light of the Beyondist understanding concerning our fellow men.

49. Chap. 18. The most advanced societies, notably Britain, have instituted such death duties in the last seventy years as suffice to phase out the larger part of ordinary family accumulations of wealth in two or three generations. That this operates only on the "larger part" is important, for considerable contributions to society have been made by individuals—Darwin, Cromwell, Jefferson, Maxwell, Newton, Washington—possessed of a secure pittance or modest property which rendered a truly independent contribution possible. A socialist and a believer in keeping a completely dispossessed proletariat will counter that a wise government gives scholarships, research grants, and art fellowships for important cultural contributions that have no immediate market negotiability. But in a communist country this requires political conventionality; in Catholic and Muslim countries what is required is religious conformity; and in countries that make grants to science it has required at least something that conventional committees can understand. What happened to Copernicus, Bruno, and Galileo in a Catholic society; what happened to investigators of genetics like Haldane, Vavilov, and Muller under Stalin and Lysenko; and what zero support Freud and Einstein received from research foundations we know. Some personal financial independence is a great aid to independence of mind, and the fact that *some* bourgeois above the level of proletariat may squander their leisure is an inescapable cost of any system of freedom to explore. Experiment is intrinsically wasteful compared to following a trodden path efficient to its own degree. Here and in many other places Beyondism stands firmly in favor of some degree of financial independence; for political independence without financial independence is a hollow mockery.

50. Chap. 18. Basically, one looks in this enigma for the justification for putting a larger charge for the same services on those who earn more—the more able and the more energetic. By the current practice it is likely to be only a matter of time before these enterprising strains are eliminated and a general level of unenterprising poverty remains.

It is quite remarkable that in a matter which so sharply concerns every citizen, idealistic and nonidealistic, one can get no public statement for principles of unequal income tax practice other than (1) that the practice descends by tradition from predatory rules (sometimes of conquerors who found it hopeless to try to collect from the poor), (2) that it is a compulsory imposition of Christian charity that the less poor support the more poor, and (3) that even in a well-organized society you cannot collect what the individual has already spent.

Apparently reasons (2) and (3) are widely accepted, though, as pointed out in other connections, (2) requires recognizing that type A (ill luck) and type B (systematic failure of social responsibility) poverty need totally different social treatment, if society is to retain its morale and its functional survival. What seems totally overlooked is that there is no argument in the name of justice for unequal income taxes if one considers the services, national and local, that an individual receives from his society—education, national defense, police protection, roads, street lighting, etc. No essential difference can be found between what is received by, say, a person earning $15,000 a year and one earning, say, $40,000 a year. If they were contracting in the open market with a private concern for the same services, they would pay essentially the same. But by social custom we accept, unquestioningly, that the second person will pay four or five times as much for the same services. Whatever the basis may have been for this Alice-in-Wonderland state of affairs, it apparently has long since ceased to be discussed.

Within at least the income range of the middle 80% of the population (excluding the grotesquely rich and the perpetually unemployed), and the defined age range from school learning to retirement, a Beyondist viewpoint would call for an absolutely equal tax. As of this year we are told the total tax income in the U.S. is $648.2 billion which calls for $2757 per person according to tax authorities. $2757 is not an uncollectable amount from all but the socially-occupationally deficient 10% of the population. This standard deduction from variable incomes would probably bring about a eugenic birth rate, and, culturally, a donation of surplus income to enterprises consistent with the values of the able and the conscientious. (The Carnegies and the Rockefellers were ahead of the government of their day in what they chose to support—education and research). The fixed tax would lead to charity as judged by the better earners. It would also—in a by no means trivial by-product—eliminate the enormous annual expenditure of time by intelligent people—accountants and citizens alike—on absurd complexities of present tax calculations.

We have considered here only the economics of income tax. But everyone knows that myriads of economic distribution schemes—from communism to tithes to "social credit"—have been proposed as ideals of social organization generally. The Beyondist recognizes first the functionality of a hierarchical economic classness, adjusted to give income to the greater contributors (workers), and in other ways discussed here. The "freak" suggestions of *one wage* have never worked and are out of touch with the realities of evolution. But a vast cleanup of unethical earnings is still needed, and rewards from "mass satisfaction, as, e.g., boxers and film stars versus medical researchers, must be devised within a natural market, perhaps by special taxes, as for cigarettes. Such suggestions of economic manipulations as the "negative income tax" and the constant political pressures for gifts to low incomes, in the form of free housing and the like should be finally cleared of their sentimentality and brought under the control of humane evolutionary goals.

It seems far too little appreciated that freedom of thought depends on capitalist freedom. When Bertrand Russell claims "freedom of thought is a prequisite of aristocracy" he really means of "someone who can support himself without state aid." He still has to get by the wall of prejudice presented by the media, but that is a challenge.

A small instance occurred at the meeting of internationally eminent social scientists at the *Institute of Psychiatry* in London called to debate Professor A. Jensen's extension (to group differences) of Sir Cyril Burt's findings on the mechanism of heredity in intelligence. Because Jensen stated the inescapable conclusion, carefully examined, of small but significant racial differences in intelligence, one newspaper produced his photograph with a label "Public Enemy." In the present writer's technical paper on psychometry, he ventured to point out that "prejudice" could exist on both sides, and that both *racist* and *ignoracist* bias needed to be dropped. The *London Times,* whose reporters were present, completely smothered vital public issues brought out by the assembled scientists, and as to my own plea for an open mind, they gave two lines to it, simply saying that "ignoracist" was a word they "preferred not to know."

51. Chap. 18. Biology is replete with examples on which a slight change of color, or form, in some members of a species results in their elimination in two or three generations. Even a slightly higher tax, rigidly applied to the more enterprising specimens of humanity, could, over a few generations, notably decrease human enterprise.

52. Chap.18. The reader will not have failed to notice that Beyondism claims to have no logical connections with the illogical notions of "right"- and "left"-wing politics. Indeed, it denies any such connections, because one cannot have logical connections with the illogical. What is right and left varies with the culture. It is well known that Americans cannot explain to foreigners, or even to one another, what basic principles separates the actions of the Democratic and the Republican party. (A captured American spy in Russia, even with fear of possible torture, was unable to give a principle that made sense to his interrogators!)

If there are X bills, each of which can be voted for or against, and no single principle binds them, there are 2^X possible voting patterns. Thus, with only 10 voting issues it would require 1024 political party platforms to satisfy the wishes of any discriminating voter with his own particular views. With two parties, one is compelled to vote for a hodgepodge of decisions that, in fact, corresponds to the wishes of very few real people. The rest go along out of loyalty, as to a football team. For example, if a person is for more expenditure on education, against more tolerance of homosexuality, for free abortion for foolish teenagers, against reduction of national defense expenditures, for later retirement of civil servants, for greater medical research expenditures, against illegal immigration, and for equal rights for women, he might as well save himself or herself voting in a Democratic vs. Republican contest, since he will cancel half his wants against the other half, whichever way he votes.

This is not the place for inspecting correlational studies regarding the actual magnitude of whatever general factor may still (empirically if not logically) exist in a right-left platform axis. It suffices that from the standpoint of ultimate human goals—rather than mere selfishness in grabbing shares of the national wealth—the right-left ideology remains a confusion, a stupid stereotype, a myth that misleads especially the millions of young people who, finding themselves with a vote, thoughtlessly embrace the nearest banner.

The Beyondist goal of what is good for human evolution potentially leads to clearly desirable, principle-consistent conclusions in every area. "Potentially" is a necessary, honest qualification, because the actual decision will often depend on social research necessary to give quantifiable answers. For example, we have argued above, in principle, that since a highly intelligent child will cost a parent more to bring up than one of average intelligence, Beyondism calls for either a larger income tax allowance per child or fully supportive state scholarships at the university level. It remains to be seen, however, from social research, to what extent a particular economic measure would change the frequency with which gifted children are produced. Such uncertainities could occur in several areas, in view of the present lack of research, but at least Beyondist principles offer, potentially, a basis for a political party of far greater internal consistency than those that have been bequeathed to us by historical accidents and questionable motives.

53. Chap. 18. The various national research fund agencies have so far, in the U.K. and the U.S.A., preserved an apolitical position (except for such instances as denial of funds to Professor Horn of Denver when he proposed to investigate negro-white intelligence differences). However, this balance seems precarious and apt to be upset by individuals with decided political views who infiltrate committees. In any case, the funds for *basic* research are an entirely trivial function of the national income. As a fair example, Ferris, the author of *Galaxies*, claims "the deep mysteries of the universe could be unravelled if the government spent as much on telescopes as on marching bands."

54. Chap. 19. We are bound to face the fact that though political right and left are essentially irrelevant to Beyondism, enthusiasts from outgrowths of these will want to ally themselves. A British Consul recently asked to describe the right wing in Britain replied, "It stands for thrift, effort, self-reliance, reduction of government involvement in society and in "social welfare." With such goals one cannot disagree; but is this a correct description?

55. Chap. 19. UNESCO, as recent critics have pointed out, has fallen from its original hopes and become a political tool of the undeveloped countries. It nevertheless does useful "routine research" providing data on a number of social indicators. Its first departure from scientific objectivity came in its attempt to rule out all psychogenetic investigation of groups. The U.S. is currently considering removing its support on account of the expensive "do-gooder" superficiality.

REFERENCES

Adelson, M. (1950). *P-technique analysis: A P-technique study of social change in the U.S., 1845-1942.* Master's Thesis, University of Illinois, Urbana.

Adorno, T. W., Frenkel-Brunswik, E., Levinson, D. J., & Sanford, R. N. (1950). *The authoritarian personality.* New York: Harper.

Allee, W. C. (1938). *The social life of animals.* New York: Norton.

Anderson, H. (1982). *The drama circle.* Minneapolis: University of Minnesota.

Anderson, I. A. (1974). *Xenophon.* New York: Scribner.

Andreski, S. (1954). *Military organization and society.* London: Routledge & Kegan Paul.

Andreski, S. (1964). Origins of war. In J. D. Carthy & F. J. Ebling, Jr. (Eds)., *The natural history of aggression.* New York: Academic.

Ardrey, R. A. (1961). *African genesis.* New York: Dell.

Ardrey, R. A. (1966). *Territorial imperative.* New York: Dell.

Ardrey, R. A. (1970). *The social contract.* New York: Athenaeum.

Arehart, J. L. (1971a). Pre-natal diagnosis: How fast, how far? *Scientific News, 100,* 44-45.

Arehart, J. L. (1971b). Genetic engineering: Myth or reality. *Science News, 100,* 152-153.

Aristotle. (1943). *Politics.* New York: Everyman's Library.

Arnold, M. (1865). *Essays in criticism.* London: Macmillan.

Baber, H. H. (1952). *Images of good and evil.* Translated by Michael Bulloch. London: Routledge & Kegan Paul.

Bacon, F. (1893). *The new Atlantis.* New York: Routledge & Sons.

Baetke, W. (1962). Die aufnahme des Christentums durch die Germanen; ein Beitrag zur Frage der Germanisierung des Christentums. Sonderaugabe. Darmstadt: Wissenschaftliche Buchgesellschaft.

Bagehot, W. (1927). *Physics and politics or thoughts on the application of principles of natural selection and inheritance to politics. Selected Essays.* London: Nelson, 1873.

Baker, J. R. (1974). *Race.* New York: Oxford University Press.

Barash, D. P. (1982). *Sociobiology and behavior.* New York: Elsevier.

Barker, E. (1948). *National character and the factors in its formation.* London: Methuen.

Barrie, J. (1920). Rectorial address at St. Andrews University.

Barth, K. (1957). *The word of God and the word of man.* Translated by Douglas Horton. New York: Harper.

Beadle, G. W. (1963). *Genetics and modern biology.* Philadelphia: American Philosophical Society.

Becker, C. L. (1932). *Heavenly city of the 18th century philosophers.* New Haven: Yale University Press.

Bell, D. (Ed.) (1970). *Toward the year 2000: Work in progress.* Boston: Beacon.

Benedict, R. (1934). *Patterns of culture.* Boston: Houghton Mifflin.

Bennett, C. A. (1933). *A philosophical study of mysticism.* New York: New York University Press.

Bentham, J. (1834). *Deontology or the science of morality.* London: Longman, Rees, Orme, Browne, Green, & Longman.

Bereiter, C. (1966). Multivariate analysis of the behavior and structure of groups and organizations. In R. B. Cattell (Ed.), *Handbook of Multivariate Experimental Psychology.* Chicago: Rand-McNally.

Berlin, I. (1963). *Karl Marx, his life and environment.* New York: Time.

Berry, J. W. (1974). Ecological and cultural factors in spatial-perceptual development. *Canadian Journal of Behavioural Science, 3,* 324-226.

Bolitho, W. (1929). *Twelve against the gods.* New York: Simon & Schuster.

Borgatta, E. F., Cottrell, L. S., Jr., & Meyer, H. J. (1956). On the dimensions of group behavior. *Sociometry, 19,* 223-240.

Borgatta, E. F., & Meyer, H. J. (1956). *Sociological theory.* New York: Knopf.

Boulding, K. E. (1964). *The meaning of the twentieth century: The great transition.* New York: Harper & Row.

Boyle, G. (1984). A re-analysis of the higher order factor structure of Motivation Analysis Test and the Eight State Questionnaire. *Personality and Individual Differences, 6,* 367-374.

Brinton, C. (1938). *The anatomy of a revolution.* New York: Norton.

Brinton, C. (1940). *Ideas and man.* New York: Norton.

Bronfenbrenner, U., & Devereux, E. C. (1952). Interdisciplinary planning for team research on constructive community behavior: The Springdale project. *Human Relations, 5,* 187-203.

Brooke, R. (1943). *Collected poems.* New York: Dodd & Mead.

Browning, R. (1895). *Complete poetical works.* Boston: Houghton-Mifflin.

Burt, C. L. (1917). *Three reports on distribution and relations of educational abilities.* London: King.

Burt, C. L. (1925). *The young delinquent.* London: University of London Press.

Burt, C. L. (1957). The distribution of intelligence. *British Journal of Psychology, 40,* 163-175.

Bury, J. B. (1920). *The idea of progress.* London: Macmillan.

Cancro, J. (Ed.) (1971). *Intelligence: Genetic and environmental influences.* New York: Grune & Stratton.

Carlyle, T. (1840). *Chartism.* (No publisher given.)

Carpenter, C. R. (1934). Field study of the behavior and social relations of howling monkeys. *Comparative Psychology Monographs, 10,* 48.

Carritt, E. F. (1952). *Morals and politics.* London: Oxford University Press.

Carr-Saunders, A. M. (1936). *World population: Past growth and present trends.* London: Oxford University Press.

Carthy, J. D., & Ebling, F. J. (1964). *The natural history of aggression.* New York: Academic.

Cartwright, D. S., & Cartwright, C. F. (1971). *Psychological adjustment: Behavior in the inner world.* Chicago: Rand-McNally.

Cartwright, D. S., Tomson, B., & Schwartz, H. (1975). *Gang delinquency.* Monterey, CA: Brooks/Cole.

Cattell, R. B. (1933a). *Psychology and social progress.* London: Daniel.

Cattell, R. B. (1933b). The conquest of obstruction. In R. B. Cattell (Ed.), *Psychology and social progress.* London: Daniel.

Cattell, R. B. (1936). Is national intelligence declining? *Eugenics Review, 27,* 181, 203.

Cattell, R. B. (1937a). *The fight for our national intelligence.* London: King.

Cattell, R. B. (1937b). Some further relations between intelligence, fertility and socio-economic factors. *Eugenics Review, 29,* 171-179.

Cattell, R. B. (1938). *Psychology and the religious quest.* New York: Nelson.

Cattell, R. B. (1942). The concept of social status. *Journal of Social Psychology, 15,* 293-308.

Cattell, R. B. (1944). The place of religion and ethics in a civilization based on science. Chap. 2 in R. Wulsin (Ed.), *A revaluation of our civilization.* Albany: Argus.

Cattell, R. B. (1945a). The cultural functions of social stratification. I. Regarding the genetic basis of society. *Journal of Social Psychology, 21,* 3-23.

Cattell, R. B. (1945b). The cultural functions of social stratification. II. Regarding individual and group dynamics. *Journal of Social Psychology, 21,* 22-55.

Cattell, R. B. (1948). Concepts and methods in the measurement of group syntality. *Psychological Review, 55,* 48-63.

Cattell, R. B. (1949). The dimensions of culture patterns by factorization of national characters. *Journal of Abnormal & Social Psychology, 44,* 443-469.

Cattell, R. B. (1950a). The principle culture patterns discoverable in the syntal dimensions of existing nations. *Journal of Social Psychology, 32,* 215-253.

Cattell, R. B. (1950b). The scientific ethics of "Beyond." *Journal of Social Issues, 6,* 21-27.

Cattell, R. B. (1950c). *Personality, a systematic theoretical and factual study.* New York: McGraw-Hill.

Cattell, R. B. (1953). A quantitative analysis of the changes in the cultural pattern of Great Britain, 1837-1937, by P-technique. *Acta Psychologica, 9,* 99-121.

Cattell, R. B. (1957). *Personality and motivation structure and measurement.* New York: World.

Cattell, R. B. (1961). Group theory, personality and role: A model for experimental researches. In F. Geldard (Ed.), *Defence psychology.* Oxford: Pergamon. Pp. 209-258.

Cattell, R. B. (1965). *The scientific analysis of personality.* London: Penguin.

Cattell, R. B. (1966). *Handbook of multivariate experimental psychology.* Chicago: Rand McNally.

Cattell, R. B. (1971). *Abilities: Their structure, growth and action.* Boston: Houghton Mifflin.

Cattell, R. B. (1972). *A new morality from science: Beyondism.* New York: Pergamon.

Cattell, R. B. (1973). The organization of independent basic research institutes symbiotic with universities. *Higher Education, 2,* 1-14.

Cattell, R. B. (1980). *Personality and learning theory.* New York: Springer.

Cattell, R. B. (1982a). Inflation and business cycles from the standpoint of psychology and sociobiology. *Journal of Social, Political & Economic Studies, 7,* 35-54.

Cattell, R. B. (1982b). *The inheritance of personality and ability.* New York: Academic.

Cattell, R. B. (1983). *Intelligence and national achievement.* Washington: Institute for the Study of Man.

Cattell, R. B. (1985). *Structured personality learning theory.* New York: Praeger.

Cattell, R. B. (1987). *Intelligence: Its structure, growth and action.* Amsterdam: North Holland.

Cattell, R. B., & Adelson, M. (1951). The dimensions of social change in the U.S.A. as determined by P-technique. *Social Forces, 30,* 190-201.

Cattell, R. B., Blewett, D. G., & Beloff, J. R. (1955). The inheritance of personality. A multiple variance analysis determination of approximate nature-nurture ratios for primary personality factors in Q-data. *American Journal of Human Genetics, 7,* 122-146.

Cattell, R. B., Bolz, C., & Korth, B. (1973). Behavioral types in pure bred dogs objectively determined by Taxonome. *Behavior Genetics, 3,(3),* 205-216.

Cattell, R. B., & Brennan, J. (1981). Population and national syntality. *Mankind Quarterly, 21,* 327-340.

Cattell, R. B., & Brennan, J. (1984). The cultural types of modern nations by two quantitative classification methods. *Sociology & Social Research, 68,* 208-235.

Cattell, R. B., Breul, H., & Hartman, H. P. (1952). An attempt at more refined definition of the cultural dimensions of syntality in modern nations. *American Sociological Review, 17,* 408-421.

Cattell, R. B., & Butcher, J. (1968). *The prediction of achievement and creativity.* Indianapolis: Bobbs-Merrill.

Cattell, R. B., & Child, D. (1975). *Motivation and dynamic structure.* London: Holt Rinehart & Winston.

Cattell, R. B., & Drevdahl, J. E. (1955). A comparison of the personality profile (16 PF) of eminent researchers with that of eminent teachers and administrators, and of the general population. *British Journal of Psychology, 46,* 248-261.

Cattell, R. B., Eber, H. W., & Tatsuoka, M. M. (1970). *Handbook for the Sixteen Personality Factor Questionnaire (16PF).* Champaign, IL: Institute for Personality and Ability Testing.

Cattell, R. B., & Gorsuch, R. (1973). The definition and measurement of national morale and morality. *Journal of Social Psychology, 67,* 77-96.

Cattell, R. B., & Gorsuch, R. (1973). Personality and socio-ethical values: The structure of self and superego. Chap. 30 in R. B. Cattell & R. M. Dreger (Eds), *Handbook of Modern Personality Theory.* New York: Teachers' College Press.

Cattell, R. B., Graham, R. K., & Woliver, R. E. (1979). A re-assessment of the factorial cultural dimensions of modern nations. *Journal of Social Psychology, 108,* 241-258.

Cattell, R. B., Kawash, G. F., & DeYoung, G. E. (1972). Validation of objective measures of ergic tension: Response of the sex erg to visual stimulation. *Journal of Experimental Research in Personality, 6,* 76-83.

Cattell, R. B., & Korth, B. (1973). The isolation of temperament dimensions in dogs. *Behavioral Biology, 9*(1), 15-30.

Cattell, R. B., & Morony, J. H. (1962). The use of the 16PF in distinguishing homosexuals, normals, and general criminals. *Journal of Consulting Psychology, 26*(6), 531-540.

Cattell, R. B., & Nesselroade, J. R. (1967). Likeness and completeness theories examined by 16P.F. measures on stably and unstably married couples. *Journal of Personality & Social Psychology, 7,* 351-361.

Cattell, R. B., & Radcliffe, J. (1961). Factors in objective motivation measures with children. A preliminary study. *Australian Journal of Psychology, 13,* 65-76.

Cattell, R. B., Radcliffe, J., & Sweney, A. B. (1963). The nature and measurement of components of motivation. *Genetic & Psychological Monographs, 68,* 49-211.

Cattell, R. B.., & Scheier, I. H. (1961). *The meaning and measurement of neuroticism and anxiety.* New York: Ronald.

Cattell, R. B., Stice, G. F., & Kristy, N. F. (1957). A first approximation to nature-nurture ratios for eleven primary personality factors in objective tests. *Journal of Abnormal & Social Psychology, 54,* 143-159.

Cattell, R. B., & Tatro, D. F. (1966). The personality factors objectively measured which distinguish psychotics from normals. *Behavioral Research Therapy, 4,* 39-51.

Cattell, R. B., Tatro, D. F., & Komlos, E. (1965). The diagnosis and inferred structure of paranoid and non-paranoid schizophrenia from the 16P. F. profile. *Indian Psychological Review, 1,* 108-115.

Cattell, R. B., & Woliver, R. E. (1981). Recurring national patterns from 30 years of multivariate cross cultural studies. *International Journal of Psychology, 16,* 171-198.

Cattell, R. B., Woliver, R. E., & Graham, R. K. (1980). The relations of syntality dimensions of modern national cultures to the personality dimensions of their populations. *International Journal of Intercultural Relations, 4,* 15-21.

Chamberlin, E. H. (1948). *The theory of monopolistic competition.* Cambridge: Harvard University Press.

Chassell, C. F. (1935). *Relation between morality and intellect.* New York: Columbia Teachers College.

Chicago Tribune. (1970, June 10). Editorial.

Chaucer, G. (1986). *Canterbury Tales.* In D. Wright (Ed.), *World's classic series.* New York: Oxford University Press.

Chesterton, G. K. (1915). *Wine, water and song.* London: Methuen.

Chomsky, N. (1957). *Syntactic structures.* s-Gravenhage: Mouton.

Churchill, R. (1908). In G. Marten (Ed.), *Churchill Companion Volume.* Boston: Houghton-Mifflin.

Clark, C. (1957). *The conditions of economic progress.* London: Macmillan.

Clark, R. W. (1969). *J. B. S.: The life and work of J. B. S. Haldane.* New York: Coward-McCann.

Clausewitz, K. von. (1943). *On war.* New York: The Modern Library.

Clavell, J. (1979). *Shogun, a novel of Japan.* New York: Delacourt.

Clemenceau, G. (1929). *In the evening of my thought.* Boston: Houghton-Mifflin.

Comte, A. (1905). *Cours de philosophie positive, 1829. (The positive philosophy).* London: Routledge.

Coon, C. S. (1962). *The origin of races.* New York: Knopf.

Cottrell, L. (1957). *The anvil of civilization.* New York: New American Library.

Cranston, M. (1963). *What are human rights?* New York: Basic Books.

Croce, B. (1945). *Politics and morals.* New York: Philosophical Library.

Curry, W. B. (1937). *The school and a changing civilization.* London: John Lane.

Darlington, C. D. (1947). *The conflict of science and society.* New York: Basic Books.

Darlington, C. D. (1969). *The evolution of man and society.* New York: Simon & Schuster.

Darwin, B. (1952). *The next million years.* Garden City, NY: Doubleday.

Darwin, C. (1871). *The descent of man.* New York: Modern Library.

Darwin, C. (1917). *The origin of species.* London: Murray, 1859.

Darwin, L. (1926). *The need for eugenic reform.* London: Murray.

Davis, K. (1949). *Human society.* New York: Macmillan.

Delhees, K. (1968). Conflict measurement by the dynamic calculus model, and its applicability in clinical practice. *Multivariate Behavioral Research, 3,* 73-96.

Delhees, K., & Nesselroade, J. (1966). Methods and findings in experimentally based personality theory. Chap. 19 in R. B. Cattell (Ed.), *Handbook of Multivariate Experimental Psychology.* Chicago: Rand-McNally.

Dennis, W. (1956). Age of productivity among scientists. *Science, 123,* 724-725.

De Tocqueville, A. (1945). *Democracy in America.* New York: Vintage Books.

Deutsch, M. (1968). *Social class, race and psychological development.* New York: Holt, Rinehart & Winston.

Dickson, L. (1969). *H. G. Wells, his turbulent life and times.* New York: Atheneum.

Diderot, D. (1775). *Oeuvres choisies.* Vol. II. *De l'interpretation de la nature.* Paris: Editions sociales, 1953-64.

Dielman, T. E., & Krug, S. (1977). Trait description and measurement in motivation and dynamic structure. Chap. 5 in R. B. Cattell & R. M. Dreger, (Eds), *Handbook of Modern Personality Theory.* Washington, DC: Hemisphere.

Djilas, M. (1962). *Conversations with Stalin.* New York: Harcourt.

Dobzhansky, T. H. (1960). *The biological basis of human freedom.* New York: Columbia University Press.

Dobzhansky, T. H. (1962). *Mankind evolving.* New Haven: Yale University Press.

Dodds, E. R. (1951). *The Greeks and the irrational.* Berkeley: University of California Press.

Draper, J. W. (1898). *History of the conflict between science and religion.* New York: Appleton.

Drawbridge, C. P. (1932). *The religion of scientists.* London: Rationalist.

Dreikurs, R. (1960). Equality: The challenge of our time. Mimeograph.

Dryden, J. (1933). In L. Bredvold (Ed.), *Best of Dryden.* London: Nelson.

Dunn, L. C., & Dobzhansky, T. (1964). *Heredity and the nature of man.* New York: Harcourt, Brace & World.

Durkheim, E. (1915). *The elementary forms of the religious life.* Glencoe, IL: The Free Press.

Ebling, F. J. (1969). *Biology and ethics.* New York: Academic.

Eddington, A. S. (1929). *Science and the unseen world.* New York: Swarthmore Lecture.

Ehrlich, P. (1968). *The population bomb.* New York: Ballantine.

Eibel-Eibesfeldt, I. (1970). *Ethology, the biology of behavior.* New York: Rinehart & Winston.

Eibel-Eibesfeldt, I. (1979). *The biology of peace and war.* New York: Viking.

Eisenhower, D. (1961, Jan. 17). Farewell Address of the President. *Proceedings of Congress.*

Eisenstadt, S. N. (1967). *Decline of empires.* New York: Prentice-Hall.

Ellis, H. (1910). *Studies in the psychology of sex.* London: Methuen.

Emmet, D. (1966). *Rules, roles and relations.* London: Macmillan.

Epstein, S. (1972). Anxiety and achievement. In C. D. Spielberger (Ed.), *The psychology of anxiety.* New York: Academic.

Eysenck, H. J. (1944). General social attitudes. *Journal of Social Psychology, 19,* 207-277.

Eysenck, H. J. (1952). *The scientific study of personality.* London: Routledge & Kegan Paul.

Eysenck, H. J. (1954). *The psychology of politics.* London: Routledge & Kegan Paul.

Eysenck, H. J. (1971). *The I.Q. argument.* New York: Library Press.

Eysenck, H. J. (1973). *The unequality of man.* London: Temple Smith.

Fehrenbacher, E. (Ed.). (1977). *A. Lincoln: A documentary portrait through his speeches and writings.* Palo Alto: Stanford University Press.

Ferris, T. (1982). *Galaxies.* New York: Stewart Tabori, & Chang.

Festinger, L., Schacter, S., & Back, K. (1950). *Social pressures in informal groups.* New York: Harper.

Fiedler, F. E. (1965, Apr.). Leadership—a new model. *Discovery.*

Fisher, R. A. (1930). *Genetical theory of natural selection.* Oxford: Clarendon.

France, A. (1920). *The garden of Epicurus.* London: Lane.

Franz, S. I. (1907). On the function of the cerebrum: The frontal lobes. *Archives of Psychology, 2,* 1-64.

Frazer, J. G. (1890). *The golden bough.* London: Macmillan.

Freedman, D. G. (1971). An evolutionary approach to research on the life cycle. *Human Development, 14,* 87-99.

Frenkel-Brunswik, E. (1954). Meaning of psychoanalytic concepts and confirmation of psychoanalytic theories. *Scientific Monthly, 79,* 293-300.

Freud, S. (1913). *Totem and taboo.* Leipzig: Helle.

Freud, S. (1928). *Future of an illusion.* London: Hogarth.

Freud, S. (1930). *Civilization and its discontents.* London: L. & Virginia Woolf at Hogarth.

Freud, S. (1961). *Moses, an Egyptian.* Translated from the German by Katherine Jones. New York: Vintage, 1939.

Friedman, M. (1968). *Dollars and deficits.* New York: Prentice-Hall.

Fulbright, J. W. (1967).*The arrogance of power.* New York: Random House.

Fuller, J. L., & Thompson, W. R. (1960). *Behavior genetics.* New York: Wiley.

Galton, Sir F. (1883). *Inquiries into human faculty and its development.* London: Dent.

Gardner, J. (1968). *No easy victories.* New York: Harper & Row.

Gibb, C. A. (1956). Changes in the culture pattern of Australia, 1906-1946 as determined by P-technique. *Journal of Social Psychology, 43,* 225-238.

Gibbon, E. (1910). *The decline and fall of the Roman empire.* London: Dent.

Gilfillan, E. (1970). *Migrations to the stars.* Washington, DC: Luce.

Gimpel, J. (1969). *Du la naissance d'une religion.* New York: Stein & Day.

Gissing, G. (1956). *By the Ionian Sea.* London: Richards.

Goldwater, B. (1979). *With no apologies.* New York: McGraw-Hill.

Gordon, M. (1953). *American people's encyclopedia.* Chicago: Spencer.

Gorsuch, R. L. (1965). *The clarification of some super ego factors.* Unpublished doctoral dissertation, University of Illinois, Urbana, IL.

Gorsuch, R. L., & Cattell, R. B. (1972). Personality and socio-ethical values: The structure of self and superego. Chap. 30 in R. B. Cattell & R. M. Dreger (Eds), *Handbook of Modern Personality Theory.* Washington, DC: Hemisphere.

Gould, J. B. (1970, Jun. 3). *World News.*

Gouldner, A., & Peterson, R. A. (1962). *Notes on technology and the moral order.* Indianapolis: Bobbs-Merrill.

Graham, R. K. (1970). *The future of man.* North Quincy: Christopher.

Graubard, M. (1939). *Man, the slave and master.* London: Dent.

Graubard, M. (1986). The biological foundation of culture. In A. McGregor (Ed.) *Evolution, creative intelligence, and intergroup competition.* Washington: Mankind Quarterly.

Graves, R. (1946). *King Jesus.* New York: Creative Age.

Gregg, P. M., & Banks, A. S. (1965). Dimensions of political systems: Factor analyses of a cross-policy survey. *American Political Science Review, 59,* 602-614.

Gregor, A. (1970, Aug.). *Proceedings of London symposium on individual differences, Aug. 19-21.* London: Institute of Psychiatry.

Grinker, R. R., & Spiegel, J. P. (1945). *Men under stress.* Philadelphia: Blakiston.

Gubser, C. J. (1969, Jul. 15). *Congressional Record,* No. 117.

Guilford, J. P. (1959). *Personality.* New York: McGraw-Hill.

Günther, H. F. K. (1927). *The racial elements of European history.* London: Methuen.

Hadden, J. K., & Borgatta, E. (1965). *American cities: Their social characteristics.* Chicago: Rand-McNally.

Haeckel, E. (1929). *The riddle of the universe.* London: Watts.

Haldane, G. B. S. (1925). *Daedalus or science and the future.* London: Kegan Paul.

Haldane, G. B. S. (1928). *Possible worlds.* London: Harper.

Hall, C. S., & Lindzey, G. (1970). *Theories of personality.* New York: Wiley.

Hardin, G. J. (1964). *Population, evolution, and birth control: A collage of controversial readings.* New York: Freeman.

Hardin, G. J. (1977). *The limits of altruism.* Lafayette, IN: Indiana University Press.

Hardin, G. J. (1982). *Grounded reason versus received formulas.* New York: Freeman.

Hardy, T. (1904). *The dynasts.* New York: Macmillan.

Harlow, H. F. (1949). The formation of learning sets. *Psychological Review, 56,* 51-65.

Harrison, G. A. (1961). *Genetical variation in human populations.* New York: Pergamon.

Haskins, C. P. (1970, Jul.-Aug.). Advances and challenges in science in 1969. *American Scientist, 58,* 365-377.

Hayek, F. A. von. (1945). *The road to serfdom.* Chicago: University of Chicago Press.

Heape, W. (1931). *Emigration, migration and nomadism.* Cambridge: Heffer.

Heidegger, M. (1949). *Existence and being.* Chicago: Regnery.

Hendricks, B. (1971). *The sensitivity of the dynamic calculus to short term change and interest structure.* Unpublished Master's thesis, University of Illinois, Urbana, IL.

Henley, W. E. (1900). *Selected poems.* London: Scribner.

Henry, D. D. (1970). *Annual report of the President of the University of Illinois.*

Herrnstein, R. J. (1971). *I.Q. in the meritocracy.* Boston: Little-Brown.

Hess, E. H. (1959). The relationship between imprinting and motivation. In M. R. Jones (Ed.), *Nebraska symposium on motivation.* Lincoln: University of Nebraska Press. Pp. 47-77.

Higgins, J. V., Reed, E. W., & Reed, S. C. (1962). Intelligence and family size: A paradox resolved. *Eugenics Quarterly, 9,* 84-90.

Hirsch, N. D. M. (1926). A study of natio-racial mental differences. *Genetic Psychology Monographs, 1,* 231-406.

Hirsch, N. D. M. (1931). *Genius and creative intelligence.* Cambridge, MA: Science-Art.

Hoagland, H. (1947). The human adrenal cortex in relation to stressful activities. *Journal of Aviation Medicine, 18,* 5.

Hoagland, H., & Burloe, R. W. (Eds). (1962). *Evolution and man's progress.* New York: Columbia University Press.

Hobbes, T. (1958). *The great leviathan.* New York: Liberal Arts.

Hofstadter, R. (1963). *Anti-intellectualism in American life.* New York: Knopf.

Hogben, L. (1951). *Science for the citizen.* New York: W. W. Norton.

Hooton, E. A. (1939). *The American criminal.* Cambridge: Harvard University Press.

Hooton, E. A. (1942). *Man's poor relations.* New York: Doubleday.

Hooton, E. A. (1946). *Up from the ape.* New York: Macmillan.

Horn, J. L. (1965). *Fluid and crystallized intelligence: A factor analytic study of the structure among primary mental abilities.* Unpublished doctoral dissertation, University of Illinois, Urbana, IL.

Horn, J. L. (1966). Motivation and dynamic calculus concepts from multivariate experiment. Chap. 20 in R. B. Cattell (Ed.), *Handbook of multivariate experimental psychology.* Chicago: Rand-McNally.

Hornbein, T. (1965). *Everest, the west ridge.* San Francisco: Sierra Club.

Housman, A. E. (1965). *The collected poems of A. E. Housman.* London: Holt, Rinehart & Winston.

Hume, D. (1938). *Treatise on human nature.* Cambridge: The University Press.

Hundleby, J., Pawlik, K., & Cattell, R. B. (1965). *Personality factors in objective test devices.* San Diego: Knapp.

Huntington, E. (1945). *Mainsprings of civilization.* New York: New American Library.

Huxley, A. (1926). *Jesting Pilate.* London: Chatto & Windus.

Huxley, A. (1932). *Brave new world.* New York: Garden City.

Huxley, J. (1953). *Evolution in action.* London: Chatto & Windus.

Huxley, J. (1957). *Knowledge, morality and destiny.* New York: New American Library.

Huxley, J., & Huxley, T. (1947). *Touchstone for ethics, 1893-1943.* New York: Harper.

Huxley, J., & Kettlewell, H. B. D. (1965). "Naturalness" of separate, segregated development. In *Charles Darwin and his world.* New York: Viking.

Huxley, T. (1893). *Evolution and ethics*. London: Macmillan.

Huxley, T. (1901). *Science and education*. New York: Appleton.

Inge, W. R. (1926). *Science and ultimate truth*. London: Longmans, Green.

Inge, W. R. (1929). *Assessments and anticipation*. London: Cassell.

James, W. (1962). The moral equivalent of war, 1910. In *Essays on faith and morals*. New York: Meridian.

James, W. (1963). *The varieties of religious experience*. New Hyde Park, NY: University Books.

Jefferson, T. (1961). *Crusade against ignorance; Thomas Jefferson on education*. New York Bureau of Publications, Teachers' College, Columbia University.

Jensen, A. R. (1972). *Genetics and education*. New York: Harper & Row.

Jensen, A. R. (1973). *Educability and group differences*. New York: Harper & Row.

Jinks, J. L., & Fulker, D. W. (1970). Comparison of the biometrical genetical, MAVA and classical approaches to the analyses of human behavior. *Psychological Bulletin, 73*, 311-349.

Johnson, D. M. (1968). Reasoning and logic. In *International Encyclopedia of Social Scientists*. New York: Macmillan. Pp 344-350.

Johnson, R. C., Dokecki, P. R., & Mowrer, O. H. (1972). *Conscience, contract and social reality*. New York: Holt, Rinehart & Winston.

Jones, R. V. (1978). *The wizard war*. New York: Coward, McCann & Geoghburg.

Jonassen, C. T. (1961). Functional unities in 88 community systems. *American Sociological Review, 26*, 399-407.

Jordan, D. S. (1914). *War and waste*.

Julian, J. W., Bishop, D. W., & Fiedler, F. E. (1966). Quasi-therapeutic effects of inter-group competition. *Journal of Personality & Social Psychology, 3*, 321-327.

Kahn, H. (1960). *On thermonuclear war*. Princeton, NJ: Princeton University Press.

Keith, Sir A. (1925). *The religion of a Darwinist*. London: Watts.

Keith, Sir A. (1946). *Essays on human evolution*. London: Watts.

Keith, Sir A. (1949). *A new theory of human evolution*. New York: Philosophical Library.

Khayyam, O. (1952). *The rubaiyat*. New York: Random House.

Khrushchev, N.S. (1970, Nov. 27). *Khrushchev remembers*. Edited and translated by C. Talbott. *Life, 69*, 32-39.

Kierkegaard, S. A. (1941). *Sickness unto death*. London: Oxford University Press.

King, R. C. (1965). *Genetics*. New York: Oxford University Press.

Kipling, R. (1940). *Inclusive verses, 1885-1932*. New York: Sun Dial.

Knapp, R. R. (1963). Demographic cultural and personality attributes of scientists. In C. W. Taylor & F. Barron (Eds), *Scientific creativity: Its recognition and development*. New York: Wiley.

Kohler, E. (1980). *The true, the good, the beautiful*. New York: Prentice-Hall.

Kretschmer, E. (1931). *The psychology of men of genius.* London: Kegan Paul.

Kroeber, A. L. (1958). *Anthropology.* New York: Harcourt.

Kropotkin, P. (1902). *Mutual aid: A factor in evolution.* New York: McClure-Phillips.

Krug, S. E. (1971). *An examination of experimentally induced changes in ergic tension levels.* Unpublished doctoral dissertation, University of Illinois, Urbana, IL.

Kuhn, T. S. (1962). *The structure of scientific revolutions.* Chicago: University of Chicago Press.

Ladd, J. (1957). *The structure of a moral code.* Cambridge: Harvard University Press.

Lange, J. (1931). *Crime as destiny.* London: Allen & Unwin.

Lanier, L. (1971, Apr. 30). New trends in university education. Honors Day Address, University of Illinois, mimeograph.

Lasswell, T. E. (1965). *Class and stratum: An introduction to concepts and research.* Boston: Houghton-Mifflin.

Lederberg, J. (1969, Nov.). Genetic engineering controlling man's building blocks. *Today's Health, 47,* 24-27.

Lehman, H. G. (1936). The creative years in science and literature. *Scientific Monthly, 43,* 151-162.

Lenski, R. (1981). *Toward a new science of man.* Washington, DC: Pimmit.

Lentz, T. F. (1927). The relation of I.Q. to size of family. *Journal of Educational Psychology, 18,* 486-496.

Lepley, R. (1944). *Verifiability of value.* New York: Columbia University Press.

Lerner, D., & Lasswell, H. S. (1951). *The policy sciences: Recent developments in scope and method.* Stanford: Hoover Institute.

Lerner, I. M. (1968). *Heredity, evolution and society.* New York: Freeman.

Levine, R. A. (1970). *The poor, ye need not have with you.* Boston: MIT Press.

Lewin, K. (1948). *Resolving social conflicts.* New York: Harper.

Lewontin, R. D. (Ed.). (1968). *Population biology and evolution.* New York: Syracuse University Press.

Light, R. J., & Smith, P. V. (1969). Social allocation models of intelligence: A methodological inquiry. *Harvard Educational Review,* 484-510.

Lindbergh, C. A. (1970). *The wartime journals of Charles A. Lindbergh.* New York: Harcourt Brace Jovanovich.

Lindsey, B. B., & Evans, W. (1925). *The revolt of modern youth.* New York: Boni & Liverright.

Linton, R. (1936). *The study of man.* New York: Appleton-Century.

Lloyd, R. (1971). Cross and psychosis. *Faith & Freedom, 24,* 1-40.

Loehlin, J. C., Lindzey, G., & Shuhler, J. N. (1975). *Race differences in intelligence.* San Francisco: Friedman.

Lombroso, C. (1911). *Criminal man.* New York: Putnam's Sons.

Lorenz, K. (1966). *On aggression.* New York: Harcourt, Brace & World.

Lumsden, C., & Wilson, E. (1981). *Genes, mind & culture, the coevolutionary process.* Cambridge: Harvard University Press.

Luria, A. R. L. S. Vygotsky and the problem of localization of functions. *Neuropsychologia, 3,* 387-392.

Lykken, D. (1981, Oct.). *Research with twins: The concept of emergenisis.* Presidential Address, Society of Psychophysiological Research, Minneapolis.

Lynn, R. (1971). *Personality and national character.* New York: Pergamon.

Lynn, R., Hampson, S., & Mullineux, J. (1987). The rise of fluid intelligence in Britain. *Personality & Individual Differences, 8,* 23-32.

MacArthur, D. (1964). *Reminiscences.* New York: McGraw-Hill.

Macaulay, T. B. (1897). *The works of Lord Macaulay complete.* Edited by Lady Trevelyon. New York: Longmans-Green.

Malinowski, B. (1937). Anthropology as basis of social science. In R. B. Cattell, J. Cohen, & R. W. M. Travis (Eds), *Human affairs.* London: Macmillan. Pp. 199-252.

Malraux, A. (1949). *The psychology of art.* New York: Pantheon.

Malthus, T. R. (1976). *Essay on the principle of population.* New York: Kelley.

Mangasarian, M. M. (1960). *The bible unveiled.* Chicago: Independent Religious Society.

Mannheim, K. (1937). Present trends in the building of society. In R. B. Cattell, et al. (Eds), *Human affairs.* London: Macmillan. pp. 278-300.

Martin, N. G., & Jardine, R. (in press). In H. Eysenck (Ed.), *Consensus and controversy.* Brighton, England: Falmer.

Marx, K. (1890-94). *Das Kapital.* Hamburg: Meissner.

Mather, K. (1953). The genetical structure of populations. *Symposium of the Society for Experimental Biology, 7,* 63.

Mathews, Dean W. R. (1963). *God in Christian thought and experience.* Digswell Place, England: Nisbet.

Maugham, S. (1938). *The summing up.* Garden City, NY: Doubleday Doran.

Mazzini, G. (1907). *The duties of man.* Everyman's, NY: Dutton.

McArdle, J. (1984). On madness in his method: R. B. Cattell's contribution to structural equation modeling. *Multivariate Behavioral Research, 19*(2-3), 245-267.

McDougall, W. (1921). *National welfare and national decay.* London: Methuen.

McDougall, W. (1924). *Ethics and some modern world problems.* London: Methuen.

McDougall, W. (1925). *Janus, the conquest of war.* London: Today and Tomorrow Series.

McDougall, W. (1934). *Religion and the sciences of life.* London: Methuen.

McDougall, W. (1977). *Is America safe for democracy?* New York: Arno.

McGregor, A. (1986). *Evolution, creative intelligence, and intergroup competition.* Washington, DC: *Mankind Quarterly.*

Mead, G. H. (1934). The ideal of social integration. In C. W. Morris (Ed.), *Mind, self and society.* Chicago: University of Chicago Press.

Mead, M. (1955). *Culture patterns and technological change.* New York: New American Library.

Meadows, D. H., et al. (1972). *The limits to growth: A report of the Club of Rome Project on the predicament of mankind.* New York: Universe.

Meeland, T., et al. (1954, Apr.). *Task Fighter: Description of Tests.* OCAFF, Fort Ord, CA, Human Research Unit No. 2.

Merritt, R. L. (1970). *Systematic approaches to comparative politics.* Chicago: Rand-McNally.

Merton, R. K. (1957). *Social theory and social structure.* Glencoe, IL: Free Press.

Mill, J. S. (1863). *Utilitarianism.* London: Parker & Bourn.

Miller, J. G. (1965). Living systems, basic concepts. *Behavioral Science, 10,* 193-237.

Moltmann, J. (1967). *Theology of hope; on the ground and the implications of Christian eschatology.* New York: Harper & Row.

Monod, J. (1971). *Chance and necessity.* New York: Knopf.

Montaigne, M. de. (1958). *Essays.* London: Penguin.

Montesquieu, de C. L. (1793). *Spirit of the laws.* London: Fingrave.

Morgan, C. L. (1923). *Emergent evolution.* New York: Holt.

Morgan, L. H. (1878). *Ancient society; or researches in the lines of human progress from savagery, through barbarism to civilization.* New York: Holt.

Morris, C. (1956). *Varieties of human value.* Chicago: University of Chicago Press.

Morris, D. (1967). *The naked ape.* London: Cape.

Morton, N. E., Chung, C. S., & Mi, M. P. (1967). *Genetics of interracial crosses in Hawaii.* Basel, Switzerland: Karger.

Mowrer, O. H. (1960). Some constructive features of the concept of sin. *Journal of Counselling Psychology, 7,* 185-188.

Mowrer, O. H. (1967). *Morality and mental health.* Chicago: Rand-McNally.

Muller, H. J. (1950). Our load of mutations. *American Journal of Human Genetics, 2,* 60-70.

Muller, H. J. (1953). *Out of the night.* New York: Vanguard.

Muller, H. J. (1966, Sep.). What genetic course will man steer? *Proceedings of 3rd International Congress on Human Genetics,* Chicago.

Murray, J. C. (1965). *Freedom and man.* New York: Kennedy.

Myrdal, G. (1965). *Challenge to affluence.* New York: Vintage.

Myrdal, G. (1968). *Asian drama: An inquiry into the poverty of nations.* New York: Pantheon.

Nadel, S. F. (1957). *The theory of social structure.* Glencoe, IL: Free Press.

Newbolt, H. (1981). *Selected poems of Henry Newbolt.* London: Hodder & Stoughton.

Nietzsche, F. (1930). *Thus spake Zarathustra.* Leipzig: Kroner.

Nietzsche, F. (1960). *Joyful wisdom.* New York: Unger.

Nietzsche, F. (1966). *Beyond good and evil.* East Hanover, NJ: Vintage.

Nietzsche, F. (1967). Genealogy of morals. In W. Kaufman (Ed.), *Basic writings.* New York: Vintage.

Noüy, L. de. (1947). *Human destiny.* New York: Longmans Green.

Oliver, R. P. (1973). *Christianity and the survival of the West.* Sterling, VA: Sterling Enterprise.

Oliver, R. (1981). *America's decline*. London: Londinium.

Oppenheimer, J. R. (1955). *The open mind*. New York: Simon & Schuster.

Otto, W. (1978). *The Homeric gods: The spiritual significance of Greek religion*. Salem, NH: Ayer.

Osler, Sir W. (1958). *A way of life*. New York: Dover.

Owen, W. (1919). *Poems*. London: Unwin.

Paddock, W. (1967). *Famine, 1975!* Boston: Little-Brown.

Paley, W. (1802). *Natural theology, as evidences of the existence and attributes of the deity, collected from the appearances of nature*. London: Faulder.

Pannenberg, W. (1970). *What is man? Contemporary anthropology in theological perspective*. Philadelphia: Fortress.

Patrick, J. M. (Ed.) (1948). *Selected essays of Francis Bacon*. New York: Appleton-Century.

Patton, M. (1947). *War as I knew it*. Boston: Houghton-Mifflin.

Pearson, K. (1909). *The groundwork of eugenics*. London: Dulace.

Pearson, R. (1974). *Anthropology*. New York: Holt, Rinehart & Winston.

Pendell, E. (1951). *Population on the loose*. New York: Funk.

Pendell, E. (1977). *Why civilizations self-destruct*. Cape Canaveral, FL: Howard Allen.

Penrose, L. S. (1948). The supposed threat of declining intelligence. *American Journal of Mental Deficiency, 53*, 114-118.

Pervin, L. A. (1975). *Personality: Theory assessment and research*. New York: Wiley.

Petrie, W. M. F. (1911). *The revolutions of civilization*. London: Harper.

Plato. (1946). *The republic*. Cleveland: World.

Polyani, M. (1958). *Personal knowledge*. London: Routledge & Kegan Paul.

Popper, K. R. (1957). *The open society and its enemies*. London: Routledge & Kegan Paul.

Price, D. de Solla. (1961). *Science since Babylon*. New Haven: Yale University Press.

Putnam, C. (1961). *Race and reason*. Washington, DC: Public Affairs Press.

Putnam, C. (1967). *Race and reality*. Washington, DC: Public Affairs Press.

Ramsey, P. (1970). *Fabricated man: The ethics of genetic control*. New Haven: Yale University Press.

Rather, D., & Gates, C. (1974). *The palace guard.* New York: Harper.

Reed, S. C., & Reed, E. W. (1965). *Mental retardation, a family study*. Philadelphia: Saunders.

Remarque, E. (1959). *All quiet on the western front*. Boston: Little-Brown.

Ricardo, D. (1911). *The principles of political economy and taxation*. London: Dent, 1817.

Richardson, L. F. (1946). The distribution of wars in time. *Journal of the Royal Statistical Association, 107*, 242-250.

Richardson, L. F. (1946). The distribution of wars in time. *Journal of the Royal Statistical Association, 107*, 242-250.

Riddle, O. (1948). *The unleashing of evolutionary thought*. New York: Vantage.

Roberts, D. F. (Ed.). (1959). *Natural selection in human populations.* New York: Pergamon.

Roberts, M. (1941). *The behavior of nations.* London: Dent.

Roe, A. (1953). *The making of a scientist.* New York: Dodd.

Rosanoff, A. J., Handy, L. M., & Plesset, R. R. (1935). The etiology of manic depressive syndromes with special reference to their occurrence in twins. *American Journal of Psychiatry, 97,* 16-30.

Rosenthal, D. (1970). *Genetic theory and abnormal behavior.* New York: McGraw-Hill.

Rowse, A. (1945). *The English spirit in history.* New York: Macmillan.

Royce, J. R. (1961). *Man and his nature.* New York: McGraw-Hill.

Royce, J. R. (1964). *The encapsulated man.* Princeton: Van Nostrand.

Royce, J. R. (1967). Metaphoric knowledge and humanistic psychology. In J. F. T. Bugental (Ed.), *Challenges of humanistic psychology.* New York: McGraw-Hill. Pp. 20-28.

Rousseau, J. J. (1913). *The social contract.* London: Dent.

Rummel, R. J. (1963). Dimensions of conflict behavior within and between nations. *General systems: Yearbook of the Society for General Systems Research, 8,* 1-50.

Rummel, R. J. (1972). *Dimensions of nations.* Beverly Hills: Sage.

Rundquist, E. E. (1933). Inheritance of spontaneous activity in rats. *Journal of Comparative Psychology, 16,* 1-23.

Russell, B. (1955). *Human society in ethics and politics.* New York: Simon & Schuster.

Russell, B. (1957). *Marriage and morals.* New York: Liveright.

Russell, B. (1968). *Autobiography.* Boston: Little- Brown.

Russett, B. M. (1968). Delineating international regions. In J. Singler (Ed.), *Quantitative International Politics.* New York: Free Press.

Sagan, C., & Schlowskii, I. S. (1966). *Intelligent life in the universe.* Oakland, CA: Holden-Day.

Salk, J. (1983). *Anatomy of reality: Merging of intuition and reason.* New York: Columbia University Press.

Santayana, G. (1896). *The sense of beauty.* New York: Dover.

Sarason, S. B., Manddler, G., & Craighill, P. G. (1952). The effect of differential instructions on anxiety and learning. *Journal of Abnormal & Social Psychology, 47,* 561-565.

Sartre, J. P. (1948). *Existentialism and humanism.* London: Methuen.

Sawyer, J., & Levine, N. (1966). Cultural dimensions: A factor analysis of the world ethnographic sample. *American Anthropologist, 68,* 708-731.

Scheier, I. H. (1958). What is an objective test? *Psychological Reports, 4,* 147-157.

Schoeps, H. J. (1967). *An intelligent person's guide to the religions of mankind.* London: Gallancy (Victor).

Schröder, C. M. (1960-68). *Die religionen der Menschheit.* Stuttgart: Kohlhammen.

Schweitzer, A. (1939). *Christianity and the religions of the world*. New York: Holt.

Sélincourt, A. de. (1962). *The world of Herodotus*. Boston: Little-Brown.

Sells, S. (1962). *Stimulus determinants of behavior*. New York: Ronald.

Shakespeare, W. (1952). *Collected works*. In W. Clarke & W. Wright, *Encyclopedia Brittanica*. Chicago: University of Chicago Press.

Shaw, G. B. (1944). *Everybody's political what's what*. New York: Dodd Mead.

Shaw, G. B. (1949). *Back to Methusaleh*. London: Constable.

Shaw, G. B. (1965). *The complete prefaces of Bernard Shaw*. London: Hamlyn.

Sheldon, W. H. (1947a). *Varieties of delinquent youth*. Cambridge: Harvard University Press.

Sheldon, W. H. (1947b). *The varieties of temperament*. New York: Cambridge University Press.

Sheldon, W. H. (1975). *Prometheus revisited*. Cambridge, MA: Schenkman.

Shirer, W. L. (1969). *The collapse of the third republic*. New York: Simon & Schuster.

Shockley, W. B. (1969, Dec. 10). Human quality problems, research taboos and eugenics. Convocation Lecture, University of Bridgeport, CT.

Short, J. F., & Strodbeck, F. L. (1965). *Group process and gang delinquency*. Chicago: University of Chicago Press.

Shwayder, D. S. (1965). *The stratification of behavior*. London: Routledge & Kegan Paul.

Sidgwick, H. (1893). *The methods of ethics*. London: Macmillan.

Simpson, G., G. (1949). *The meaning of evolution*. New Haven: Yale University Press.

Simpson, J. (1926). *Landmarks in the struggle between science and religion*. New York. (No publisher given.)

Sims, V. M. (1928). *The measurement of socio-economic status*. Bloomington, IL: Public School Publishing.

Singer, J. D. (Ed.) (1965). *Human behavior and international politics*. Chicago: Rand-McNally.

Skinner, B. F. (1971). *Beyond freedom and dignity*. Cambridge: Harvard University Press.

Smith, E. D., & Vetter, H. J. (1982). *Theoretical approaches for personality*. New York: Prentice-Hall.

Snow, C. P. (1959). *The 2 cultures and the scientific revolution*. Cambridge: Harvard University Press.

Snow, C. P. (1961). *Science and government*. Cambridge: Harvard University Press.

Solzhenitsyn, A. (1976). *A collection of critical essays*. K. Feier (Ed.). New York: Prentice-Hall.

Sorokin, P. A. (1927). *Social mobility*. New York: Harper.

Sorokin, P. A. (1937). *Social and cultural dynamics*. Vol. 3. New York: American Book.

Spearman, C. (1930). *Creative mind*. London: Nisbet.

Spencer, H. (1892). *Principles of ethics.* London: Williams & Norgate.

Spengler, O. (1928). *Decline of the West.* New York: Knopf.

Spengler, O. (1934). *The hour of decision.* New York: Knopf.

Spielberger, C. D. (Ed.). (1966). *Anxiety and behavior.* New York: Academic.

Spuhler, J. N. (Ed.). (1967). *Genetic diversity and human behavior.* New York: Viking Fund Publication.

Stephen, J. F. (1873). *Liberty, equality, fraternity.* New York: Holt.

Stevens, S. S. (1952, Apr.). The NAS-NRC and psychology. *American Psychologist, 7,* 119-124.

Stoddard, J. L. (1922a). *Revolt against civilization.* New York: Freeland.

Stoddard, J. L. (1922b). *The rising tide of color.* New York: Scribner.

Stricker, L. (1978). *Dimensions of social stratification for whites and blacks.* Princeton, NJ: ETS (RM 98-6).

Stricker, L. (1981). *A factor analysis of social status variables.* Princeton, NJ: ETS.

Stumpfl, C. (1929). In G. Boring (Ed.), *History of experimental psychology.* New York: Appleton-Century-Crofts.

Sumner, G. (1959). *Folkways.* New York: New American Library.

Sweney, A. B., & Cattell, R. B. (1962). Relationships between integrated and unintegrated motivation structure examined by objective tests. *Journal of Social Psycholoigy, 57,* 217-226.

Tarde, G. (1903). *The laws of imitation.* London: Macmillan.

Taylor, C. W., & Barron, F. (Eds.). (1963). *Scientific creativity: Its recognition and development.* New York: Wiley.

Tennyson, A. L. (1908). *Poetical works.* London: Macmillan.

Terman, L. M. (1926). *Genetic studies of genius. I. A thousand gifted children: II.* (With Catherine M. Cos, et al.) *The early mental traits of three hundred geniuses.* London: Harrap.

Thomas, L. (1979). *The medusa and the snail.* New York: Bantam.

Thomson, G. M. (1964). *The twelve days: 24 July to 4 August, 1914.* New York: Putnam.

Thorndike, E. L. (1939). *Human nature and social order.* New York: Macmillan.

Thurstone, L. L. (1944). *A factorial study of perception.* Chicago: University of Chicago Press.

Thurstone, R. (1977). Causation of Binet I.Q. decrements. *Journal of Educational Measurement, 14,* 197-202.

Tillich, P. (1954). *Love, power, and justice.* New York: Oxford University Press.

Tillich, P. (1955). *Biblical religion and the search for ultimate reality.* Chicago: University of Chicago Press.

Tinbergen, N. (1951). *The study of instinct.* Oxford: Clarendon.

Tinbergen, N. (1959). Behavior, systematics and natural selection. *Ibis, 101,* 119.

Toffler, A. (1970). *Future shock.* New York: National General.

Toland, J. (1970). *The rising sun: The decline and fall of the Japanese empire.* New York: Random House.

Tolstoy, L. (1894). *The kingdom of God is within you.* Translated by A. Delano. London: Scott.

Toynbee, A. J. (1947). *A study of history.* New York: Oxford University Press.

Toynbee, A. J. (1952). *Greek civilization and character.* New York: Mentor.

Treitschke, H. G. (1916). *Politics.* New York. (No publisher given.)

Tryon, R. C. (1940). Genetic differences in maze learning ability in rats. In *Yearbook of National Society for the Study of Education.* Vol. 39. Pp. 111-119.

Truman, H. S. (1947, Mar. 12). *Congressional Record.*

Tuchman, B. (1967, Nov. 7). Address to National Conference on Higher Education, Chicago.

Tuttle, D. J. (1951). *The trail of deceit.* Boston: Houghton-Mifflin.

Udry, J. R. (1966). *The social context of marriage.* Philadelphia: Lippincott.

Unamuno, M. de. (1926). *The tragic sense of life.* Paris: Gaurmard.

United States Office of Education. (1971). *United States Office of Education Report for 1970.* Washington, DC: Government Printing Office.

Unwin, J. D. (1934). *Sex and culture.* London: Oxford University Press.

Van Court, M. (1986). The persistence of dysgenic trends in intelligence. *Eugenics.*

Vandenberg, S. G. (1965). *Methods and goals in human behavior genetics.* New York: Academic.

Veblen, V. (1899). *The theory of the leisure class.* New York: Macmillan.

Vidal, F. (1971). *Problem solving: Méthodologie géneral de la creativité.* Paris: Dunod.

Vining, D. R. (1982). Fertility differentials and the status of nations: A speculative essay on Japan and the West. *Mankind Quarterly, 22,* 311-354.

Voltaire, F. (1946). *Candide.* New York: Appleton-Century-Crofts.

Waddington, C. H. (1953). Genetic assimilation of an acquired character. *Evolution, 7,* 118-126.

Waddington, C. H. (1962). *The nature of life.* New York: Atheneum.

Wallas, G. (1914). *The great society.* London: Macmillan.

Ward, M. (1967). *Robert Browning.* New York: Holt.

Watson, J. B. (1914). *Behavior: An introduction to comparative psychology.* New York: Holt, Rinehart & Winston.

Weber, M. (1956). *The protestant ethic.* New York: Scribner, 1904.

Weber, M. (1968). Objectivity in social science. In E. A. Shils & H. A. Finch (Eds), *The methodology of the social sciences.* New York: Free Press, 1949.

Wells, H. G. (1903). *Mankind in the making.* London: Chapman & Hall.

Wells, H. G. (1905). *A modern utopia.* London: Chapman & Hall.

Wells, H. G. (1920). *The outline of history.* London: Cassell.

Wells, H. G. (1930). *The open conspiracy.* London: Hogarth.

Wells, H. G. (1931). *What are we to do with our lives?* London: Heineman.

Wells, H. G. (1940). *The rights of man: Or, what are we fighting for?* New York: Penguin.

Westermarck, E. A. (1932). *Ethical relativity.* New York: Harcourt, Brace.

Weyl, N. (1973). Population control and the anti-eugenic ideology. *Mankind Quarterly, 14,* 63-82.

Weyl, N. (1977). *Karl Marx: Racist.* New Rochelle, NY: Arlington House.

Whitaker, R. (1976). *A plague on both your houses.* Washington, DC: Luce.

White, A. D. (1896). *A history of the warfare of science with theology in Christendom.* London: Constable.

Wiener, N. (1954). *The human use of human beings.* Boston: Houghton-Mifflin.

Wilkie, W. L. (1943). *One world.* New York: Simon & Schuster.

Williams, R. J. (1956). *Biochemical individuality.* New York: Wiley.

Williams, R. J. (1969). Heredity, human understanding and civilization. *American Scientist, 57,* 237-243.

Wilson, D. S. (1983). The group selection controversy: History and current status. *Annual Review of Ecology, 14,* 159-167.

Wilson, E. O. (1975). *Sociobiology: The new synthesis.* Cambridge: Harvard University Press.

Wilson, W. (1917, Apr. 2). *Congressional Record.*

Winborn, B. B., & Jansen, D. G. (1967). Personality characteristics of campus political action leaders. *Journal of Counselling Psychology, 14,* 509-518.

Wolfe, D. (1971). *The uses of talent.* Princeton, NJ: Princeton University Press.

Woods, H. (1906). *Mental and moral health in royalty.* New York: Duell, Sloan & Pearce.

Wrigley, C. (1963). *A multivariate study of United Nations General Assembly voting records.* East Lansing: Michigan State University. Mimeograph.

Young, K. (1922). *Mental differences in immigrant groups.* Eugene: University of Oregon Press.

Young, M. (1958). *The rise of the meritocracy.* London: Thames & Hudson.

Zirkle, C. (1949). *Death of a science in Russia: The fate of genetics as described in Pravda.* Philadelphia: University of Pennsylvania Press.

Müller, H. J. 189
Mussolini, B. 239

Napoleon 127
Nesselroade, J. R. 207, 255
Newbolt, H. 59, 137
Newton, I. 161
Nietzsche, F. W. 6, 49, 62, 72, 80, 126, 132, 159, 163, 169, 231, 252

Oliver, R. P. 103, 106, 145
Osler, W. 249
Otto, W. F. 72
Owen, R. 145
Owen, W. 59, 155

Paine, T. 105
Paley, W. 80, 148
Pascal, B. 124, 161
Pasteur, L. 79
Paul, St. 83, 130, 131, 149
Pavlov, I. 110
Pearson, R. 30, 199
Pendell, E. 139, 166, 212, 215-216
Pervin, L. A. 152
Planck, M. 228, 254
Plato 49, 52, 145, 161, 163, 191, 220, 235, 249
Proudhon, P. J. 113, 115, 194
Putnam, C. 206
Pythagoras 163

Remarque, E. 134
Roberts, D. F. 210
Rosanoff, A. J. 57
Rousseau, J. J. 105, 120, 126, 145
Rowse, A. 198
Rummel, R. J. 26, 212, 221, 226
Russell, B. 55, 143, 152, 169, 246
Russett, B. M. 26

Sagan, C. 68, 120, 221
Salk, J. 221
Santayana, G. 200
Sawyer, J. 26
Schlowskii, I. S. 68
Shakespeare, W. 94, 129
Shaw, G. B. 52, 79, 105, 126, 199, 223-224
Sheldon, W. H. 38, 195, 203, 251
Sims, V. M. 215
Skinner, B. F. 50, 115, 155
Smith, A. 121, 241

Smith, E. D. 152
Snow, C. P. 124
Solzhenitsyn, A. 8, 252
Spearman, C. 9
Spencer, H. 10, 14, 40, 252, 253
Spengler, O. 26, 103, 212
Stice, G. 108, 134, 168
Stoddard, J. L. 109, 111, 186
Stricker, L. 213, 215
Stumpfl, C. 57
Sumner, G. 251
Swift, J. 126

Tarde, G. 54
Tatsuoka, M. M. 155, 193
Tennyson, A. L. 6, 156, 199
Terman, L. M. 102, 110, 193
Thomas, L. 66
Thoreau, H. D. 170
Thorndike, E. L. 52, 94
Thurstone, R. 56
Tillich, P. 148
Toffler, A. 19, 123, 183, 221
Toynbee, A. J. 53, 58, 85, 96, 212, 246
Trotsky, L. 111, 114, 249
Tuttle, D. J. 71

Van Court, M. 119, 211, 212, 213, 215
Vandenberg, S. G. 36, 205
Vetter, H. J. 152
Vining, D. R. 119, 211, 212, 213, 215
Voltaire, F. 169, 253

Waddington, C. H. 169, 221
Wallas, G. 229
Washington, G. 203
Watson, J. B. 36
Weber, M. 164
Wells, H. G. 145, 188, 199, 223, 229
Weyl, N. 72, 111-112, 182, 186, 191, 196, 250, 253
Whitaker, R. 84
Williams, R. 166, 221, 253
Wilson, E. O. 20, 22, 128, 169, 210, 221, 226, 253
Woliver, R. E. 26-27, 168
Woods, H. 39
Wordsworth, W. 238

Young, M. 52, 212, 222, 245

Zirkle, C. 108

320

After teaching at Harvard and Duke Universities, Professor Cattell was, for thirty years, Research Professor and Director of the Laboratory of Personality and Group Behavior at the University of Illinois. He is responsible for numerous advances in research methodology, the discovery of fluid and crystallized intelligences, and of primary and secondary personality structure. He is the author of 41 books, over 450 research articles, and many standardized tests of personality and ability that are used worldwide. These efforts have more recently culminated in the VISAS systems, an integrated and comprehensive theory of personality. He has five children, three with doctorates in medicine or psychology, and has set up the Cattell Research Institute in his "retirement" in Hawaii, to explore the psychology of socio-political problems. Dr. Cattell is the recipient of the Darwin Fellowship, the Wenner-Gren Prize of the New York Academy of Science, the Psychometric Award of APA/Educational Testing Service, and the Dobzkansky Award of the Behavior Genetics Society.